STONEHENGE

THE BIOGRAPHY OF A LANDSCAPE

STONEHENGE

THE BIOGRAPHY OF A LANDSCAPE

TIMOTHY DARVILL

For Colin Renfrew and Arthur ApSimon

First published in 2006 by Tempus Publishing
Paperback edition first published in 2007

Reprinted in 2008 by
The History Press
The Mill, Brimscombe Port,
Stroud, Gloucestershire, GL5 QG
www.thehistorypress.co.uk

Reprinted 2010

British Library Cataloguing in Publication Data.
A catalogue record for this book is available from the British Library.

ISBN 978 07524 4342 3

Typesetting and origination by
Tempus Publishing Limited
Printed and bound in England.

CONTENTS

ILLUSTRATIONS AND TABLES

TEXT FIGURES

COLOUR PLATES

TABLES

PREFACE

As long ago as AD 1130 the Lincoln cleric known to us as Henry of Huntingdon extolled Stonehenge as one of the wonders of Britain. Today, nearly a million people journey to Salisbury Plain to visit Stonehenge every year. They come from all over the world – tourists, travellers, students, and academics – just to spend a few hours struggling to understand the grey monoliths, the surrounding earthworks, and the grassy barrows that pimple the landscape. For some the monument itself seems small compared with its reputation, but most find it awesome. Back in the nineteenth century the antiquarian and Liberal parliamentarian Sir John Lubbock (later Lord Avebury) described Stonehenge as 'the most exciting of our megalithic monuments' (1865, 50), while more than a hundred years later the modern antiquarian and former lead singer with The Teardrop Explodes, Julian Cope, suggested that it is 'an outrageous and magical drama imposed on the landscape' (1998, 224).

A few visitors take time to venture beyond the car-park and the 'heritagescape' that now surrounds the stones to follow the network of footpaths that provide easy access to outlying monuments such as the Cursus, Woodhenge, and Durrington Walls. Some picnic on the barrows. Some enjoy the openness of the countryside. A few immerse themselves in the antiquity of a landscape that contains one of the most dense concentrations of prehistoric remains anywhere in the world. Indeed, it is for this reason that the Stonehenge landscape enjoys almost every form of legal protection and special-area status available in the United Kingdom. The Stonehenge Triangle in which the stones stand, Woodhenge, and a few smaller pockets of land are held in the Guardianship of the State, looked after on a day-to-day basis by English Heritage. More than 850ha of the surrounding countryside is owned by the National Trust, managed as working farmland in ways sympathetic to the conservation of archaeological remains and as accessible as possible to the general public. The whole landscape is an Area of Special Archaeological Significance defined by Wiltshire County Council. Within an area of 135 square kilometres centred on Stonehenge there are more than 300 Scheduled Monuments of National Importance, some 293 Listed Buildings, and 12 Conservation Areas. In November 1986 an area of land totalling 2600ha was inscribed on the World Heritage List established by UNESCO, the southern component of the Stonehenge, Avebury, and Associated Sites World Heritage Site (WHS number C373).

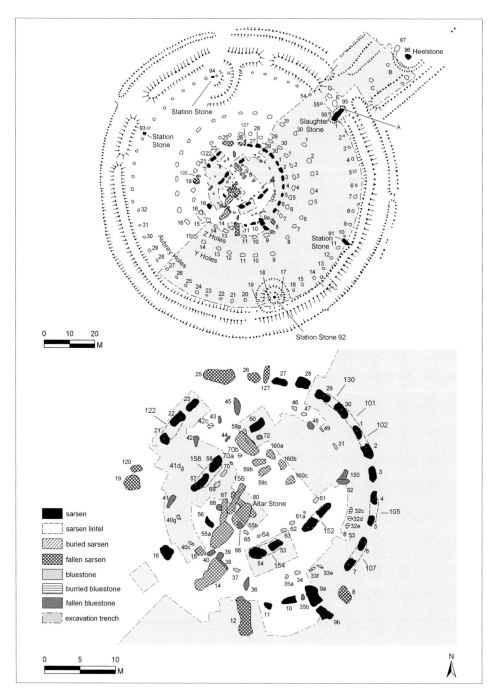

1 Stonehenge: schemes for numbering the stones and other related features. Top: Full monument. Bottom: Detail of the central setting, comprising the Sarsen Circle, Bluestone Circle, Sarsen Trilithons, and Bluestone Horseshoe. *After Petrie 1880, Plate I, with additions from Newall 1959; Cleal et al. 1995, figures 13, 14; and Pitts 1982*

Over the past three centuries or so many books and papers have been published about Stonehenge and its landscape, some of exceptional interest and importance. At the turn of the twentieth century Jerome Harrison provided a bibliography of more than 940 works by some 732 authors that had come to his attention until that time (Harrison 1902), and in the last century or so that list has multiplied several times over as the bibliography at the end of this volume demonstrates. Highlights of later twentieth- and early twenty-first-century literature relating to Stonehenge and its world include: the seminal work simply entitled *Stonehenge* by Richard Atkinson, first published in 1956 and later revised in the light of new dating evidence (Atkinson 1979); surveys by the Victoria County History of Wiltshire (Grinsell 1957; Crittall 1973; Crowley 1995), the Royal Commission on the Historical Monuments of England (RCHM 1979; 1987; McOmish et al. 2002), and the Trust for Wessex Archaeology (Richards 1990); excavation reports (e.g. Wainwright and Longworth 1971; Ashbee et al. 1989; Cleal et al. 1995); conference reports (e.g. Cunliffe and Renfrew 1997); and synthetic overviews by Burl (1987), Wainwright (1989), Richards (1991; 2004; 2005), Bender (1998), Pitts (2001a), Chippindale (2004), and Worthington (2004). However, few have dealt with the full depth of the wider landscape in terms of the great span of time represented and the wealth of connections that exist between people, places, and monuments across time and space. This is the aim of the present book; a contribution that goes beyond the history of individual sites and structures to unfold a more holistic view of a landscape that is, in a very real sense, a living, breathing creature with its own peculiar biography (see Chapter 1).

A few words of explanation are needed with regard to some of the conventions adopted here. Places in the county of Wiltshire are referred to simply by their common name and, when first mentioned in a section, tied to their civil parish as obtained in 2004. For convenience, however, the modern parish of Wilsford-cum-Lake is referred to simply as Wilsford. Places in the British Isles beyond Wiltshire are referred to by their name and county; those elsewhere in the world by their name and country.

By convention the barrows of Wiltshire are referred to by the name of the parish in which they stand and a serial number. The numbers were initially assigned by Edward Goddard (1913), massively expanded by Leslie Grinsell in what remains the definitive listing (1957), and later supplemented through surveys by the Royal Commission on the Historical Monuments of England (RCHM 1979). In some publications barrow numbers are prefixed by the letter 'G' for Goddard/Grinsell, but for clarity this is omitted here.

Although Sir Richard Colt Hoare provided a cunning alpha-numeric system for identifying the extant stones of Stonehenge itself (1812, opp. 145), the most commonly used system is that developed by Professor Flinders Petrie during his surveys in June and September 1877 (Petrie 1880). This system assigns a unique number to each stone with letters denoting individual fragments of broken stones (*e.g.* 59a, b, c etc.). The order begins at the northeast-oriented axis and runs clockwise. Numbers 1 to 30 are the uprights of the outer Sarsen Circle (allowing numbers for the blank spaces); 31 to 49 the Bluestone Circle; 51 to 60 the Sarsen Trilithons; 61 to 72 the inner Bluestone Horseshoe; 80 the Altar Stone; and 91 to 96 the outlying stones. The lintels are numbered 100 more than their higher-numbered supporter. Illustration *1* shows a plan of the site with the stones numbered according to this system as well as the numbering schemes applied to other features (the Aubrey Holes and the Z- and Y-Holes).

Following excavations in the early 1950s, Professor Richard Atkinson proposed a three-period scheme for the development of the monument. These were identified by Roman numerals as Stonehenge I, II, and III; period III being further subdivided into three phases a–c (Atkinson 1956, 58–9). Many subsequent publications used this scheme, and variations of it, but in 1995 a seminal volume reporting all the twentieth-century excavations at Stonehenge proposed a new scheme that was in part at least tied into a new series of dates for the main episodes of construction and reconstruction. This scheme identifies three main phases denoted by arabic numerals 1–3. Phase 3 is subdivided into 3i–3vi for the central stone setting and associated features and 3a–c for the peripheral features that cannot precisely be associated with elements of the central setting (Cleal et al. 1995, 466–70).

The chronology used here is a backward projection of the modern Gregorian calendar expressed in years BC and AD. Dates BC are mainly based on calibrated radiocarbon ages. Where specific dates are cited they are expressed as a date-range calibrated from the original age determination at two standard deviations ($\sigma 2$) which broadly equates with the 95 per cent confidence limits; the laboratory number and original uncalibrated age determination in years BP (Before Present) is also given. All radiocarbon age determinations have been calibrated using OxCal version 3.5 (Bronk Ramsey 2000) with atmospheric data published by Stuiver et al. (1998).

There remains much to see and enjoy in the Stonehenge landscape, and many happy hours can be spent there exploring the downland, wandering through the many villages of the Avon and Till valleys, or exploring the small town of Amesbury. For those prepared to stay longer there is local accommodation, good food, and some excellent English pubs that provide a warm welcome. Beyond the immediate environs of the landscape itself there are two important museum collections that are well worth visiting: Devizes Museum run by the Wiltshire Archaeological and Natural History Society in Long Street, Devizes, to the north, and the Salisbury and South Wiltshire Museum in the Cathedral Close, Salisbury, to the south.

I have dedicated this book to Colin Renfrew and Arthur ApSimon, experts both in Stonehenge and in its landscape (Chapter 1) whose patient instruction encouraged me and many others to explore this site, its setting, its relationships, and its implications for understanding the prehistory of northwest Europe.

Timothy Darvill
Winter Solstice 2005

ACKNOWLEDGEMENTS

Many individuals and organizations have assisted with the preparation of this book. Special thanks are due to Vanessa Constant for producing the illustrations and tracking down and exploring source material, and to Arthur ApSimon, Paul Ashbee, Mick Aston, Alastair Bartlett, David Batchelor, Bob Bewley, Roy Canham, John Chandler, Jeff Chartrand, Ros Cleal, Andrew Crookston, Simon Crutchley, Andrew David, Sue Davies, Bruce Eagles, Marianne Eve, Andrew Fitzpatrick, Lesley Freeke, Vince Gaffney, Tom Gaskar, John Gater, Sarah Green, Teresa Hall, Lorna Haycock, Martyn Henderson, David Hinton, Jim Keyte, Melanie Pomeroy-Kellinger, Andrew Lawson, David Miles, Robert Moody, Patricia Moore, Christopher Musson, Richard Osgood, Mike Parker Pearson, Louise Pearson, Mike Pitts, Colin Renfrew, Paul Robinson, Bronwen Russell, Miles Russell, Isobel Smith, Paul Stamper, Neville Stokes, Yvette Staelens, Charles Totterdell, Geoff Wainwright, Gerry Waite, Katy Whitaker, Tim Williams, and Martin Wright for providing information, helpful suggestions, and constructive criticism. Peter Kemmis Betty and Laura Perehinec at Tempus Publishing ensured the smooth progress of the book through the press. Frances Brown kindly worked on the proofs during the hottest week of the summer. My cousin Mary Lanning of Keynsham reminded me of several poorly known accounts of Stonehenge and unearthed the photograph reproduced as illustration 107 in a family album. Yvette Staelens not only made the reconstruction reproduced as illustration 17 but also helped with the proof-reading and provided much-needed loving support while the text of this book was in preparation.

The following have kindly allowed the reproduction of photographs and illustrations: Mick Aston (5; 61); the British Library (7); English Heritage (35; 75; 91; 112; 116); Gifford and Partners (75; 116); GSB Prospection (75); Christopher Musson (36); Salisbury and South Wiltshire Museum (52); Yvette Staelens (17); Wessex Archaeology (58D; 116); and the Wiltshire Buildings Record (104; 105).

Roy Canham and staff at the Wiltshire County Council Sites and Monuments Record kindly provided information used in the construction of distribution maps and plans. Extracts from Ordnance Survey mapping have been used in the construction of a number of maps and are reproduced by permission of Ordnance Survey on behalf of HMSO. Crown Copyright 2006. All rights reserved. Ordnance Survey Licence number

100045276. Administrative boundaries are taken from the 1991 Census digital boundary data provided by EDINA UKBorders which were constructed with the support of the ESRC and JISC and use boundary material which is copyright of the Crown and ED-LINE Consortium.

1

STONEHENGE
AND ITS LANDSCAPE

Only the sheep heard the noise, although any New Year revellers out late on 31 December 1900 might have felt the earth move like never before. For on that stormy night one of the great sarsen uprights on the west side of Stonehenge's outer ring collapsed onto the grass with a thud. The lintel it supported came crashing down behind, breaking into two pieces as it hit the ground. This was not the first time that pieces of Stonehenge had fallen; just about a century before, on 3 January 1797, the southwestern Sarsen Trilithon (Stones 57, 58 and 158) had succumbed to the forces of gravity. And there were several other disasters before that. But unlike these earlier events, the falls of New Year's Eve 1900 marked a watershed in the monument's recent history. Before then the site looked after itself, 'sweet, huge heaps of stones' as the sixteenth-century English soldier and poet Sir Philip Sidney so eloquently described it in his posthumously published sonnet *The Seven Wonders of England* (Sidney 1962). Afterwards, restoration, conservation, care, and management came to play an increasingly significant role in the way the site was treated and the regard in which it was held. Building on concerns that surfaced in the press during the last quarter of the nineteenth century, committees were formed to help protect the monument, plan its future, and shape the surrounding landscape. The stones were fenced-off in May 1901 and the monument known in medieval times as the Giants' Dance was caged and tamed as never before. More than a dozen stones were re-erected, replaced, or straightened between 1901 and 1964, starting with the tallest remaining upright (Stone 56) that once formed half of the southwestern Sarsen Trilithon (Gowland 1902; *2*). Stone 22 and its lintel that fell on that fateful last night of the nineteenth century were raised back into position in 1958, and now form the backdrop to one of the most favoured views of the monument (*3*). A programme of research excavations under the auspices of the Society of Antiquaries of London was undertaken between 1919 and 1926, directed by Lt-Col. William Hawley, and further excavations were carried out by Richard Atkinson and others between 1950 and 1964 in advance of conservation work in the central part of the monument. Tracks and footpaths were diverted, car-parks built, and visitor facilities installed. By the end of the twentieth

2 The centre of
Stonehenge showing the
partly collapsed remains of
the Great Trilithon with
Stone 56 standing, Stone
55B to the left, and the
lintel, Stone 156, in the
foreground with Stone 68
behind. The Altar Stone
is visible below Stones
55B and 156. To the right
is Stone 69 and behind
is Stone 57 with its lintel
(Stone 158). *Photograph:
Timothy Darvill, copyright
reserved*

century more than half a million people a year were passing through the turnstiles to
tour the monument, and perhaps as many again simply looked through the fence for a
distant glimpse of the stones. The Summer Solstice became such a major festival that in
2005 around 20,000 people of all ages and many diverse beliefs spent the night around
the stones to the sound of drums and singing before witnessing a glorious sunrise.

Sticking out of the grass like the wicket of some long-abandoned game of cricket,
the stones of Stonehenge have become an icon of Britain's prehistoric past that is
familiar the world over (*colour plate 1*). But Stonehenge was not 'discovered' in the way
that many world-famous archaeological sites were. The weathered stones that dominate
the site have stood sentinel over their surroundings for more than 4000 years. Anyone
passing across the southern part of Salisbury Plain in later prehistoric, Roman, medieval,
or recent times would have seen a structure only a little different from that visible today.
Many did, and from the sixteenth century AD onwards we have a panoply of descriptions,
commentaries, speculations, verses, drawings, paintings, photographs, sculptures, dances,
and songs that record and reflect upon what they saw.

Stonehenge itself is largely responsible for attracting the attention of so many people over the years, for unusual places often become spiritual meccas and intellectual challenges. In a sense Stonehenge is unique, but this uniqueness derives not so much from the form of the structure itself as from its survival through 50 centuries and the combination of elements that were brought together over many generations to make up the ensemble that we see today. For Stonehenge is not an isolated monument, either in time or in space. It is quite wrong to think of it as a discrete entity, even though that is how it is often portrayed and how we experience it as visitors following the prescribed circumjacent pathway. Instead we must blank from view the trappings of modern visitor management and think of a landscape – a wide open space that has, quite literally, been a stage on which successive generations have lived out their lives against a backdrop of undulating downland, amid the ever-changing scenery of monuments and structures, and using props and objects from near and far. Some of those actors never left the stage and still lie buried in the barrows and cemeteries that are now themselves part of the landscape. Others came and went, connecting the Stonehenge landscape to wider worlds in Britain and beyond.

3 View of Stonehenge looking eastwards from the modern tourist path around the site. To the left are Stones 21, 22, and 122, two of which fell in 1900 and were re-erected in 1958; in the centre is the southwestern Sarsen Trilithon (Stones 57, 58, and 158) which fell in 1797 and was re-erected in 1958; and to the right is one of the uprights of the Great Trilithon (Stone 56) which was straightened in 1901. *Photograph: Timothy Darvill, copyright reserved*

SPACE AND ENVIRONMENT: LANDSCAPE AND FORM

Physically, the Stonehenge landscape is classic chalk downland occupying a prime position in central southern England (4). The underlying geology comprises layers of milky-white chalk formed 135 million years ago during the Cretaceous period. The highly calcareous Middle and Upper Chalk that outcrops in the Stonehenge area gives rise to fairly rich neutral or alkaline free-draining soils. It also provides suitable geochemical conditions for the preservation of a wide range of archaeological materials.

Within the Upper Chalk there are tabular seams of dark-coloured flint, a siliceous material ideal for the manufacture of cutting edges for tools and weapons and widely exploited in prehistoric and later times. Geologically later than the chalk, and once perhaps covering it, was a layer of very hard, dense sandstone known as 'sarsen'. However, this layer was broken up and redistributed through denudation and subsequent geomorphological activity over millions of years with the result that scatters of sarsen boulders occur sporadically across the chalklands of southern Britain from Dorset to Kent. Sometimes known as 'greywethers' because they resemble, from a distance, a flock of sheep, these boulders range from less than 1m across to massive blocks up to 4m long and weighing more than 60 tons. Like flint, sarsen was widely exploited in prehistoric and later times, mainly as a material for constructing monuments and buildings.

Central southern Britain was subject to major geomorphological changes during the late Pliocene and Pleistocene periods some 2 million to 10,000 years ago (Kellaway 1991; 2002). Periglacial conditions during the Pleistocene Ice Age in particular led to the formation of superficial deposits such as clay-with-flints, chalky drift, and loess which can be found capping the eroded and denuded chalk bedrock to thicknesses of up to 1m. These deposits are less calcareous than the chalk beneath, and locally provide important parent material for the formation of soils that can be classified as rendzinas, brown calcareous earths, and argillic brown earths, some of which are rather stony (Findley et al. 1984; Richards 1990, 6–7; Darvill 1991, 37–45).

It was during the later stages of the Pleistocene Ice Ages that the basic topography of the area was established. Forming part of the southern edge of Salisbury Plain, the area is dominated by two rivers: the Avon to the east and the Till to the west. Both run broadly north to south through the landscape, subdividing it into three principal geo-topographical units (4). They drain southwards, the Avon being the main river, emptying into the English Channel at Christchurch in Hampshire. The River Till is a north-bank tributary of the Wylye which flows into the Avon via the Nadder at a confluence near modern-day Salisbury. Both the Avon and the Till run through relatively narrow but pronounced valleys typically 1km wide. A low terrace consisting of loamy, flinty drift flanks the Avon Valley, showing the river has changed its gradient at least once in its long history.

The downland east of the Avon rises steadily from around 100m OD along the river valley to about 140m OD at Silk Hill just 2.5km east of the river and 204m at Beacon Hill

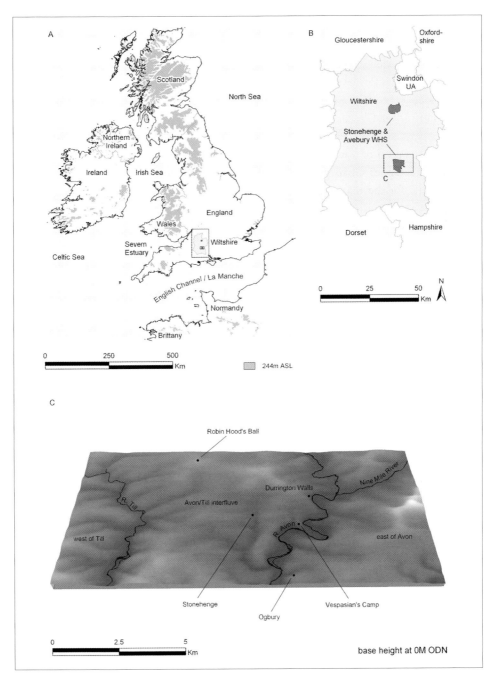

4 Stonehenge and its landscape. A: The position of Stonehenge within northwest Europe. B: County of Wiltshire with the two sections of the Avebury, Stonehenge and Associated Monuments World Heritage Site marked. C: Topographic model of the Stonehenge landscape showing the rivers and main landscape zones. *Drawings by Vanessa Constant: using ESRI® Data and Maps 2004 for outlines and EDX Engineering Inc. data at 50m intervals for topography*

still further beyond. A relatively elevated plateau represented by Boscombe Down, Earl's Farm Down, Bulford Field, Milston Down, Ablington Down, and Figheldean Down is characterized by thin soils and extensive views to the west.

The central block of downland, between the Avon and the Till, is more undulating and relatively low-lying with most of the land between 70m and 100m OD. Today it is characterized by large open fields and isolated clumps of trees. The highest points are at about 140m OD in the south near Druid's Lodge, and at Larkhill in the north. Several named areas of downland can be recognized: Lake Down, Horse Down, Wilsford Down, Normanton Down, Stonehenge Down, Winterbourne Stoke Down, Durrington Down, Knighton Down, and Alton Down. Throughout this region there are numerous small dry or seasonally running river systems, for example Stonehenge Bottom, and low eminences and ridges such as King Barrow Ridge. Stonehenge itself lies on such an eminence at about 100m OD towards the eastern side of the interfluve.

The land east of the Till is very similar in character to the central block, again with numerous small valley systems running eastwards and westwards from the main river. Parsonage Down and High Down are the two main areas of downland.

Clothing this distinctive landscape has been a succession of vegetation regimes reflecting changing climate and the impact of animal and human communities using the area. Details are considered in later chapters, but in outline a series of five main stages can be recognized (Allen 1997).

Holocene Wildwood characterizes the period from before 8000 BC down to about 4000 BC. The Boreal climate was relatively warm and dry. The chalkland at this time had a thick cover of brown earth or argillic brown earth soils (perhaps up to 1m thick) supporting open woodland dominated by hazel and pine. Vegetation was not static, and periods of more open conditions may have punctuated a generally more closed woodland.

Tamed Wildwood characterizes the period from 4000 BC to 3000 BC, as the impact of human communities increased. Elm, ash, oak, hazel, and yew dominated the woodland, but the extent of woodland was reducing and several buried soil profiles suggest that areas of grassland were already established by 3000 BC. Some cereal cultivation was practised, probably in small clearance plots or 'gardens'. Domesticated cattle are well represented; pig and sheep are present in small numbers. The native fauna is known to include red deer, roe deer, and beaver, but other species may well have been present too (perhaps including brown bear, wolf, wild cattle, wild pig, horse).

Emergent downland characterizes the period from about 3000 BC down to 1600 BC, with the balance between woodland and grassland shifting so that for the first time grassland predominated. The existing range of domestic animals continued to be represented, although the relative abundance of species changed slightly, with some sites showing a higher proportion of pig than cattle. Sheep were poorly represented until well into the second millennium BC. Wheat and barley were cultivated but little is known about the wild plant species in this phase. Woodland included oak, hazel, blackthorn, and hawthorn/whitebeam/rowan.

Farmed downland characterizes the period from about 1600 BC down to AD 1500. Formal fieldsystems were established in this period and provide the framework for mixed agriculture that included both arable and pasture. Wind-blown sediment trapped in archaeological features suggests that some arable land was left as open ground for part of the year. Elsewhere, the grazing was characterized by open short-turfed grassland. Ridge and furrow cultivation typical of the early second millennium AD cuts earlier fieldsystems in several areas. Cereals cultivated in the area included emmer wheat, bread wheat, club wheat, spelt, and barley. The woodland included birch, holly, beech, and oak. Cattle, horse, sheep/goat, pig, dog, chickens, red deer, fox, hare, raven, and frog were amongst the animals present in the landscape.

Pasturelands characterized much of the Stonehenge landscape from AD 1500 down to the early twentieth century, although detailed studies are absent and generalization is therefore extremely difficult. The higher ground, more remote from settlements along the main river valleys, was open grassland; nearer the settlements there was a higher incidence of cultivated ground. The eighteenth century was probably the all-time low-point in the level of woodland cover in the landscape. Deliberate planting began soon after, and in the nineteenth century a number of fairly substantial plantations were added. Since the early twentieth century there have been a number of changes to the environment of the central part of the Stonehenge landscape. Intensive military usage until 1950 gave way to a period of agricultural intensification in the wake of clearing away many of the former military installations.

Over the last 10,000 years or so represented by this sequence there has been considerable soil erosion, softening slopes and making the valley floors flatter. Both the Avon and the Till meander through their valleys and have built up fairly well-developed alluvial flood plains from material washed off the surrounding uplands. Some of the seasonal valleys and dry valleys that carried rivers in earlier times also contain alluvial deposits. In some cases this may mask underlying archaeological evidence, and certainly preserves useful environmental sequences (Allen 1997, 120; Cleal et al. 2004). Elsewhere in the landscape there are build-ups of colluvium resulting from the down-slope movement of soil and sediment. Accumulations up to 1.5m thick are known within the southern part of the interior of Durrington Walls (Wainwright and Longworth 1971, 23). Rather less substantial deposits were revealed in a slight hilltop saddle occupied by Coneybury Henge (Richards 1990, 124), and may be inferred from the presence of lynchets associated with early fieldsystems. More recently, deposits of colluvium have been recognized on Coneybury Hill (WA 1993a), on the west side of the River Avon below Durrington Walls (Richards 1990, 263), and within and around the foot-slopes of Vespasian's Camp where its accumulation may be dated to the later prehistoric, Roman, and medieval periods (Hunter-Mann 1999). However, a sampling programme involving the investigation of eight locations within the context of the Stonehenge Environs Project in 1981–2 failed to identify significant deposits in some promising locations (Richards 1990, 210–11) and it must be concluded that erosion in this part of Salisbury Plain has been less severe than in some other parts of the chalk downlands across southern Britain.

TIME AND TRADITION: LANDSCAPE AND BIOGRAPHY

These physical qualities of the landscape are only part of the picture. If we cast aside the nineteenth- and early-twentieth-century preoccupation with trying to separate nature from culture by imposing simplistic dualisms we find that landscapes have strongly social aspects. People dwell in landscapes. They shape them. They give each tiny element of them special meaning and value. The landscape is seen not for itself, but rather as reflection of the human condition and the tensions between order and disorder in everyday life. Each generation inscribes its own impressions and removes some of the marks left by their predecessors. Connections between disparate elements are forged, and monuments assembled and changed. The rhythms of life are played out through engagements with stone, wood, water, earth, and sky; through the rotations of the sun, moon, and stars; through experiences of the wind, rain, snow, and heat; and by movements across the land, up hills, down valleys, over streams, through woods, and along trackways tramped by ancestors real and imagined. Colours, sounds, textures, and the play of light all contribute to the reality of landscape just as much as they do in the images captured by the nineteenth-century Dutch masters of landscape painting. For archaeology, the landscape becomes a set of interlocking but infinitely reworkable spaces that people have defined, shaped, and made relevant to their everyday lives: the earthwork enclosure separating an inside from an outside; the Avenue linking the enclosure to the River Avon; and the carefully chosen axes for monuments to be aligned on the rising midsummer sun to the northeast and the setting midwinter sun to the southwest (5).

Uniting this holistic view of the landscape is the idea of 'biography' – an account of the course of its life, a dissection and demonstration of how it was made and how it worked (Wells 1934). Like any living being, the landscape has an essential personality over which there is a changing set of characteristics that develop and mature as its life unfolds. External influences shape appearances, sensibility, and understanding. Equally, each being alters events going on around them, affecting the life of others in predictable and unpredictable ways. There exists a complicated web of relationships, which in the case of landscape can be played out over very long periods of time. In a very real sense the landscape is the most ancient 'living' thing we regularly encounter: far older than the trees, woods, rivers, animals, and human communities that form part of it. The cycles of change are equally complicated and convoluted, involving many interconnected scales and wavelengths.

Compared with the longevity of the constructed world, the lives of individuals, families, and even recognizable social groups are short. Tensions can therefore be recognized between the long-term cycles of climate change, environmental succession, and the decay of inorganic materials, and the short-term cycles of human life, memory, and the decay of organic materials. To help explore such matters the Annales School of historical thought, established by Marc Bloch and Lucien Febvre in the late 1920s and later developed by Fernand Braudel in the 1950s and '60s, provides some useful perspectives that focus on

5 Connecting time and space: an aerial view of Stonehenge and the Avenue looking southwest. The modern A344 cuts across the Avenue just before it meets the ditch enclosing Stonehenge. Also visible is the modern visitor path around the outside of the monument. *Photograph: Mick Aston, copyright reserved*

three kinds of history (Bintliff 1991). In particular, their idea of the *longue durée* as a view of deep time provides a useful way of thinking retrospectively about the structures of slow but deep-seated change beyond the experience of individuals except through abstract thought. More recognizable are the medium-term structures representing demographic cycles, evolving ideology, and social histories preserved and perpetuated through collective memory and the cross-generational transmission of knowledge about the world. And most recognizable of all are the short-term structures, the sequence, history, and context of particular events that can be experienced by individuals during their own lifetime. Axiomatic to this approach is the notion that people themselves simultaneously think about their world at all three scales, thus creating a dialogue between the present and both the past and the future – what has happened and what might happen – which not only gives meaning to their lives but provides a motor that both drives and controls social change. Focusing on people, things, relationships, and meanings is in many ways the raw material of biography; as American philosopher Ralph Emerson once said, 'there is properly no history; only biography' (1841, i).

6 Colin Renfrew (left) and Arthur ApSimon (right) explaining the intricacies of Stonehenge during a visit in July 1977. *Photographs: Timothy Darvill, copyright reserved*

Creating a biography of the Stonehenge landscape naturally requires a body of raw material from which to work. In large measure this is physical evidence for what happened within the landscape over the course of time: who did what, when, where, and why as represented by archaeological traces and remains. But it is also metaphysical in the sense that these remains cannot speak directly to us. They need to be interpreted, decoded, and disassembled in order to contribute, and that can only be done within particular frameworks of thought and philosophical structures. Chapter 2 looks at how Stonehenge itself and the Stonehenge landscape have been conceived, understood, and portrayed over the last millennia or so, and what evidence we have available with which to investigate it today. Using such materials, Chapters 3 to 12 unfold a biography of the landscape reflecting recognizable phases in its life to date. Key moments of change and development are explored, and connections and relationships through time and across space investigated.

No biography can ever be complete, especially one relating to a life that it not yet over. The Stonehenge landscape will endure far beyond what can be visualized here, perhaps until it is swept away by the next Ice Age tens of thousands of years hence. More immediately, as will be discussed in Chapter 12, the opening of the twenty-first century AD looks to be as much a turning point for the Stonehenge landscape as the early years of the twentieth century were before.

Any biography is inevitably partial, told from the perspective of the biographer on the basis of the materials to hand. My own involvement with the Stonehenge landscape relates to just a fragment of its long history. It started with childhood visits and a time when the stones seemed massive and the landscape vast; it continues to this day with a close involvement in the development of sustainable research for the area (Darvill 2005). However, comprehending the site and its surroundings owes much to the guidance of the two archaeologists to whom this book is dedicated: Colin Renfrew and Arthur ApSimon (6). During the later 1970s and early 1980s both were part of the Department of Archaeology in the University of Southampton and brought to that community their skills, knowledge, and wisdom. Arthur ApSimon had researched the metalwork and pottery of the early second millennium BC in great detail and excavated at the thirdmillennium BC settlement near Downton in the Avon Valley south of Salisbury (ApSimon 1954; 1972; Rahtz and ApSimon 1962). By contrast, Colin Renfrew brought to the Stonehenge landscape a series of novel theoretical perspectives that focused on understanding the social organization of fourth- and third-millennium BC Wessex, and an interest in radiocarbon dating that conclusively showed Stonehenge and its related monuments to be over a thousand years earlier than supposed prototypes in Greece and the eastern Mediterranean (Renfrew 1968; 1973a; 1973b). The work of both men shows how critical it is to pay attention to the detail of archaeological data when developing long-term narratives of prehistory, and how theoretical underpinnings determine the character of our interpretations.

2

FINDING THE STONEHENGE LANDSCAPE
PAST AND PRESENT

Assembling a biography of the Stonehenge landscape involves recourse to many interconnected sources: archaeological excavations, drawings and plans, geophysical surveys of subsurface remains, aerial photographs, folklore, placenames, historical records, and of course the land itself. Such studies have been going on for more than three centuries, creating a mountain of finds and publications. But investigation and recording do not happen in isolation. Scholars find what they are looking for, what they are programmed to see, what their view of the world tells them is significant. And it is the same for artists, poets, and writers when they draw inspiration from a subject such as Stonehenge and its surroundings. Just as the pattern of investigation in the Stonehenge landscape represents in microcosm the history of archaeology generally, so too the interpretation of Stonehenge and its surrounding monuments reflects the changing philosophical traditions characteristic of the discipline and the intellectual world beyond.

Viewed through the long perspective offered by descriptions and depictions of Stonehenge spanning nearly a thousand years, the cycle of changing traditions can be seen in stark outline and mapped onto shifting attitudes towards the landscape in general. Andrew Sherratt has proposed a useful model with which to analyse these changes, what he calls the European Cultural Dialectic (1996a, 142). This identifies two broadly parallel trajectories of thought, each using ideas taken from a range of other disciplines including philosophy, art history, and literature. Such borrowings are not always strictly in sync with the application of ideas elsewhere. Indeed, with reference to Stonehenge, the development of competing interpretations reveals an idiosyncratic pattern of thought that probably owes much to the maverick character of those responsible for each successive contribution.

The first trajectory in Sherratt's model is predominantly 'enlightenment' in its approach, providing essentially evolutionary narratives in which order, hierarchy, and progression are paramount. Models of change are deterministic, and analysis is largely comparative. This set of attitudes can be traced from the classical revivals of the Renaissance in fourteenth-century Europe, through the Age of Enlightenment in the seventeenth and eighteenth centuries, to positivist science from the early nineteenth century, and, most recently, modernist and processualist views current from the mid-twentieth century.

The second trajectory is predominantly 'romantic' in its vision, with genealogical narratives focusing on meaning, action, growth, and descent. It is grounded in contextualist and relativist modes of thinking to produce accounts of the past that are largely interpretative. This line of approach comes into sharp view during the Reformation in Europe in the early sixteenth century, but its concern for the roots of northern peoples and the local origin of archaeological remains can be glimpsed amongst the mythical histories of medieval times. Later periods favouring such approaches include the Romanticism of the eighteenth century, Nationalism in the late nineteenth and early twentieth centuries, and, currently, post-modernism and its counterpart in post-processual archaeology from the late 1980s onwards.

While each of these trajectories unfolds in parallel, the dialectical element of Sherratt's model emphasizes the periodic shift in dominance between the two trajectories. Phases of popularity, stability, and contentment with one line of thinking lead to disenchantment, challenge, and revolt, and consequently a shift back to the other approach. At any one time there is a favoured, rather visible, dominant tradition on one trajectory, while research on the parallel line takes on a reduced significance until the next shift in emphasis rekindles attention. The picture is rather akin to what Kuhn (1970) has elsewhere modelled as 'paradigm shifts', and what Sterud (1973) called a 'paradigmatic view'. For Stonehenge, these changing approaches can be seen not only in the pattern of archaeological work and the resulting reports and accounts, but also in the way the site and its surroundings are depicted in contemporary art.

In the remainder of this chapter the way that information about Stonehenge and its associated monuments has gradually accumulated in relation to the European Cultural Dialectic is considered in some detail. Starting from the earliest accounts, the pattern of discovery, investigation, and interpretation is set against the changing background of successive dominant modes of thinking and ways of looking at the world (*Table A*).

GREEKS, ROMANS, AND BRITONS

Writing sometime around 330 BC the Greek historian Hecataeus of Abdera provided a tantalizing yet brief mention of ancient sanctuaries and temples in the land of the Hyperboreans, the place from which the north wind blows which is usually identified as the British Isles. Many scholars have cautiously identified the temple referred to as Stonehenge (e.g. Lockyer 1909, 51–2; Oldfather 1935, 36–7 n.2; Atkinson 1979, 183). Unfortunately, Hecataeus' original text perished long ago, although extracts survive in later histories such as the *Bibliotheca Historica* compiled by Diodorus Siculus around 8 BC. In translation (Oldfather 1935, 37–41) this tells us that:

Table A Summary of the main intellectual traditions relevant to the study of the Stonehenge landscape with selected examples of key exponents. The shaded sections of the table represent the dominant interpretive tradition during each period.

	ENLIGHTENMENT (Positivist: explanations with evolutionary narratives based on order, hierarchy, and progression)	ROMANTICIST (Relativist: interpretations and understandings with genealogical narratives focused on meaning, action, growth, and descent)
To 1400		AGE OF MYTH AND LEGEND Henry of Huntingdon (1130); Geoffrey of Monmouth (1140); Alfred of Beverley (1143); Wace (1155); Giraldus Cambrensis (1187); Neckham (1215); Robert of Gloucester (1278); Langtoft (1307); Higden (1327); Mannyng (1338) Manuscript depiction 1 (Merlin); Manuscript depiction 2 (squared-up circle)
1450–1530	EUROPEAN RENAISSANCE *Chronicle of England* (1480); John Rastall (1530)	
1530–1600	Polydore Vergil (1534); Lambarde (1580)	REFORMATION Leland (1545/1709); Folkerzheimer (1562); Stow (1565); de Heere (1573–5); Camden (1586) Lucas de Heere 1573–5; RF 1575; William Smith 1588
1600–1720	ENLIGHTENMENT Jones and Webb (1655); Charleton (1663); Fuller (1655); Aubrey (1693a; 1693b) John Speed 1625; Anon. 1716	Bolton (1627): Gale (1705)
1720–1800	Gale (1740) Philip Crocker 1720; David Loggan 1727; George Wood 1736	ROMANTICISM/'VOLKGEIST' Stukeley (1740); Wood (1747); Smith (1771); Maurice (1796); King (1799) Thomas Hearne 1779; Thomas Rowlandson 1784; Thomas Girtin 1794; William Turner; James Bridges; Thomas Jones 1774

Period	Theoretical approach / References
1800–1910	**POSITIVISM** 📖 Colt Hoare (1812); Lubbock (1865); Thurnam (1871); Ramsey et al. (1868); Long (1876); Petrie (1880); Barclay (1895); Lockyer (1909); Gowland (1902) 🎨 John Inchbold 1872 📖 Duke (1846); Herbert (1849) 🎨 William Blake 1820; J M W Turner 1825–7; William Overend Geller (1832); John Constable 1835; Copley Fielding 1835; Thomas Cole 1836; Samuel Rush Meyrick & Charles Hamilton Smith 1815; Barbara Boudochon 1870
1910–65	**NATIONALISM/CULTURE-HISTORY PERSPECTIVE** 📖 Cunnington (1935); Grinsell (1957) 📖 Stevens (1924); Stone (1924); Cunnington (1929); Piggott (1938; 1951); Atkinson (1956) 🎨 Heywood Sumner 1924; Edward Bawden 1931; Julia Trevelyan 1960; Edward McKnight Kauffer 1931
1965–85	**MODERNISM/PROCESSUALISM** 📖 Hawkins (1966a); Renfrew (1968; 1973a; 1973b); Hoyle (1966); Wainwright & Longworth (1971); RCHM (1979); Burgess (1980); Pitts (1982) 📖 Hawkes (1967); Bergström (1974); Chippindale (1983a); Richards & Thomas (1984); Thorpe & Richards (1984); Richards (1985) 🎨 Henry Moore 1971–3 (see Spender 1974)
1985–	**POST-MODERNISM/POST-PROCESSUALIST** 📖 Burl (1987); Ashbee et al. (1980); Richards (1990); Richards (1990); Cleal et al. (1995); 📖 Chippindale (1986); Chippindale et al. (1990); Bender (1992; 1993; 1998); Anderson et al. (1996); North (1996); Barrett (1994; 1997); Darvill (1997a); Whittle (1997); Parker Pearson & Ramilisonina (1998); Pitts (2001a); Pollard & Ruggles (2001); Heath (2002); Worthington (2004) 🎨 Carry Akroyd 1985; Charlie Sheard 1987; Peter Fowler 2005

📖 Books and papers etc. (see Harrison 1902 for works before 1800; later works in the bibliography below)

🎨 Painting and drawings etc. (see Chippindale 1986a; 1987; 2004; Dimbleby 2005; and Hatchwell 1969 for further details)

in the regions beyond the land of the Celts there lies in the ocean an island no smaller than Sicily … Leto was born on this island and for that reason Apollo is honoured amongst them above all other gods; and the inhabitants are looked upon as priests of Apollo, after a manner, since daily they praise this god continuously in song and honour him exceedingly. And there is also on the island both a magnificent sacred precinct of Apollo and a notable temple which is adorned with many votive offerings and is spherical in shape. Furthermore, a city is there which is sacred to this god, and the majority of its inhabitants are players on the cithara; and these continually play on this instrument in the temple and sing hymns of praise to the god, glorifying his deeds … certain Greeks visited the Hyperboreans and left behind them there costly votive offerings bearing inscriptions in Greek letters … They say also that the moon, as viewed from this island, appears to be but a little distance from the earth and to have upon it prominences, like those of the earth, which are visible to the eye. The account is also given that the god visits the island every nineteen years, the period in which the return of the stars to the same place in the heavens is accomplished … At the time of this appearance of the god he both plays on the cithara and dances continuously the night through from the vernal equinox until the rising of the Pleiades, expressing in this manner his delight in his successes.

Leaving aside the obvious propaganda, Aubrey Burl has plausibly used the 19-year cycle of visits to suggest that Hecataeus was referring to a lunar temple, quite possibly the great stone circle and avenue at Callanish, Lewis, in the Hebrides. This site fits the requirements and might have been recorded by Pytheas during his voyages around Britain in the late fourth century BC (Burl 2000a, 205; cf. Cunliffe 2001). However, the clear reference to Apollo is at odds with this view and suggests either that Burl is mistaken or that Hecataeus has conflated several strands of information. The latter is quite likely and we may have embedded in this fragment of text several important insights if only we could unscramble it. In particular, the reference to Apollo is of interest as he is one of the ancient gods of the sun, of uncertain origin, who was associated with divination, prophecy, and healing (Guirand 1959, 119–29). Accepted into the Roman Pantheon, Apollo may also be equated with a range of Celtic deities associated with healing, including Grannus, Phoebus, Belenus, and Burno (Green 1986, 161–4). In ancient times it was believed that Apollo spent much of the year at Delphi in southern Greece, but for the three months of the year centred on the Winter Solstice he moved northwards to the land of the Hyperboreans (Salt and Boutsikas 2005), a theme we shall revisit in Chapter 5.

Curiously, none of the later Greek and Roman historians whose works include sections dealing with Britain, for example Caesar (51 BC), Strabo (AD 20), Pliny (AD 77), and Tacitus (AD 97), make reference to Stonehenge or its associated monuments. The same is true for the early British historians writing between AD 560 and AD 796, for example Gildas, Bede, and Nennius. Only with the emergent scholarly interest in describing the physical world and the wonder of places and things during medieval times does the spotlight of enquiry pick out such curiosities as Stonehenge.

AGE OF MYTH AND LEGEND

The earliest explicit historical reference to Stonehenge is by Henry of Huntingdon (1084–1155), Archdeacon of Huntingdon, in his seven-volume work *Historia Anglorum* written about AD 1130. He refers to the monument as one of the four 'wonders' of England (Harrison 1902, 65):

> The second is at Stanenges [Stonehenge], where stones of a wonderful size have been erected after the manner of doorways, so that doorway appears to have been raised upon doorway, nor can anyone conceive by what art such great stones have been so raised aloft, or why they were there constructed.

A few years later, around AD 1136, Geoffrey of Monmouth provided a more rounded account of Stonehenge, and possible answers to Henry's questions, in his *Historium Regum Britanniae* (Thorpe 1973). Geoffrey (1100–54) was a cleric living near Oxford and was able to draw on a wide range of sources, including a book of Breton folklore obtained from his friend Walter, Archdeacon of Oxford. In his account of Stonehenge he relates a legend, the story of Aurelius Ambrosius, King of the Britons, who sought to commemorate 480 of his nobles treacherously slain by Hengist the Saxon in about AD 470. Aurelius consults the prophet/wizard Merlin as to what a fitting memorial might be, and Merlin advises acquiring a stone structure known as the Giants' Dance (*Chorea Gigantum*) from Killaraus in Ireland. This was done with supernatural help from Merlin.

Geoffrey's book was very popular in the Middle Ages and was widely read both in Britain and abroad. The tale of Aurelius and Merlin was widely repeated through the later twelfth and thirteenth centuries, for example by Wace in about 1171; in the *Topographia Hibernica* by Giraldus Cambrensis of about 1187; in a work by Robert of Gloucester dating to about 1278; and in Thomas of Malmesbury's *Eulogium Historiarum* of 1366 (Barclay 1895, 131–2; Legg 1986 for selected transcriptions). Although written down perhaps 3000 years after the construction of Stonehenge, Geoffrey's story is widely believed to embody genuine folk-memories, including the acquisition of stones from a distant source in the west of Britain (Piggott 1941; Atkinson 1979, 185).

Two illustrations of Stonehenge are known from fourteenth-century manuscripts. One shows Merlin building the monument, much to the amazement of mere mortal onlookers; the other depicts a rather squared-up perspective view of the monument (Chippindale 1983a, figures 14 and 15). Here, as with the oral traditions, Stonehenge is the real-world incarnation of something created in a mythical age whose exact meaning is lost; a place where worlds collide and a challenge is presented to the inquiring mind.

RENAISSANCE REVISIONISM

The transition from the medieval world to the modern order is represented by the revival of learning and fresh interests in classical antiquity that characterized the Renaissance from around AD 1400 onwards. This led to the first challenge to Geoffrey of Monmouth's account. It is found in the anonymously authored *Chronicle of England* compiled in the mid-fifteenth century and published by William Caxton at Westminster in 1480 (Atkinson 1979, 186; Chippindale 2004, 25). Here, the retold version of Geoffrey's tale is represented as just that, a story. The questioning, inquiring intellect inherent to Renaissance thinking can also be seen in the comments made by John Rastall (1530) to the effect that some of the stones at Stonehenge were made of artificial cement.

THE REFORMATION AND STONEHENGE

Religious revolution and the reconstruction of western Christendom in northern Europe in the early sixteenth century cut short the first flush of Renaissance thinking in Britain. It engendered an intellectual detachment from the classical world, and refocused on the origins and autonomy of northern peoples. John Leland was at the heart of the early development of such thinking with reference to the antiquities of England as the King's Antiquary in the service of Henry VIII from 1533 onwards. Although the site of Stonehenge is not included in Leland's *Itinerary*, elsewhere he repeats Geoffrey of Monmouth's story with one significant variation in which Merlin obtains the stones, not from Ireland, but from a place on Salisbury Plain (Leland 1709, 1, 42–8).

A young Protestant German scholar, Herman Folkerzheimer, came to England in 1562, and in the company of Bishop Jewel of Salisbury visited Stonehenge. Interpretation was a challenge to both men, but the bishop ventured that in his opinion the stones had been set up as trophies by the Romans because the actual positioning of the stones resembled a yoke (Chippindale 2004, 30). This was the first recorded proposal that the Romans might be responsible for the structure, although the manner in which it is stated reveals the Reformationist perspective on the possibility.

Other commentaries of the period include that by Lucas de Heere, a Flemish Protestant who fled to England in 1567. Between 1573 and 1575 he prepared a guide to Britain that included a detailed account of Stonehenge and a picture which is the earliest known to have been drawn at the site itself (7), and interestingly included two barrows as well as Stonehenge (see Bakker 1979). Only slightly later in date are a watercolour by William Smith produced in 1588, and a rather unreal stylized engraving by an unknown artist with the initials 'RF' dated 1575. The foreground of this view includes two men digging into a barrow from which they have already removed some giant bones.

Within the same tradition was William Camden's history and topography of Britain first published in Latin in 1586 as the *Britannia*, and subsequently enlarged and reprinted

7 Watercolour of Stonehenge by Lucas de Heere, drawn 'on the spot' in 1573–5. *Reproduced by permission of the British Library Add. MS 28330, fo.36*

many times. The edition of 1600 included an illustration of Stonehenge (an incompetent re-engraving of the RF print of 1575 already referred to) and a description. Camden refers to Stonehenge as 'a huge and monstrous piece of work' and in a comment redolent of the age he laments 'with much grief, that the Authors of so notable a Monument are thus buried in oblivion' (see Legg 1986, 60–1).

ENLIGHTENMENT AND THE ENGLISH RENAISSANCE

The Enlightenment of the seventeenth and early eighteenth centuries in Britain returned the focus of interpretation to scientifically based thinking. Two problems relating to Stonehenge began to command attention: where did the stones come from, and how did they get to Salisbury Plain? William Lambarde (1580) addressed both by emphasizing what can be achieved by dedicated groups of people who in this case brought the stones from north Wiltshire (Chippindale 2004, 36–7 for summary).

Developing interest in providing detailed descriptions of things may have resulted in the idea, perpetuated in folklore, that the stones were difficult to count; although the removal of stones at this time may have sustained the myth. Speed's map of Wiltshire published in 1625 shows the beginnings of a more geographically aware view of the land, and Chippindale (2004, 46 and figure 30) has speculated that a picture dated 21 June 1716 which shows people exploring the monument might reflect an early interest in Stonehenge astronomy.

The spirit of inquiry so typical of the Enlightenment is reflected in the idea of investigating archaeological sites by digging into them to find out what lies beneath the turf. This practicestarted early at Stonehenge. In 1620, for example, George, Duke of Buckingham, had a hole dug in the middle to see what was there (Chippindale 2004, 47). Later reports suggest that the 'heads and horns of stags and oxen, charcoal, arrowheads, rusty armour and rotten bones' were found (quoted in Long 1876, 49) and there is more than a suspicion that the diggings were at least partly responsible for the fall of Stone 55. The duke also examined round barrows on King Barrow Ridge, in one of which was found a 'bugle-horne tip't with silver at both ends' (Long 1876, 39). This work so intrigued the monarch of the time, James I, that while staying at Wilton in 1620 he commissioned the well-known neo-classical architect Inigo Jones to make a survey and study of Stonehenge. As it turned out, much of the fieldwork was done after the king's death in 1625, mostly during visits to Wiltshire between 1633 and Jones' own death in 1652. The work of producing the publication was completed by John Webb, Jones' assistant (Jones and Webb 1655). Again following Enlightenment thinking, Jones was adamant that the structure was built by Roman architects using Tuscan proportions (*8*).

Further evidence of Renaissance interest in debate and the resolution of intellectual questions in relation to Stonehenge comes from the work of John Aubrey (1626–97). Commanded to investigate the site by Charles II, Aubrey worked at Stonehenge in 1666, using fieldwork, surveys, planning, and observation to create a new plan of the site that challenged Jones' idealized classically inspired reconstructions. His *Monumenta Britannica* was incomplete and unpublished at the time of his death, but survived in manuscript form until its eventual publication in 1980 (Aubrey 1693a; 1693b). Aubrey's contribution to the understanding of the stones was his resort to another aspect of classical antiquity by invoking in a rather confused way the ancient Druids, as mentioned by Caesar, Tacitus, and others, as the architects and users of Stonehenge and the other stone circles in Britain. This conclusion, reached in old age after decades of discussion and speculation, perhaps reflected the shifting intellectual climate that by about 1700 was again favouring a more locally orientated vision of the past (see Piggott 1937). Indeed, throughout the seventeenth century, contrary views circulated alongside those of Jones, Aubrey, and others, keeping alive earlier Romanticist views. In 1624, Edmund Bolton declared that Stonehenge was the tomb of the British queen Boadicea (1627, 182–4), while in 1663 Dr Walter Charleton, physician to Charles II, proposed that

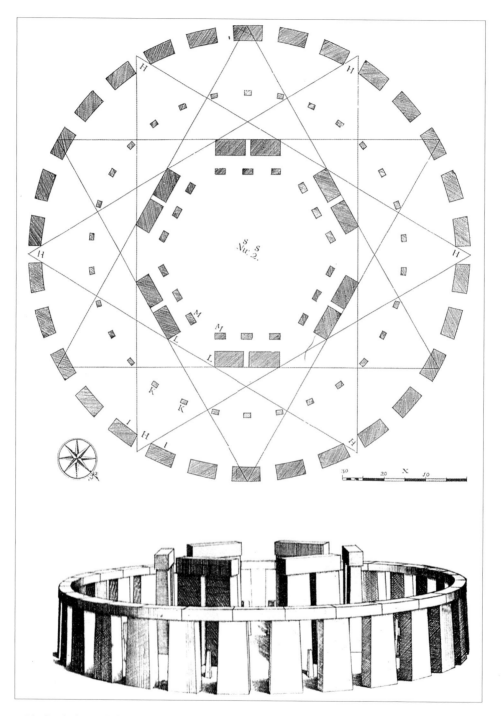

8 Idealized plan and elevation of Stonehenge by Inigo Jones published in 1655. To make the site fit his model he has added an extra trilithon and arranged the two innermost settings as a regular hexagon. *From Jones and Webb 1655*

the builders of Stonehenge were the Danes of the ninth century AD, noting analogies with megalithic structures in Denmark. Especially important in view of the prevailing political situation was the proposal that Stonehenge had been the coronation place of the Danish kings (see Chippindale 2004, 61). A little later, in 1705, Samuel Gale was perpetuating the idea that Stonehenge was rude and barbarous, a peculiarly British monument (Nichols 1790, 24).

ROMANTIC VISIONS

Straddling the transition from the intellectual traditions of the Enlightenment to those of Romanticism was one of the great antiquaries of the eighteenth century, William Stukeley (1687–1765). Stuart Piggott (1985, 24) argued that Stukeley's upbringing meant that for the first half of his life he continued the style of fieldwork, travelling, measuring, and observing on the ground, so central to the work of Jones and Aubrey, continuing these traditions well into the 1730s because he was provincial, old-fashioned, and out of date. The five seasons of fieldwork that William Stukeley undertook in the early eighteenth century represented the first extensive investigation of the landscape as a whole. Starting in about 1720, the work included drawing and describing Stonehenge and its setting. In 1721 he found the Stonehenge Avenue leading northeastwards away from the stones, and on 6 August 1723 he discovered the long, narrow embanked enclosure north of Stonehenge that he called the *cursus* (Piggott 1985, 93). Together with Lord Pembroke he dug into 13 barrows (12 round and 1 oval) in 1722–3, most of them in Amesbury and Wilsford parishes (Atkinson 1984).

Piggott argued that in the second half of his life, from the late 1730s onwards, Stukeley was drawn into the changed intellectual mood of the metropolis. In his book *Stonehenge: a temple restor'd to the British Druids* published in 1740 he described the results of his fieldwork, but also revealed his newly found Romantic leanings. He dismissed the idea of Roman, Danish, Saxon, Phoenician, or any other overseas involvement, instead arguing with almost religious zeal for the primary contribution of native Britons. In particular he emphasized the role of the Druids in building and using Stonehenge. The subtitle of his study shows his desire to overturn existing, and by then intellectually inferior, explanations of the site and 'restore' it to its place in history (9). In discussing his discovery of the Avenue, Stukeley also noted its alignment on the rising sun on midsummer day; here was a connection between the human world and the natural world that so interested the Romantic thinkers of the mid-eighteenth century. As Piggott (1985, 153) observed: 'Stukeley's delight in the English countryside is an endearing feature ... an almost sensuous pleasure in the mild English landscape of the Wiltshire Downs.' But Ronald Hutton (2005) has challenged Piggott's analysis, arguing instead that Stukeley's ordination as a cleric in the Anglican Church reflected changing religious attitudes that also had profound implications for his scholarship.

9 A peep into the *Sanctum Sanctorum*: William Stukeley's slightly fanciful reconstruction of the central area of Stonehenge, complete with Druids inside and out, 6 June 1724. *From Stukeley 1740, Tab. VII*

Belief in a Druidical origin for Stonehenge and connections with astronomy can be traced through the later eighteenth century, and beyond. The internationally-renowned English astronomer Edmund Halley visited the site in 1720, probably in the company of Stukeley (Lockyer 1909, 54). Fifty years later John Smith suggested that the site could be astronomically explained and that it was a temple for observing the motions of the heavenly bodies (1771).

The Romantic visions of Stonehenge created in the mid-eighteenth century come through most clearly in the depictions of it made in the later eighteenth and early nineteenth centuries (Chippindale 1987, 18–21). The Sublime tradition is represented by an astonishing number of fine paintings. The works of Thomas Hearne in 1779, Thomas Rowlandson in 1784, Thomas Girtin (*Stonehenge with a stormy sky*) in 1794, William Turner of Oxford, James Bridges, and many others provide marvellously theatrical pieces that stand up well alongside the watercolour masterpieces by J M W Turner (*c.*1825–8) and John Constable (*c.*1835). Thomas Cole's narration of landscape history published in 1836 shows Stonehenge in Arcadia, replete with nymphs and shepherds (Chippindale 2004, figure 68). Druidical images also come through with great force. In 1815 a view by Samuel Rush Meyrick and Charles Hamilton Smith entitled the *Costume of the original* *inhabitants of the British Isles* shows a grand conventional festival with banners carrying snake designs draped over the trilithons, the ark of the covenant from Old Testament traditions, and the costumes themselves from medieval Europe (Chippindale 2004, figure 61). Other illustrations in similar vein abound, Druids and hordes in full measure.

Even as these images were being prepared, however, the pendulum of radical thinking was swinging back towards the more explanatory traditions that built on the discipline of Renaissance observation and by the early nineteenth century revealed itself in positivist science.

POSITIVISM AND THE EMERGENT SCIENCES

Relatively little fieldwork took place during the later eighteenth century, although two barrows within Vespasian's Camp were excavated in 1770, probably in the course of landscaping works (RCHM 1979, 22). The art of excavation was revived at the very end of the century by William Cunnington (1754–1810) who in 1798 dug under the stones of the fallen southwestern Sarsen Trilithon (Stones 57, 58, and 158) and found Roman pottery (Cunnington 1975, 10–11). This was reported by the young topographer John Britton in his *Beauties of Wiltshire* as proof of a Roman date for the monument, but others were more cautious.

Cunnington started working for H P Wyndham, MP for Wiltshire, excavating barrows with great fervour such that by 1801 he had opened 24 around Stonehenge. In 1802 Cunnington again excavated at Stonehenge, and soon after came to be employed by Sir Richard Colt Hoare (1758–1838), a well-connected, wealthy landowner living at Stourhead (Meyrick 1948; Sandell 1961). Colt Hoare's travels in Europe, and the extensive network of contacts that they brought him, prompted a desire to write a new history of Wiltshire. This he did between 1808 and his death in 1838. The spirit of the age is reflected in the motto he cited at the head of the first volume: 'we speak from facts, not theory' (Colt Hoare 1812, 7); the facts in question being the results of Cunnington's excavations. Stonehenge and its surroundings are included in the first volume of *The Ancient History of Wiltshire* (Colt Hoare 1812, 113–78), the account being accompanied by numerous high-quality illustrations, made by Philip Crocker, and the first detailed map of the archaeology of the Stonehenge environs (*10*).

The most spectacular discovery made by Cunnington was the richly furnished burial at Bush Barrow (Wilsford 5) uncovered in September 1808. It contained an inhumation with accompanying grave goods. These included a bronze axe, three daggers, one of which had a hilt decorated with gold, a stone sceptre, and two gold lozenges (Colt Hoare 1812, 203–5). But Colt Hoare and Cunnington did not confine their investigations to barrows. Cunnington excavated at Stonehenge at least three times before his death in 1810. Work also took place at Rox Hill, and numerous other sites described in *Ancient Wiltshire* were 'tested by the spade' in various ways.

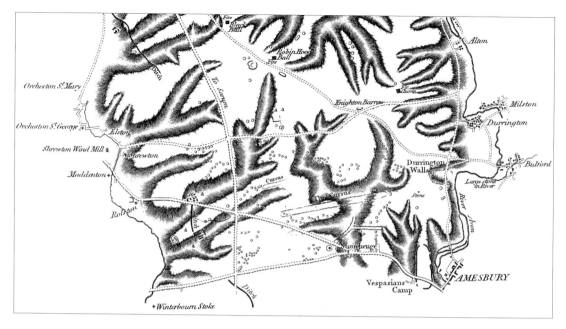

10 Early map of the Stonehenge landscape from Sir Richard Colt Hoare's *The Ancient History of Wiltshire. From Colt Hoare 1812, opp. 170*

Cunnington's and Colt Hoare's work naturally inspired others to engage in excavation. Amongst them the Revd Edward Duke (1779–1852), who inherited Lake House in 1805. In 1810 he excavated mounds within the barrow cemeteries at Lake, Wilsford Down, and Lake Down. Although these excavations were small-scale, Duke attempted grand interpretations on a wide canvas. He suggested, for example, that the early inhabitants of Wiltshire had portrayed in their monument-building a vast planetarium or stationary orrery. He saw the earth being represented by Silbury Hill while the sun and the planets revolving around it were marked by a series of earth and stone 'temples' in which Stonehenge was supposed to represent Saturn (Duke 1846).

After a lull of about 40 years, investigations of sites around Stonehenge continued in the later nineteenth century with the campaigns of John Thurnam, medical superintendent at the Devizes Asylum (Piggott 1993). He opened long barrows and round barrows in the Stonehenge landscape between 1850 and 1873, mainly because of an interest in human remains and the anthropology of early populations. His results were published in site-specific reports, in two general papers (1868; 1871), and in the *Crania Britannica* (Davies and Thurnam 1865).

The achievements of these nineteenth-century fieldworkers were considerable, but it was not until the second half of the nineteenth century that their value could really be appreciated as the results of intellectual and theoretical scientific thinking in spheres such as stratigraphy, evolution, and artefact sequences came to the fore. John Lubbock's book *Prehistoric Times* was first published in 1865 and applied to Britain the so-called Three-Age subdivision of the prehistoric past that had been developed 50 years earlier in Denmark. Lubbock placed Stonehenge and most of the barrows around about into a period back beyond the Bronze Age, a more ancient period than even the most adventurous antiquaries had previously ventured to suggest (Lubbock 1865). Ironically, as prehistorians were attempting to fit Stonehenge into an essentially evolutionary model of the ancient past, Charles Darwin himself was at Stonehenge in June 1887 studying the way that fallen stones became buried. He suggested that earthworms had played a major role in the submergence of some of the stones (Darwin 1888, 154).

Scientific approaches were not confined to chronology, sequence, construction, and decay. John Thurnam's excavations focused not on grave goods but on human remains (Marsden 1974, 57–64; Piggott 1993), allowing him to suggest that the skulls from barrows divided into two types: dolicocephalic from long barrows and bracycephalic from round barrows. These he associated with different and successive racial or ethnic groups (Thurnam 1871, 543–4). Meanwhile, in 1868, Sir A C Ramsey was the first geologist to point out the similarity of some of the bluestones of Stonehenge to the igneous rocks of Pembrokeshire (Ramsey et al. 1868; see also Maskelyne 1878 and Thomas 1923).

Astronomical lines of inquiry also submitted to science with observational work by Lockyer in 1901 following nearly two decades of studies elsewhere in the world. His findings led him to connect Stonehenge and the temples of ancient Egypt, and to endorse, in a scientific way, earlier suggestions that Stonehenge had been a solar temple serviced by astronomer-priests (Lockyer 1909, chapter 44).

In 1874 and 1877, Professor Flinders Petrie surveyed Stonehenge in detail and published his enumerated plan in *Stonehenge: plans, description, and theories* (1880). Characteristic of the positivist traditions behind his investigations is the fact that this book is divided into two sections: facts and theories. His numbering of the stones remains in use today. Petrie also suggested the need for detailed excavations at Stonehenge to find evidence to accurately date the construction of the circles. He proposed a way of excavating a stonehole while supporting the stone in a wooden cradle, but it was Professor William Gowland who, in 1901, first scientifically excavated a stonehole (Gowland 1902). In concluding his report, Gowland suggested that Stonehenge was constructed in the period of transition from stone to bronze (1902, 86) and that the 'purpose for which Stonehenge was erected … [was] a place of sanctity dedicated to the observation or adoration of the sun' (1902, 87). Following an interest in what today would be called comparative ethnography, Hawley included in his report a print showing sun-worship in Japan (1902, pl. vi).

Dating the construction of Stonehenge, and by implication some of the associated structures, was a major issue during the nineteenth and early twentieth centuries. Lockyer used astronomical data to suggest that the main stone settings visible today were built about 1700 BC (Lockyer 1909, 78). About the same time the well-known

Swedish prehistorian Oscar Montelius proposed a chronology for the British Bronze Age based on cross-dating typologically distinct artefacts with pre-classical civilizations in Greece and Italy. He proposed that the Copper Age (Period 1) dated to between 2500 and 2000 BC and the early Bronze Age (Period 2) followed at 2000 to 1700 BC (Montelius 1908, 162). Following Gowland, he further suggested that the stone structures at Stonehenge already existed by his Period 2 and were thus erected before 2000 BC; a conclusion that can now be supported by radiocarbon dating (cf. Montelius 1908, 115; Cleal et al. 1995, 168).

The synthetic volume on Stonehenge by Edgar Barclay (1895) usefully marks the end of this period of scientific inquiry and enlightenment thinking. By the early years of the twentieth century there are signs that the world was moving on, with subtle shifts in the way ancient communities were studied and understood.

NATIONALISM AND CULTURAL HISTORIES

Romantic interpretations of Stonehenge and its surroundings did not die out during the nineteenth century, although they were eclipsed by the brightness of the brash, authoritative scientific inquiries of the age. However, during the early twentieth century there was renewed interest in interpretative studies, partly as a reaction to the scientific focus of the previous century or so and partly because of the political climate in Europe and beyond with its inherent concern for nationalism and identity. Attention shifted away from questions such as when Stonehenge was built, and for what purpose, towards an interest in who built it, what influenced them, and where they came from. Culture histories that recognized the distinctiveness of communities and sought interpretations based on migration, colonization, and invasion were favoured. Two publications of 1924 capture these changes in their content: *The stones of Stonehenge* by E Herbert Stone; and *Stonehenge today and yesterday* by Frank Stevens. Both also reflect the changing mood of the times in their style and presentation, Stevens' book benefiting from specially commissioned drawings by the Arts and Crafts illustrator Heywood Sumner.

Vere Gordon Childe, by far the most notable exponent of the cultural-historical approach in European prehistory, suggested (1940, 106) that:

> like the fabric of an English cathedral, the stones of Stonehenge mirror the fortunes of a community. Neither the construction of the Aubrey Circle nor even the erection of Lintel Circle and Horseshoe … would be beyond the power of a prosperous pastoral tribe profiting from the grazing of Salisbury Plain and the products of its flint-mines.

Who that community was can be found in the work of another great scholar of the period, Stuart Piggott. In 1938 he defined the Wessex Culture in classic Childean terms (Piggott 1938, 52) as:

A highly individual culture whose origin lies in an actual ethnic movement from N. France. The nature of the evidence – finds from the richly-furnished graves of chieftains – presents us with a view of the material equipment of an aristocratic minority. The basic folk culture appears, from the slight evidence available, to have been similar to the food-vessel culture of the greater part of Britain north of the Thames at this time.

Childe himself (1940, 135) described them as a 'small ruling class expending their accumulated surplus wealth on luxury trade with far-flung connections', but disagreed with Piggott's proposal that they were invaders from Brittany (Childe 1940, 141–3).

Investigations of the cultural associations of all the various elements of Stonehenge and its neighbouring monuments, the sequences of events represented there, and the local and long-distance associations demonstrated by finds and replicated ideas formed the main fields of inquiry between 1910 and the mid-1960s. It was these approaches that influenced the campaigns of early professional archaeologists in the area. Systematic excavation lay at the heart of many inquiries, as it had during the nineteenth century.

Following the presentation of Stonehenge to the Nation in 1918 a campaign of works was initiated with the combined purpose of exploring the site and assisting in its consolidation. The work was directed by William Hawley between 1919 and 1926; with further work by Robert Newall and George Englehart in 1929. In all, about half of the ditch circuit and approximately 40 per cent of the interior were examined (see *1*). Further excavations, again linked to the needs of restoration, took place between 1950 and 1964 under the auspices of Richard Atkinson, Stuart Piggott, and J F S Stone, and in 1950 and 1952 by Robert Newall (Cleal et al. 1995, 11–12). For many years the results from these campaigns were only available as interim accounts (Hawley 1921; 1922; 1923; 1924; 1925; 1926; 1928; Atkinson et al. 1952; Newall 1952; Piggott 1954a; 1959a), but in 1995 a consolidated report on all twentieth-century excavations provided a much-needed summary and a treasure-chest of previously unpublished information (Cleal et al. 1995).

Many other research papers on Stonehenge were of course published in timely fashion. Work on the origins of the bluestones developed earlier thinking and helped fuel what has since become a long-running controversy on the relative merits of human agency as against glacial action as a means of transportation (Thomas 1923; see Thorpe et al. 1991, table 5). It was also during this time that seemingly authentic rock art was noted on a number of stones (Crawford 1954; see Thurnam 1866 for an earlier discussion of the possibility that such art may be present).

Prior to the Second World War the emphasis shifted away from a preoccupation with barrows to include an interest in other classes of site. Mr P Farrer observed sections cut by pipe-trenches through the bank of Durrington Walls and the central part of the Stonehenge Cursus in 1917. Dr J F S Stone, a chemist based at Porton Down with a great passion for archaeology, excavated at numerous sites along Countess Road and around Ratfyn that were brought to light in the 1920s and 30s through property development, road-widening, or the laying of pipelines. He also directed work at a mini-henge on the east side of Fargo Plantation that had come to light when Boy Scouts found prehistoric pottery in upcast from rabbit burrows (Stone 1939). Excavations were carried out at a newly discovered Roman villa at Upavon in 1907 (Anon 1930), Casterley Camp in 1912 (Cunnington and Cunnington 1913), and Winterbourne Stoke in 1925 (Newall 1926). Surface collections were also assuming a more prominent place in archaeological research, evident for example in the work of Laidler and Young (1938) on King Barrow Ridge.

Aerial photography played an increasingly important role in the documentation of sites in the Stonehenge landscape as the twentieth century unfolded. The first successful aerial photographs of an archaeological site in Britain were of Stonehenge, taken from a military balloon by Lt Sharpe in the summer of 1906 (Capper 1907; but see also Barber 2005). Crawford and Keiller included images of Ogbury Camp, Bush Barrow, Amesbury Down, and Stonehenge in their now classic volume *Wessex from the air* (1928). The discovery of Woodhenge though aerial photography in 1926 led to very extensive excavations by Benjamin and Maud Cunnington (last of three generations of archaeo-logically inclined Cunningtons) between 1926 and 1928 (Cunnington 1929). In addition, they excavated four ring-ditches/barrows immediately south of Woodhenge and the enclosure known as The Egg (Cunnington 1929, 49).

Investigations associated with the construction of military facilities on the south side of Salisbury Plain made important contributions to the archaeology of the area before, during, and after the Second World War. In 1930 Amesbury 85 was examined before the construction of an airfield at Boscombe Down (Newall 1931), the subsequent expansion of which called for further excavations in 1948–9. This was one of the largest excavations carried out in the area up until that time and such was the scale of the work that a drag-line excavator was used to remove ditch fills; it is one of the earliest cases in Britain where heavy plant was used in an archaeological excavation (Richardson 1951, figure 5).

Post-war decommissioning of military installations and increases in demand for cultivated land led to large tracts of landscape around Stonehenge being ploughed up between 1945 and the early 1960s with the result that earthworks were levelled and important sites destroyed. The biggest casualties were among round barrows (see for example Grinsell 1978a, 5). Campaigns of excavations were launched, in most cases after sites had already been heavily damaged. There were major investigations at: Amesbury 101 in the 1920s (Passmore 1940); Wilsford 51–4 on Normanton Down in 1958 (Smith 1991); 18 barrows near Shrewton in 1958–60 (Green and Rollo-Smith 1984); Wilsford 2–5 in 1959 (Grimes 1964); 12 barrows in Amesbury and Winterbourne Stoke between 1959 and 1961 (Gingell 1988); Wilsford 1, 33, and 33a in 1960 (Field 1961); Amesbury 51 in 1960 (Ashbee 1978a); and Amesbury 70 and 71 in 1961 (Christie 1964; 1970). The excavation of the pond barrow Wilsford 33a between 1960 and 1962 led to the discovery of the Wilsford Shaft, a 30m-deep pit cut into the solid chalk perhaps as a well or ritual feature (Ashbee et al. 1989). Excavations at the west end of the Cursus, and at barrow Winterbourne Stoke 30 within the Cursus (Christie 1963), have since allowed the restoration of the Cursus's western terminal and barrow 30 to their pre-1950 appearances.

One of the first geophysical surveys in Britain was undertaken using a Megger Meter at the so-called long mortuary enclosure on Normanton Down in 1957–8, no doubt encouraged by Richard Atkinson's enthusiasm for remote sensing prior to excavation. The site was subsequently excavated and dated to the late fourth millennium BC (Vatcher 1961, 160; and cf. Clark 1990, 12–13).

In the post-war years the range of sites recorded expanded, and the opportunities for small-scale investigations at known monuments increased greatly. Flint mines were discovered and recorded east of the Stonehenge Inn in 1952 (Booth and Stone 1952). A pipe-trench through Durrington Walls in 1950–1 revealed possible structures to the south of the enclosure and these were explored further in 1952. It was charcoal from this excavation that provided material for radiocarbon dating, as it turned out the first two radiometric dates on archaeological material from the British Isles (Piggott 1959b). Another essentially research-driven excavation was carried out at Robin Hood's Ball in August 1956 to assess the age and nature of the earthworks long known to antiquarians (Thomas 1964).

The 1950s and early 1960s in particular were a period characterized by works of synthesis and review, triggered by the new excavations by Atkinson, Piggott, and Stone. Atkinson's volume *Stonehenge*, first published in 1956, appeared before the excavation was finished, although it was later updated (Atkinson 1979). One of the most important, but generally rather ignored, studies was that by Stuart Piggott published in 1951 and thus pre-dating Atkinson's well-known volume by five years. Taking account of the interim reports from Hawley's work and Newall's overview (1929a), Piggott re-examined the 'two-date theory' (1951, 275). This proposed that the encircling ditch, bank, Aubrey Holes, and cremation deposits were of an earlier date than the centrally situated stone circles (see R H Cunnington 1935, 74–5). In broadly accepting it he developed a three-stage sequence for the construction of the monument which he termed Stonehenge I, II, and III respectively (Piggott 1951). It was this basic sequence that Atkinson used in modified form in 1956 (Atkinson 1956, 58–77).

By the mid-1960s the cultural-historical approaches to Stonehenge and surrounding sites that had been fuelled by decades of excavation and fieldwork began to run out of steam. A resurgent interest in more scientific, explanatory approaches again surfaced and served to redirect attention.

PROCESSUALISM

Two lines of inquiry about Stonehenge that had lain dormant for a period came back to life in the mid-1960s. In 1966 Gerald Hawkins published a book entitled *Stonehenge decoded* in which he speculatively expanded the astronomical aspects of Stonehenge, suggesting that it was in effect a giant computer used for the prediction of eclipses and other astronomical events. Although it was a line of argument that built on similar statements 60 years previously it hit the mood of the times and generated a lot of interest that continued for many years after (Colton and Martin 1967; 1969; Hawkins 1966a; 1966b; Newham 1966; 1972; Thatcher 1976; Thom 1974; 1975). It caused much debate, in relation to both the astronomy and the interpretation of the archaeological features (Atkinson 1966; Hoyle 1966; 1973 Hawkins 1973; Hawkins et al. 1967; Moir 1979), and in terms of the increasing conflict of position between an essentially Romantic role for archaeology and an Enlightenment role (Hawkes 1967). A recent review by Ruggles (1997) picks up the fall-out from these various debates.

A second area of controversy was rekindled by G A Kellaway with a restatement of the argument that the bluestones from west Wales arrived at Stonehenge by glacial action rather than human agency (Kellaway 1971). Again, this matter was widely aired with a variety of contrary views taken through the later 1970s and beyond (e.g. Atkinson 1974; 1979, 105–16; Kellaway 1991; 2002; Thorpe et al. 1991; Darrah 1993; Ixer 1997a; 1997b); Burl 2000b; Castleden 2001, and will be considered further in Chapter 5.

The exchanges that surrounded the rediscovery of these questions were entirely typical of the increasing influence of modernist thinking in both the humanities and the sciences. Axiomatic to this was an internationalizing tendency in which general laws and principles were sought. In archaeological studies this is reflected in reactions to the essentially static, cultural-historical frameworks by those interested in dynamic models which address, in a testable way, questions of how and why things are as they appear to be. It was a way of thinking initially called the New Archaeology, but later characterized as 'processualism' or 'Social Archaeology' (Renfrew 1973b).

Although the dating of Stonehenge itself and the surrounding monuments had been at the focus of research efforts during the early twentieth century, it was not until radiocarbon dating was developed in the 1950s that absolute dates became available. By the late 1960s enough had been obtained to show that some traditional models based on cross-dating and diffusion were fundamentally flawed. Colin Renfrew's paper 'Wessex without Mycenae' published in 1968 started the demolition of many long-cherished ideas (11), a process continued with increasingly devastating effect when the calibration of radiocarbon ages to calendar years allowed greater ease of comparison between radiometric determinations and historically documented events (Renfrew 1968; 1973a). By the mid-1970s it was not only the chronologies that were being called into question but the whole purpose and nature of archaeological interpretation. Renfrew suggested that the future lay in the study of cultural process through the analysis of different fields of activity, different subsystems of the cultural system to use a cybernetic analogy, which if properly understood should give the information needed to understand the workings of the culture as a whole (Renfrew 1974, 36). Stonehenge and its associated monuments have been widely used in exploring such a processual approach to prehistory, amongst them Renfrew's own study of social change in the area (Renfrew 1973a).

Excavations and surveys continued, but were now set within a more formal 'problem-orientated approach' with specific questions to be answered by defined

11 The Lion Gate at Mycenae, Greece. The style of architecture represented in the gateway and the Cyclopean walling was once thought to provide a prototype for elements of Stonehenge. Radiocarbon dating showed that the walls at Mycenae were built *c.*1350–1250 BC while the Phase 3 stone circles at Stonehenge date to *c.*2500–2400 BC. *Photograph: Timothy Darvill, copyright reserved*

techniques. Two investigations undertaken at Stonehenge in 1978 show the pattern. Alexander Thom uncovered the northwestern Station Stone (Stone 94) in order to determine its original position. Meanwhile, in the same year, John Evans made a cutting through the outer ditch in order to recover environmental samples (Evans 1984). By far the largest excavations in the immediate vicinity of Stonehenge were those connected with the construction of extensions to the car-park in 1966 and 1979, the creation of an underpass and associated works in 1967, and a whole range of pipe-trenches and cable-laying in 1968 and 1979–80 (*12*). Faith and Lance Vatcher undertook much of this work, with later seasons by Mike Pitts and the Central Excavation Unit of English Heritage (formerly the Department of the Environment). In total, these investigations added considerably to what was known about the area immediately around Stonehenge, and included major discoveries that fundamentally changed understandings of the monument: a partner for Stone 96 (the Heelstone); postholes dating to the eighth millennium BC and an early treehole in the western end of the car-park; and the so-called Palisade Ditch north and west of Stonehenge. There were also opportunities to explore the eastern end of the Avenue near the Avon west of Amesbury in advance of house-construction (Smith 1973).

12 Excavations directed by Mike Pitts beside the A344 north of the Heelstone in advance of laying a new telephone cable in June 1979. *Photograph: Timothy Darvill, copyright reserved*

Elsewhere, a wide range of construction works, pipe-trenches, and cable-laying led to numerous watching briefs and small-scale excavations, as for example at Amesbury 25 and 103 barrows in 1978–9 (Pitts 1980). Rather more substantial excavations took place in advance of tree-planting on the later prehistoric and Roman site southwest of Durrington Walls in 1970 (Wainwright 1971).

Alterations to the road network around Amesbury in the later 1960s provided numerous opportunities for archaeological investigation. Works included the construction of a dual carriageway along the A303 in the eastern part of the Stonehenge landscape, the creation of a by-pass around the north side of Amesbury (also A303), construction of a roundabout and modification to the road alignments at Longbarrow Crossroads, and the realignment of the A345 through Durrington Walls. All revealed important finds and structures. The single largest operation was at Durrington Walls where extensive excavations took place between 1966 and 1968. As at Boscombe Down earlier, earthmoving machinery was extensively used by Geoffrey Wainwright to uncover a large area for excavation, here using highly manoeuvrable JCBs to remove topsoil and clear the site (Wainwright and Longworth 1971, 10); the approach caused disquiet in the archaeological community at the time but set a pattern much followed since (Wainwright 2000b, 913). Amesbury 39, excavated in 1960, in advance of widening works on the A303, was subsequently reconstructed with a revetment to support the underlying chalk (Ashbee 1980). The most unexpected find associated with the A303 widening was probably the so-called 'plaque-pit' west of King Barrow Ridge (Harding 1988): a small chalk-cut pit containing two rather unusual decorated chalk plaques datable to the later third millennium BC.

As an essentially scientific school of thought, processualism promoted the scientific study of sites and materials and it was in such an environment that technical studies of ancient materials from around Stonehenge flourished: amber (Shennan 1982; Beck and Shennan 1991), shale (Brussell et al. 1981; Pollard et al. 1981), metal (Britton 1961; Ottaway 1974), faience (McKerrell 1982), and stone (Howard in Pitts 1982).

Contextual information to set alongside the work at individual monuments was provided by two surveys. The first, *Stonehenge and its environs* provides a review of field monuments in the area (RCHM 1979), expanding and updating an earlier listing compiled by Leslie Grinsell (1957). Second was the extensive Stonehenge Environs Survey directed by Julian Richards and undertaken between 1980 and 1986. This work included systematically fieldwalking all available cultivated land (*c.*750ha), excavations at 15 sites ranging in date from the fourth to the first millennium BC, and the sampling of dry-valley fills (Richards 1990). By the time the Stonehenge Environs Survey was published, however, challenges to the theoretical basis of social archaeology were mounting and in a seminal paper published in 1984 Ian Hodder poignantly asked how 'can a scientific archaeology devoted to the testing of theories against data cope with verifying statements about ideas in prehistoric people's heads?' (1984, 25).

POST-PROCESSUALISM

In the summer of 1985 clashes between the Wiltshire police and a convoy of New Age travellers hoping to hold a festival at Stonehenge to mark the Summer Solstice culminated in the 'Battle of the Beanfield' (Chippindale 1986b; Worthington 2005). It was a confrontation that resonated beyond the obvious issues of power, authority, and control, touching the very heart of post-modernist views of the world in which all activity is political, and spilling over into archaeology to further fuel critiques of processualism.

Central to post-processualist archaeology is the notion that the past and present cannot be separated because it is us here in the present day who create and validate all the categories of material and dimensions of the past that we choose to explore. The questions we pose, and the answers we find, are always created in the present out of our particular embodied historical and social context. Thus post-processualism is relativist in its outlook and seeks interpretations rather than explanations. In this view the past can be understood in various ways, through multiple narratives which may compete for acceptance (multi-vocality) and through the construction of non-linear narratives that simultaneously represent a range of standpoints. Christopher Chippindale's book *Stonehenge complete*, first published in 1983, and the volume *Who owns Stonehenge?* (Chippindale et al. 1990) were among the first attempts to consider the changing and often contested meaning of Stonehenge itself. Later, Barbara Bender took the arguments out into the landscape through various papers (Bender 1992; 1993) and a full-length book *Stonehenge: making space* (Bender 1998). Similar themes are also included in the English Heritage *Teacher's handbook to Stonehenge* (Anderson et al. 1996) where the emphasis is placed on how to read the archaeology rather than the presentation of a definitive narrative.

Interpretative reviews of Stonehenge and its landscape include works by: Nick Thorpe and Colin Richards (1984) on the decline of ritual authority in Wessex during the third millennium BC as Beaker pottery becomes widespread in Britain; Colin Richards and Julian Thomas (1984) on ritual activity and structured deposition at Durrington Walls; the present author on symbolic landscapes (Darvill 1997a); Alasdair Whittle on structures and meanings (1997a); and Mike Parker Pearson and Retsihisatse Ramilisonina (1998) on the social use of space across the Stonehenge landscape.

Another illuminating area of research that developed during the early 1990s involved exploring the phenomenology of landscape in an attempt to understand how it was experienced as people engaged with it (see Tilley 1994). Following these ideas a team based at Birmingham University developed an interactive CD-ROM visualizing the landscape around Stonehenge and allowing journeys through real-and-imagined worlds (Exon et al. 2001).

One practical effect of making the past a powerful part of the present is the way in which the distinctions between past and present become blurred. The use of Stonehenge as the setting for a story or as a powerful image has a long history, but from the late 1960s its appearance in popular and historical fiction, poetry, art, advertising, and 'pop' culture has become considerably more common (see Grinsell 1986; Chippindale 2004; Darvill 2004a). By the end of the 1990s the range of Stonehenge-inspired literature was very considerable, and included best-sellers by Edward Rutherford (1987) and Bernard Cornwell (1999) among others.

Alongside these post-processualist projects a good deal of more traditional archaeology continued to flourish and will, in due course, no doubt provide the bedrock upon which the next turn of the cultural dialectic will be founded. In the field of landscape studies, for example, the analysis of the changing environment provides a key element that also bears on changing land-use (Richards 1990; Allen 1995; 1997). Detailed plotting of aerial photographs and the application of new methods of remote sensing (Bewley et al. 2005) allow ever more vestigial earthworks to be identified and mapped. Extensive geophysical surveys provide increasingly detailed views of subsurface features (David and Payne 1997). Radiocarbon dates add precision to prehistoric chronologies (Bayliss et al. 1997), while studies of historic sources (Crowley 1995) and the expansion of archaeological interests to cover remains from the modern era allow new understandings of life during recent centuries.

The need for investigations directly related to site management and conservation works can be seen in the excavation of new pathways into Stonehenge (Bond 1982), the recording of barrows on King Barrow Ridge and in Luxenborough Plantation damaged by storms in 1987 and 1990 (Cleal and Allen 1994), and extensive geophysical work at Durrington Walls and in the Stonehenge Triangle (David and Payne 1995, 73–113).

Survey work within the army's Salisbury Plain Training Area has been in progress since the early 1980s (R W Smith 1981; DLA 1993). More recently, site surveys and the consolidation of existing work was carried out by the Royal Commission on Ancient and Historical Monuments and presented as a wide-ranging synthesis (McOmish et al. 2002).

The application of approaches to the assessment and evaluation of sites prior to the determination of planning permissions, as set out in PPG16 (DoE 1990), but widely used before this time, introduced new kinds of archaeological investigation to the roster. At Butterfield Down, Amesbury, excavations in advance of a housing development revealed prehistoric, Roman, and Saxon remains (Rawlings and Fitzpatrick 1996). At Figheldean excavations and watching briefs for pipeline schemes allowed the excavation of later prehistoric and Romano-British enclosures and occupation sites (Graham and Newman 1993; McKinley 1999). Field evaluation followed by targeted excavation of selected areas revealed pits containing Beaker pottery at Crescent Copse, Shrewton (Heaton and Cleal 2000). In the far northwest corner of the Stonehenge landscape a pipeline scheme revealed, and then permitted the excavation of, an area of Romano-British settlement and part of a small cemetery of the same date (McKinley and Heaton 1996). And most recently, rich Beaker burials have been found at Amesbury in advance of constructing a new school (Fitzpatrick 2002; 2003a), and on Boscombe Down as a result of renewing a water-pipe (Fitzpatrick 2003b; 2004a). The largest excavation in the Stonehenge landscape, covering an area in excess of 10ha at Boscombe Down, was completed in 2004 and revealed numerous prehistoric and later features including a pit circle about 50m in diameter which dates to the late third millennium BC (Fitzpatrick 2004b).

Two major development schemes deserve special mention because of the extent of the work involved: the Stonehenge visitor centre proposals; and the A303 roadline improvements. These two schemes form what is known as the Stonehenge Project (English Heritage and National Trust 1999) and are considered further in Chapter 12.

Despite the wealth of literature produced under the rubric of post-processual archaeology, there have been very few research-oriented investigations since 1980. Small-scale excavations were carried out at Vespasian's Camp in 1987 (Hunter-Mann 1999), and also at the Netheravon Roman villa site in 1996 for an episode of the Channel

Four television series *Time Team* (Rawlings 2001). However, the launch in 2004 of the Stonehenge Riverside Project (Parker Pearson et al. 2003; 2004) offers hope that a new phase of research is dawning and that it will engage with a wealth of emerging questions and themes (Darvill 2005).

LANDSCAPE AND BIOGRAPHY

As the above discussion shows, the Stonehenge landscape is one of the most extensively investigated tracts of countryside in Britain, but there is still much to find out and much to learn. The sheer volume of material is now so great that more than a lifetime would be needed to read and digest it all. In the following chapters, therefore, results from a selection of the excavations and surveys noted above will be used to illustrate and support a biography of the landscape, starting from its birth and early development and ending with the twentieth century.

3

TUNDRA PLAINS AND WOODED WORLDS
(TO 4000 BC)

People first visited the Stonehenge landscape as much as half a million years ago, a time when northwest Europe would have looked and felt very different from how it is today. From at least one million years ago the northern hemisphere has experienced what is sometimes referred to as the Ice Age. This period, known to geologists as the Pleistocene, saw fluctuating climatic conditions in which very cold phases were interspersed with warm periods. The cold glacial periods were characterized by the southward expansion of the polar ice-cap and the local development of glacial systems around upland regions, beyond which, in periglacial areas, was arctic tundra. The warmer periods, interglacials, variously saw the establishment of forest cover or open savanna conditions. In simple terms there were four main glacial phases (Beestonian, Anglian, Wolstonian, and Devensian) between which were three interglacials (Cromerian, Hoxnian, and Ipswichian), but within these main blocks there were many fluctuations and changes that can be modelled in some detail through the examination of ice-cores from Greenland and ocean-floor sediments from the north Atlantic. The last glacial phase, the Devensian, seems to have ended about 12,000 BC, and it now seems that we are living in an interglacial (known as the Flandrian) of the kind seen several times before. How long it will last we cannot tell, but global warming, melting ice-caps, and changing weather patterns such as we now hear so much about are all entirely typical of the tumultuous trends seen in previous interglacials.

Even at their maximum extent no ice-sheets are known to have extended as far south as Salisbury Plain, although their influence was certainly felt. During glacial periods the area would have been subject to permafrost and freeze-thaw conditions that cracked the underlying bedrock and created solifluction and cryoturbation features such as ice-wedges, frost polygons, festoons, and involutions (Evans 1968). The break-up and uneven distribution across the landscape of sarsen boulders may in large measure be attributed to periglacial solifluction processes (Bowen and Smith 1977, 187). During periods of global warming, when the ice-caps and glaciers melted, torrents of surface water and swollen rivers moved loose rocks, sediments, and any humanly created artefacts or other remains, mixing them and depositing them as superficial layers of sand, gravel, and coombe rock in river valleys and clay-with-flints across the downlands. Gradual erosion during the warmer interglacials removed or re-sorted some of these deposits but left others untouched. The fact that it all happened several times over adds to the complexity and makes the task of sorting it all out less than easy.

Excavations at Durrington Walls in 1966–8 allowed the careful examination of a layer of coombe rock in the base of the shallow valley running through the site. This suggested that the valley had been carved out during a period of extreme cold, but that conditions had been moist enough for solifluction and the formation of the coombe rock. This possibly happened during the middle part of the Devensian glaciation (also known as the Weichselian) c.30,000 to 50,000 BC. Later frost weathering created a series of involutions within the bedrock surface in which there was a snail fauna suggestive of an open tundra environment, although the dating of this horizon is extremely uncertain (Wainwright and Longworth 1971, 334).

Spreads of clay-with-flints are mainly confined to small areas of the higher ground west of the River Avon (13), but river and valley gravels are widely distributed along the Avon and its tributaries, and along the Till (Piggott 1973a). In places they are sealed below deposits of alluvium that probably formed in later prehistoric times. But what evidence is there for human activity during the Pleistocene Ice Age? What happened after the Devensian glaciation? And how did people adjust to the changing conditions at the start of the present interglacial?

ONCE UPON AN ICE AGE

Preserved *in situ* occupation deposits from Pleistocene times are extremely rare in Britain, and in this regard the Stonehenge landscape is no exception. What we do have are secondary, *ex situ* remains mixed into naturally formed deposits, and occasional stray finds.

Two findspots in the Avon Valley have yielded Pleistocene faunal remains. Grinsell (1957, 27) reported teeth of mammoth and woolly rhinoceros from a spot in Amesbury parish, probably a gravel pit, while a mammoth tooth was found during gravel quarrying in Durrington parish (Stevens 1921; Grinsell 1957, 65). Both finds serve to illustrate something of the range of animal species in the area during the late Pleistocene even though attributing them to a specific phase is not possible from present evidence. The discoveries also confirm the great potential of the gravel terraces in this section of the valley as sources of information about the area at this early date.

Tools and weapons left by human communities exploiting the area between 500,000 and 170,000 BC have been found at five sites within the Stonehenge landscape, although in some cases details of their discovery are scant and in some cases even the exact findspot is not known (13). On typological grounds all may tentatively be assigned to the Hoxnian interglacial or early stages of the Wolstonian glacial phase and may well be associated with

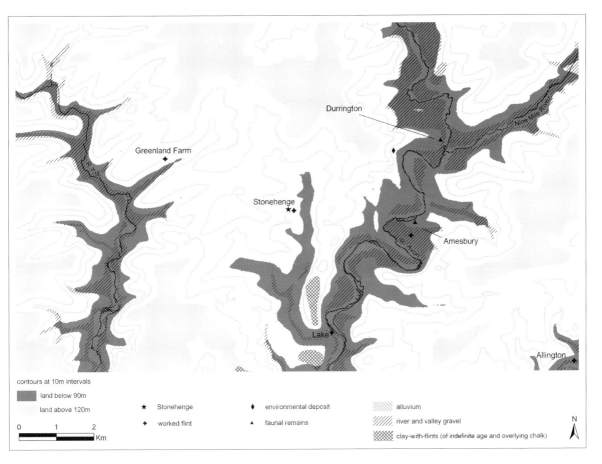

13 Map of the Stonehenge landscape showing Pleistocene deposits and recorded sites and findspots dating to before *c.*10,000 BC. *Drawing by Vanessa Constant: Wiltshire SMR and various archaeological sources over mapping from EDX Engineering Inc. data at 50m intervals and Ordnance Survey © Crown Copyright 2006. All rights reserved. Licence 100045276*

the activities of *Homo erectus*, the first hominid species to colonize northern latitudes. At Lake in the Avon Valley, finds made in terrace gravels during the later nineteenth century include at least two ovate handaxes probably of Acheulean tradition (*14D*) as well as struck flakes (Evans 1897, 627–8; Roe 1969, 13). A handaxe from south of Amesbury Abbey may also derive from the river gravels, while two handaxes from Allington came from deposits in the valley of the River Bourne (WA 1993b, AV3–1).

There are also finds on the interfluves between the main rivers. A handaxe from 'near Stonehenge' (WA 1993b, AV3–3) may be of Acheulean tradition; while in 1992 a group of three handaxes (*14A–c*) and associated worked flints of Acheulean tradition was found on an upland field situated on a spur on the north side of the Wylye Valley just outside the Stonehenge landscape at Stapleford (Harding 1995).

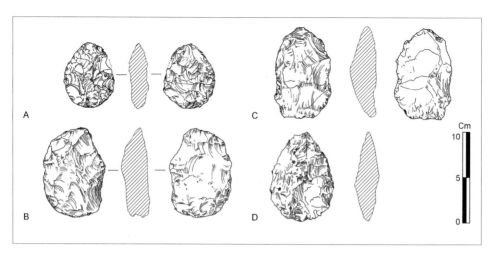

14 Flint implements of the period 500,000–100,000 BC from the Stonehenge landscape. A–C: Stapleford. D: Lake. *Drawings by Vanessa Constant: A–C after Harding 1995, 12; D after Evans 1897, figure 468*

Of slightly later date is a flint core of 'tortoise' type found southwest of Greenland Farm, Winterbourne Stoke (Anon 1973). This may be related to the Mousterian industries of the Ipswichian interglacial or early Devensian, 170,000–25,000 BC, that are often associated with the cultural traditions of *Homo neanderthalensis* (Roe 1981, 233–52).

Further searches in the river gravels and elsewhere will no doubt reveal additional finds that will enrich this rather sparse picture of life in Devensian and earlier times. That the area was more densely occupied than present evidence suggests is fairly certain. The Avon and the Till form the headwaters of one of the main rivers feeding the Solent River that in Pleistocene times joined a mighty river flowing east to west through what is now the English Channel (Bridgland 2001). Gravel terraces along the middle and lower reaches of the Solent River, for example south of Salisbury and at the confluence of the Avon and Stour around Bournemouth, are extremely rich in tools and worked flint of these early periods (Harding and Bridgland 1998; Wymer 1999, map 23; Hosfield 2001). All of this material must ultimately have derived from landscapes further to the north through which these ancient rivers once ran.

EARLY POSTGLACIAL COMMUNITIES (12,500–7000 BC)

Following a break in the occupation of northwestern Europe between about 25,000 BC and 12,500 BC, the coldest part of the Devensian glaciation, modern humans (*Homo sapiens sapiens*) recolonized the region from the south and east (Housley et al. 1997). Sea-level was sufficiently low at this time for both the North Sea and the English Channel to be dry land so that what we know as the British Isles were essentially an extension of the North European Plain. The territories occupied by human communities were large, the populations mobile hunter-gatherer groups whose tools and weapons related closely to the animals and plants they exploited and the environmental conditions they found themselves living in. A succession of cultural groups have been recognized and many were related, if not in some cases closely tied, to communities whose homelands extended eastwards into what is now Belgium, the Low Countries, and southern Scandinavia, or southwards into northern France.

The first communities to recolonize Britain were Creswellian tool-using groups (12,500-11,500 BC) who were contemporaries of Magdalenean communities in France and probably closely related to the Hamburgian communities of Belgium and the Low Countries (Breest and Veil 1991; Jacobi 1991). None of the distinctive flint tools and weapons of these groups such as the trapezoidal blunted-back blades, scrapers, piercers, and burins have yet been found in the Stonehenge landscape, but these communities were big-game hunters and it is possible that the mammoth remains already referred to from gravels at Amesbury and Durrington belong to this early postglacial period.

Throughout much of the time that Creswellian groups occupied southern Britain the environment gradually got warmer and poorly vegetated open tundra turned to open steppe. However, about 11,500 BC temperatures stabilized or perhaps cooled slightly with the result that areas of scrubby woodland dominated by birch and willow dotted the countryside. Animal species that thrived on the open steppe disappeared and were replaced by large vertebrates such as red deer, elk, horse, and wild cattle. Technologies and cultural traditions changed too with the development between 11,500 and 10,500 BC of assemblages characterized by the presence of 'penknife points' – curve-backed blades blunted along the back and around one end but razor-shape along the straight cutting edge. Shouldered points, round thumb-nail scrapers, end scrapers, and burins are also represented in styles that suggest close affinity with the Federmesser industries of adjacent continental Europe (Barton 1999, 24–8).

A continuing climatic deterioration and increased aridity into a period known as the Younger Dryas between about 10,500 and 9000 BC prompted yet further changes to the plants and animals available to the hunter-gatherer communities of southern Britain. Wild horse and reindeer grazed on open grasslands as tree-cover diminished. Tools and weapons also changed with the development of what are called 'long blade' industries which are related to the Ahensburgian traditions of northern Germany (Barton 1999, 28–32). Low-lying settlements in river valleys were favoured by these communities and one of the type-sites of the period is Hengistbury Head, Dorset, overlooking the confluence of the rivers Avon and Stour (Barton 1992).

The end of the Younger Dryas cold stadial is marked by a period of rapid climatic warming and environmental change leading to a period of vegetation succession during which the chalkland of southern Britain developed thick cover of brown earth or argillic brown earth soils (in places up to 1m thick) supporting open woodland dominated initially by hazel and pine. The changing character of the environment is neatly illustrated by the results of pollen analysis from a transect through the northern floodplain of the Avon east of Durrington Walls. This shows that vegetation at the very base of the available sequence (1.6m below the present ground surface) comprised open herbaceous plant communities dominated by sedges and grasses, but that sharp increases in tree pollen indicating colonization by birch, pine, hazel, and oak soon followed (Cleal et al. 2004, 231).

Culturally, the period 9000-7500 BC is characterized by flintworking and styles of material culture found widely across northern Europe and known as the Maglemosian. Developing from the earlier 'long blade' industries, worked flints include obliquely blunted points, microliths, and what have come to be called 'broad-blade assemblages'. One of the most extensive sites of this period in central southern Britain is at Downton beside the River Avon south of Salisbury. Here structural evidence in the form of scoops, cooking pits, and stakeholes was found as well as a large flint assemblage (Higgs 1959). Interestingly, like Stonehenge, Downton also lay within an area that was heavily used in the later third and early second millennia BC (Rahtz and ApSimon 1962).

No extensive Maglemosian flint scatters are known within the Stonehenge landscape, but, unusually, there is evidence for constructions of the period near Stonehenge itself (15). The most securely dated comprise three substantial postholes and a treehole found during the construction of the Stonehenge car-park north of the modern A344 in 1966 (Vatcher and Vatcher 1973). About 100m to the east was a pit (known as Pit 9580) found during alterations to the visitor centre in 1988–9 (Cleal et al. 1995, 43–7). Charcoal dates posthole A to 8560–8200 BC (HAR-455: 9130±180 BP), posthole B to 7550–6550 BC (HAR-456: 8090±180 BP), and the base of the recut secondary fill of Pit 9580 to 8300–7750 BC (GU-5109: 8880±80 BP). The date of the treehole is not known although it is sometimes assumed to be contemporary and may in fact have been the focus of this small cluster of features (16). Their wider context in terms of potential relationships with areas outside the investigated trenches is unknown, but will perhaps be explored one day. No artefacts are associated with any of the features, but they are distinctive in having an abundance of pine charcoal which Allen (in Cleal et al. 1995, 52) associates with the Boreal biostratigraphic subdivision of the Flandrian. The pollen sequence and mollusca profile from Pit 9580 provide the first evidence for the character of the Boreal woodland actually within the chalklands: a birch, pine, hazel mix.

Together, this small but dispersed group of features suggests that the landscape hereabouts was somehow regarded as special by this time, worth marking, and deserving of repeated visits. The posts that once stood in the Stonehenge car-park are widely interpreted as similar to the totem-poles of indigenous North American communities (e.g. Allen in Cleal et al. 1995, 55–6; Allen 1997, 125–6) and as such would represent the first appearance of monumental features in the landscape. They may have been painted or carved with intricate designs that narrated stories of the world, or the imagery may have been more subtle and grounded in the modification of the natural world (17). Certainly the posts themselves were whole trunks of pine, each between 0.6 and 0.8m

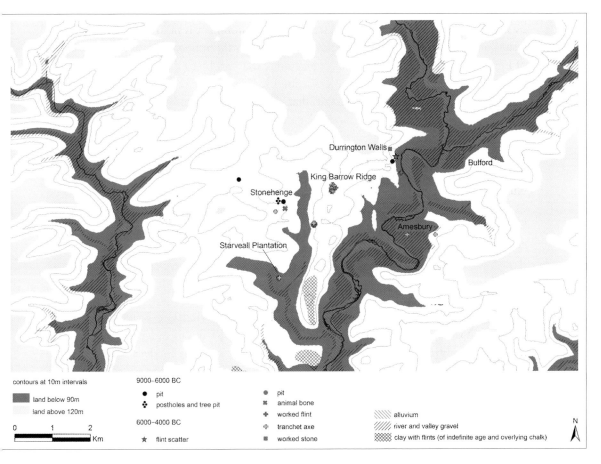

15 Map of the Stonehenge landscape showing the distribution of recorded sites and findspots dating to the period *c.*9000–4000 BC. *Drawing by Vanessa Constant: Wiltshire SMR and various archaeological sources over mapping from EDX Engineering Inc. data at 50m intervals and Ordnance Survey © Crown Copyright 2006. All rights reserved. Licence 100045276*

in diameter standing 3–4m out of the ground. Whether all three posts stood at the same time is unclear. The radiocarbon dates can be spread out over anything between 300 and 1600 years so while it is possible that they represent some unity in construction it is equally possible that they represent two successive replacements of an original marker.

Pit 9580 was nearly 2m across and about 1.3m deep. It had clearly been recut and reshaped at least once, suggesting periodic visits to the site by those who knew of its presence and purpose. The almost complete absence of finds from the successive fills suggests that it was not a storage pit or a rubbish pit, but rather an attempt to delve into the earth. A large piece of pine charcoal from the primary fill might suggest the deposition of a burnt branch or timber liberated from elsewhere. The juxtaposition of a pit and massive upright posts in relation to a tree may also be relevant, if it is accepted

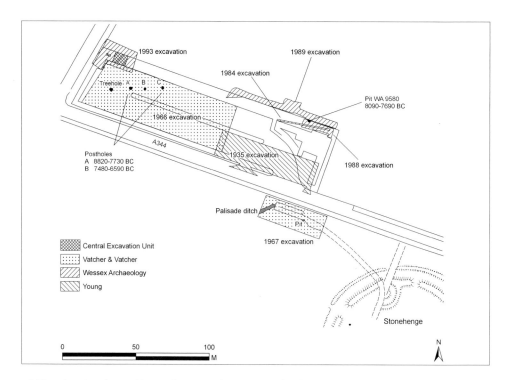

16 Plan showing the position and extent of excavations for the car-park, visitor facilities, and underpass below the A344 with recorded archaeological features indicated. *Drawing by Vanessa Constant: after Cleal* et al. *1995, figure 24*

that the treehole is broadly contemporary. Like the constructed features, the tree serves to link an underworld below the ground with the world of mortals on the face of the earth and the sky above, but in this case through the artifice of a single living thing. In a way the erection of posts and the digging of a pit presages the construction some 5000 years later of Stonehenge itself. There may indeed be reason to imagine a long-lived more-or-less continuous theme running through the early life of this landscape which revolves around recurrently cutting pits into the earth and setting-up posts and stones as markers. It is a routine that we shall return to in later chapters.

Pits that are potentially contemporary with the example in the Stonehenge car-park have been found at two other sites nearby; more may await recognition through the review of published excavation reports. Below Winterbourne Stoke 30 round barrow, situated within the western end of the Stonehenge Cursus, there was an oval hollow about 1.8 by 2.8m in extent. Stratigraphically it pre-dates the barrow and contained only pine charcoal as an indicator of its age (Christie 1963, 377 and 381). Similarly, a subsoil hollow or shallow pit beneath the bank at Woodhenge contained abundant flecks of charcoal and a slightly calcined core-trimming flake perhaps of the sixth or seventh millennium BC, associated with a woodland fauna (Evans and Wainwright 1979, 73, 162 and 192–4).

INSULAR POSTGLACIAL HUNTER-GATHERERS

Environmental changes continued as mean temperatures rose. Rises in relative sea-level flooded low-lying land thus creating the North Sea and the English Channel so that by about 7000 BC the British Isles were more-or-less as they appear today. Vegetation changed too with the relatively open conditions of the Boreal woodland giving way to a more closed oak, elm, and hazel dominated Wildwood. Human populations as well as animal populations may have contributed these changes. Charcoal dated to 8300–7100 BC (GU-3239: 8640±40 BP) from a depth of 1.6-1.45m below the northern floodplain of the River Avon east of Durrington Walls suggests that peat was beginning to form in the bottom of the valley at this time (Cleal et al. 2004, 231).

The period 7500–4000 BC is widely regarded as a period of supreme interest and importance because it embraces the transition from essentially hunter-gathering lifestyles to agricultural subsistence systems. Most of the period is characterized by small and obliquely blunted microliths and core tools, although insufficient assemblages from central southern England are known to allow accurate characterization. By the very end of the period, around 4000 BC, there is the first appearance of novel implements such as leaf-shaped arrowheads and polished axes, ceramics, the construction of earth and stone monuments, and the deliberate opening up of the environment. Such changes seem abrupt in the archaeological record, but in reality probably spanned several generations and involved the gradual adoption by local populations of lifestyles, economies, and ritual practices that were already well established on the adjacent continental mainland. For three and a half millennia the physical isolation from Europe as a result of rising sea-levels led to cultural isolation and the development of increasingly insular and regionalized technologies and material culture.

About 30 findspots of material dating to the period 7500–4000 BC are known in the Stonehenge landscape (Radley 1969; Wymer 1977; Coady 2004), most of them single pieces of worked flint or smaller localized scatters (*15*). Strangely though, the extensive fieldwalking surveys for the Stonehenge Environs Project revealed very little evidence of this period beyond a light scatter of microliths (Richards 1990, 16). This may be a result of inappropriate sampling strategies being applied, but another possibility is that the picture is biased by the fact that later prehistoric alluvium and colluvium is sealing land surfaces occupied in this period. Richards (1990, 263) cites the results of a sample excavation through a colluviual bench on the western side of the River Avon below Durrington Walls which revealed an *in situ* blade-based flint industry with microliths. More recently, in 2004, field evaluations west of Countess Farm carried out in connection with planning the A303 improvements revealed a hollow in the bedrock with associated flintwork sealed beneath a layer of alluvium/colluvium (J Keyte pers. comm.). Neither of these assemblages would have been identified through fieldwalking and they only came to light because of targeted excavations; other similar deposits no doubt await discovery along the main river valleys and may in due course change our picture of settlement in the seventh, sixth, and fifth millennia BC.

The distribution of findspots as currently recorded shows an interesting concentration on the Avon–Till interfluve especially along King Barrow Ridge (*15*). At least five tranchet axes/adzes have been found to date (*18*), mainly on the downland, including a possible example from the 1935 excavations in the Stonehenge car-park (Cleal et al. 1995, figure 203) and one from 'a field near Stonehenge' (Wymer 1977, 333). A piece of animal bone from the packing of Stonehole 27 in the Sarsen Circle at Stonehenge has been dated to 4340–3980 BC (OxA-4902: 5350±80 BP), possibly a piece of residual material sealed in a later feature but indicative of pre-henge activity that is otherwise invisible (Cleal et al. 1995, 188–90 and 529).

East of the Avon there are very few finds of this period, although the balance may be redressed by pits found during excavations at Boscombe Down Sports Field that have yet to be fully published. No sites at all are currently known in the western part of the Stonehenge landscape.

Little can be said about either the technological or the cultural relationships of the seventh- to fifth-millennium BC material from around Stonehenge as there is simply not enough of it to judge. In general, however, the area lies in a border region between

17 Reconstruction drawing of the tree and posts dated to *c.*7500 BC found in the Stonehenge Car-park. View looking southeast. *Drawing by Yvette Staelens, copyright reserved*

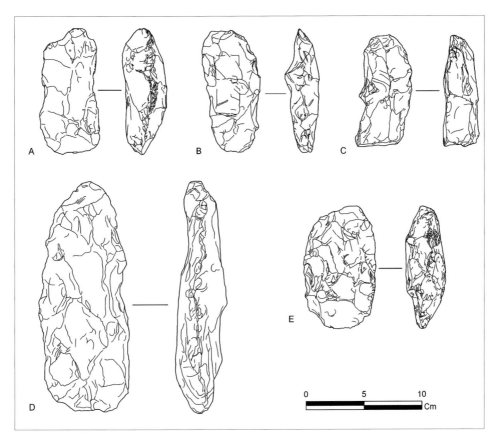

18 Tranchet axes from the Stonehenge landscape. A: Starveall Plantation. B: Tumulus 22. C: Holders Road, Amesbury. D: King Barrow Ridge. E: near Stonehenge. *Drawings by Vanessa Constant: implements in Devizes Museum (A, B, D, and E) and Salisbury and South Wiltshire Museum (C)*

two of Jacobi's putative technologically defined social territories: the South Western technology to the south and west, and the Wealden technologies to the east (Jacobi 1979, 68). Slight evidence for contacts within these territories and further afield is represented by imports to the region. A flake of Portland chert found in 'a field near Stonehenge' must have been brought from outcrops on the south coast (Wymer 1977, 333; cf. Palmer 1970). And a perforated-dolerite pebble hammer, probably from the Welsh Marches, was found inside Durrington Walls (Crawford 1929, 49–50; but cf. Roe 1979, 36) although its exact date is not known. Rankine (1956, 159–60) lists two additional hour-glass perforated pebbles from the Stonehenge landscape – from Bulford and Winterbourne Stoke – but again little is known about the circumstances surrounding these finds, their origins, or indeed their date. As with several of these finds they may be just as relevant to what happened in the Stonehenge landscape during the fourth millennium BC, the subject of the next chapter.

4

MOUND-BUILDERS
(4000–3000 BC)

Long-term and deep-seated environmental changes across southern Britain began to make their impact felt on the Stonehenge landscape in the centuries either side of 4000 BC. By this time the climate was more Atlantic in feel, with temperature ranges similar to those of today but with a slightly higher rainfall (Piggott 1973b, 284; A G Smith 1981,133–44). River systems gradually changed their regime so the very character of the principal valleys altered. Peat was growing in the Avon Valley creating a marshy, rather wet, valley floor which, if the evidence of the Somerset Levels is any guide, might have needed wooden trackways to cross. There is evidence that the Wildwood clothing the higher ground in the Stonehenge landscape was diminishing, perhaps through clearance as a source of timber, as a means of creating open areas, or perhaps simply as a consequence of a greater human presence. Occasional storms and gales may have played a role. Below the Amesbury 39 round barrow on King Barrow Ridge there were eight or more tell-tale tree-throw pits (Ashbee 1980, 7) suggesting that perhaps the great storms of October 1987 and January 1990 had equally destructive prehistoric counterparts. Tree-throws have also been noted below the long mortuary enclosure on Normanton Down (Vatcher 1961, figure 3) and may account for the natural hollows below Wilsford 52 (Smith 1991, 20). More were certainly found beside the present A303 during field evaluations for the proposed road-improvement scheme in 2003–4.

Charcoal from sites scattered through the Stonehenge landscape suggests the presence of elm, ash, oak, hazel, and yew, but Mike Allen (1997, 127) describes the vegetation cover in this period as a 'complex mosaic … with areas of ancient denser woodland, light open mixed hazel and oak woodland and clear-felled areas of shrubs and grassland for grazing, browse, cultivation, and occupation'. Some cereal cultivation was practised, probably in small clearance plots or 'gardens'. Hazelnuts and tubers are represented amongst palaeobotanical material recovered from fourth-millennium BC sites (Richards 1990, 251). Buried soils of this period sealed beneath later monuments include rendzinas such as normally develop under grassland. But the soils are also thinner than in earlier millennia, suggesting perhaps that erosion was already having an impact.

Wild animals roamed the land, including red deer, roe deer, brown bear, wolf, wild cattle, wild pig, and horse. Beavers lived in the rivers, and brown trout was present amongst the animal remains recovered from a large pit at Coneybury (Richards 1990, 57). Domesticated species are also represented in the area from soon after 4000 BC: cattle, pig, and sheep. These are amongst the earliest domesticated animals known in Britain and DNA evidence suggests that they were not the products of local domestication but rather introductions from Europe (Bollongino et al. 2005; Larson et al. 2005). Wheat and barley were grown in the area during the fourth millennium BC and these too must have been introduced from continental Europe. Together with the biological manipulation of production and reproduction in animals, the use of domesticated plants is often seen as the hallmark of simple farming economies adopted by people living in the British Isles. Changes to the way these groups viewed their surroundings, what they believed, and how they rationalized what they saw around them were also part of the picture at this critical time in the life of the landscape and the relationships people had with it. Colin Renfrew has argued that a common proto-Indo-European language spread northwestwards from its origins in the Near East in tandem with the adoption of farming economies (Renfrew 1987; 1996). This would have provided a dimension of cultural identity not previously recognized, and perhaps provided the basis for closer inter-regional contacts throughout northwest Europe. But while the population of southern Britain may have increased in the period 4000 BC to 3000 BC, it is likely that most were direct descendants of earlier occupants of the area. DNA studies suggest that more than 85 per cent of the genes in today's white Britons come directly from early postglacial hunter-gatherer groups (Miles 2005, 67). It is perhaps not surprising therefore that some of the long-established traditions of the region were perpetuated through into the fourth millennium and beyond. One of these involved setting up markers; the other necessitated digging into the ground perhaps as a way of approaching the underworld and the powers believed to reside there.

PITS AND SHAFTS

A geophysical survey of Coneybury Hill to the east of the Avon in 1980 unexpectedly revealed a discrete, strong magnetic response. Subsequent excavations showed it to be a large pit nearly 2m across and more than 1.25m deep that had been cut into the chalk bedrock (Richards 1990, 40–61). Known as the Coneybury 'Anomaly' (19), this pit dates to the early fourth millennium BC, 4050–3640 BC (OxA-1402: 5050±100 BP). When first dug it had fairly straight sides and a flat bottom. It was left open for a few days or weeks after it was dug and lenses of chalk wash began to accumulate around the base. Within a short period a mass of ash-rich soil containing abundant pottery, animal bone, and worked flints was dumped into the pit creating a layer some 20cm thick right across the floor. Several basket-loads must have been involved, and a few of the larger items such

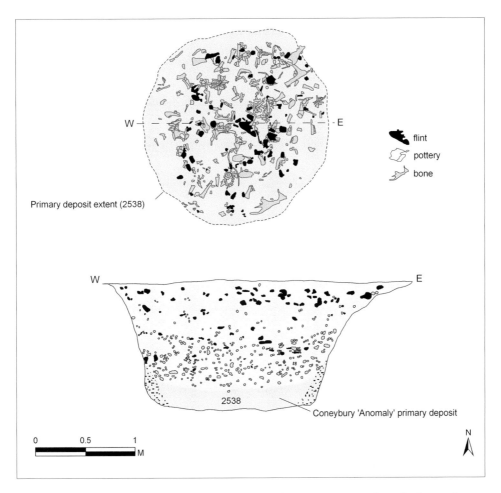

19 The Coneybury 'Anomaly' excavated in 1981. *Drawing by Vanessa Constant: after Richards 1990, figure 24*

as broken deer antlers seem to have been placed, perhaps deliberately, around the edge. Oak and hazel were recognized among the fragments of charcoal, also blackthorn and hawthorn. High phosphate levels suggest that originally there had been other organic material here too, a few grains of wheat indicating that it was perhaps food-waste. The animal bones included the remains of at least 10 domestic cattle, several wild roe deer, 2 red deer, and 1 pig. A few bones from a beaver and a brown trout were also present. At least 41 ceramic vessels were represented, all locally manufactured but in mainly plain styles common throughout southwestern England during the early fourth millennium BC. Cups and small bowls predominated, but there is at least one large, deep vessel that could have served as a communal cooking pot. The worked flints included 47 flint scrapers, 2 leaf-shaped arrowheads, and part of a broken ground flint axe, as well as flakes, blades, and cores. It seems likely that all this material had been taken from a midden somewhere in the vicinity and brought to the site as some kind of ceremonial deposit. Interestingly, Mark Maltby's analysis of the animal bones suggests that they represent a major butchery episode and that meat from the roe deer was probably consumed immediately after butchery. In contrast the dressed cattle and red deer carcasses were consumed elsewhere, perhaps preserved by smoking for later use. The presence of calves of red deer, cattle, and roe deer, assuming they were all born in the spring, suggests that this event happened in the summer months, perhaps a feast or celebration of some kind spread over several days or weeks, that culminated in a proportion of the waste debris being ceremoniously taken up onto Coneybury Hill and buried in a freshly dug pit. Once the deposit had been made the pit seems to have been abandoned to the elements. The upper parts started to decay and fall in; the slow accumulation of silts and chalky rubble with occasional later finds intermixed shows that it remained visible as a pronounced hollow for at least 1000 years.

Longevity is also a feature of another chance discovery made in 1960 on Wilsford Down, 2.5km east of Coneybury. Here, Edwina Proudfoot intended excavating what appeared to be a recently bulldozed round barrow (Wilsford 33a) of a type known as a pond barrow. Typical of its type, this comprised a shallow depression about 12.6m across, surrounded by a low bank. Once excavations began, however, the site proved to be anything but typical and certainly not a conventional pond barrow. Instead the low bank enclosed a rock-cut shaft about 30m deep (20). The excavation of this extraordinary feature continued through into 1961 and 1962 under the charge first of Peter Gray and then Paul Ashbee (Ashbee et al. 1989). Debate continues as to the purpose and date of the shaft, the only real certainly being that it was not until the early Roman period that it had completely silted-up to the point where it was no longer recognizable. Prior to this the main fill seems to have accumulated during the second and first millennia BC, marked by a neat sequence of stratified pottery and a series of radiocarbon dates for pieces of bone that became incorporated into the fill as it built up. For most of its depth the shaft was round in cross-section and about 2m in diameter. The lowermost 2m or so was waterlogged when excavated, but it was clear that over time the level of the local water table had fluctuated and that while the lower part had always been waterlogged at times the water table had risen to a point just over 20m down. More significantly, the very bottom section of the shaft was narrower than the rest and showed abundant evidence of having been constructed using only antler picks. The finds from this lowermost section included a double-ended flint scraper, a selection of flint flakes and blades, a piece of hard flint and sand tempered pottery, and, most significant, pieces of a wooden container radiocarbon dated to 3650–3100 BC (OxA-1089: 4640±70 BP). Finds from the same general area and above date to the second millennium BC and may relate to a period of refurbishment when the shaft was cleared out and the sides tidied up (see Chapter 6). Samples from the early wooden container were rerun with a similar result, and tests were carried out to check for contamination resulting from conservation, with negative results (Ashbee et al. 1989, 68–9).

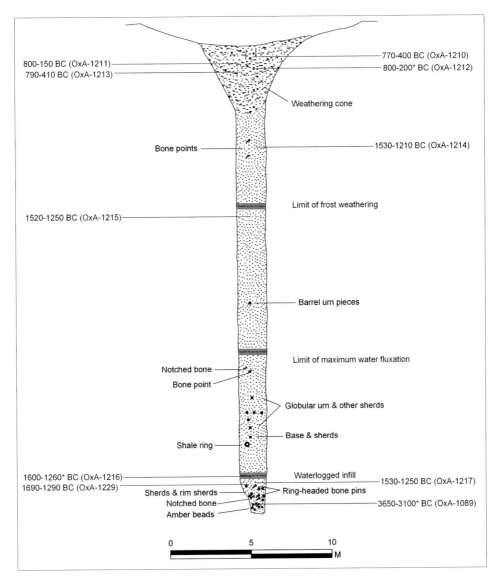

20 The Wilsford Shaft. *Drawing by Vanessa Constant: after Ashbee* et al. *1989, figure 7*

Single pits and clusters of small pits, also of the fourth millennium BC, are known in two other parts of the Stonehenge landscape (*21*). The first is along King Barrow Ridge and Vespasian's Ridge to the north of Coneybury. During the upgrading of the A303 a single pit dated to 3800–3100 BC (OxA-1400: 4740±100 BP) was found on the top of King Barrow Ridge, but details are scant (Richards 1990, 65–6). On the east side of the ridge another pit containing large fragments of three Windmill Hill Ware bowls was found beneath Amesbury 132 during excavations in 1959 (Gingell 1988, 39–41; *22* A, D, and H).

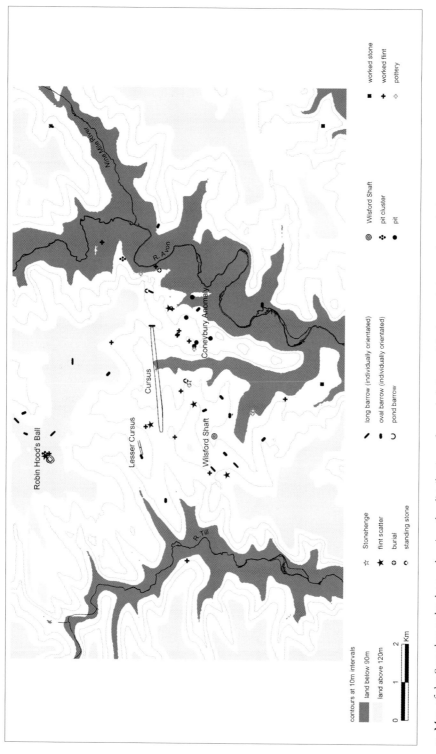

21 Map of the Stonehenge landscape showing the distribution of recorded sites and findspots dating to the period *c.*4000–3000 BC. *Drawing by Vanessa Constant. Wiltshire SMR and various archaeological sources over mapping from EDX Engineering Inc. data at 50m intervals and Ordnance Survey © Crown Copyright 2006. All rights reserved. Licence 100045276*

Legend:

contours at 10m intervals

land below 90m
land above 120m

0   1   2 Km

Stonehenge
flint scatter
burial
standing stone

Wilsford Shaft
pit cluster
pit

long barrow (individually orientated)
oval barrow (individually orientated)
pond barrow

worked stone
worked flint
pottery

Robin Hood's Ball

Cursus

Lesser Cursus

Wilsford Shaft

Coneybury Anomaly

Nine Mile River
R. Avon
R. Till

The second group of pits is around Robin Hood's Ball in the northern part of the Stonehenge landscape. Here a roughly circular cluster of shallow pits was revealed during the investigation of a dense scatter of worked flints immediately northeast of Robin Hood's Ball (Richards 1990, 61–5: Site W83). The pits contained pottery, worked flint, and animal bone. The pottery was mainly of the plain Southwestern Series typical of the area, but at least one decorated piece of rim belongs to the Southern Decorated Series found widely across southeastern England and divisible into local styles such as Windmill Hill Ware on the north Wessex Downs and Abingdon Ware around the middle and upper Thames Valley. Some pottery tempered with gabbroic rock fragments from The Lizard, Cornwall, was also present (Cleal and Raymond in Richards 1990, 234) demonstrating long-distance contacts and suggesting that what was placed in these pits was somehow rather special. Unusually, the worked flints included more than 200 scrapers as well as a more typical array of leaf-shaped arrowheads and considerable amounts of knapping debris. Although poorly preserved, the animal bones included pieces of cattle, pig, and sheep/goat; two animal bones were radiocarbon dated to 3800–3100 BC (OxA-1400: 4740±100 BP) and 3650–2900 BC (OxA-1401: 4550±120 BP), suggesting that these pits gradually accumulated, one at a time, over several centuries.

Individual pits, shafts, clusters of pits, and groups of pits and shafts together must have been a relatively common and widespread feature of fourth-millennium BC and later landscapes in the British Isles. Examples include: Kilverstone and Eaton Heath in Norfolk (Garrow et al. 2005; Wainwright 1973); Hurst Fen, Suffolk (Clark et al. 1960); Goodland, Northern Ireland (Case 1973); Billown Quarry, Isle of Man (Darvill 2003); and, in central southern England, Windmill Hill, Wiltshire (Whittle et al. 2000, 141–4), and Down Farm, Dorset (Green and Allen 1997). Many seem to be associated with, or link to, sink-holes or collapse structures in the underlying bedrock that would have created natural depressions or gaping holes inexplicable to contemporary minds but perhaps seen as evidence for activity by the spirits of the underworld. It is in such contexts that the deposition of individual objects or domestic rubbish taken from middens or occupation areas should be seen. With reference to the Goodland evidence, Humphrey Case asked 'what can have been the significance of settlement-rubbish?' concluding that 'it became directly associated in the mind of early man with fertile soil … with desirable conditions' and that 'similar practises of sympathetic magic have universal and consolatory roles in primitive societies' (Case 1973, 193). Feasting and working flint may equally be part of the activities connected with the recurrent periodic use of these places in the landscape, some of which lie close to formal enclosures or causewayed camps as at Robin Hood's Ball.

ROBIN HOOD'S BALL

More than 100 causewayed camps and related enclosures have been identified across the British Isles since their recognition as distinctive monuments in the early years of the

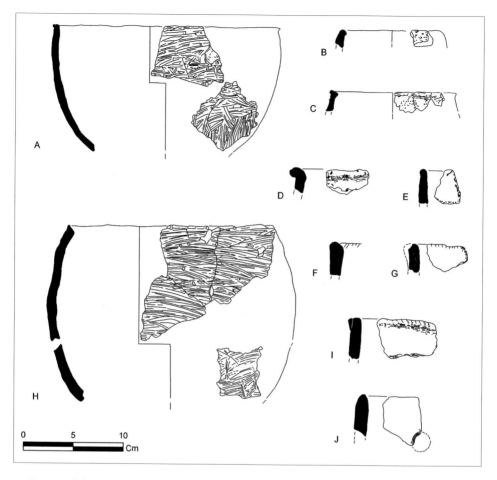

22 Pottery of the early fourth millennium BC. A, D, and H: Amesbury 132. B and C: Winterbourne Stoke 46. E and G: Wilsford 51. F: Wilsford 54. I and J: Wilsford 52. *Drawings by Vanessa Constant: A, B, C, D, and H after Gingell 1988, figures 18 and 34; E, F, G, I, J after Smith 1991, figure 13*

twentieth century (Oswald et al. 2001). Robin Hood's Ball is at present the only certain example within the Stonehenge landscape, situated on the higher ground almost exactly half way between the Avon and the Till some 4.5km northwest of Stonehenge itself (*21*). The inner enclosure at Yarnbury was once though to be an example too (Curwen 1930, 37), but this was disproved by Cunnington's excavations there in 1932 (Cunnington 1933b). Another likely looking site that has yielded finds of the fourth millennium BC is Ogbury, but further work would be needed to confirm this (cf. Crawford and Keiller 1928, 150–2).

Curiously, Robin Hood's Ball was recognized as an earthwork and described in some detail by Richard Colt Hoare at the beginning of the nineteenth century (1812, 176). He noted damage to the site by ploughing, and later it was further disturbed by the construction of rifle-butts for military training. The site was included in the first published list of British causewayed camps (Curwen 1930, 35–7), but it was Stuart Piggott who first mapped the true character and shape of the earthworks using aerial photographs (1954b, figure 3 and plate I). Four trenches excavated by Nicholas Thomas through the earthworks in 1956 confirmed the date and cultural affinities of the site (Thomas 1964; Oswald et al. 2001, 157; McOmish et al. 2002, 31–5).

Morphologically, Robin Hood's Ball comprises two roughly concentric circuits of interrupted ditches with low internal banks enclosing an area of about 3ha (23). The inner circuit is sub-circular, the outer circuit pentagonal in outline. Both circuits show flattened faces towards the southeast and both seem to have entrances opening in the same direction; a single centrally placed entrance in the inner circuit and a pair of wider gaps in the outer circuit. Other possible entrances may be noted in the outer circuit, including what looks like a blocked entrance marked by the short length of out-turned ditch in the west side. The overall impression is that the whole enclosure is oriented to the southeast and its elevated position certainly gives extensive views in this direction. It may indeed be significant that it overlooks the head of a tributary valley of the Avon known as Stonehenge Bottom (see below).

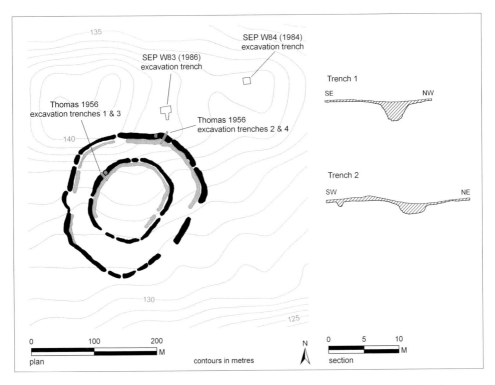

23 Robin Hood's Ball causewayed enclosure, Figheldean. *Drawing by Vanessa Constant: after Thomas 1964, figures 2 and 3; Oswald* et al. *2001, figure 1.4; and Richards 1990, figure 34*

Thomas' excavations showed that, at least in the areas he examined, the inner ditch was deeper, wider, and more steep-sided than the outer ditch. Both, however, showed evidence for periodic recutting, suggesting that the site was refurbished from time to time either because it was felt that boundaries had be maintained or because use of the site was itself intermittent and reoccupation meant redefinition. Detailed surveys of the earthworks endorse the idea of periodic remodelling of the enclosure, especially on the north side where the ditch has a braided course (Oswald et al. 2001, 5). The surviving earthworks show that the outer ditch was constructed as a series of elongated pits with narrow causeways except for the entrances. Both ditch circuits show the remains of internal banks which, unlike the ditches, look to have been continuous except for the entrances. The outer bank survived to a height of 0.6m and Thomas' excavation showed that it was carefully made of chalk rubble interleaved with turf and soil. A posthole found below the outer bank may pre-date it, but equally it may have been the socket for a post supporting a timber fence along the back edge.

As at other causewayed camps in southern Britain, the ditch fills contained quantities of cultural debris, some perhaps deliberately deposited but much of it preserved simply because hollows in the ground act as natural traps for rubbish and waste. The distribution of material within the small areas excavated suggested that the focus of occupation was the area between the ditches, and one pit was found in this area just behind the outer rampart in Trenches 2 and 4. Further support for this distribution of activity comes from the analysis of phosphate levels in the ditch fills. Only in the middle and upper fills of the inner ditch was there any evidence of phosphate levels suggestive of occupation, and even these were not especially high. The nature of the soil preserved below the bank suggested relatively open, grassland conditions obtained on this hilltop when the enclosure was built, again hinting that the view may have been important. Indeed, the presence of cultural debris below the bank of the outer earthwork may suggest that the site was already a centre of attention even before the enclosure was built.

Overall, portions of about 30 pottery vessels were found, mainly in the inner ditch and around, within, and under the outer bank. These included simple bowls and cups whose cultural affinity again lay with the plain Southwestern Series. The surface finishes were interesting as about 44 per cent were brown in colour, 32 per cent red, 22 per cent black, and 2 per cent grey. This contrasts with the assemblage from the Coneybury 'Anomaly' where 55 per cent of the pottery was grey in colour and only 15 per cent brown. Exactly what particular colours meant is not known, but reds and browns seem to be closely associated with death and the setting sun at chambered tombs of this period (Jones 1999; Bradley 2000). About 24 of the vessels at Robin Hood's Ball were tempered with flint or flint in combination with other widely available materials and these probably originated on the surrounding chalk downlands. Four or five vessels contained fragments of oolitic limestone or shell which Ian Cornwall and Henry Hodges suggested came from somewhere along the Jurassic ridge at least 50km away to the northwest (Cornwall and Hodges 1964). More interesting still, one or two finely made open bowls contained fragments of igneous rock that has since been recognized as gabbro from the Lizard Head in western Cornwall some 270km distant to the southwest (Peacock 1969; Harrad 2004). A broken sherd of this ware had been marked with incised criss-cross lines in a style that is increasingly recognized on objects and structures of fourth- and third-millennium BC date (Darvill and O'Connor 2005, 295).

Wide geographical links were also revealed amongst the worked flint and stone from the site. A large flake of greensand from the Warminster area was found in the cutting through the inner boundary (Thomas 1964, 20). Flint may also have been brought to the site from sources across the Wessex Downs; six worked pieces were found in the excavations – two end scrapers, a serrated blade, a composite point with a hollow scraper below, another hollow scraper/spokeshave, and a retouched flake probably used as a knife. The animal remains were dominated by cattle bones (69 per cent) followed by sheep/goat, red deer, and pig. Amongst the burnt material forming the matrix of the ditch fills, associated with cultural debris, there was an abundance of oak with lesser amounts of ash and hazel. Several pieces of pottery showed cavities left by plant fibres that adhered to the surface of the vessel during manufacture, but only one could be identified to species: a grain of emmer wheat.

Given the small size of the 1956 excavations at Robin Hood's Ball it is impossible to draw detailed conclusions, but the amount of cultural debris represented is sufficient to imply a significant focus of occupation, whether periodic or on a more permanent basis in the centuries following 3700 BC. Elsewhere in the Stonehenge landscape there is other evidence for occupation during the fourth millennium BC that might be linked with the use of Robin Hood's Ball.

SETTLEMENTS AND OCCUPATION

No houses of the fourth millennium BC are known in the Stonehenge landscape, although by comparison with examples elsewhere they would probably be timber-framed rectangular structures built as communal longhouses for extended families (Darvill 1996). However, a general impression of the distribution of activity in the Stonehenge landscape can be gained from the work of the Stonehenge Environs Project (Richards 1990). Against a light scatter of material right across the area surveyed, four zones stand out as flint scatters indicating a greater density of activity. From east to west these are: King Barrow Ridge, Stonehenge Down, Durrington Down, and Wilsford Down (see *21*). It is notable that much the same pattern is borne out by the presence of cultural material within and below later barrows and earthworks in these areas. Moreover, as noted earlier, in the case of King Barrow Ridge and Wilsford Down there is evidence of tree-throw pits below barrows which suggests that perhaps people were taking advantage of natural clearings in the woodland for the siting of settlements.

On King Barrow Ridge ground flint axes are well represented, especially on the east side (Richards 1990, figure 157), and may in part coincide with the scatter of apparently ceremonial pits containing selected deposits that were discussed above. Slightly different is the material incorporated into the mound of Amesbury 39 on the west side of King Barrow Ridge overlooking Stonehenge Bottom. Worked flint, animal bone, and pottery including 11 featured-sherds of Windmill Hill ware probably derive from some kind of settlement in the area (Ashbee 1980, 18).

Stonehenge Down, west of Stonehenge, revealed a mixed scatter of worked flint including scrapers, axes, and other basic tools (Richards 1990, figure 157). To the north, across Durrington Down, scrapers and other classes of flint tool dominated the assemblage recovered (Richards 1990, figure 157). On the northwest side of the Down a selection of Windmill Hill ware and part of a carinated bowl typical of the Southwestern Series was recovered from the ditch fills of Winterbourne Stoke 46, perhaps derived from the same source deposit as the flint scraper and scatter of animal bone also recovered (Gingell 1988, 55–8; see *22* B and C).

On Wilsford Down flint scatters were dominated by scrapers, but included a few axes, arrowheads and other items (Richards 1990, figure 157). Pottery was recovered from below three out of the four barrows (Wilsford 51–54) excavated by Earnest Greenfield in 1958, in the case of 52 amounting to more than 200 sherds from the upper fills of natural features below the mound (Smith 1991, 34–5; see *22* E–G and I–J).

One area not covered in detail by the Stonehenge Environs Project may be added: the Avon Valley west of King Barrow Ridge. Excavations in 1966 beneath the northern enclosure boundary of Durrington Walls revealed an area of old ground surface that preserved a dense concentration of cultural material suggestive of a nearby settlement. No postholes, pits, or other cut features were present, although a line of large postholes discovered during earthmoving operations nearby in 1967 may possibly be related (Wainwright and Longworth 1971, 14–6). Parts of at least 21 round-bottomed pots were present, mainly plain, attributable to the Windmill Hill Ware of the Southern Decorated Series. Bowls, jars, and cups are all represented in flint-tempered fabrics that were probably locally made. Over 800 pieces of struck or worked flint include a complete but well-used polished flint axe, four scrapers, a chopping tool, three utilized flakes, a retouched blade, and a leaf-shaped arrowhead. More than 80 pieces of animal bone were recovered but these were not studied separately from the much larger assemblage relating to the use of the main enclosure during the third millennium BC. An important environment sequence based on samples taken through the buried soil and covering bank showed that the fourth-millennium BC occupation was loosely associated with clearance of woodland in the area, perhaps for cultivation (Wainwright and Longworth 1971, 192). Charcoal from the occupation provided a radiocarbon date of 3550–2600 BC (NPL-191: 4400±150 BP). Nowhere else below the banks of Durrington Walls was such dense occupation found, although even in the southern sector it was clear that the area was well used in the fourth millennium BC; charcoal from the old ground surface here yielded dates of 3650–3000 BC (GRO-901: 4584±80 BP) and 3510–3090 BC (GRO-901a: 4575±50 BP), although they should be treated with some caution as they derive from bulk samples and were measured at a time when radiocarbon dating itself was still in its infancy.

All of these five settlement areas appear fairly discrete, and all lie between the Avon and the Till. It is also a pattern supported by equally strong negative evidence. A selection of six round barrows in the Lake barrow cemetery excavated in 1959 produced no residual material of the fourth millennium BC (Grimes 1964). Likewise none of the 18 round barrows excavated by Charles Green near Shrewton between 1958 and 1960 (Green and Rollo-Smith 1984). And the same applies to the four round barrows east of the Avon excavated in September 1956 (Ashbee 1984a). In this regard it is also noteworthy that if the landscape had been fairly open at the time then four out of the five areas were intervisible with Robin Hood's Ball; the only exception being the focus of activity in the Avon Valley near Durrington Walls (Batchelor 1997, plan 7).

LONG BARROWS

Scattered amongst the ceremonial areas and settlement zones is a series of 20 distinctive long mounds that were closely associated with the burial of the dead and in many senses define these fourth-millennium BC communities as the first mound-builders in the area. Surveys and investigations since the eighteenth century show that two main types of mound can be recognized on the basis of shape and size (*24* and *25*): small rather squat mounds generally less than 45m long which are known as oval barrows, and larger elongated rectangular or trapezoidal examples typically over 50m in length which are classic long barrows.

Long barrows represent a fairly short-lived tradition that started about 3800 BC and lasted for perhaps five or six centuries. Similar monuments showing only slight regional variations were built right across the British Isles, sometimes superseding smaller existing structures. Ultimately, the inspiration for long barrows seems to derive from continental Europe and can plausibly be linked to a way of thinking about the world in which houses for the dead echoed in their shape, size, and layout the traditional longhouse occupied during life (Ashbee 1984b, 87–99; Bradley 1998, 36–50; Darvill 2004b, 67–80).

At least seven long barrows can be recognized in the Stonehenge landscape. None has been fully excavated although three-quarters of them have been dug into at some stage by antiquarian investigators. All lie between the Avon and the Till, mainly on hill-spurs and low ridges where the orientation of the mound aligns with the natural grain of the landscape. They are not set in especially conspicuous positions, but they do bunch together slightly and in two cases it seems that adjacent long barrows share a common orientation.

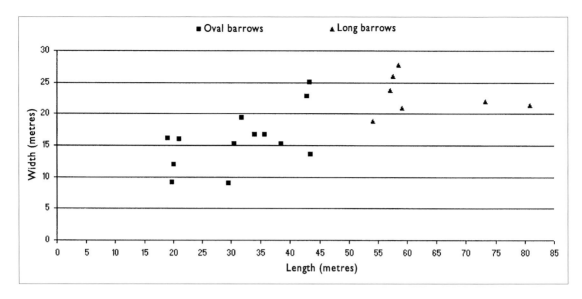

24 Graph showing the size ranges of long barrows and oval barrows in the Stonehenge landscape.
Drawing by Vanessa Constant: measurements from Grinsell 1957 and various additional sources

The largest is Amesbury 42 at the east end of the Stonehenge Cursus (25D). It is now completely flattened, but Leslie Grinsell records it as being 80m long, 21m wide, and originally over 1.1m high (1957, 137). Excavations by John Thurnam revealed at least three burials and some cattle bones, but details are scant (Thurnam 1868). The excavation of a single section across the eastern ditch, berm, and mound edge in 1983 revealed evidence for at least two phases of construction but no material suitable for dating either was recovered (Richards 1990, 96–109). A second well-known long barrow is Winterbourne Stoke 1 at Longbarrow Crossroads, the best-preserved such barrow in the area and easily visible from the A303 and the A360 (*colour plate 2*). Grinsell records this example as being 73m long by 21m wide and originally over 3m high (1957, 146). There has been no modern excavation here, and the work carried out by Thurnam in 1863 is inadequate for anything more than a very superficial understanding of the site. What appears to have been a primary burial was represented by the remains of an adult male in flexed position and accompanied by a flint implement. Six, probably secondary, burials were also discovered.

John Thurnam also excavated Figheldean 31 to the southeast of Robin Hood's Ball where he seems to have found a deposit of dark earth and a single skeleton (Grinsell 1957, 140). Nothing is known of what lies inside the other long barrows. The examples northeast of Robin Hood's Ball and the Knighton Barrow (Figheldean 27: *colour plate 3*) appear never to have been investigated, while Winterbourne Stoke 71 to the southeast of Longbarrow Crossroads (RCHM 1979, 1) and the example southwest of Woodhenge (McOmish 2001, figure 4.3) are known only through aerial photography.

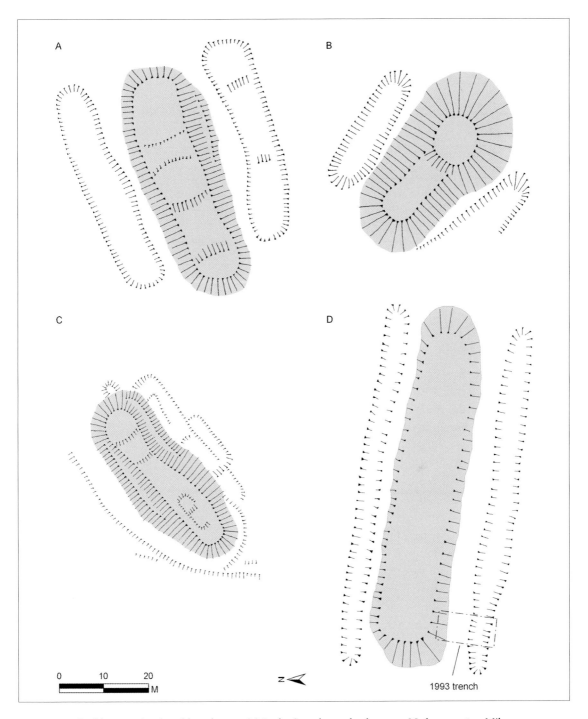

25 Oval barrows (A–C) and long barrow (D) in the Stonehenge landscape. A: Netheravon 6. B: Milston
1. C: Durrington 24. D: Amesbury 42. *Drawing by Vanessa Constant: A after McOmish* et al. *2002, figure 2.4;*
B after Canham 1983, figure 2.25; C after McOmish et al. *2002, figure 2.8C; D after Richards 1990, figure 64*

Suggestions that there was once a long barrow with a stone chamber at one end somewhere near West Amesbury (Lukis 1864, 155; Cunnington 1914, 408; Grinsell 1957, 137; Corcoran 1969, 294: WIL 13) may be linked with other speculations on the presence of megaliths near Stonehenge (Newall 1966). Desmond Bonney (1981) has plausibly argued that at least part of this tradition arises from the misidentification of stones in illustrations within the 1725 edition of Inigo Jones' book *Stonehenge*, but it is also possible that what is being referred to corresponds with the ploughed-out remains of an oval barrow (Amesbury 104) identified through aerial photography (RCHM 1979, 1). An elongated mound at Totterdown Clump south of Woodhenge (Durrington 63–65) has often been considered to be a long barrow (Colt Hoare 1810, 170; Grinsell 1957, 140), but later studies of aerial photographs show that it is probably a row of three close-set round barrows (RCHM 1979, 1).

From what little we know, all the long barrows in the Stonehenge landscape are earthen long barrows (Ashbee 1984b) in which a timber chamber or mortuary house lay at one end of the mound (usually the eastern end) occupying only a small part of the overall structure. Fresh corpses would be placed in the outer part of the chamber, but as they decomposed individual bones or parts of the body were moved progressively further into the chamber. Skeletal elements were often piled up and ordered into discrete heaps, and there are suggestions that bones were removed from some long barrows and placed in ceremonial pits or the ditches of causewayed camps. Strangely, there is no direct evidence for this at sites in the Stonehenge landscape; indeed the apparent scarcity of human remains from contexts dating to the fourth millennium BC in the area is notable and slightly exceptional.

OVAL BARROWS

Following his excavations at Winterbourne Stoke 35 in May 1865, John Thurnam endorsed earlier suggestions that oval barrows be recognized as distinct from long barrows, noting that oval barrows belong 'to a different and more recent period than the true long barrows, and to the same age as the circular barrows of the ordinary bowl and bell shapes' (Thurnam 1869, 41). Since Thurnam's day these stumpy barrows have sometimes been regarded as simply the short end of a wide size-spectrum of long barrows, but work in Sussex (Drewett 1975; 1986) and Oxfordshire (Bradley 1992) has endorsed Thurnam's distinction and shown the class to be long-lived through the fourth and third millennia BC. During the later stages of this tradition they do indeed overlap the use of round barrows, and at this time tend to cover single burials. In sum, oval barrows are generally less than 45m long, rather squat in outline with curved side ditches, and considerably easier and quicker to build than long barrows. The earliest examples typically cover small wooden chambers or platforms, and it is mainly this kind that appears in the Stonehenge landscape (Darvill 2004b, 52–6).

About a dozen oval barrows can be recognized around Stonehenge (*21* and *25*), mainly between the Avon and the Till but spilling across the Avon to the east as well. The excavation of an example at Netheravon Bake to the northeast of Robin Hood's Ball (Richards 1990, 259) confirms that such barrows were being built during the fourth millennium BC as an antler from the base of the ditch here yielded a radiocarbon date of 3710–3350 BC (OxA-1407: 4760±90 BP). Equally early is Woodford 2 near Druid's Lodge, immediately south of the Stonehenge landscape. Here excavations by Lance and Faith Vatcher in 1963 (Harding and Gingell 1986, 15–22) revealed an oval mound 20 by 14m flanked by short, slightly curved quarry ditches. A timber chamber or mortuary house had probably stood under the northern half of the mound, perhaps associated with human remains that in due course became covered by a layer of flints. A group of six large pits had been dug on the site before the barrow was built, possibly some kind of open-cast flint mine. Unfortunately, the excavation seems to have been rather hurried, and poorly recorded, with the result that it is now very hard to make much sense of what was found.

Antiquarian excavations at five oval barrows around Stonehenge fill some of the gaps that modern work has left exposed, but this class as a whole deserves to be better understood through a new campaign of research. Thurnam's work on Winterbourne Stoke Down revealed a burial, perhaps originally in a wooden chamber of some sort, at the west end of the barrow. The remains of a tall adult male were apparently found, together with three flint leaf-shaped arrowheads and a very fine laurel-leaf spear-tip. At least one pot was found near the centre of the mound, and a secondary burial dating to the mid-third millennium had been dug into the top near the east end (Thurnam 1869, 42–3; Grinsell 1957, 202 inexplicably lists this site as three confluent bowl barrows). A similar picture was found at Amesbury 14 on Normanton Down where excavations in 1866 revealed three skeletons at the southeast end of the mound, two of them with cleft skulls perhaps as result of wounds received in battle (Cunnington 1914, 382). One of the two rather disarticulated skeletons found by Thurnam in 1865 at the southeast end of the Netheravon 6 barrow (*25A*) near Robin Hood's Ball also had a cleft skull. At Wilsford 30, excavations by William Cunnington revealed four skeletons 'strangely huddled together' on what sounds like the floor of an unrecognized timber chamber at the broader eastern end of the mound (Colt Hoare 1812, 206). And a variant of the theme can be glimpsed from Colt Hoare's excavations at Winterbourne Stoke 53 where the burial zone at the east end of the mound comprised a platform on which was found a deposit of burnt human bone mixed with marl and covered by a large pile of flints (Cunnington 1914, 407).

ROUND BARROWS AND PIT GRAVES

Surprisingly, none of the investigated round barrows in the Stonehenge landscape shows conclusive evidence of being constructed during the fourth millennium BC, despite the occurrence of such monuments elsewhere in southeastern England (Kinnes 1979). Rather interesting in this connection is a crouched inhumation found in 1932 at Woodhenge, Totterdown, during tree-planting. The burial lay in a circular pit with its head to the south. A few pieces of plain pottery seemingly of Southwestern Series were present in the fill of the grave (M E Cunnington 1935; RCHM 1979, 7). Although possibly covered by a round barrow, this could equally be a pit grave of a type also distinctive of the fourth millennium BC but little studied (Kinnes 1979, 126–7).

LONG ENCLOSURES AND CURSUSES

Alongside the great earth and stone barrow mounds in the area there were at least three elongated enclosures defined on the ground by ditches with low internal banks. Like the barrows, these form part of a widespread tradition found right across the British Isles during the middle and later part of the fourth millennium BC (Barclay and Harding 1999).

At the small end of the size spectrum is the long mortuary enclosure on Normanton Down excavated by Faith Vatcher in 1959 (Vatcher 1961). Approximately 36 by 21m, this enclosure is defined by a discontinuous ditch with an internal bank (26C). The remains of a structure, possibly a portal of some kind, lay inside what appears to be an entrance through the earthwork at the southeast end. A radiocarbon determination from one of the 11 antler picks found in the ditch gives a construction date of 3550–2900 BC (BM-505: 4510±103 BP). Richard Atkinson suggested that enclosures such as this were used as excarnation areas for human corpses before the disarticulated remains were gathered up and placed within the chamber of a long barrow or oval barrow (Atkinson 1951a). The proximity of the Wilsford 30 oval barrow just 100m north of the long mortuary enclosure might support this argument, but no human bone was found in the Normanton enclosure. Indeed, very little at all was found apart from the antler picks that had been used to dig the ditch; a few animal remains, and one sherd of Peterborough Ware came from the upper ditch fills. Current interpretations focus on the use of these enclosures as open-air shrines or assembly places for ceremonies foreshadowing the appearance of much longer enclosures known as cursuses. Two of these have been found in the Stonehenge landscape.

The so-called Lesser Cursus lies on Winterbourne Stoke Down about 2.5km north of the Normanton Down long mortuary enclosure. It too is associated with an oval barrow, Winterbourne Stoke 35, which stands a few metres beyond its western end. Levelled by ploughing between 1934 and 1954, the Lesser Cursus was investigated in 1983 as part of the Stonehenge Environs Project (Richards 1990, 72–90). Three trenches were cut into different parts of this large monument, showing that there were at least two main phases to its construction. Phase 1 comprised a slightly trapezoidal enclosure 200 by 60m whose ditch may have been recut more than once and in part at least deliberately back-filled (26A1). In Phase 2 this early enclosure was remodelled by elongating the whole structure eastwards by another 200m. This extension comprised only two parallel side ditches, making the whole thing about 400m long with a rectilinear enclosure at the west end with entrances in its northeast and southeast corners giving access into a second rectilinear space, in this case open to the east (*26A2*). A sample of antler from the Phase I ditch has been dated to 3650–2900 BC (OxA-1404: 4550±120 BP) and, rather inconsistently, antler from the Phase II ditch to 3650–3050 BC (OxA-1405: 4640±100 BP). A detailed geophysical survey of the site by Alastair Bartlett in 1983 revealed the presence of an irregular oval enclosure, *c.*15m across, off-centre between the flanking ditches near the eastern end. Its date is unknown, but there is the slight suggestion that it comprises a series of intercutting pits. The same survey also found a pair of entrances into the western enclosure, one roughly in the centre of each of the long sides. Numerous anomalies suggestive of pits were noted within and around the western enclosure, and a possible hengi-form monument of the third millennium BC was identified just to the north (David and Payne 1997, 87–9).

The largest cursus in the area is the Stonehenge Cursus, an impressive earthwork first recognized by William Stukeley on 6 August 1723. Overall, it is nearly 3km long, and between 100m and 150m wide, and is defined throughout its perimeter by a chalk rubble bank and external ditch. It is one of very few cursuses in the British Isles that remains standing as a visible earthwork, although part of what can be seen at the western end is a reconstruction based on its appearance prior to being bulldozed in the late 1950s. Four episodes of excavation have taken place at various points, the results serving to emphasize its varied form and scale (RCHM 1979, 13–15 and Richards 1990, 93 for summaries). The most recent excavations, in 1983, made two cuttings through the southern ditch but recovered no significant dating evidence (Richards 1990, 95–6). An antler pick recovered from the floor of the ditch of the southern boundary in 1947 (Stone 1948, 13) has been dated to 2890–2460 BC (OxA-1403: 4100±90 BP) but Richards has plausibly argued that it derives from an intrusive cut into the ditch fills and is thus not primary (1990, 96). Finds from the ditch fill include a sherd of undistinctive pottery, a fragment of bluestone, a piece of sarsen rubber, and a stone maul (Stone 1948, 15). The total excavation of the Winterbourne Stoke 30 bowl barrow in the western terminal of the Cursus (now restored) provides the only substantial view of an area within the interior of the Cursus. However, although a few pre-barrow features were noted none could be securely dated or certainly associated with the Cursus (Christie 1963). Neither was the barrow itself securely dated as the primary burials were unaccompanied cremations. A substantial assemblage of struck flint recovered from the 1959 excavations of the Cursus ditch includes the remains of *in situ* flint working at a time when the ditch was freshly dug. On technological grounds this flint working belongs to the third millennium BC (Saville 1978, 17). Taking all the evidence so far available from the Stonehenge Cursus together it seems likely that it was built towards the end of the fourth millennium BC and continued to be used through into the first half of the third millennium BC, spanning an important phase in the development of the Stonehenge landscape as the next chapter will show.

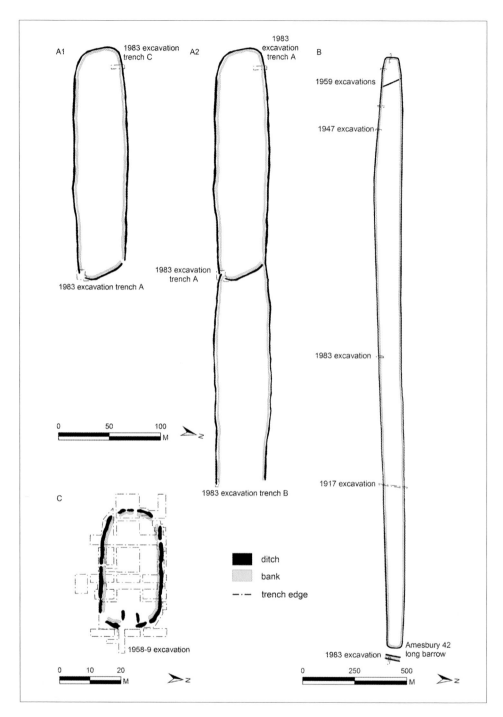

26 Long enclosures. A: The Lesser Cursus (A1: Phase 1. A2: Phase 2). B: Stonehenge Cursus. C: Normanton Down long mortuary enclosure. *Drawing by Vanessa Constant: A and B after Richards 1990, figures 43 and 62; C after Vatcher 1961, figure 2*

In its design and construction the Stonehenge Cursus was a massive undertaking, the largest in the area until that time (*26B*). Aubrey Burl (1987, 44) estimates that more than 7100 cubic metres of chalk was moved to build the Cursus, a task needing at least 40,000 person-hours, toil that involved running a structure between the high ground of Winterbourne Stoke Down in the west to King Barrow Ridge in the east, crossing Stonehenge Bottom and the stream that probably flowed through it along the way. Curiously, the northern side of the Cursus is fairly straight and could have been set out using thin posts to act as ranging rods, but the south side is not exactly parallel and was perhaps set out using off-sets that varied slightly so that there are in fact three separate straight sections connected by slight dog-legs. Like its neighbour the Lesser Cursus, the far western end of the Stonehenge Cursus seems to have been separated off with a cross-ditch to form a small but discrete space. Standing in the western terminal, now reconstructed to its pre-1950s appearance, there are extensive views in all directions but especially dominant are the rolling plains flanking the River Till. The eastern terminal has long since disappeared, but it is perhaps no coincidence that the largest of the three long enclosures in the area is associated with the largest long barrow, Amesbury 42, which must once have formed an impressive and dominant skyline feature just a few metres east of the Cursus' terminal. Here at the eastern end of the Cursus there are also extensive views, but from this point it is the Avon Valley and its surroundings that attract attention.

Exactly how cursus monuments were used is far from clear, but their shape and form lend themselves to marking a special pathway across the landscape while guiding the progress and gaze of anyone undertaking such a journey. Many attempts have been made to retrace the steps of the ancients along cursuses (*e.g.* Tilley 1994, 143–201; Brophy 1999, 127–9; Johnston 1999) with varying degrees of insight. In the case of the Stonehenge Cursus a leisurely stroll from one end to the other takes between 45 minutes and an hour. The two ends are intervisible, but from the lowest point in Stonehenge Bottom only the central section of the monument remains in view. Looking southwards at about the midpoint Stonehenge stands bold against the skyline, but when the Cursus was new little if any of that had yet been built.

As it is oriented roughly east to west, various attempts have been made to give the axis of the Stonehenge Cursus some kind of astronomical significance (e.g. Lockyer 1909, 155; North 1996, 178–85). Little of this stands up to detailed scrutiny beyond the rather obvious conclusion that the progress of the sun across the sky from its rising in the east to its setting in the west at about the time of the autumn and spring equinoxes is mirrored on the ground by the orientation and form of the Cursus in such a way that physical progression from east to west and back again could be seen as a metaphor for the passage of a solar day. Equally, the journey from east to west could have been an allegory for a human lifespan from birth to death: the first light of the rising sun in the eastern sky kindling new life from the ancestral remains deep in the Amesbury 42 long barrow through to the last rays of the setting sun carrying away the breath of those waiting in the western terminal as evening closes.

A LAND IN TRANSITION

Around 4000 BC the Stonehenge landscape may have seemed a rather small-scale and youthful place, with occupation scattered amongst clearings in the Wildwood. But as the fourth millennium unfolded the landscape and its occupants matured and had a greater impact on each other than at any time before. Perhaps people were trying to tame the land, trying to understand its powers and moods in relation to their own, and trying to rationalize their knowledge of the sky, the earth, and the ground beneath as a structured system: a cosmology of their world. Pits and shafts were dug into the ground following an age-old tradition, and used for some purpose that suggests respect for what lay beneath. The remains of the dead were only very rarely placed in the ground; instead the ground itself was raised to form great mounds over wooden chambers or platforms on or in which the dead were laid as if sleeping in their ancestral home. Only when the flesh had gone, the life-forces were spent, and their death was complete, could the bones be moved to make way for others.

As in earlier times, it is likely that wooden posts stood in the Stonehenge landscape during the fourth millennium BC as markers of some kind. One possible example is represented by a neatly cut posthole found in 1968 on King Barrow Ridge during work to lay an electricity cable (Cleal et al. 1994, 60). Over 0.5m across and 0.7m deep, there were sherds of a small cup in the lower fill; if it had indeed once held a post it would have stood in an impressive position on the western brow of the ridge.

It is possible that stones also served as markers. There are two contenders, although neither is securely dated. One is the Cuckoo Stone, a substantial block of natural sarsen over 2m long, 1.5m wide, and 0.6m thick (*colour plate 20*) that now lies prostrate on the axis of the Stonehenge Cursus some 900m beyond its eastern terminal. Although recorded by Colt Hoare (1812, map opp. 170), the site has never been investigated (Cunnington 1929, 11). A second, still larger stone is the Heelstone just outside Stonehenge (*colour plate 10*). Aubrey Burl has speculated that this pillar pre-dated the main development of Stonehenge (Burl 2000a, 353), and may even be one of the reasons that Stonehenge developed where it did. Excavation of the socket in which the Heelstone sits in 1953 revealed rather little except some sherds of Beaker pottery from upper levels which allow the erection of the Heelstone to be dated to the late third millennium BC or earlier (Cleal et al. 1995, 272–4). The stone itself is one of the few undressed sarsens at Stonehenge, and at 4.8m tall above-ground with a further 1.2m buried it is also one of the largest sarsens present. Moreover, its position more-or-less at the top of the slope leading down into Stonehenge Bottom means that this stone above all others is easily seen by anyone looking southwards while walking the eastern half of the Stonehenge Cursus.

As for the site of Stonehenge itself, there is no evidence for any structures; the discovery of a single sherd from a Southwestern Series ceramic bowl from the bank on the southeastern side may also be regarded as a part of the overall background noise caused by activity right across the landscape (Cleal et al. 1995, 350). Settlements were scattered around about, perhaps in clearings in the Wildwood, but overlooking them was the enclosure at Robin Hood's Ball, another considerable communal building effort and perhaps the place where dispersed extended family groups periodically came together for social intercourse, trading, feasting, and ceremonies such as walking the Cursus and visiting nearby long barrows and oval barrows. It is possible that some people travelled a considerable distance to the join the festival, perhaps bringing with them items and materials from their homelands as well as stories and news of distant events. The style of pottery most common in the Stonehenge landscape through the fourth millennium BC suggests strong cultural links with communities in southwestern Britain. Pottery actually brought from Cornwall is here in small amounts, suggesting that the Avon Valley was pretty near the far eastern extremity of this particular exchange network. However, there is also pottery imported from the

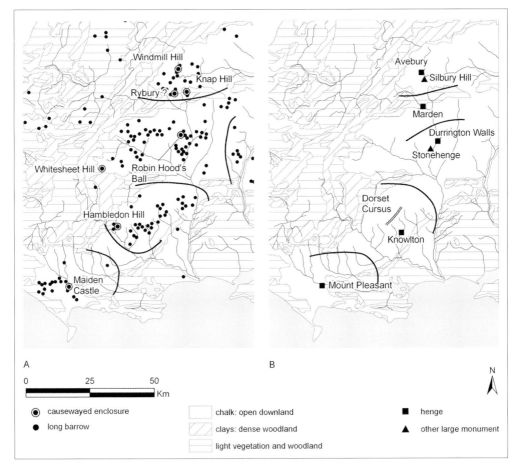

A

B

N

0   25   50
Km

◉ causewayed enclosure   ☐ chalk: open downland   ■ henge

● long barrow   ▨ clays: dense woodland   ▲ other large monument

                       ☐ light vegetation and woodland

27 Social territories in prehistoric Wessex: Renfrew's 1973 model of developing organizational scale. A: Fourth millennium BC. B: Third millennium BC. *Drawing by Vanessa Constant: after Renfrew 1973a, figures 3 and 4*

limestone lands to the north and, from stylistic evidence, perhaps also from territories away to the east and northeast. Quality raw flint may also have been imported to the region, and exotic stone from still further afield suggests long-distance ties or at least participation in chains of exchanges between communities that over time could move prestige items long distances. A jadeite axe found long ago in 'a barrow near Stonehenge' (Campbell Smith 1963, 164 no. 41) is one such object that started its life more than 900km away in the Alps of northern Italy or Switzerland (Campbell Smith 1965; Ricq-de Bouard 1993).

Despite the generally high level of aerial reconnaissance in the region, Robin Hood's Ball seems to be a fairly isolated enclosure spatially associated with a relatively discrete cluster of long barrows and oval barrows and fitting well with a dispersed pattern of enclosures across central southern Britain (Ashbee 1984b, figure 6; Oswald et al. 2001, 80). This pattern was interpreted by Colin Renfrew (1973a, 549) in terms of emergent chiefdoms linked to territories each focused around one or two causewayed enclosures (Ashbee 1978b, figure 22). Up to half a dozen such territories can be identified across central southern Britain (27A), the concentration of monuments within each suggesting that these were perhaps some of the most densely occupied parts of the country at this time. The presence of arrowheads and cleft skulls amongst the burials of people living in the Stonehenge landscape shows that these were not necessarily peaceful times. Nationally, nearly 10 per cent of crania from long barrows and oval barrows show signs of interpersonal violence (Schulting and Wysocki 2005), and it might be that tensions between groups served to reinforce the need for defined territories, strong leadership, long-distance alliance structures, and the creation of distinct local identities through building monuments and securing exotic resources. Socially at least, the people of the Stonehenge landscape were strong enough to change their world in ways that still cause awe and wonder. As one of a series of foci along the main rivers running into the heart of southern Britain from natural harbours at Christchurch and Poole in the back of Bournemouth Bay (27B), the face of the Stonehenge landscape changed around 3000 BC to reflect reformed traditions and new cultural imperatives.

5

SACRED CIRCLES AND MAGICAL RINGS
(3000–2000 BC)

Sometimes change happens slowly, but sometimes, as in the Stonehenge landscape during the third millennium BC, it happens fast. In a sense these ten centuries formed the character of the landscape that has endured down to the present day even if its face has changed. For the third millennium BC really was the 'Age of Stonehenge'.

It has been suggested that in some parts of Britain the beginning of the third millennium BC saw a hiatus in the expansion of agricultural communities and a shift in settlement patterns connected to soil exhaustion, scrub growth, and woodland regeneration (Whittle 1978; Smith 1984, 116–17; and see also Davies and Wolski 2001). But there is no evidence for this in the Stonehenge landscape, and Mike Allen has argued that after 3000 BC the balance between woodland and grassland shifts so that, for the first time in its history, grassland predominated. The process by which this happened is seen in terms of people expanding initial clearances (Cleal et al. 1995, 477; Allen 1997, 129–33). Many of the main monuments established at this time were constructed within areas of grazed downland, although the classic henge at Coneybury provides an exception as it was built in a small woodland clearing that had become overgrown (Richards 1990, 157–8).

Climate studies suggest that the Atlantic conditions of the fourth millennium BC gave way to more continental conditions during the third. This was the Sub-Boreal bioclimatic stage, with slightly drier and warmer summers and colder winters (Tinsley 1981, 210–11). Summer air temperature may have been up to 1.5°C higher than today (J A Taylor 1980, figure 3.1). This would give rise to changes in the altitude of the tree-line in upland areas, but probably made little difference to the overall character of the vegetation on the downlands of central southern England. Charcoal from archaeological sites in the Stonehenge landscape suggests that woodland included oak, hazel, blackthorn, and hawthorn/whitebeam/rowan (Richards 1990, 252–3). Palaeobotanical remains give a flavour of vegetation in the wider landscape; a range of grasses as well as onion couch, chickweed, stinging nettle, hazel, and hawthorn (Richards 1990, 251). Wheat and barley were cultivated and their charred remains have been found at many sites of this period. Evidence for ploughing, perhaps with a rip-ard, is preserved below the mounds of

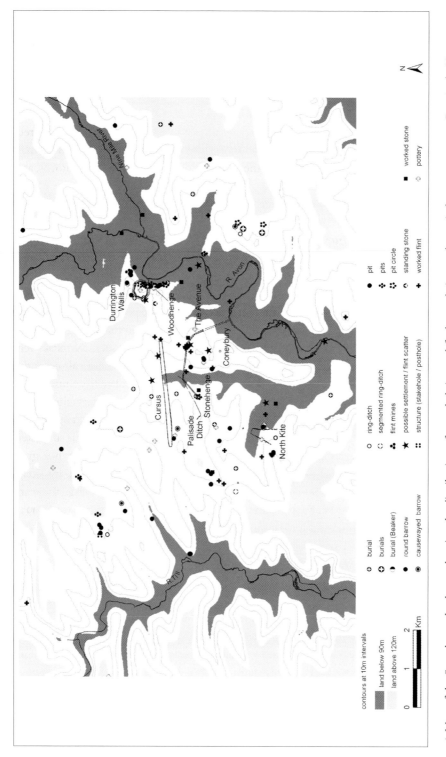

28 Map of the Stonehenge landscape showing the distribution of recorded sites and findspots dating to the period c.3000–2000 BC. *Drawing by Vanessa Constant: Wiltshire SMR and various archaeological sources over mapping from EDX Engineering Inc. data at 50m intervals and Ordnance Survey © Crown Copyright 2006. All rights reserved. Licence 10004 5276*

Amesbury 70 and 71 (Christie 1964, 33; 1967, 347). The increasing extent of cultivation through the early second millennium BC may account for the accumulation of sediments in the secondary fills of earlier ditches at sites that had fallen out of use, but soil erosion as such does not seem to be a major problem at this period.

The existing range of domestic animals continued to be represented, although the relative abundance of species changed slightly with some sites showing a higher proportion of pig than cattle. Sheep are poorly represented until well after 2000 BC. There is no direct evidence of animal extinctions in the area at this time, and the range of wild animals probably remained similar, with cattle, pig, sheep, goat, dog, red deer, roe deer, aurochs, and mallard represented by preserved remains.

Broad-brush overviews of such a long period of time inevitably hide short-term and localized changes that would have been experienced by people living at the time. In his studies of patterns in tree growth in the British Isles, Mike Baillie has noted two marked events represented by reductions in tree growth for several years, one centred on 3190 BC the other on 2345 BC. These he correlated with evidence from cores through the Arctic ice-cap, which themselves link back to major volcanic eruptions (Baillie 1999, 54). As a result, weather patterns changed, skies darkened for a few years, people at the time may have wondered what was happening in the heavens, and perhaps myths and legends were born and then passed down through the generations. To what extent such things actively prompted social change is less clear, but it is true that novel forms of material culture in the form of Peterborough Ware and Grooved Ware pottery began to circulate from just before the turn of the fourth millennium BC, and by about 2400 BC Beaker pottery along with new styles of worked stone and the first metal objects in the form of gold, copper, and bronze ornaments, tools, and weapons make an appearance. Humphrey Case has suggested that Beaker pottery from around Stonehenge belongs to all three successive typological Styles (1–3) within his regional Group D, which occurs widely across southwestern England and Wales and shows continuing cultural affinity with that area. However, there are also quantities of Group B Beakers which cluster in eastern England (Case 1993, 246; 1995). Long barrows, causewayed enclosures, and some of the elongated enclosures had fallen out of use by 3000 BC, at least in terms of their original roles. A few existing monuments, such as the Cursus, continued in use into the early third millennium BC at least, but new structures appeared, mainly of round form (*28*). Traditional interest in digging pits, creating pit clusters, and raising stones and posts continued, but the scale and pattern of use was transformed. After 3000 BC size mattered and the cost in human terms of building monuments and acquiring materials escalated out of all proportion compared with what had gone before.

DARK SIDES OF THE MOON

One of the first new monuments is at Stonehenge itself where a circular earthwork was constructed around 2950 BC. This is technically known as Stonehenge Phase 1, while

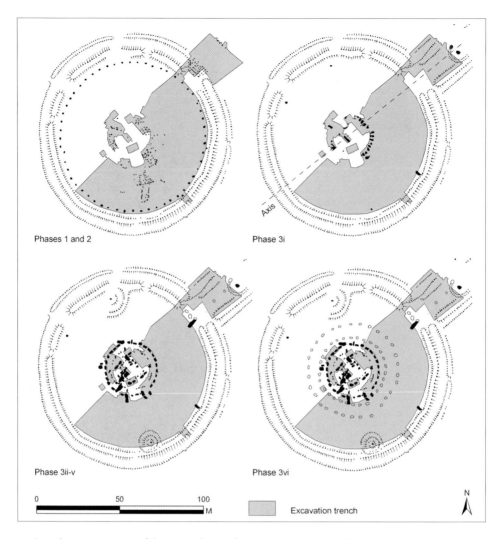

Phases 1 and 2

Phase 3i

Phase 3ii-v

Phase 3vi

0   50   100
|_____|_____| M

Excavation trench

N

29 Stonehenge: summary of the main phases of construction and use. Phases 1 and 2: 2950–2600 BC. Phase 3i: 2600–2500 BC. Phase 3ii–v: 2500–2000 BC. Phase 3vi: 1800–1600 BC. *Drawing by Vanessa Constant: after Newall 1959 with additional information from Cleal et al. 1995 and various other sources*

subsequent developments in the interior between 2900 and about 2600 BC are referred to as Phase 2 (*29*). At first, Stonehenge comprised a ditch flanked on the inside by a bank and, for part of its circumference, a small counterscarp bank outside the ditch. The area enclosed is fairly flat, about 90m across, and commands good views in all directions. There were at least three entrances, the widest one opening towards the northeast, a slightly smaller opening towards the south, and a possible third very much smaller gap opening to the south-southwest. When first dug the ditch was typically 1.2-1.6m deep and up to 4.2m wide.

In 1932 the 'henge' part of Stonehenge was expropriated by Christopher Hawkes to provide the name for a newly recognized class of circular earthworks which were regarded as sacred enclosures (Kendrick and Hawkes 1932, 83). Further defined by Richard Atkinson (1951b) and Geoffrey Wainwright (1969), such monuments are characterized as having a distinctive arrangement in which the ditch lay inside the bank. Ironically, on these grounds, Stonehenge itself would not classify as a henge, but it is now recognized that henges represent a heterogeneous family of monuments with more than half a dozen variations, most of which occur in the Stonehenge landscape. The earliest, sometimes known as *formative henges* (Harding 2003, 13), have ditches outside the banks, as with: Stonehenge 1; Flagstones, Dorset (Woodward 1988); Priddy 1–4, Somerset (Tratman 1967); Llandegai A, Gwynedd (Lynch and Musson 2001, 36–48); and Castell Bryn-Gwyn, Anglesey (Wainwright 1962). These may be considered ancestral to the *classic henges*, with their ditches inside the bank, although even here there are regional variations: ditchless examples at Meini-Gwyr, Pembrokeshire (Darvill and Wainwright 2003, 22–30), Mayborough, Cumbria (Topping 1992), and numerous sites in Ireland (Condit and Simpson 1998); a bankless example at Ring of Brodgar, Orkney (Renfrew 1979, 39–43); and examples with banks between pairs of concentric ditches across midland and northern England as at Thornborough, North Yorkshire (Harding 2000) and Maxey, Cambridgeshire (Pryor et al. 1985, 59–70). Small henges of less than 10m across are termed *hengi-forms* (Wainwright 1969) or *mini-henges* (Harding and Lee 1987), while the four rather large irregularly shaped henges in the Avon/Frome river catchment of central southern England – Marden and Durrington Walls in Wiltshire and Knowlton and Mount Pleasant in Dorset – are usually referred to as *henge-enclosures* (Harding and Lee 1987).

BUILDING THE FIRST STONEHENGE

The ditch defining Stonehenge 1 was dug as a series of connected pits following the tradition seen at causewayed enclosures across northwest Europe through the fourth millennium BC. Links with the past are also represented by a series of ox jaws, ox skulls, and bones of red deer placed in the ditch near the entrances into Stonehenge. Radiocarbon dating shows that these pieces were already between 50 and 850 years old when deposited in the freshly cut ditch about 2950 BC. Treatment of the ditch also echoed earlier practices. In most of the excavated sections there was an initial primary fill caused by slippage from the bank and the erosion of the side walls which quickly stabilized with the formation of a thin soil and turf cover. Soon, however, selected areas were deliberately refilled with clean chalk rubble while other sections eroded gradually. A few lengths of ditch were recut down to the primary fills and sometimes beyond, suggesting periodic visitations that perhaps involved physically redefining the boundary even if only partially or as a symbolic act.

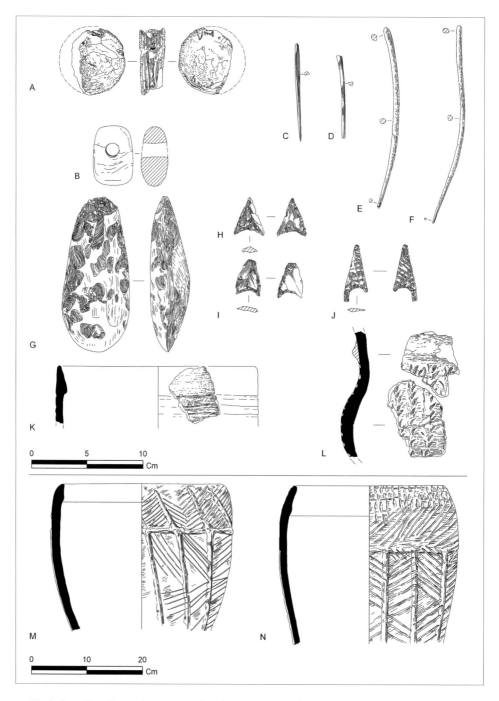

30 Finds from Stonehenge (A, B, E, F, K, L) and Durrington Walls (C, D, G–J, and M–N). A: Ceramic object. B: Macehead. C–F: Bone pins. G: Polished flint axe. H–J: Projectile points. K, M, and N: Grooved Ware; L: Beaker pottery. *Drawing by Vanessa Constant: after Cleal* et al. *1995, figures 192, 195, 216, and 228; and Wainwright and Longworth 1971, figures 33, 65, 73, 74, and 79*

The bank must have been fairly irregular as it eroded and was used as a quarry for chalk to refill sections of ditch. When first built it was perhaps 1.5–2.0m high, but it would have quickly compacted to form a rise no more than 1.5m high that a standing adult could easily see over. In contrast to the ditch, relatively little of the bank has ever been excavated. A cutting made in 1954 in the northeastern sector revealed a line of postholes more-or-less down the centre line of the bank, suggesting either a pre-bank fence or a timber palisade running along the top of the bank (Cleal et al. 1995, figure 56).

Inside the enclosure things were happening too, and over the first half of the third millennium BC a succession of wooden structures and earth-cut features were created. Immediately inside the bank was a ring of 56 equally spaced holes, known as the Aubrey Holes, dug sometime around 2800 BC. Much debate surrounds the interpretation of these holes, but initially at least all or most of the 34 examples that have been investigated seem to have held upright wooden posts, yet again perpetuating a far older tradition. Some of the posts seem to have rotted *in situ* while others were pulled out. The hollows where the posts once stood continued to attract attention and were remembered even when not especially visible. At least 24 of the excavated Aubrey Holes had small pits cut into the top of them to receive deposits of cremated bone. Some of these burials were associated with skewer pins (*30E–F*) that might have been used to secure a leather bag containing the cremation itself. Pieces of antler, animal bone, and occasional flint and chalk objects were also represented, as well as a curious ceramic object from Aubrey Hole 29 (*30A*). This item is sometimes considered to be a vase-support similar to those of the Chasseen cultures of western France (Piggott 1938, 76–7), although indigenous British parallels amongst Grooved Ware assemblages may also be relevant (Cleal et al. 1995, 360–1).

More than 50 deposits of cremated bone representing perhaps as many as 70 individuals were deposited in the top of the eroding bank, in the gradually accumulating ditch fills, and around the edge of the enclosed area. As with the cremations in the Aubrey Holes, few were accompanied by grave goods. An exception is a small cremation from just inside the bank on the southeast side which was associated with a perforated polished-stone ovoid macehead, beautifully made from a piece of black and white folded gneiss (*30B*). The source of this piece lies among the granite-rich landscapes of northern and western Britain and perhaps suggests that people were bringing the cremated remains of their loved ones or kinsfolk from some distance away to be laid to rest within this earthwork enclosure.

Posts, fences, and wooden structures
More than 120 postholes have been recorded and plotted within the excavated areas inside Stonehenge; many more have no doubt been lost through later activity. Not all are necessarily contemporary, and making sense of them is impossible. Some may have been arranged in circles broadly concentric with the Aubrey Holes, others as short arcs of between five and ten posts that formed screens if not whole circuits. Near the southern

entrance there is a rectangular setting of posts that may have formed the framework for a small building some 11 by 3m, or perhaps created a passageway to guide the path of those entering through the southern entrance. On the causeway between the ditch terminals of the northern entrance there are six roughly parallel lines of posts running concentrically with the line of the ditch. Four very large postholes in a line 20m outside the northern entrance once held substantial timber uprights and together with the posts in the entrance have often been interpreted as markers so that people standing in the centre of the enclosure could accurately observe celestial events (see below). More prosaically, these posts probably supported screens or gateway structures that served to control access or views into the interior.

The use of the site as a cremation cemetery, and for whatever activities were connected with the use of the timber post-settings and structures, inevitably led to casual losses and the deliberate deposition of both everyday objects and special items. Amongst the former are a few pieces of Grooved Ware pottery representing perhaps four or five vessels in all, less than 150 pieces of worked flint, about 20 pieces of worked stone, and a handful of bone skewer pins, points, part of a spatula, and a chisel. Amongst the worked flint was an *in situ* cluster of knapping debris in the primary fill of the ditch immediately west of the northeastern entrance, much working waste in the form of cores and flakes from elsewhere, and a scatter of scrapers, fabricators, and a denticulate flake. The worked stone was mainly pieces of chalk shaped into balls, of which 12 were represented, a block carrying a small cup-mark, a small perforated slab, pieces fashioned into the form of axes, and a piece of tabular chalk incised with what appears to be a simple chevron pattern.

The decorated slab finds haveparallels with other pieces from the area (see below), but also notable is the cup-marked stone. This appears to be a piece of mobiliary rock art of a type not uncommon in fourth-, third-, and second-millennium BC contexts in the British Isles (Beckensall 1999, 145) and possibly associated with the female gender. Thomas (1952) lists a further three similar 'cups' or cup-marked chalk blocks from the Stonehenge landscape, one from Wilsford and two from Woodhenge. Another was found at Southmill Hill, Amesbury, in 1974 (Anon 1976, 134).

WHY STONEHENGE?

Why an earthwork enclosure was built at this particular place is far from clear. It may simply have been a suitably flat open area that was available for the construction of a fairly extensive structure. Geomancy or divination may have drawn people to the spot. There may have been some natural feature already present that has not yet been recognized, a tree perhaps, or if Aubrey Burl's speculations are right perhaps it was the massive sarsen block known as the Heelstone (Stone 96, also 'Heel Stone') that provided a focus (Burl 1991; 2000a, 353). What we can say is that the spot lies in the centre of a natural amphitheatre in the landscape, commands extensive views onto the surrounding ridges, and, conversely, can be seen from a good distance away. Much attention has been given to possible astronomical orientations and the alignment of particular elements of the monument with celestial events. In the 1960s C A Newham proposed that the lines of postholes across the northern entrance were used to mark moonrises over several 18.6-year cycles to create an exact indication of the extreme northern lunar limit (Newham 1966; 1972). Aubrey Burl recognized difficulties with Newham's scheme but maintained the case for associating these early phases in the life of Stonehenge with an interest in lunar cosmologies, concluding that 'such observation has been part of Neolithic religious practices and had a long history amongst the prehistoric inhabitants of Britain, Ireland, and Brittany for many centuries' (2000a, 354). However, a critical review of the data by Clive Ruggles (1997, 214–18) leaves no hard evidence supporting meaningful lunar alignments, or indeed any other celestial alignments, embedded in the form or layout of the monument in its early phases. Other possibilities therefore have to be considered.

Looking at the sacred geography of the landscape as a whole provides one interesting line of exploration. Elsewhere I have suggested that in the third millennium BC the Stonehenge landscape was notionally seen as having two sectors, one to the southeast and the other to the northwest. This 'linear binary' system in the social use of space finds expression in the distribution of monuments and also in the design of Stonehenge itself which may be seen as a metaphorical representation of the landscape (31). In this view the main axis of the site represents the binary sectoring of space while the River Avon, which notionally lies in the southeastern sector, may be considered to enter through the northern entrance and leave through the southern entrance. The posts and bank may somehow represent the edge of the 'world' where the uncleared forest began and the hills rise up beyond, while two positions later marked by barrows (see below) seem to correspond with known and possible fourth-millennium BC enclosures (Darvill 1997a, 179–81). Looking only at Stonehenge, Josh Pollard and Clive Ruggles show that the primary NE–SW axis is also represented in the patterns of deposition seen in the objects and materials included in the ditch fills. They suggest that, through sustained ritual practice, the motions of the moon became increasingly referenced, especially through the deposition of cremations, and also hint at further, more complicated, radial divisions which might prefigure later developments at the site and include a symbolic quartering primarily demarcated by solstitial rising and setting points (Pollard and Ruggles 2001, 69; cf. Burl 1994, 91).

Around 2600 BC there seems to be a slight hiatus in the use of Stonehenge, perhaps short-lived, but represented in the environmental sequence from the northern ditch fill studied by John Evans in the late 1970s (Evans 1984). He found evidence for localized regeneration of scrubland, and while Mike Allen (in Cleal et al. 1995, 168–9) has questioned how representative Evans' section might be, there is a possible social context for the relative neglect of Stonehenge for perhaps a decade or two as attention focused on projects elsewhere in the landscape, amongst them digging pits and building other kinds of henge.

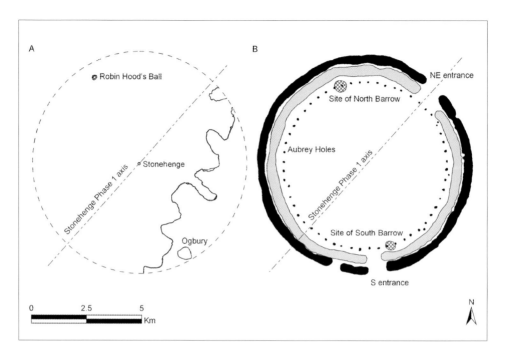

31 Comparison between the Stonehenge landscape (A) and the Phase 1–2 monument at Stonehenge (B). *Drawing by Vanessa Constant: after Darvill 1997a, figure 5*

PITS AND PIT CLUSTERS

Pits and shafts perpetuate earlier traditions throughout the third millennium BC, especially on King Barrow Ridge. Investigation of an extensive flint scatter on the northern part of the ridge as part of the Stonehenge Environs Project included the excavation of 12 sample trenches. Four areas revealed pits and scatters of stakeholes, trench J/K having three small circular pits grouped around a natural hollow that might have resulted from a tree-throw strangely reminiscent of the much earlier features in the Stonehenge car-park (see Chapter 3). Finds from the King Barrow Ridge pits included heavily decorated Peterborough Ware, Grooved Ware, pig bones in some quantity as well as smaller amounts of cattle and sheep/goat, flint working waste in the form of spent cores and flakes, flint tools including scrapers and arrowheads, and a bone point. One of the pits was dated to 3800–2900 BC (OxA-1396: 4700±150 BP), another to 3550–2850 BC (OxA-1397: 4500±120 BP) suggesting yet again the progressive accumulation of dug features at this site. Also notable is the fact that the phosphate levels in the earlier of the two dated pits showed a comparable concentration to that recorded in the Coneybury Anomaly (see Chapter 4), but the other pits sampled showed very low levels of phosphate. It is almost as if places once used for occupation were remembered and celebrated by later periodic visits.

Further south on King Barrow Ridge is the so-called 'Plaque Pit', named because it contained two square chalk plaques bearing incised decoration (*32*). The pit was discovered and excavated in 1969 during the widening of the A303 (Vatcher 1969; Harding 1988; Cleal and Allen 1994). Sherds of Grooved Ware, an antler pick, and animal bones were also found in the pit and two radiocarbon dates place the material in the early third millennium BC. These are amongst the earliest dates for Grooved Ware in southern Britain and illustrate the potential of the evidence from the Stonehenge landscape to help illuminate the appearance of this highly distinctive ceramic tradition. A seemingly isolated posthole containing sherds of Grooved Ware was found nearby during the laying of an electricity cable in 1968 (RCHM 1979, 33; Cleal and Allen 1994, 60–2, the large post it once contained again perhaps perpetuating a tradition established by an earlier posthole in the same area on the west side of the ridge (see Chapter 4).

Excavations at Butterfield Down, Amesbury, revealed a number of pits that can be assigned to the middle or later third millennium BC on the basis of the pottery and worked flint present. Pit 2 contained an extremely large Beaker vessel, one of the largest known in southern England, and because of its completeness considered to be in a non-domestic context (Rawlings and Fitzpatrick 1996, 37). A decorated chalk plaque of the same date was found nearby (Rawlings and Fitzpatrick 1996, 22–3).

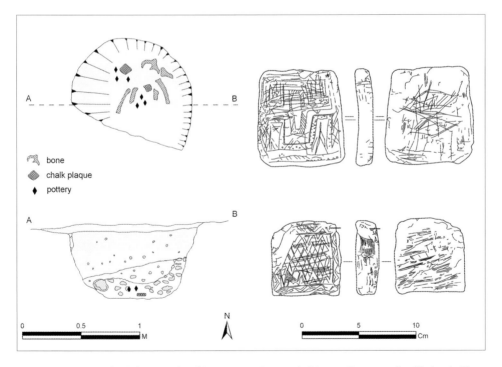

bone
chalk plaque
pottery

32 King Barrow Ridge 'Plaque Pit' and it contents. *Drawing by Vanessa Constant: after Cleal and Allen 1994, figure 5 and Harding 1988, figure 2*

One of the two chalk plaques from the Plaque Pit carries an incised image in the form of an opposing Greek key pattern set within a tram-line frame; the other has a cross-hatched design within a tram-line frame (Harding 1988). The example from Butterfield Down also has a tram-line frame, the interior being filled with parallel lines (Rawlings and Fitzpatrick 1996, 23). All three pieces may be linked with the decorated slab from the ditch at Stonehenge (Cleal et al. 1995, 403–4), and the plaques from the area carry images that compare with the decoration found on Grooved Ware and Beaker pottery, and as motifs within British rock art traditions.

CLASSIC HENGES

Three classic henges have been identified in the Stonehenge landscape (*33*): Coneybury, Woodhenge, and Winterbourne Stoke Down. All appear to have a single ditch set inside a bank with a single entrance. They are all smaller than Stonehenge, and belong to the group of Class 1 henges found widely scattered across Britain according to the typology expanded by Richard Atkinson (1951b, 82, following Piggott and Piggott 1939).

Coneybury lies on high ground west of the Avon. For many years it was regarded as a ploughed-out round barrow, but aerial photography in the 1950s called this view into question and its status was confirmed through surveys and a carefully designed sample-excavation in 1980 as part of the Stonehenge Environs Survey (Richards 1990, 123–58; *33*C). Grooved Ware pottery was found in the primary ditch fill and internal features while Group B Beaker pottery was common in secondary contexts. The central area of the monument was occupied by a timber structure of some kind, but as at Stonehenge its form cannot be determined. A radiocarbon date of 3100–2450 BC (OxA-1408: 4200±110 BP) from animal bones in the primary fill of the ditch suggests this is a relatively early classic henge by comparison with others across the British Isles, a conclusion supported by a date of 3350–2700 BC (OxA-1409: 4370±90 BP) for animal bone from a pit within the henge. These dates also show that the monument is broadly contemporary with Stonehenge 1 and 2.

Woodhenge occupies high ground on the west side of the Avon, immediately south of, and partly intervisible with, Durrington Walls. It was identified through aerial photography in December 1925, and the interior and trenches through the boundary earthwork were excavated by Captain and Mrs Cunnington in 1926–8 (Cunnington 1929) and subsequently restored for public display by marking the postholes with concrete blocks (*colour plate 19*). A further section through the bank and ditch was cut in 1970 and provided additional environmental evidence (Evans and Wainwright 1979). The site has a broad ditch and narrow external bank with a single entrance opening to the northeast (*33*B). The interior is occupied by six oval concentric rings of postholes generally believed to be the foundations of a large timber structure, possibly roofed, although like other examples in the area a source of much debate (Pollard 1995a and

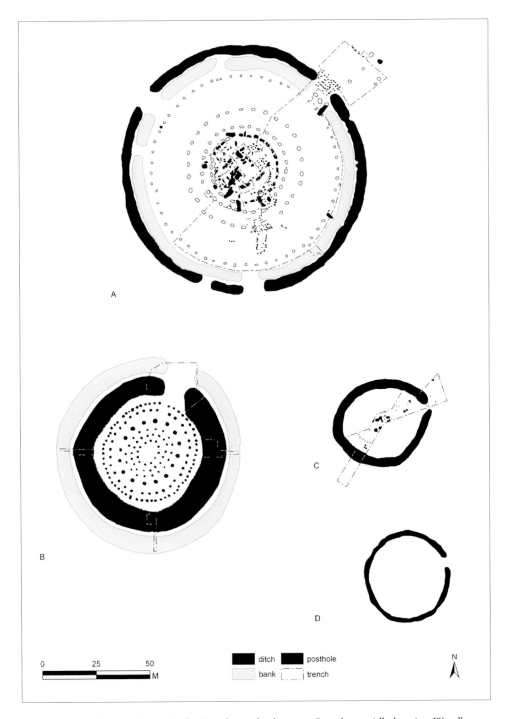

33 Formative and classic henges in the Stonehenge landscape. A: Stonehenge (all phases). B: Woodhenge.
C: Coneybury. D: Winterbourne Stoke. *Drawing by Vanessa Constant: A after Cleal* et al. *1995, figure 36;* B
after Cunnington 1929, plate 3; C *after Richards 1990, figure 97;* D *after David and Payne 1997, figure 13*

see below). A grave containing the burial of a child was found near the centre of the site, and two sockets for standing stones were located on the southeast side. Grooved Ware was found in many of the internal features and in the ditch fill. Radiocarbon dates of 2470–2030 BC (BM-677: 3817±74 BP) and 2340–1970 BC (BM-678: 3755±54 BP) suggest that the site was built and used in the second half of the third millennium BC, later than Coneybury but contemporary with Stonehenge Phase 3i–v and the use of Durrington Walls. Analysis of the distribution of finds within the site suggests patterning to the social use of space with evidence for feasting in the form of discarded pig bones mainly in the eastern half while the western half appears rather clean (Pollard 1995a, figure 7). However, caution is needed in the interpretation of these patterns as contextual information on the source of most finds is poor and it is possible that events long after the use of the structure itself influenced the distribution of material (see Chapter 6).

A third possible classic henge has been defined by geophysical survey on Winterbourne Stoke Down (David and Payne 1997, figure 13A; 33D). Like Coneybury, this site has for years been listed as a round barrow (Winterbourne Stoke 74) but a single entrance through the ditch opens to the east-northeast which, together with its size and position, makes this a likely henge that deserves further investigation. No internal features have been detected.

MINI-HENGES

Mini-henges are often found in close association with classic henges and cursus monuments, as with the two examples so far recognized in the Stonehenge landscape (34). The best known is at Fargo Plantation some 100m south of the Stonehenge Cursus. Excavated in 1938 (Stone 1939) the structure comprises a slightly oval ditch broken by a pair of opposing entrances. The internal space measures about 4m by 6m; in the centre was a pit containing an inhumation and two cremations. Beaker pottery of typologically late Style 3 within Group B was associated with the inhumation, suggesting that the use of this monument extends into the early second millennium BC.

A second mini-henge measuring about 5m across is known through geophysical survey in the area immediately north of the Lesser Cursus (David and Payne 1997, figure 8). It is noteworthy that the orientation of this example is almost at right-angles to the Fargo example (34B). Both, however, are small but perfectly formed Class II henges. No doubt others await discovery in the area.

DURRINGTON WALLS – A HENGE-ENCLOSURE

At the opposite end of the size spectrum to mini-henges are the massive henge-enclosures: great sub-circular enclosures usually found beside rivers in valley-bottom or valley-side locations. Durrington Walls is one of four prime examples within the

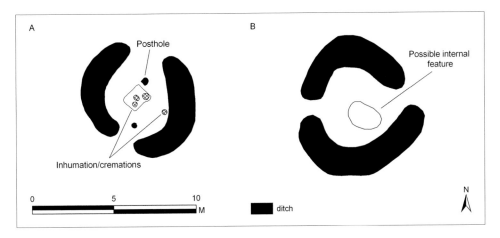

34 Mini-henges in the Stonehenge landscape. A: Fargo Plantation. B: Winterbourne Stoke Down. *Drawing by Vanessa Constant: A after Stone 1939, plate II; B after David and Payne 1997, figure 8*

catchment of the Hampshire Avon in central southern England. Early excavations by J F S Stone, Stuart Piggott, and A St J Booth took advantage of observations made during the laying of a water-pipe through the site, their main trench being on the outer edge of the bank on the south side (Stone et al. 1954). This work showed that the site was closely associated with the users of Rinyo-Clacton-style pottery, nowadays known as Grooved Ware, and charcoal from under the bank was used for the first radiocarbon determinations made on material from the British Isles. Both dates centre on about 3200 BC (GRO-901: 4584±80 BP and GRO-901A: 4575±50 BP) and while famously described at the time by Stuart Piggott as 'archaeologically inacceptable' (1959b, 289) they are now believed to be a fair guide and suggest that the enclosure was built in the first few centuries of the third millennium BC, broadly contemporary with Stonehenge 1–2. A far more extensive excavation, one of the largest of its day, was undertaken in 1966–8 when the main A345 road through the site was realigned (Wainwright and Longworth 1971). Geophysical surveys and further excavations carried out when the site became the focus of the Stonehenge Riverside Project (Parker Pearson et al. 2003; 2004) provide a fairly detailed picture of this important monument (35).

Straddling a broad, dry valley on the east side of the Avon, the boundary earthworks of the henge-enclosure are massive (Crawford 1929) and still impressive today. The ditch is up to 18m wide and 6m deep; the bank, separated from the ditch by a berm varying between 10m and 20m across, is some 27–30m wide and preserved to a height of 2m in some places. Piggott's excavations along the outside of the bank on the southeast side suggested that here at least there may have been some kind of timber revetment (Stone et al. 1954, 163) but this was not found elsewhere. There are certainly two entrances, each more than 20m wide, one to the southeast providing ready access down to the Avon and one to the northwest giving access to the higher ground running off in this direction.

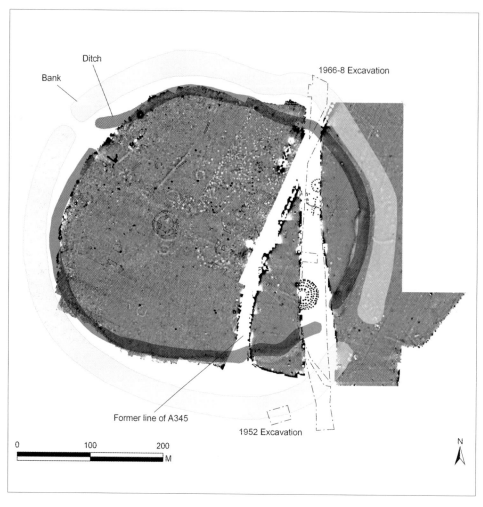

35 Henge enclosure at Durrington Walls showing the extent of excavations 1952 and 1966–8
in relation to the results from subsequent geophysical surveys. *Drawing by Vanessa Constant: after
Wainwright and Longworth 1971, figure 3 over geophysical survey data kindly supplied by English Heritage*

Two further entrances are suspected as a result of topographic and geophysical surveys,
one on the south side providing access to nearby Woodhenge and another opening
northwards towards what is now the Packway. Both of these last-mentioned entrances
were probably blocked towards the end of the enclosure's life. Piles of antler picks on
the floor of the ditch attest the digging methods used and estimates suggest that perhaps
900,000 person-hours would have been needed to build the encircling earthwork alone
(Wainwright and Longworth 1971, 197). Radiocarbon dates on charcoal, antler, and bone
from the base of the enclosure ditch accord with dates from under the bank and confirm
that construction work took place during the first half of the third millennium BC.

Internally, Durrington Walls covers about 11ha, an area roughly 374m by 396m. In the slice through the eastern side revealed in the 1966–8 excavations there were two circular timber-framed structures represented by postholes (*36*). The Northern Circle had been heavily damaged by later cultivation and was poorly preserved. Two successive phases were represented. The first was circular, about 30m across, with an entrance to the southwest and a fence running off to the south. This was replaced by a smaller but more substantial structure, again circular in plan but now only 15m across. Four large posts in the centre were surrounded by a ring of smaller posts forming the outer wall with an entrance opening to the south. In plan, this structure is fairly typical of houses of the third millennium BC (Darvill 1996), and it may have been set within a palisaded compound with its main gate to the south. A path marked by posts that once perhaps supported hurdlework, or some kind of fence, approaches the compound from the south and suggests that space within Durrington Walls was ordered and structured. A single radiocarbon date of 2900–2000 BC (NPL-240: 3905±110 BP) from an antler in one of the central posts on the Northern Circle is the only secure dating evidence for the use of this structure.

The Southern Circle was rather better preserved than its northern counterpart and of quite different scale (*36B*). Again, however, there seem to be two main phases. The first comprised a circular structure about 30m in diameter with four concentric rings of large timber posts. The entrance, perhaps porched, was to the southeast. A fence running tangentially to the structure on a NE–SW axis might well be part of a compound providing demarcated space for this building, the larger scale of the posts either side of the entrance gap perhaps indicating some elaboration of the façade, as would be appropriate to its position immediately inside the southern entrance to the henge-enclosure. An antler pick from one of the postholes relating to this phase of the structure dates to 2600–1700 BC (NPL-239: 3760±148 BP) suggesting a late third-millennium BC date for its construction. In its second phase the Southern Circle was expanded to a structure nearly 40m across, with six nearly concentric rings of posts. The postholes were cut deep into the chalk and many were provided with a ramp to facilitate the erection of the post. More than 340 antler picks had been left in the postholes as work progressed. A substantial entrance opens to the southeast and it is notable that immediately outside was a spread of gravel surfacing, while inside the building on this side the floor comprised rammed chalk. There was a hearth in the centre, while short lines of stakeholes suggest furniture, fittings, or perhaps small screens. The outer wall seems to have been replaced at least once, but the central timbers, seemingly all of oak, remained in place for the duration of use. Three radiocarbon dates on charcoal and antler from this phase are consistent with the construction and use of the building in the second half of the third millennium BC, and this accords with the discovery of Style 3 Beaker pottery along with Grooved Ware in some of the postholes and related deposits. Outside the Southern Circle to the northeast was a substantial hollow, edged on three sides by the stakeholes of a light fence, in which had accumulated a midden of debris including broken flint tools, bone pins, antler picks, pottery, and animal bone.

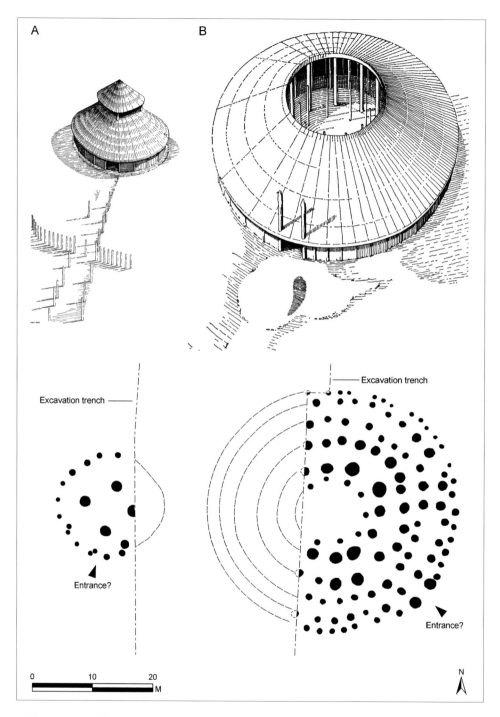

36 Durrington Walls: reconstruction and ground-plan of the Northern Circle (A) and Southern Circle (B). *Drawing by Vanessa Constant: after Wainwright and Longworth 1971, figures 12, 17, 84, and 87. Reconstruction drawings reproduced courtesy of Christopher Musson*

Geophysical surveys across unexcavated parts of Durrington Walls suggest that several other timber structures and further fences exist (David and Payne 1997, 91–4), while excavations outside the southeastern entrance have revealed traces of rectangular structures and a metalled pathway leading towards the Avon (Parker Pearson et al. 2004; 2006).

Much debate surrounds the interpretation of the excavated timber structures, some authorities seeing them as roofed or part-roofed buildings (Piggott 1940; Wainwright and Longworth 1971, 362–77) that could have formed dwellings or a sanctuary. Others favour formal arrangements of free-standing posts (Parker Pearson 1993, figure 58; Gibson 1998a, 97–121; 37), perpetuating earlier traditions and perhaps representing wooden memorials to the dead. Without indications of superstructure in the form of building materials it is hard to choose between these views, but the existence of a midden/rubbish heap outside the structure may suggest that people attempted to keep an enclosed space relatively odour-free.

Likewise, the overall use and role of the site has been hotly contested, with the excavator favouring an essentially residential/habitational interpretation (Wainwright 1975; 1977) while others interpret the distribution of finds as indicating essentially ritual activities and feasting (Richards and Thomas 1984, 214–15; Albarella and Serjeantson 2002). However, such simplistic distinctions between domestic and ritual activity are not especially helpful in the prehistoric context and both most likely happened side by side (Bradley 2005, 10–16). A useful study comparing the assemblages from the two excavated structures was carried out by Colin Richards and Julian Thomas in the early 1980s. They showed that there were fundamental differences between the material associated with

37 *Time Team* reconstruction of the Durrington Walls Southern Circle as a series of free-standing post rings at Upavon, Wiltshire, in July 2005. *Photograph: Timothy Darvill, copyright reserved*

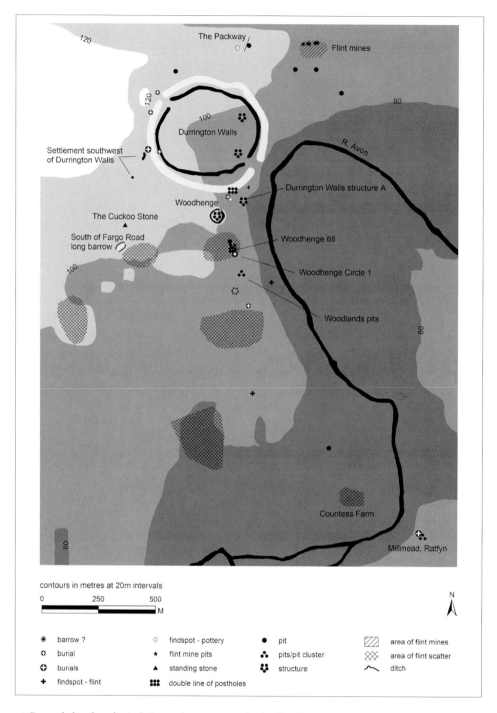

The Packway
Flint mines
120
120
100
Durrington Walls
Settlement southwest
of Durrington Walls
R. Avon
80
Durrington Walls structure A
Woodhenge
The Cuckoo Stone
South of Fargo Road
long barrow
Woodhenge 68
100
Woodhenge Circle 1
Woodlands pits
80
Countess Farm
80
Millmead, Ratfyn

contours in metres at 20m intervals

0   250   500
                                M

N

	barrow ?		findspot - pottery		pit		area of flint mines
	burial		flint mine pits		pits/pit cluster		area of flint scatter
	burials		standing stone		structure		ditch
	findspot - flint		double line of postholes				

38 Recorded archaeological sites and monuments in the Durrington Zone. *Drawing by Vanessa Constant: Wiltshire SMR and various archaeological sources over mapping from EDX Engineering Inc. data at 50m intervals and Ordnance Survey © Crown Copyright 2006. All rights reserved. Licence 100045276*

each circle. The Northern Circle was dominated by a limited range of plain Grooved Ware, functional flint artefacts such as scrapers and knives, and cattle bones. By contrast the larger Southern Circle had a wide range of mainly decorated Grooved Ware, prestigious flint artefacts such as transverse arrowheads, numerous bone points, and a faunal assemblage dominated by pig bones (Richards and Thomas 1984). Here then may be evidence of essentially domestic dwellings across the northern and perhaps western parts of the site, with a big prestigious club-house just inside the southeastern entrance where large groups of people could meet together. Interestingly, after this building was no longer used, and its above-ground structure vanished, pits and scoops were dug into the top of the former postholes and backfilled with domestic refuse presumably taken from the midden or the occupation surface within the building. This does not seem to have happened at the Northern Circle and may be seen as part of a set of ritual practices played out early in the second millennium BC (see Chapter 6).

Durrington Walls did not stand in isolation, it was part of an intensive zone of activity along the west side of the Avon (38). A formal pathway so heavily used that it became a hollow-way seems to have connected the southeast entrance with the River Avon, and a similar path may be imagined leading southwards to Woodhenge. The 1951–2 excavations revealed occupation debris outside the bank on the southeast side (Stone et al. 1954); the 1966–8 work yielded evidence of ditches, hollows, and a rectangular post-built structure outside the henge to the southeast (Wainwright and Longworth 1971, 44–6); and in 2005 several rectangular buildings were identified outside the southeastern entrance to the north of the pathway leading to the river (Parker Pearson et al. 2006).

The construction of each the timber building inside Durrington Walls required a great deal of timber from mature trees and must have taken a heavy toll on local woodlands. Up to 3.5ha of forest timber would have been needed for each structure (Wainwright and Longworth 1971, 223). A detailed examination of the pig bones from the site also reminds us how important it is to see the site in its local environment. Work by Umberto Albarella and Sebastian Payne (2005) shows that many of the pig bones display butchery marks, leaving little doubt that they represent food remains. The pigs themselves were mainly young, domesticated, and between nine months and three years old when slaughtered. It is suggested that many were slaughtered during winter-time, and from the presence of injuries and fragments of flint projectile point remaining embedded in the bones some or all of these animals may have been taken in the chase (Albarella and Serjeantson 2002). Taken together, the evidence from Durrington Walls suggests a fair-sized more-or-less permanently resident population that was periodically swelled by visitors or pilgrims who came for festivals from far and wide and perhaps participated in hunting rituals and celebrations focused on the club-house. These may well be tied to the use of other monuments in the area, for example Stonehenge, Woodhenge, Coneybury, and the Cursus, and no doubt involved setting up temporary camps outside the earthworks and around about.

SETTLEMENTS AND RESIDENCE

Beyond the immediate vicinity of Durrington Walls the intensity of occupation along the west side of the Avon Valley continues for some distance to both north and south, much of it known as a result of small-scale developments and chance finds (*38*); Julian Richards has labelled this area the 'Durrington Zone' (1990, 269–70).

To the north, half a dozen pits and scoops were found in 1991 during the construction of a pipeline parallel to The Packway (Cleal et al. 2004, 220–3). These contained small amounts of pottery, animal bones, and worked flint, but their overall context could not be determined in the limited areas investigated.

Southwest of Durrington Walls, excavations in advance of tree-planting in 1970 revealed evidence for a settlement comprising four pits used for the disposal of rubbish and a shallow ditch all associated with Grooved Ware, worked flints, and antler picks (Wainwright 1971, 78–82). Radiocarbon dates of 2150–1740 BC (BM-702: 3597±76 BP) and 1980–1600 BC (BM-703: 3473±72) suggest that these pits were contemporary with the later use of Durrington Walls.

Directly south, Woodhenge Circle 2 (Durrington 68) preserved a setting of postholes that has been reconstructed as the remains of a house (Cunnington 1929, 45 and plate 39; Pollard 1995b). It is typical of others around the country (Darvill 1996, 107), and very similar in plan to the Northern Circle within Durrington Walls (*39*). Further south still, the Woodlands pit group was found in the garden of a house called Woodlands in Countess Road in 1941 and explored further in 1947 (Stone and Young 1948; Stone 1949). There were four pits in all, each oval in plan and rather shallow. They contained Grooved Ware, part of a Group VII stone axe from North Wales, and a wide range of worked flint, worked stone, animal remains, fish remains, marine shells, and carbonized hazelnut shells. More recently, field evaluations on the site of the proposed Stonehenge visitor centre at Countess Road East revealed a possible pit, a section of ditch, and a substantial collection of flint working debris provisionally dated to the third millennium BC (WA 1995; 2003; 2004).

There is some evidence that intensive occupation also extends east of the Avon. Similar material was found at Ratfyn in 1920 (Stone 1935; Wainwright and Longworth 1971, 5–6), for example, including a ditch and pits. Finds included human remains, Grooved Ware, a stone axe-hammer, worked flints, animal bones, and a large scallop shell suggesting links with the coast.

Although less intensive than in the Durrington Zone, the Stonehenge Environs Survey revealed at least four other areas within the Stonehenge landscape between the Avon and the Till with evidence of occupation during the third millennium BC, in most cases focused around one of the henges or mini-henges discussed above. Each area is mainly represented by a flint scatter, stray finds of pottery and other distinctive items, structural remains preserved below later monuments, and collections of material incorporated into the fabric of later earthworks. To an extent these represent the continuation of areas already used in the fourth millennium BC (see Chapter 4) and serve to emphasize

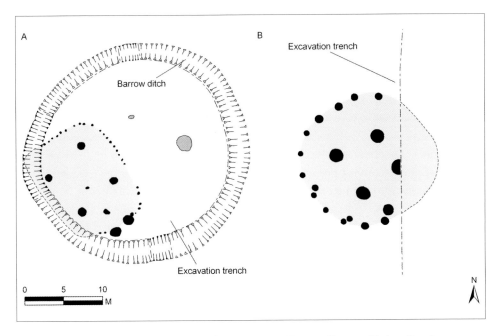

39 Houses of the third millennium BC in the Durrington Zone. A: Preserved below Durrington 68. B: Durrington Walls Northern Circle. *Drawing by Vanessa Constant: after Pollard 1995b, figure 2 and Wainwright and Longworth 1971, figure 17*

a degree of continuity in the disposition of occupation. It is notable, however, that the amount of material that can be assigned to the third millennium BC that is scattered across the landscape as background noise between these areas – especially pottery – is rather greater than for earlier times and strongly suggests an overall increase in the scale and extent of activity.

The west side of King Barrow Ridge remained a focus of occupation, perhaps connected with some of the ceremonial pits and Coneybury Henge already referred to. The Amesbury 39 barrow and several other mounds along the ridge incorporated Peterborough Ware, Grooved Ware, and Beaker pottery in the matrix of the mound (Cleal and Allen 1994, 62–5 and 70); Amesbury 133, a twin bell barrow on the east side of the ridge, sealed a large hollow containing Peterborough Ware and the remains of an antler, while Grooved Ware and Beaker pottery were recovered from the buried soil (RCHM 1979, 4; Gingell 1988, 39).

Wilsford Down, occupying the high ground south of Stonehenge, has fairly dense concentrations of worked flint of the third millennium BC as well as scatters of Peterborough Ware, Grooved Ware, and typologically early Style 1 Beaker (Richards 1990, 271; Cleal et al. 1995, figures 78 and 225). The Winterbourne Stoke Henge stands at the western end of this spread of activity. Sample excavation of sixteen, 5m by 5m, trenches revealed one feature and abundant worked flint in the ploughsoil. Areas of high phosphate concentrations suggested occupation within the sampled area, perhaps connected with flint working (Richards 1990, 158–71). Nearby, excavations of the round barrows in Lake Wood revealed Peterborough Ware and early Style Beaker pottery within and under mounds 36f, 37, 38, and 39 (Grimes 1964).

Stonehenge Down to the west of Stonehenge yielded a fairly discrete and rather dense scatter of worked flint as well as Peterborough Ware and Grooved Ware (Richards 1990, figure 158). Few barrows have been excavated in this area to provide additional information, but its location overlooking Stonehenge and its possible association with the Palisade Ditch discussed further below make this a promising area for further research.

North of the Stonehenge Cursus and extending across onto Durrington Down is a fourth extensive scatter of worked flint and pottery of the third millennium BC perhaps somehow associated with the mini-henge in Fargo Plantation (Richards 1990, figure 158). Flint knapping debris in the ditch of the Stonehenge Cursus seems to be of third millennium BC date (Saville 1978, 17) and perhaps shows that this activity was carried out on the edge of a settlement zone. Sample excavation of five 5m by 5m trenches adjacent to Fargo Plantation with the intention of investigating a spread of material from the second millennium BC also revealed a surprising amount of pottery and worked flint of the third-millennium BC, but no features of the period (Richards 1990, 194–208).

To these can be added other areas outside the Stonehenge Environs Survey. In the Till Valley, Beaker pottery was found at Winterbourne Stoke 39 and 47 (Gingell 1988, 54), but the largest assemblage from the area is from Winterbourne Stoke 51–4 excavated by Earnest Greenfield in 1958. Here 144 sherds of Peterborough Ware, 49 sherds of Grooved Ware, and 5 sherds of Style 3 Beaker pottery were found in pre-barrow contexts (Smith 1991, 34–8). Six pits containing Beaker pottery were excavated at Crescent Copse near Shrewton in 1997 (Heaton and Cleal 2000) but nothing is known of their wider context. The same applies to a cluster of three pits found in 1940 during military digging on Knighton Down, Durrington, and a group of pits found at the Rollestone Grain Store in 1996 (Anon 1998, 164).

On the high ground east of the Avon, Amesbury 61 yielded a range of Beaker pottery (Ashbee 1984a, 76–9), while further south excavations at Butterfield Down have provided some evidence for occupation in the later third and early second millennium BC in the form of two pits and a linear ditch associated with Beaker pottery and worked flints (Lawson 1993; Rawlings and Fitzpatrick 1996, 10 and 37–8). It is also now recognized that here too are some of the richest burials of the period not just in the Stonehenge landscape but in the whole of northwest Europe (see below).

PALISADE DITCH AND ENCLOSURES

Immediately west and north of Stonehenge is a linear ditch, known as the Palisade Ditch or the Gate Ditch (see 28). Traced through geophysical survey (David and Payne

1997, 87) and aerial photography for a distance of more than 1300m, the Palisade Ditch has only been smapled through small-scale excavations in 1953, 1967, and 1978 (Cleal et al. 1995, 155–61). Each of the excavated sections differs in detail, but most show a V-profile ditch cut to support upright timber posts which can be interpreted as a palisade or stockade. Dating is uncertain, but there is late second-millennium BC pottery from the uppermost fills of the palisade itself, and in the 1967 trench a crouched inhumation burial dated to the mid-first millennium BC cut into the top of the ditch (Cleal et al. 1995, 157). When the Palisade Ditch was first excavated there was nothing comparable known to provide a wider context, but since the later 1970s a number of very large palisaded enclosures have been discovered and sampled (Gibson 1998b; 2002). Among these is a pair of enclosures in the valley of the River Kennet south of Avebury (Whittle 1997b, 53–138). A third-millennium BC date is consistent with the evidence from the Stonehenge Palisade Ditch, although whether it should be seen as a full enclosure or simply a linear boundary remains to be determined. If it was a full enclosure then a projected extent based on the shape and size of better-recorded examples means that it could include the spreads of occupation debris noted earlier on Stonehenge Down and Durrington Down. More significant, its impact on the appearance of Stonehenge would also have been considerable. It is possible that Stonehenge was simply a small monument immediately outside a much larger enclosure in rather the same way that Woodhenge lies just outside the great henge-enclosure of Durrington Walls.

A second possible enclosure, just as poorly understood, is the so-called North Kite (see *28*). This lies south of Stonehenge on the eastern side of the Till/Avon interfluve. The site was recognized by Colt Hoare (1812, map opp. 170) and recorded from the air by Crawford and Keiller (1928, 254) as a large three-sided earthwork enclosure, roughly trapezoidal in plan, which they regarded as being Romano-British in date. Since the 1920s the North Kite has been badly damaged by ploughing, and it lies amid a series of later prehistoric boundaries and fieldsystems that rather confuse attempts to understand it. Two round barrows of the second millennium BC in the Lake barrow cemetery stratigraphically overlie the southwestern boundary of the North Kite (RCHM 1979, 26), while small-scale excavations undertaken in 1958 suggested a date in the later third or early second millennium BC and confirmed the absence of a fourth side (Annable 1959, 229). Further excavations in 1983 as part of the Stonehenge Environs Project yielded Peterborough Ware and Beaker pottery from the buried soil below the bank, broadly confirming the previously suggested date (Richards 1990, 184–92). The scale of the enclosure is impressive: the axial length is at least 400m (north–south) by 150m at the narrow northern end, expanding to 300m wide at the southern end. An unexcavated ring-ditch (Wilsford 93) lies roughly in the centre of the open southern end. The only comparable excavated monument is the rather earlier, fourth-millennium BC, trapezoidal ceremonial structure at Godmanchester, Cambridgeshire, with an axial length of 336m and a maximum width of 228m (McAvoy 2000).

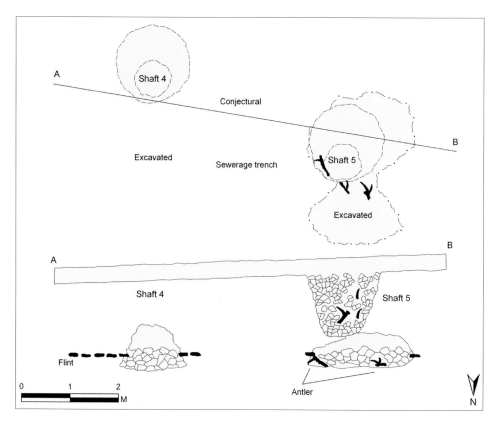

40 Flint mines at Durrington: plan and section of shafts 4 and 5. *Drawing by Vanessa Constant: after Booth and Stone 1952, figures 1 and 2*

FLINT MINES

Flint mines were recorded east of the Stonehenge Inn in 1952 (*40*). Three were shallow open-cast scoops about 0.6m deep while three others were rather deeper shafts that included low galleries and undercutting to optimize the amount of flint extracted (Booth and Stone 1952; Wainwright and Longworth 1971, 6). These finds have not been followed up but are amongst just three confirmed mining sites in Wiltshire (Barber et al. 1999). It may be noted, however, that a substantial collection of flint working debris was found during field evaluations for the proposed Stonehenge visitor centre at Countess Road East only about 1km south of the Durrington flint mines. The bulk of the assemblage of more than 1500 pieces derives from the production of core tools, either functional items such as axes or knives or perhaps prestige items such as flint replicas of bronze daggers (WA 2004, 11). Chipped flint axes with the appearance of being roughouts for making polished implements have been found in the Stonehenge landscape, for example at Bulford and Winterbourne Stoke.

HERE COMES THE SUN

Around 2550 BC attention again focused on Stonehenge with a period of refurbishment that saw the monument transformed from a fairly ordinary, and by this time rather obsolete, monument into something special and unique. Stone structures began to be erected in the interior, thus starting more than six centuries of building and rebuilding. Although provisionally divided into six architecturally coherent phases (3i–vi: Cleal et al. 1995, 167–331) changes during the later third millennium BC are perhaps better seen as a single evolving long-term project whose final outcome was, of course, never exactly clear to those actually doing the work. It is assumed that all the earlier timber posts and structures had rotted and were easily cleared to make way for these new structures, but again we must always beware of imposing modern views of construction site management onto the distant past, and it may be that work started amid a tangle of decaying and partly collapsed timbers.

What was built more-or-less in the centre of the existing earthwork enclosure utilized as many as 82 blocks of dolerite, rhyolite, and tuff – collectively known as bluestones – that ultimately derive from the Preseli Hills of southwest Wales (see below). Whether these stones arrived gradually over a long period of time, or were the result of a concerted effort to get the raw materials for this project, is not known. Some authorities postulate the presence of bluestones on Salisbury Plain as far back as the mid-fourth millennium BC and have even proposed a pre-Stonehenge bluestone monument somewhere in the area (Stone 1948, 18). Certainly this is possible since spotted dolerite was used in the construction of the portal dolmen at Pentre Ifan, Pembrokeshire (Grimes 1948) as early as 3800 BC, and stone axes of the same material, known as petrological Group XIII, may have been circulating during the fourth millennium BC although none have been found in securely stratified contexts (Williams-Thorpe et al. 2006). However, there are other, more plausible, explanations that can be offered for this extraneous material and these will be considered below as they are part of the evolving history of the monument.

The ground plan of the first bluestone monument at Stonehenge (Phase 3i: Cleal et al. 1995, 169–88) is poorly known because it was wholly removed during later reconstructions. Only the eastern sector has been firmly established through excavation although some information is available about the western part as localized excavations here provide glimpses of relevant features. Richard Atkinson (1979, 58–61) suggested that the dumb-bell-shaped sockets he first found in 1954 (the Q- and R-Holes) were the remains of a round or slightly oval Double Bluestone Circle with an overall diameter of about 26m. Later interpretations have sometimes favoured an incomplete structure, perhaps of rectangular or horseshoe form (e.g. Cleal et al. 1995, 188), but in fact Atkinson's original idea stands up remarkably well to computer modelling that uses all the excavated features of this phase in a single structure (*41*).

Little is known about the pillars that made up the Double Bluestone Circle as it was only their sockets and a few broken stumps that were recorded during the excavations. It is assumed, however, that the stones were reused in later remodellings and that most are

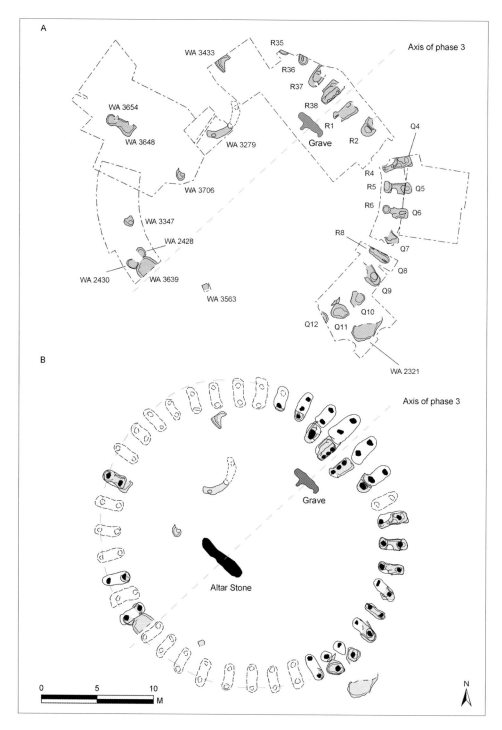

41 Stonehenge Phase 3i Double Bluestone Circle. A: Excavated evidence. B: Reconstructed plan.
Drawing by Vanessa Constant: after Cleal et al. *1995, figures 80 and 81*

therefore still on the site today. Certainly, a handful of the bluestones used in Phases 3iv–v show various signs of shaping that are irrelevant to their later position and thus perhaps indicate something of the architectural design of the earlier structure. Stone 68, for example, has a groove running along one edge (*42*) which might fit with the tongue worked onto one face of Stone 66 to form some kind of screen or conjoined block. Stones 67, 69, and 70 also show facets and worked features, but the purpose of these cannot now be determined. Stones 150 and 36 each have a pair of mortises on one face, suggesting that they were once the tops of bluestone trilithons (*colour plate 9*), perhaps radially set trilithons flanking the entrance into the circle. Overall, the form and construction of the early Double Bluestone Circle may have been more complicated than commonly supposed.

The main entrance into the Double Bluestone Circle was to the northeast and was emphasized by additional bluestones set inside the inner circuit and perhaps by the trilithons already referred to. The new axis created by this arrangement of stones aligns on the rising midsummer sun as it appears over the horizon at Sidbury Hill. It is possible that a large slab of greenish sandstone known as the Altar Stone (Stone 80) lay horizontally within the circle at its focus (Burl 2001), with various other stones within the enclosed space forming further structural elements, including a small arc of two or three stones in the northwest quarter. A shallow grave immediately inside the entrance setting and set transversely to the principal axis was excavated in 1926. Although the area has been heavily disturbed in later times, the presence of Beaker pottery may suggest a burial of this period within the circle (Cleal et al. 1995, 265).

Left: 42 Stonehenge: Stone 68 with a linear groove down the western (right-hand) side. *Photograph: Timothy Darvill, copyright reserved*

Above: 43 Stonehenge: Station Stone 93. *Photograph: Timothy Darvill, copyright reserved*

Four sarsen boulders showing little sign of shaping were set up within the earthwork enclosure at the corners of a rectangle some 80m by 30m, perpendicular to the principal axis (*43*). These so-called Station Stones seem to define two sets of sight-lines that have astronomical significance: the two short sides follow the same alignment as the principal axis and therefore sight onto the rising midsummer sun and the setting midwinter sun; the two long sides align on the major limiting moon rising in the south (full in summer) or setting in the north (full in winter) which would happen every 18.6 years (Ruggles 1997, 218–21). This set of alignments was retained in later phases of rebuilding, and perhaps elaborated (*44*).

Changes were made to the earthwork enclosure when the Double Bluestone Circle was added. Richard Atkinson suggested that a section of ditch to the southwest of the original northeastern entrance was filled and levelled, and a corresponding section of the bank removed, in order to align the entrance on the new principal SW–NE axis through the Double Bluestone Circle (1979, 72–3). This is disputed by Cleal et al. (1995, 138–9) who present evidence for the localized refilling of the ditch at several points around its circuit and link it to the general ritual cycle of ditch use. Either way, the enclosure ditch hereabout was full by the time the stone circles were built.

Two stones seem to have been set up immediately outside the entrance: the Heelstone (Stone 96) which may already have been there (*colour plate 10*) and a partner-stone to the northwest (Stone 97), the socket for which was discovered in 1979 (Pitts 1982, 83). Viewed from the centre of the circle these two stones would have provided an accurate sight-line to the rising midsummer sun with the sun rising in the gap between them.

Outside the remodelled entrance a pathway or Avenue was built. Despite more than 20 excavations across the Avenue, and extensive geophysical surveys, there is still great uncertainty about its exact date and phasing of its construction. Ultimately, it ran for a distance of about 2.5km, connecting Stonehenge with the River Avon at West Amesbury. However, there is some reason to believe that it was built in two stages, first a straight 530m length from Stonehenge directly northeastwards to Stonehenge Bottom, followed sometime later by a much longer and more sinuous section from Stonehenge Bottom across to the River Avon (see below). Geophysical surveys in Stonehenge Bottom in 1990 revealed slight traces of a junction between the two sections (Cleal et al. 1995, figure 265), suggested also by a detailed survey of the earthworks (RCHM 1979, figure 5), but excavations are needed here to further clarify the matter. In its putatively primary stage, the Avenue was defined on either side by a low bank with an external ditch. It is possible that standing stones were set at intervals along the banks, although none survived into modern times (Cleal et al. 1995, 506–10). The overall width of the Avenue tapered slightly from about 27m in Stonehenge Bottom down to 21.5m as it approached the enclosure around Stonehenge. Strangely, the earthworks of the Avenue never actually joined the ditch at Stonehenge; a gap about 1.8m wide was found between them.

Little is known about the northeastern terminal of the Avenue in Stonehenge Bottom except that a small, round mound stood on the southeast side. The topography of

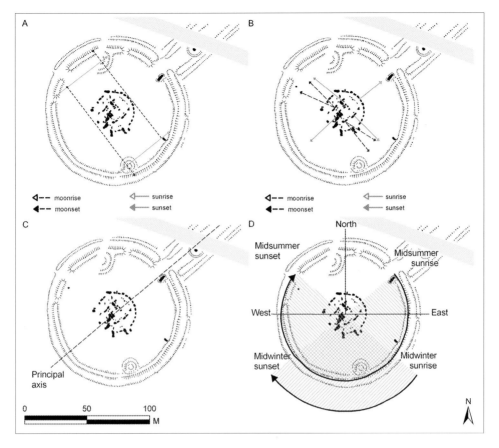

44 Stonehenge showing the main proposed astronomical axes and alignments. Alignments proposed by Gerald Hawkins for the early phases of Stonehenge (A) and through the central trilithons (B). C: The principal NE–SW axis projected onto Phase 3 of the monument. D: Schematic representation of the principal solar movements in relation to Phase 3 of the monument. *Drawing by Vanessa Constant: A and B based on Hawkins 1966a, figures 11 and 12; C after Cleal* et al. *1995, figure 79; D after Atkinson 1987, 11*

Stonehenge Bottom near this point suggests that a small stream flowed along the floor of the valley in ancient times, as indeed it has within living memory (Richards 1990, 211); Lake, the small settlement where Stonehenge Bottom joins the main Avon Valley, takes its name from the Old English *lacu* meaning 'streamlet' (Gover et al. 1939, 372).

Few finds can be related to the Double Bluestone Circle and activity contemporary with it. Two sherds of early Style 1 Beaker pottery came from stone socket Q5, fragments of antler from Q6 and one of the R-Holes, a piece of chert from Q7, and a piece of flint from one of the R-Holes (Cleal et al. 1995, 184). Radiocarbon dates on antler from an R-Hole and bone from a Q-Hole (2149–1750 BC (I-2384: 3570±110 BP) and 2460–2040 BC (OxA-4901: 3800±45 BP) respectively) are considered unreliable determinations (Cleal et al. 1995, 185). Some of the Beaker pottery recovered from later contexts may be residual from this phase in the use of the monument, and Humphrey Case has emphasized the strength of the Beaker associations with this and later structures at the site (1997, 165) which relate to a period when Beakers indicated a rather circumscribed exclusive culture (Needham 2005). Case also noted the presence of a small tubular-sheet copper or bronze bead typically associated with Beaker pottery from the disturbed upper fill of Aubrey Hole 18 (1997, 165).

No other stone circle in the British Isles is quite like the Double Bluestone Circle at Stonehenge, although various complex ring-cairns or ring-cairn circles in western Britain have concentric rings of orthostats edging their banks (Lynch 1972, 62-3). The rectangular setting represented by the four Station Stones is slightly more familiar and Aubrey Burl has drawn attention to broadly comparable structures in southwest Britain and Brittany (Burl 2003).

EVER INCREASING CIRCLES

Change continued at Stonehenge through the later centuries of the third millennium BC. The Double Bluestone Circle of Phase 3i was dismantled and Stone 97 in the entrance removed. Ditches were dug around the Heelstone (Stone 96) and also around the southeastern and the northwestern Station Stones (Stones 92 and 94) as if to mark these out as somehow special. Perhaps the unworked sarsen blocks themselves were of some magical or historical interest, or the place that they marked was somehow revered. It was all part of the on-going project of change and reshaping that in a sense cleared the ground for the creation of the great stone structure visible on the site today. The burial of an adult male with evidence of traumatic pathology suggesting death caused by arrow-shot was found in a grave dug into the northwest sector of the enclosure ditch may relate to this phase of clearance as it dates to 2400–2140 BC (Evans 1984; Cleal et al. 1995, 533).

The exact sequence of building represented though Phases 3ii–v is far from clear and the main components are often difficult to relate to one another, although the main pattern of development can be recognized (see 29). The principal NE–SW axis was maintained, perpetuating an interest in the midsummer sunrise and midwinter sunset (see below). Four roughly concentric settings of stones were constructed in the centre of the enclosure on this axis, reusing some of the bluestones taken from the Phase 3i monument and adding to them a series of massive sarsen blocks brought from the north Wessex Downs.

At the focus was the so-called Altar Stone (Stone 80; *colour plate 14*), a greenish coloured block of sandstone, now broken in two but originally 5m long by 1.1m wide by 0.53m thick, from the Senni Beds of Devonian Old Red Sandstone somewhere between Kidwelly and Abergavenny in South Wales (Ixer and Turner 2006). Probably reused from Phase 3i, there has been some debate about whether this stone was set horizontally or vertically; the former now being preferred on the grounds that it would not have got to its present position if it had been felled from an upright position by the collapse of Stones 55 and 156 sometime before AD 1575 (Burl 1997; 2001). Around the Altar Stone was an oval setting of 24 or 25 bluestones, all of them carefully selected spotted dolerite from just one or two outcrops on or around Carn Menyn, Pembrokeshire. These relatively large bluestones are all shaped and well finished, and were arranged to be graded in height, with the taller examples in the southwest sector and the shortest to the northeast.

Outside the Bluestone Oval was a horseshoe setting of five massive Sarsen Trilithons (*colour plate 11*), the largest being to the southwest with successively more squat examples to the northeast and the open end of the horseshoe facing on the principal axis to the northeast. Alasdair Whittle has pointed out that each trilithon seems to incorporate a well-dressed stone to the left as viewed from the centre of the site paired with a relatively rough more pock-marked pillar to the right (1997a, 155–61). In all cases the lintels seem to have been shaped and fitted onto the uprights with primitive mortise and tenon joints formed in stone. Some trial and error seems to have been involved with this as Stone 156 has mortises in both faces.

Outside the Trilithon Horseshoe is a ring of about 40 bluestones (*colour plate 12*), again probably reused from Phase 3i, but in this case comprising mainly natural boulders and blocks with little if any formal shaping. They include a variety of spotted and non-spotted dolerite, rhyolite, and tuff, that derive from a range of outcrops around the main Carn Menyn ridge (Bevins et al. 1989; Thorpe et al. 1991; Williams-Thorpe et al. 2006). The juxtaposition of the Bluestone Oval and the Bluestone Circle in terms of the stones selected for their construction physically replicates rather faithfully the geographical arrangement of stone outcrops in north Pembrokeshire: Carn Menyn and Carn Goedog at the focus providing the stones for the central setting (Bluestone Oval/Horseshoe) and other outcrops around about providing stones for the outer circle (Bluestone Circle). The pillars forming the Bluestone Circle at Stonehenge were roughly graded in height with the tallest examples to the southwest, but the pair of stones flanking the principal axis to the northeast were perhaps carefully selected for their shape. The one to the left of the axis/entrance as viewed from the centre of the site (Stone 49) has a bevelled top while the one to the right (Stone 31) has a flat top (*45*), perhaps evidence of sexual dimorphism in the form of male and female stones respectively (Darvill 2004c, 51–2).

The outermost stone setting is the Sarsen Circle with its uprights and lintels (*colour plate 13*). Sixteen uprights remain standing. There is some question as to whether this was ever a complete circle as most of the stones that would have formed the southwestern sector are missing and have been absent from the site since at least the sixteenth century AD (Ashbee 1998). However, earlier robbing of the structure is quite possible and it certainly gives the structure great coherence to envisage a complete ring of 30 uprights capped by 30 shaped lintels. The gap between the uprights averages 1.8m, but the gap between Stones 1 and 30 on the principal axis to the northeast is 2.1m and this seems to have been the main entrance into the central area of the site. All of the surviving elements of this circle seem to have been carefully shaped with a slightly convex curve (entasis) to correct the visual illusion of curving inwards that straight sides otherwise would give. The height of the uprights is also graded to produce a horizontal top to the ring of lintels despite the fact that the ground dips to the southwest and thus requires taller uprights in this sector. The lintels are also shaped and were secured to their supporting uprights by mortise and tenon joints. As with the construction of the Sarsen Trilithons, mistakes were made when the stones were shaped and Stone 122 has four mortises, two at each end. The lintels were secured to each other by an upright ridge on one end that slots into a groove on the end of the next stone. One slightly unusual feature of the Sarsen Circle is that Stone 11 in the southeast sector is only half a stone, narrower than the rest and less than 2m high; the gap between the top of the stone and the lintels that it supported was presumably filled with timber bracing.

Even in this developed form, the pattern of circles, horseshoe, and oval did not remain static. One particularly visible change was the removal of five or six bluestones from the northeastern sector of the Bluestone Oval to turn it into a Bluestone Horseshoe of 19 pillars, open on the principal axis to the northeast. Where these superfluous stones went is not known for sure, but some may well have been taken off-site and broken up. Certainly there are fragments of bluestone (spotted dolerite) in a number of nearby monuments, with a slight concentration in the area of Fargo Plantation (Stone 1948; 16–18; Thorpe et al. 1991, figure 4). It is possible that one stone was taken to the long barrow variously known as Boles Barrow or Bowls Barrow, on Imber Down, Heytesbury, some 19km away, where it was incorporated into blocking deposits or some kind of secondary structure within this complicated and poorly understood monument (*colour plate 4*). The Boles Barrow bluestone was found during excavations by William Cunnington in 1801 (Hoare 1812, 87–8), but not recognized until a year or two later (Cunnington 1920; 1924). Subsequent excavations by Cunnington in 1803 (Hoare 1812, 88), John Thurnam in 1864 (1865, 472–3), and William (Jn) and Henry Cunnington in 1885-6 (Cunnington 1889) failed to reveal any further bluestones, but equally did nothing to resolve the context of the original stone. Nor is it wholly clear what became of the stone. The bluestone block now in Salisbury Museum labelled as coming from Boles Barrow is by no means certainly the stone in question, and from its size and shape looks rather like a trophy from some antiquarian visit to Stonehenge at a time when removing bits of stone as charms or curiosities was considered acceptable (cf. Cunnington 1924; Burl 2000b). All we can really say is that the 1801 excavation focused on the east end of the monument where they found the remains of a stone or timber chamber with burials spread across the floor and 'a great pile of stones and flints raised lengthways along the centre of the barrow over them … this pile (in form like the ridge of a house) was covered with marl' (Cunnington 1924, 432). As such it sounds as if much of this deposit of stone was some kind of blocking, and certainly many other long barrows in central and western England show clear evidence of disturbance, secondary use, and deliberate filling in the later third millennium BC, notably, for example, at the West Kennet long barrow near Avebury (Piggott 1962a; Darvill 2004b, 173–86).

45 View from the centre of Stonehenge northeastwards along the principal axis, through the gap between Stones 31 and 49 in the Bluestone Circle and Stones 1 and 30 in the Sarsen Circle to the Heelstone (Stone 96) in the middle distance. *Photograph: Timothy Darvill, copyright reserved*

Changes were also taking place around the periphery of the site, especially in and around the entrance. Three or possibly four large stones were at one stage set up in the entranceway through the earthwork. Two or three were later removed; the fourth one was toppled and remains prostrate on the ground today as the so-called Slaughter Stone (Stone 95). At least two further stones lay more-or-less on the principal axis immediately outside the entrance and together with the Heelstone may at various times have marked the alignment of the midsummer sunrise. In thinking about the arrangement of stones in and around the entrance in the later phases of Stonehenge's existence Aubrey Burl has suggested similarities with structures at other henges in the British Isles and proposed that at one stage at least there was a short, corridor-like entrance arrangement delimited by standing stones (Burl 1994; 1997; 2001). There is no evidence of changes to the Avenue in the later third millennium BC, and if the two-phase development of this feature is accepted then throughout this period its northwestern terminal was in Stonehenge Bottom, physically linking the monument with a small watercourse.

Leaving aside the detail of all these changes and remodellings at Stonehenge, what comes through the millennia loud and clear is the longevity of the significance that must have been attached to the place. Obtaining all the stones, setting them up, and periodically remodelling the site was not a small undertaking, and could probably have been achieved only through the energy of some centralizing authority (Renfrew 1973a; 1973b). To anyone walking up the Avenue towards the stones in their later manifestations the appearance of the monument against the southwestern horizon would have been spectacular and no doubt awe-inspiring. There was simply nothing else in northwest Europe quite like it. First into view would have been the top of the great southwestern Sarsen Trilithon, then the Sarsen Circle and the stones that stood in the entranceway, and finally as the circles drew nearer the earthwork and peripheral structures. Any sounds being made in the interior would spill out through the narrow gaps in the Sarsen Circle, and at night any bright light in the interior would also fan out through these same gaps. Only when actually standing in the northeastern entrance gap between Stones 1 and 30 would it be possible to see what was going on in the interior and identify the smaller settings of the Bluestone Circle, Bluestone Oval/Horseshoe, and the Altar Stone. Although the interior of the site now feels rather cluttered, this is largely because the fallen stones prevent easy movement; originally the central area would have felt relatively open and spacious.

Finds from the stoneholes and the interior of these circles, ovals, and horseshoes are sparse in the extreme. A few sherds of pottery, occasional pieces of flint, a piece of a Group I greenstone axe from Cornwall, and a few fragments of bone and antler. A skeuomorphic axe and perhaps a phallus both carved from lumps of chalk may also relate to this phase of the monument (Cleal et al. 1995, 348–463). Extending right across the central area of the monument was a spread of stone flakes and chips – the Stonehenge Layer as it is sometimes called – in places nearly 0.5m thick and representing the accumulation of debris from shaping the sarsens and bluestones. Quartzite, rhyolite, and dolerite hammerstones and mauls used in the flaking, battering, and crushing of the sarsen and bluestone pillars are also represented. Part of a Group III axehammer from Cornwall was found in the Stonehenge Layer. Precise dating for most of the structural elements of the Phase 3ii-vi monument is also lacking, although the Sarsen Circle was probably built between 2620–2480 BC, the Sarsen Trilithons 2440–2100 BC, the Bluestone Circle 2280–2030 BC, and the Bluestone Horseshoe 2270–1930 BC (Cleal et al. 1995, 532–3).

Analogies for most of the separate elements that make up the later phases of Stonehenge can be found scattered across northwest Europe, although nowhere else do they seem to have been assembled together in one place in quite the same way. Plain circles are common and widespread (Barnatt 1989; Burl 2000a), and in southwestern Britain, the territory traditionally associated with the builders of Stonehenge, there are monuments comprising concentric stone circles: a pair at The Sanctuary near Avebury, Wiltshire (Cunnington 1931), and three at Yellowmead, Devon (Barnatt 1989, 63). The Bluestone Oval is exactly matched by the structure at Bedd Arthur, Pembrokeshire, overlooking the bluestone outcrops on Carn Menyn (46), itself one of a series of such monuments around the Irish Sea basin (Darvill and Wainwright 2003). Aubrey Burl has argued that the horseshoe arrangement of stones seen in the Trilithon Horseshoe and the Bluestone Horseshoe connects with monuments across the British Isles and the Atlantic coastal regions of France (Burl 1997; 2003), a view subsequently challenged by Scarre (1997) who prefers the autonomous development of these structures in each area.

1 Stonehenge looking north from Normanton Down. *Photograph: Timothy Darvill, copyright reserved*

2 Winterbourne Stoke 1 long barrow at Longbarrow Crossroads. *Photograph: Timothy Darvill, copyright reserved*

3 Knighton Barrow (Figheldean 27). *Photograph: Timothy Darvill, copyright reserved*

4 Boles Barrow (Heytesbury 1). *Photograph: Timothy Darvill, copyright reserved*

5 Sarsen erratics at Lockeridge, West Overton, Wiltshire. *Photograph: Timothy Darvill, copyright reserved*

6 Spotted dolerite outcrops at Carn Menyn, Pembrokeshire. *Photograph: Timothy Darvill, copyright reserved*

7 Spotted dolerite from Carn Menyn, Pembrokeshire in fresh fracture. *Photograph: Timothy Darvill, copyright reserved*

8 Excavations through the boundary wall of the Carn Menyn Enclosure, Pembrokeshire, in April 2005. The scale totals 1m. *Photograph: Timothy Darvill and SPACES, copyright reserved*

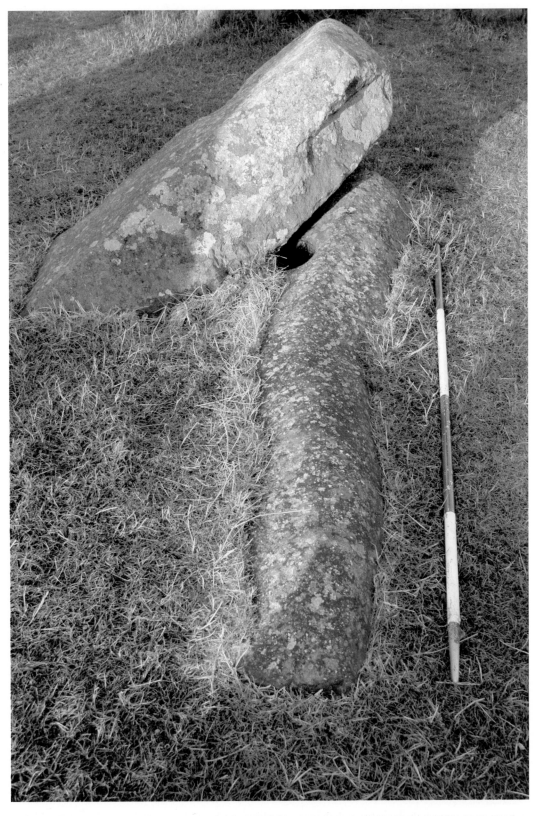

9 Stonehenge: Stones 150 (foreground) and 32 within the Bluestone Circle at Stonehenge. Stone 150 appears to have been reused from an earlier structure. The scale totals 2m. *Photograph: Timothy Darvill, copyright reserved*

11 Stonehenge: southwestern Sarsen Trilithon, Stones 57, 58, and 158 re-erected in 1958. *Photograph: Timothy Darvill, copyright reserved*

12 Stonehenge: interior view of the northeast sector of Stonehenge showing bluestones 32 (foreground), 31, 49, 48, 47, and 46 and (right) sarsen uprights 1, 30, 29, and 28. The scale totals 2m. *Photograph: Timothy Darvill, copyright reserved*

13 Stonehenge: viewed from the northeast upon passing through the earthwork enclosure. The fallen Slaughter Stone (Stone 95) lies centre-left; other now missing stones beyond and right of the Slaughter Stone originally framed the view into the circle directly ahead. *Photograph: Timothy Darvill, copyright reserved*

14 Stonehenge: recumbent Altar Stone (Stone 80) at the centre of the interior space. Parts of the fallen southwestern Sarsen Trilithon (Stones 55 and 156) overlie the red-coloured sandstone Altar Stone. The scale totals 2m. *Photograph: Timothy Darvill, copyright reserved*

15 Bell barrow Amesbury 11 looking west with Stonehenge in the near distance, top-right. *Photograph: Timothy Darvill, copyright reserved*

16 Bush Barrow (Wilsford 5) looking east. *Photograph: Timothy Darvill, copyright reserved*

17 Bowl barrow Amesbury 35 in the Old King Barrow cemetery. *Photograph: Timothy Darvill, copyright reserved*

18 New King Barrows following clearance of the covering woodland after heavy storm damage in October 1987 and January 1990. *Photograph: Timothy Darvill, copyright reserved*

19 Woodhenge reconstructed in colour-coded concrete pillars. *Photographs Timothy Darvill, copyright reserved*

20 The Cuckoo Stone west of Woodhenge. Scale totals 1m. *Photograph: Timothy Darvill, copyright reserved*

21 Targeted excavations in June 1991 of low–relief fieldsystem boundaries east of Fargo Plantation. *Photograph: Timothy Darvill, copyright reserved*

22 Linear earthwork on Wilsford Down to the southeast of Longbarrow Crossroads. Looking east. *Photograph: Timothy Darvill, copyright reserved*

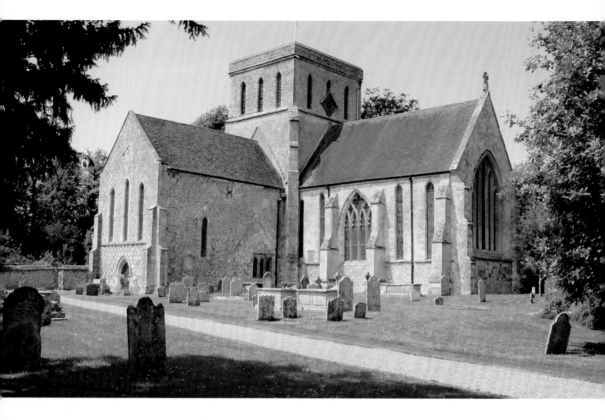

26 Sunrise at the 2005 Summer Solstice celebrations. *Photograph: Timothy Darvill, copyright reserved*

27 Modern stone circle constructed at Butterfield Down, Amesbury, on the edge of a new housing development *c.*1998. *Photograph: Timothy Darvill, copyright reserved*

46 Bedd Arthur stone oval in the Preseli Hills, Pembrokeshire, looking eastwards towards Carn Menyn. *Photograph: Timothy Darvill, copyright reserved*

It should also be remembered that these stone settings are only part of the picture and that more-or-less identical structures were often made in wood. Indeed, the Sarsen Trilithons and Sarsen Circle provide potent reminders of this because their very construction seems to embody techniques of jointing that draw on conventional techniques more familiar to carpenters than stonemasons (Gibson 1998a).

Whether, during its prime, the stones of Stonehenge were painted or decorated in some way cannot now be determined, but it is tempting to think that they may have been. The different colours represented by the stones selected for its construction — reds and grey/blues — would have provided some contrasts and perhaps communicated special meanings to those who encountered them. What is certain is that 11 stones are known to carry decoration in the form of rock art panels comprising lightly pecked motif (*47*): Stones 3, 4, 5, 9b, 23, 29, 30, and 120 in the Sarsen Circle and 53, 55a, and 57 in the Trilithon Horseshoe (Cleal et al. 1995, 30–3). Other panels may await discovery (see Goskar et al. 2003), but at present unhafted axe blades represented blade-up are the most common motifs, although the dagger, knife, torso, and quadrilateral motifs have prompted the most discussion because of their similarity with images used in several parts of Atlantic Europe including France and Spain (cf. Burl 1997; Scarre 1997; and see Loveday 1999). Overall, this is the largest group of rock art panels currently known in southern England and deserves greater attention. Standing at the very centre of the monument facing the Altar Stone and the Great Trilithon, one would see images of Breton-style figurines and an axe-haft would be seen to the right on Stone 57 of the southwestern trilithon while a dagger and more than a dozen axes would be visible to the left on Stone 53 of the southeastern trilithon (Burl 2001, figure 3).

BEYOND STONEHENGE: SOURCING AND MOVING THE STONES

It has long been recognized that the stone circles at Stonehenge comprise blocks from several different sources, some of which are not local to Salisbury Plain. Geological

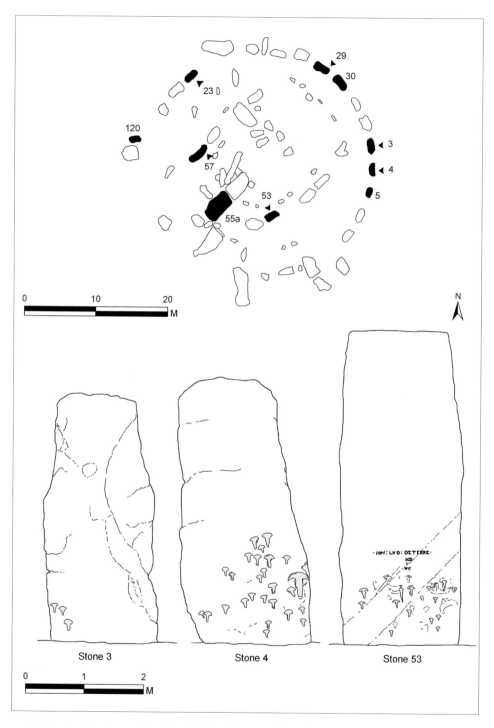

47 Rock art at Stonehenge. Top: Distribution of stones with prehistoric engravings. Bottom: Axes and other motifs on Stones 3, 4, and 53. *After Cleal* et al. *1995, figures 17, 18, and 20 with additions*

studies of the stones that remain standing, as well as stumps, discarded fragments, working waste, and tools recovered through excavations, show that overall at least 18 main types of rock are represented (*Table B*). Of these, the flint represented as tools and the chalk represented as carved objects are essentially local to the area, as too perhaps are quartzite and pyrite. Greenstones from Cornwall representing Petrological Groups I, Ia, III, and XVI all relate to imported polished implements – axes and an axehammer. Fragments of glauconitic sandstone and oolitic limestone suggest that perhaps there were once structural components made of these materials which must derive from the Jurassic outcrops of western or northwest Wiltshire or beyond. Similar contacts are shown during the fourth millennium BC through the tempering agents used in making pottery (see Chapter 4). This leaves three groups of rock, all demonstrably used as structural components: sarsen, sandstones, and bluestone.

Sarsen

Sarsen is a very hard kind of sandstone formed almost exclusively of pure silica in the form of quartz grains bound together with siliceous cement. It accounts for more than three-quarters of the rock found at Stonehenge, and was the main material used for the construction of the Phase 3ii-iv circles. The Heelstone (*colour plate 10*), Slaughter Stone, and the four Station Stones appear to have been natural blocks of sarsen used without significant modification, and the same may apply to some or all of the other peripheral stones now missing. By contrast, the components of the Sarsen Trilithon Horseshoe and the Sarsen Circle have all been extensively worked to create 40 pillars and 35 lintels, although as noted above there are some differences of treatment amongst the uprights of the Trilithon Horseshoe which may have symbolic meaning. Projections (tenons) and sockets (mortises) were also made for securely joining the stones together in a manner highly reminiscent of woodworking joints. This shaping was done by first flaking the natural blocks to achieve the basic form, and then pecking and grinding to produce the required surface finish. Traces of the working are very clear in certain light (*48*). The two largest sarsen pillars are Stones 55 and 56, the latter still standing and comprising a block nearly 10m long when the portion below ground is included. This stone is estimated to weigh about 40 tons (Richards and Whitby 1997, 234). More typically the blocks used in the Sarsen Circle each weigh about 25 tons, the lintels about 6 tons. Much debate, and some experimentation, has been carried out as to how the stones were put into position (e.g. Stone 1924b; Atkinson 1961; 1979, 129–39; Richards and Whitby 1997; Adamson 2002). Archaeological evidence shows that the uprights were raised in a socket with one vertical side and one sloping side so that they could be toppled into position and then hauled upright; experiments show this is perfectly feasible, with a team of about 150 people being needed for the biggest stone and commensurately fewer for the others (Richards and Whitby 1997, 252). Raising the lintels is possible using a rising platform or with a temporary ramp, and again experiments have illustrated the possibilities (Garfitt 1980; Hogg 1981; Pavel 1992; Richards and Whitby 1997).

Table B Summary of the main types of rock and their sources represented at Stonehenge during the period c.3000–2000 BC

STONE	ALTERNATIVE NAMES	STRUCTURAL COMPONENTS	FRAGMENTS AND DEBRIS	IMPLEMENTS AND TOOLS	SOURCE AREA
Ophitic dolerite[†]	Diabase; diabasic dolerite; greenstone; syenite; spotted dolerite	✓	✓	Axe	SW Wales: Preseli Hills (Group XIII/XXIII) Carn Menyn, Carn Gyfrwy, Carn Goedog, Cerrig Marchogion, Carn Breseb
Rhyolite (bluish)[†]	Hornstone; felstone; porphyrite; felsite; siliceous schist; brecciated rhyolite; spherultic rhyolite; ignimbrites	✓	✓	Axe	SW Wales: Pembrokeshire
Rhyolite (grey)[†]	[as bluish rhyolite]	✓	✓		SW Wales: Preseli Hills
Basic tuffs[†]	Calcareous ash or tuff; agglomerates; scistose rock; calcareous chloritic schist	✓	✓		SW Wales: Preseli Hills (?near Moel Trigarn)
Sarsen (saccaroid)		✓	✓	Mauls, hammerstones	Marlborough Downs
Sarsen (quartzitic)		✓	✓	Mauls, hammerstones	
Grey-green micaceous sandstone	Palaeozoic Sandstone; Cosheston Sandstone; Devonian Old Red Sandstone	✓	✓		South Wales: Senni Beds
Metasandstone	Argillaceous flagstone; Lower Palaeozoic sandstone		✓		?South or mid-Wales
Glauconitic sandstone			✓		?North Wiltshire

Material	Petrology			Artefact type	Source
Oolitic freestone					?NW Wiltshire/Cotswold Hills
Pyrite		✓	✓		?
Greenstone	Uralitized gabbro; epidiorite			Polished axe	Mount's Bay, Cornwall (Group I)
Greenstone	Uralitized gabbro; epidiorite			Polished axe	Mount's Bay, Cornwall (Group Ia)
Greenstone	Epidiorite			Polished axehammer	Marazion, Cornwall (Group III)
Greenstone	Epidotized intermediate tuff			Polished axe	Lake Distict (Group VI)
Greenstone	Sheared diabase			Polished axe	Cornwall (Group XVI)
Greenstone	Quartz dolerite			Polished axe	Whin Sill, Northumberland (Group XVIII)
Folded gneiss				Polished macehead	?
Quartzite				Hammerstone	?
Chalk				Balls, discs, phallus, axe, carved piece	Chalklands of southeastern England
Flint				Scrapers, points, knives, fabricators, arrowheads, working waste	Chalklands of southeastern England

†These rocks are usually included within the broadly defined class of 'Bluestones' at Stonehenge

48 Stonehenge: outer face of fallen Stone 59a, formerly one of the uprights forming the northwestern Sarsen Trilithon, showing marked evidence of shaping and working the surface of the stone. *Photograph: Timothy Darvill, copyright reserved*

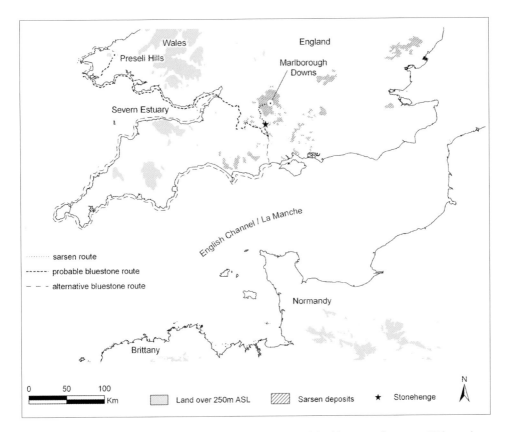

49 Possible routes used in the transportation to Stonehenge of the bluestone from west Wales and the sarsen stones from the Marlborough Downs. *Drawing by Vanessa Constant: routes after Atkinson 1979, figures 4 and 5; distribution of natural sarsens after Bowen and Smith 1977; outline and topographic base from ESRI® Data and Maps 2004 and EDX Engineering Inc.*

Petrological and petrographic studies by Hilary Howard of sarsen samples from the 1979–80 excavations suggest that two main kinds of sarsen are represented: a coarse sugary saccaroid variety and a quartzitic ultra-hard variety (Howard in Pitts 1981, 119–23). The former was the most common. Both kinds no doubt derive from the spread of natural sarsen boulder-fields occurring sporadically right across the chalklands of southeastern England from Dorset in the west to Kent in the east (Bowen and Smith 1977), but exactly where within this extensive catchment is far from clear (49). Traditionally, it is assumed that the Marlborough Downs east and south of Avebury represented the source area (e.g. Atkinson 1979, 116) because it is here that appropriately sized boulders can be found down to the present day (*colour plate 5*). Fieldwork in the area has also identified possible extraction sites (M Pitts pers. comm.). But other areas must also be considered, and further work to characterize the sarsen at Stonehenge, and compare it with a wide range of potential sources, is urgently needed.

Moving the sarsen blocks from their source to Stonehenge, anything between a few metres for those obtained locally and 40km or more for distant sources such as the Marlborough Downs, must have involved overland routes (*49*). Rollers, sledges drawn over movable rails, and perhaps A-frame sleds are obvious possibilities supported by ethnographically attested cases of stone-moving by communities with comparable technology to that available in Britain in the third millennium BC (Smith 1866; Garfitt 1979); some have also been replicated in experimental contexts. Perhaps as many as 200 people would have been needed to drag the largest sarsen, a slow but not impossible feat (Richards and Whitby 1997, 238–9).

Sandstones

Apart from the glaoconitic sandstone from north Wiltshire already mentioned there are two kinds of older and much harder sandstone from further afield. Several fragments of metasandstone of Lower Palaeozoic age have been found within the enclosure, including pieces from Aubrey Holes 1 and 5. The source of this material is currently unknown (Ixer and Turner 2006, 8), but may possibly lie in central or southern Wales. Rather different is the grey-green micaceous sandstone used for the Altar Stone (Stone 80) at the focus of the monument. Fragments resulting from the shaping and dressing of this large block are also known. Once thought to originate in the Cosheston Beds of the Milford Haven area of southwest Wales, recent petrological studies suggest that in fact it comes from the Senni Beds of Devonian Old Red Sandstone that outcrop in a broad band across South Wales from west of Kidwelly to the Welsh Marches (Ixer and Turner 2006, 8).

Bluestones

Since the late nineteenth century it has been recognized that the bluestones at Stonehenge derive from igneous and metamorphic outcrops far to the north or west of Salisbury Plain (Ramsey 1868; Maskelyne 1878; Cunnington 1884; Teall 1894; Judd 1902). But it was not until Herbert Thomas' studies of geological formations in southwest Wales in the course of his work as petrographer to the Geological Survey that the dolerites, rhyolites, and tuffs that collectively comprise the bluestones were securely tied to outcrops in and around Carn Meini towards the eastern end of the Preseli Hills of north Pembrokeshire (Thomas 1923; *colour plate 6*). Subsequent studies using an increasingly sophisticated range of petrological techniques to examine the mineralogy of the rocks, and geochemical analysis to characterize the very composition of the material, have added detail to the picture. It is now clear that the dolerites derive wholly or mainly from Carn Menyn (one of the group of carns known as Carn Meini) and Carn Goedog (Thorpe et al. 1991; Ixer 1997a; Williams-Thorpe et al. 2006) while most of the rhyolites and tuffs can be matched amongst outcrops of the Fishguard and Sealyham Volcanic Groups peripheral to the dolerite dykes that dominate the structure and scenery of the region (Thorpe et al. 1991, 140–4; but cf. Howard in Pitts 1982, 116–17 for other sources). Although there is more work to be done on pinpointing the geological origins of each individual type of stone it is already clear that the general pattern of rock outcrops in the Preseli landscape is matched by the disposition of bluestones at Stonehenge, at least during its later phases (50). The Bluestone Oval/Horseshoe in the centre of the monument comprises exclusively dolerite blocks and all of the four examples sampled by the Open University researchers led by Richard Thorpe proved to originate in a compact area no more than 3km across centred on Carn Menyn. By contrast, the Bluestone Circle surrounding the central settings is a mish-mash of stones of many different types; the 11 samples studied by the Open University team represented at least eight different sources including dolerites, rhyolites, and tuffs from outcrops scattered over a fairly wide area along and around the main Preseli ridge. It is a pattern broadly translated from one context to another that must have some bearing on the interpretation and meaning of these rocks and what they represent.

Thomas' conclusion that the Stonehenge Bluestones derived from west Wales naturally rekindled interest in the tale set out by Geoffrey of Monmouth in the later fourteenth century which told of Merlin the magician/prophet bringing the stones from Ireland and setting them up on Salisbury Plain (Stone 1924a, 65). Stuart Piggott in particular unpicked the jumbled myth, legend, and fantasy of Geoffrey's *Historia Regum Britanniae* to conclude that we may have a story handed down through oral tradition long enough to ensure its incorporation in the tales that accumulated in the Dark Ages of Wessex before being preserved in the myths of the Celtic West, 'finally entering the body of written record of the Middle Ages among the legendary miscellanea of a romantic medieval ecclesiastic who may have fancied it as a fairy-tale' (Piggott 1941, 319). Many since have ridiculed the idea and questioned the veracity of Geoffrey's history, Aubrey Burl, for example, declaring that 'the legend is no more than a monkish mixture of Merlin, magic and imagination' (1985, 182). But as Grahame Clark pointed out long ago, 'one reason why historical sources are so valuable is that they help to establish continuity between prehistoric and modern societies, providing the essential link between archaeological material and analogies drawn from recent folk-culture' (1952, 4), a view that underpinned Leslie Grinsell's meticulous studies of the folklore of Stonehenge (1975; 1978b). All commentators agree that Geoffrey of Monmouth embroidered and elaborated the story, connecting it all with his hero, Arthur, using contemporary geographical perspectives to speak of places that might be understood by his readers, conflating all the many elements of Stonehenge into a single entity, and perhaps even joining several stories together as one (Thorpe 1973). Underneath though are the critical ideas that some at least of Stonehenge was brought from a land far to the west and set up on Salisbury Plain, that achieving this involved many people and the intervention of a magician, that the stones themselves were regarded as having special powers, and that the stones had to be set up at Stonehenge just as they were at their source.

How the Bluestones got from north Pembrokeshire to Salisbury Plain, a distance of 220km as the crow flies, has also been a source of much debate and speculation. As early as 1901, J W Judd suggested that glacial action might be responsible (Judd 1902, 116–18), drawing of course on what at the time were relatively new theories in the field

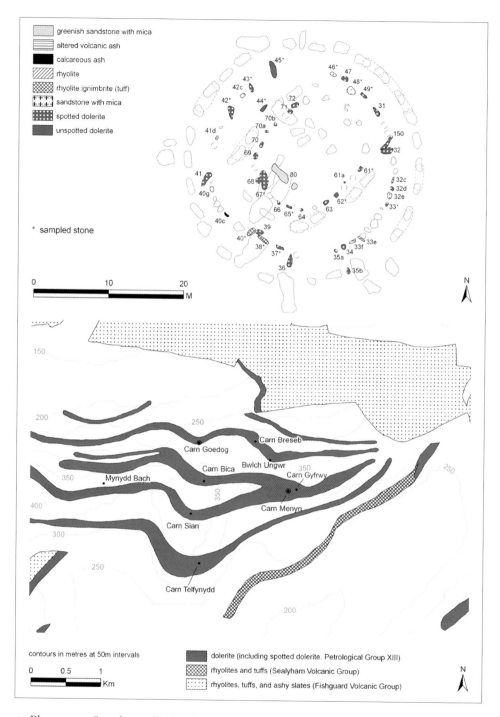

50 Bluestones at Stonehenge (Top), and as outcrops in the Preseli Hills of north Pembrokeshire (Bottom). *Drawings by Vanessa Constant: top after Cleal* et al. *1995, figure 15 and Thorpe* et al. *1991, figure 1; bottom after Evans 1945 and Bevins* et al. *1989*

of geology. Despite Thomas' arguments against such possibilities (1923, 252–4) the idea persisted and was reinvigorated by G Kellaway in a series of papers published from the early 1970s (Kellaway 1971; 1991; 2002). Proving the glacial model has underpinned the researches of Richard Thorpe and others at the Open University (Thorpe et al. 1991; Williams-Thorpe et al. 1995; 1997), and continues to be championed by Aubrey Burl (Burl 2000b) and debated by others (Ixer 1997b) despite a mountain of hard scientific evidence to the contrary. Christopher Green (1997) has argued on geological grounds that the glacial derivation of the specific rocks represented at Stonehenge is impossible, while James Scourse (1997) has shown that there are simply no known glacial movements that could have moved rocks in an easterly direction from the Preseli Hills to Salisbury Plain at any time in the last million years or so. Drawing also on glaciology, Rodney Castleden has marshalled and neatly presented all the geological and geomorphological arguments before reiterating Thomas' conclusion that 'alluring as the Glacial Drift theory may appear, it must reluctantly be set aside for want of convincing evidence' (Castleden 2001, 18).

Surprisingly perhaps, while these scientific arguments have been raging over the last 30 years or so, there has been very little archaeological investigation of the Preseli Hills to provide a social context for the bluestone sources. W F Grimes worked in the area through the 1920s and 30s but published very little (Grimes 1929; 1938; 1939), while much the same applies to the extensive walk-over surveys of the area carried out in the early 1980s by Peter Drewett and students from the Institute of Archaeology in London (Drewett 1987). In 2001, however, the present author and Geoffrey Wainwright established a new long-term project known as SPACES (Strumble-Preseli Ancient Communities and Environment Study) to identify, map, and investigate the archaeology of a modest study area that includes the bluestone outcrops (Darvill and Wainwright 2002a; 2002b; Darvill et al. 2003). Already it is clear that there was a high level of activity across the Preseli Hills during the fourth and third millennia BC represented by dolmens, portal dolmens, long barrows, circles, standing stones, and enclosures. At Bedd Arthur overlooking the craggy outcrops of Carn Menyn there is an oval setting of bluestones of such similar shape, size, and orientation to the Bluestone Oval at Stonehenge that the two must be closely connected, if not the work of the same people (51). Moreover, investigations in 2004 revealed a stone wall defining an area of ancient stone extraction on the very top of Carn Menyn (colour plate 8) and broken monoliths of directly comparable proportions to dolerite blocks at Stonehenge lie scattered round about (Darvill and Wainwright 2002b). Here, lest there be any remaining doubts, is an archaeology for people coming to the Preseli Hills to extract monoliths for the construction of monuments, and if Geoffrey of Monmouth is to believed, perhaps the site of the 'Giants' Ring' (Thorpe 1973, 196).

Why the particular stones available in and around the Preseli Hills should have been chosen for Stonehenge is one of those questions that cannot be solved by archaeology. But there are a number of possibilities. At a general level it is clear that people living on Salisbury Plain during the fourth and third millennia BC belonged to communities

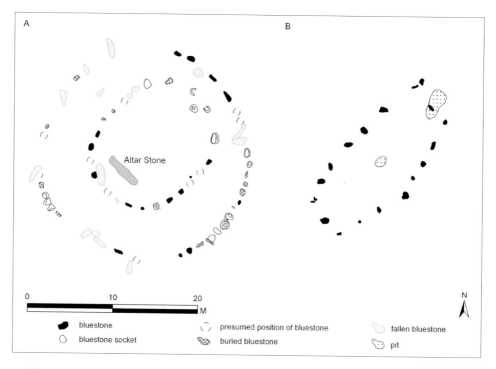

51 Bluestone ovals. A: Stonehenge, Wiltshire (Phase 3iv). B: Bedd Arthur, Pembrokeshire. *Drawing by Vanessa Constant: A after Cleal et al. 1995, figure 117; B after Darvill and Wainwright 2003, figure 3*

whose pottery and trading links connected with people across southwestern Britain. Thus the Preseli Hills might well have been within the territory of their own people. More specifically, stone was clearly important to these people, it was regularly moved considerable distances, and it presumably carried meanings and messages that were as much about the outcrop from which a particular stone derived as the stone itself. In this sense the Preseli Hills were a special, magical, place, perhaps the home of the gods or the birthplace of the ancestors. As David Kaiser has suggested (2003), the outcrops themselves might coincidentally have appeared as something else, perhaps a face or the outline of a person – a *simulacrum*. The stone itself, with its distinctive white spots, may have been held in high regard for perceived magical properties (*colour plate 7*), and we might also note the unusual acoustic qualities of some of the stones, which make a ringing sound when struck (see Fagg 1956; 1957). One of the most persistent claims relates to the healing powers of these stones, incidentally noted by Geoffrey of Monmouth (Thorpe 1973, 196) and still believed in relatively recent centuries (Grinsell 1975, 7–8). If the correspondence between the geographical arrangement of stone sources in the real landscape and the placement of the stones in the monumental landscape of Stonehenge is any guide then it is Carn Menyn and perhaps Carn Goedog that were the focus of attention, twin peaks for the people of Wessex to contemplate.

Physically moving the bluestones from the Preseli Hills to Salisbury Plain was no mean feat; whether they trickled along a well-known route over centuries or millennia one or two at a time or were transported *en masse* over a few years or decades. Several routes have been suggested (see *49*), most using rivers and the sea to allow water-borne methods perhaps involving boats or canoes lashed together. The shortest route, about 420km, involves overland movement off the hills down to the Western Cleddau from where they could follow the river downstream to Milford Haven, along the coast of South Wales, across the Severn Estuary, inland along the Bristol Avon, portage to the headwaters of the Hampshire Avon, and then downstream to a suitable point near modern-day Amesbury from where they would again be hauled overland to Stonehenge itself. An alternative route around the Southwest Peninsula is over twice as long at about 1000km, but involves no portage until the final leg of the journey and generally stronger rivers. Rodney Castleden cites the presence of several Cornish stone axes at Stonehenge as evidence for this route (2003, 21) and certainly there is good evidence for long-shore trading and the use of the Hampshire Avon as a major thoroughfare in prehistoric times (Sherratt 1996b). Less fully explored are wholly overland routes which would have involved carrying stones or moving them on rollers, sledges, or sleds. In contrast to the sarsen stones, the bluestones are far more manageable in size, the largest weighing only about 4 tons.

A CULT CENTRE AND ORACLE?

The idea that Stonehenge was a sanctuary or temple of some kind, at least through its later life, is widely recognized and generally accepted even though many suggestions have been made regarding the deities celebrated and the cosmologies embedded in its structure. For Inigo Jones and John Webb it was for Roman gods, for Walter Charleton Norse gods, and for John Aubrey and William Stukeley a temple for the Druids. To John Smith in the eighteenth century it resembled a 'serpent's egg' (1771), while to Anthony Perks and Darlene Bailey in the twentieth century the whole thing resembles the structure of the human vulva with the birth canal at its centre (2003). Taking a rather different approach Mike Parker Pearson and Retsihisate Ramilisonina (1998) draw formal analogies with the use of stone amongst Madagascan communities to suggest that the stone structures at Stonehenge and other stone circles in Britain should be seen as belonging to the ancestors, a stone version for the dead of the timber circles used for ceremonies by the living. Behind this lies a set of metaphorical associations between ancestors and stone, and a structuring principle involving increasing hardness as people moved from the domain of the living to the spirit world of the dead. It is an interesting idea and certainly helps open our minds to new ways of seeing the site, but it seems overly simplistic to reduce Stonehenge to a single explanation based on modern-sounding binary oppositions between life and death :: wood and stone. For some reason Stonehenge was the only henge in the area whose wooden structures were replaced with stone features. Why did the same not happen at Woodhenge and Coneybury? Why was Stonehenge constantly being remodelled and changed over a period of perhaps a thousand years?

Over time Stonehenge got larger, more grand, and more complicated in terms of the elements retained and the new parts added. Picking up on this John Barrett (1997) has emphasized the architectural order inherent to the structure and the way this might be perceived and understood by those entering the circle after walking up the Avenue from Stonehenge Bottom. In a similar vein, Alasdair Whittle (1997a) stressed the three-dimensional nature of the structure, suggesting that in its architecture we may glimpse notions of inclusion and exclusion, unity and division, and that in its later manifestation at least there may be some kind of three-dimensional hierarchy. The spirits and celestial beings that were being represented in its concentric structure might somehow tie back into contemporary ideas of the earth and its creation (1997a, 150–1). Indeed, it may not be too far-fetched to imagine the structure as a model of the world as its builders saw things. But to get deeper into the purpose and use of Stonehenge itself requires some consideration of possible underlying cosmologies and belief systems.

Ancient religion is a topic that archaeology has generally avoided, mainly because it is difficult, involves a degree of speculation, and inevitably draws cross-cultural comparisons through time and across space. In a brave attempt to reverse this trend Kristian Kristiansen and Thomas Larsson (2005) have developed a plausible and archaeo-logically grounded outline of the cosmological systems embedded in the lives and practices of north European societies between the later third and early first millennia BC. They show how long-distance connections and alliances between local elites provided for the transmission of religious, political, and social knowledge across large parts of Europe such that many ideas found in the Near East and Mediterranean were also familiar in central and northern Europe. These ideas found expression in such things as the structure of monuments, the manufacture and decoration of particular objects, the deposition of objects, and the motifs used in rock art. Following the work of Garrett Olmsted (1994) tracing the Indo-European religions of the Greek and Roman world back into Pre-Indo-European times, Kristiansen and Larsson draw on Hittite, Mycenean, and Assyrian pantheons, rituals, and myths to explore contemporary European cultures. Fundamental here is the recognition of three realms: upper (the sky), middle (the earth), and lower (the netherworld/underworld) each associated with particular gods and symbols. The upper realm divides into two spheres, day and night, that are controlled by a pair of gods who are twins. Twins also rule in the other realms, and Olmsted contends that dialectical tensions between twins is a critical aspect of Pre-Indo-European religion that later diminished in significance (1994, 87–8). Bound into this representation of the world is the dynamic element of the sun's daily journey through the upper and lower realms: rising in the east, passing across the sky, setting in the west, travelling through the underworld, and then reappearing again in the east to renew the cycle (Kristiansen and Larsson 2005, 306–7). Central to this model is a focus on the sun as the significant celestial object, and the netherworld as a place dominated by water. Both are ideas well established in the Middle East and southeastern Europe during the early third millennium BC, and which spread widely through central and northern Europe as part of the package of thinking associated with the adoption of Beaker pottery (Kristiansen and Larsson 2005, 140).

Across southern Britain there are subtle changes in the layout and form of the monuments clustered together at ceremonial centres that can be traced to the middle centuries of the third millennium BC. It is most visible in the realignment and reshaping of monuments, together with their enlargement. Thus at Dorchester on Thames, Oxfordshire, for example, the long mortuary enclosure was replaced by a much longer cursus on a slightly different angle (Bradley and Chambers 1988), while at Godmanchester, Cambridgeshire, the great trapezoidal enclosure was replaced or extended by a slightly realigned cursus monument (McAvoy 2000), and at Eynesbury and Brampton, both also in Cambridgeshire, cursuses are again reoriented away from the axes embedded in earlier monuments (Malim 1999). These are small but fundamental changes, with the NE–SW (midsummer sunrise/midwinter sunset) and NW–SE (midwinter sunrise/midsummer sunset) orientations becoming dominant. At Stonehenge the changes at around 2600 BC that were outlined earlier in this chapter were closely associated with the appearance of Beaker pottery and relate very explicitly to referencing the movement of the sun, and to a lesser extent the moon, and the creation of an attachment to water.

Clive Ruggles has convincingly argued that there is very little if any intentional lunar or solar orientation in the early phases of Stonehenge, but with the creation of the Double Bluestone Circle and the Avenue we have a clear interest in the Summer and Winter Solstices: the rising midsummer sun and the setting midwinter sun. At about the same time the four Station Stones set on the corners of a perfect rectangle perpetuate the solstitial orientation along their short sides while observations down the long NW–SE sides align on the major limiting moon rising in the south (full in summer) or setting in the north (full in winter) which would happen every 18.6 years (Ruggles 1997, 218–21). These basic patterns are retained, and in some instances enhanced, in later rebuilding, and thus architecturally embed three astronomical cycles relating to a basic cosmology charting the movement of the sun and marking the passage of time: solar years, lunar months, and a metonic era each equating to 18.6 of our solar years. Juxtaposing the movements of the sun and moon in such a way is a feature of many early cosmological and calendrical schemes (Hodson 1974), often reflecting concerns about day and night, the transition between the two, and the movements of one celestial body while the other is visually dominant.

As a device for representing the passing of time – time-indication – observing the daily cycle of the sun and marking the two solstices provides secure and observable moments that in a slightly informal way can chronometrically anchor key festivals and events to the routine of daily life. Conveniently, it divides the year into two seasons – summer and winter – according with the binary division of the middle realm into two spheres which we might imagine to be ruled by a pair of deities each perhaps presiding over their respective festivals and celebrations associated with the seasons.

As a device for time-reckoning, that is the application of systematic long-term continuous counting systems to allow the actual or abstract location of an event or happening within a prescribed calendar of regular divisions, the periodicity of lunar events provides the prompts. For the short-term the 30 stones of the Sarsen Circle around the outside of the monument equates very closely to the 29.53 days of the lunar cycle between full moons (Hawkins 1964; 1973, 183), especially when it is remembered that Stone 11 is only a half-sized stone. Seen in this way, each stone in the Sarsen Circle could therefore relate to a specific day in the lunar month. On a longer scale the metonic cycle of 235 lunar months between extreme moonrise or moonset positions provides a means of blocking together the monthly cycles into larger units that equate to 18.6 solar years.

Neither the time-indication devices nor the time-reckoning apparatus are in themselves likely to be reasons why Stonehenge was constructed, each being ancillary facilities built into its structure to facilitate and programme its real purpose. Rather it was the life of the sun attaining its daily passage through the upper and lower realms that was perhaps of greatest interest to those occupying the middle realm. At the summer solstice the sequence focused on beginnings. The sun would rise over Sidbury Hill at Larkhill to the northeast of Stonehenge notionally emerging from the waters of the underworld to shine along the line of the Avenue into the centre of Stonehenge before riding across the sky and then setting into the low hills of Winterbourne Stoke Down to the northwest. At the Winter Solstice the focus was on endings, the sun rising in the east over Boscombe Down, crossing the sky and then setting over Wilsford Down, at a position framed by the Great Trilithon and directly in line with the principal axis and the Avenue leading back to the underworld.

Presiding over these events in the centre of Stonehenge are the five Sarsen Trilithons which in a very real sense might be considered conjoined deities, pairs of gods or rulers born at the same time from a single union who may also represent male/female, day/night, summer/winter oppositions. The Great Trilithon to the southwest, the largest and most prominent, is set astride the principal axis and might cautiously be identified with a pair of deities representing day and night: the sun and moon. In both the Greek and Roman pantheons these might be seen as Apollo (male solar deity) and Artemis (female lunar deity), twins fathered by Zeus and born of Leto. These powerful deities also represent divination, prophecy, healing, music, and causing the fruits of the earth to ripen (Apollo), and the forests, hunting, agriculture, and childbirth (Artemis); both were associated with the ability to cause sudden death (Guirand 1959, 119–33). Some confusion surrounds the origins of Apollo and Artemis, but there are clear parallels back into Assyro-Babylonian cosmologies of the third and fourth millennia BC, with Apollo perhaps cognate with Shamash the sun god who was responsible for divination and Artemis with his wife Aya. Other origins are possible, however, including the rather intriguing idea, if the Greek historian Diodorus is to be believed, that Leto, mother of Apollo and Artemis, was born on an island (?Britain) inhabited by the Hyperboreans (Oldfather 1935, 39) and that Apollo had a special place in the hearts and rituals of these communities.

Identifying possible deities for the other four Sarsen Trilithons is more difficult as the full pantheon of the period has yet to be worked out. Barclay (1895, 97–110) suggests early equivalents of the Roman gods associated with the seasonal festivals: Mercury (Spring), Jupiter (Summer), Mars (Autumn), and Saturn (Winter), but these seem rather contrived and do not fit well with the idea of two seasons. Hawkins (1973, 77) by contrast links those on the east side to sunrise and moonrise and those on the west side to sunset and moonset, but does not associate these events with specific deities. It may be notable, however, that, in Greek mythology, when Leto gave birth to Apollo and Artemis on the island of Delos, Poseidon provided shelter and protection by raising the waves over the island and supporting them on four pillars (Guirand 1959, 122). Could the centre of Stonehenge be the symbolic birthplace of the ancient sibling gods later known as Apollo and Artemis?

The bluestones are different. They are the critical elements in the developing importance of the site for they first give the place its special character, setting it apart from other henges in southern Britain. Their significance is such that they were retained and perhaps augmented in all subsequent remodellings of the site. They might be seen quite literally as people, petrified guardians or ancestors keeping watch over a sacred place, or perhaps as pieces taken from one sacred spot to enhance the significance and special powers of another. One such power might be to assist shamans make prophecies or, as Geoffrey of Monmouth suggested (Thorpe 1973, 196), heal the sick.

Taking the structure of Stonehenge in its late phase as a totality, the concentric circles can be seen as elements in a complicated structure with deeply embedded cosmological references, as well as the means to determine when rituals and ceremonies should take place. At its heart was the Altar Stone that provided the focus for events in the central area, perhaps a seat or a platform to accommodate those presiding over events. Framing it were the stones that made this place special, shaped pillars from a sacred place far away to the west (the Bluestone Horseshoe) that together with the natural blocks forming the Bluestone Circle replicate the exact arrangement of outcrops in that distant land. Towering over the central space, giving extra power and meaning to the events that took place there, are the Sarsen Trilithons, each perhaps representing a twin deity. Enclosing the whole sanctuary is a boundary (the Sarsen Circle) whose pillars perhaps represent the days of the lunar month and help to provide a time-reckoning system that fixes the cycle of festivals and ceremonies.

Whether or not such symbolism is broadly right is impossible to say, but any temple is likely to embody multiple layers of meaning, providing metaphors in its architecture that structure ritual and guide participants through the performances they are involved in. What is unusual about Stonehenge is its longevity, its seemingly constant reconstruction, the huge investment of time and labour in its construction, and the integration of ideas not just from other parts of the British Isles but from further afield as well. In the last of these Stonehenge is unique in the British Isles, although taking account only of the first three Avebury comes close behind as it draws only on indigenous traditions. Something makes Stonehenge different from the other stone circles and ceremonial centres scattered across Britain and it is possibly something that developed over time rather than being somehow implicit to the spot.

One possibility is that Stonehenge was an oracle, a place to which people made pilgrimages in order to contact the supernatural, the gods, or the dead, possibly at specific times of the year, to learn about the future, to know a little of their own fate, and if associated with healing then perhaps also to seek the help of the gods in overcoming some ailment (Curnow 2004, 1–8). What makes oracles different from other kinds of temples is the direction of the communication. At oracles the gods don't instigate the talk, they respond. Hard to prove with reference to a site more than 4000 years old, but oracles were common in the ancient world and many had roots extending back into the third millennium BC (Alcock and Osborne 1994). Some later became very famous indeed. At Stonehenge there are strong links with solar–lunar interests and perhaps with deities that in later prehistoric times were seen as Apollo and Artemis. Both have earlier incarnations and in the case of Apollo he represents the whole field of divination, prophecy, and healing. At Delphi, perhaps the most famous and reliable oracle in the classical world, Apollo was available for consultation during the month of Delphinios in the West Greek lunar calendar, which Alun Salt and Efrosyni Boutsikas (2005) have shown was marked by the heliacal rising of the constellation Delphinus. However, Apollo did not stay in Delphi the whole year; during the winter he was believed to move to the land of the Hyperboreans (James 1962, 242–5; Salt and Boutsikas 2005, 570). Hecataeus' description of Apollo's temple, sacred precinct, and 'city' (Oldfather 1935, 39) makes one wonder if here is a thinly garbled reference to Stonehenge, the Cursus, and the great enclosure of Durrington Walls. Winter-time gatherings have been suggested at Durrington Walls on the basis of the discarded animal remains (Albarella and Serjeantson 2002). And if Apollo did visit for relatively short defined periods then small wonder that time-indication and time-reckoning devices were embedded in the very architecture of his sanctuary as no supplicant would want to miss an appointment with the supernatural.

BARROWS AND BURIALS: THE STONEHENGE PEOPLE

At least some of the people who built and used Stonehenge remained in the landscape they knew for eternity. Some were laid to rest within the henges already described, and for a period at least Stonehenge seems to have been a major focus for cremation burials (Cleal et al. 1995, 451–61). More typically, the deceased were buried under a barrow or in one of the flat graves known to date from the third millennium BC (Piggott 1973c, 340).

Some of these monuments perpetuate earlier traditions, but most contrast markedly with structures from previous millennia and are now associated with Grooved Ware and Beaker pottery. They are mainly round, but more significantly the burials themselves are set below-ground in the earth in pits or shafts. The shape of the burial monuments perhaps reflects the much wider interest in round things and might ultimately be linked to sun-symbolism. The placing of the dead below ground suggests changing attitudes towards the spirits and deities of the underworld and perhaps the unification of the dead with the nether-regions through the kind of cyclical cosmology briefly outlined above and discussed in detail by Kristiansen and Larsson (2005, 251–319).

Secondary burials in long barrows and oval barrows

There is no evidence that any long barrows or oval barrows were built in the Stonehenge landscape during the third millennium BC, although elsewhere in southern Britain the use of oval barrows continues down to 2500 BC and perhaps beyond (cf. Drewett 1986; Bradley 1992). Interest in earlier examples of these monuments is, however, represented by the insertion of secondary burials into existing structures. Amongst oval barrows five contracted burials, one seemingly accompanied by a Beaker, were found by Thurnam in Wilsford 34 (Cunnington 1914, 405–6), two secondary inhumations were found in Amesbury 14 (Grinsell 1957, 137), and one at Wilsford 30 (Grinsell 1957, 145). Amongst the long barrows, Figheldean 31 yielded a crouched inhumation accompanied by a Style 3 Beaker towards the southeast end of the mound (Grinsell 1957, 140), while Amesbury 42 contained a crouched adult and an infant (Cunnington 1914, 383–4).

Bowl barrows

One early kind of barrow that did continue to be popular through the third millennium BC is the simple hemispherical mound with or without a surrounding ditch that is generally known as a bowl barrow (Kinnes 1979 and see Chapter 4). However, unless these mounds are dated it is impossible to separate them from the ubiquitous second millennium BC examples. Within the Stonehenge landscape as a whole there are some 639 round barrows and 308 ring-ditches, an unknown proportion of which (perhaps 10–15 per cent) date to the third millennium BC.

A few bowl barrows of the third millennium BC covered cremation burials. Circle 2 to the south of Woodhenge (Durrington 68), for example, contained an off-centre pit-grave with a cremation and three sherds of Grooved Ware (Wainwright and Longworth 1971, 3).

Commonly, the main burials under bowl barrows at this time were inhumations. Some such barrows are of a single phase, but upon excavation a fair proportion prove to be multi-period structures representing the successive remodelling of the mound associated with the deposition of further burials. At Amesbury 71 the first phase of a multi-phase barrow comprised a continuous ring-ditch about 7m in diameter, within which was a sub-circular ring of stakes surrounding a central grave pit that was covered by a low barrow. This was later covered by a larger mound (Phase II) containing stake circles and enclosed within a ring-ditch about 23m in diameter. The central grave pit of the Phase II monument cut into the Phase I grave pit, disturbing the earlier burial. A radiocarbon date of 2900–2100 BC (3960±110; NPL-77) was obtained from charcoal in the grave of the Phase II monument (Christie 1967, 339–43).

Amesbury 22 covered the primary burial of an adult male in the bottom of a shaft cut some 1.2m into the underlying chalk, above which was a secondary grave that included a Beaker pot (Grinsell 1957, 150). At Durrington 7 excavations in 1983 as part of the Stonehenge Environs Project revealed a ditchless bowl barrow some 11m in diameter with a flint cairn over an oval grave-pit containing the crouched inhumation of a juvenile accompanied by a large cattle (?aurochs) lumbar vertebra, a fragment of antler, and the cremated remains of a second juvenile (Richards 1990, 171–84). A radiocarbon determination on a sample of bone from the inhumation returned a date of 2500–1750 BC (3700±100; OxA-1398). Rather similar is Wilsford 87f where a primary inhumation, seemingly without any accompanying grave goods, was succeeded by a cremation accompanied by deer antlers (Grinsell 1957, 199). At Winterbourne Stoke 56, Colt Hoare revealed a primary adult male burial accompanied by a deer antler, above which was a cremation accompanied by a Beaker (Grinsell 1957, 202). Bulford 27 may be yet another example. The primary burial here was an adult male laid to rest in a rock-cut pit and accompanied by a Stage I battleaxe of quartz dolerite from the Whin Sill in Northumberland (Group XVIII; Roe 1979, 42). This grave was also covered by a cairn of flints. Around about, on the original ground surface, were the inhumations of three men of fine physique. They had been buried with their heads towards the centre of the barrow, their bodies tightly doubled up but their forearms missing in each case. Over these were the skeletons of seven children, perhaps added when the large bowl barrow some 42m in diameter and 3m high was built (Hawley 1910, 616–17). Shrewton 27, excavated by William Cunnington, also had a primary burial accompanied by a Stage V battleaxe, this one of Hissington picrite from the Welsh Marches (Group XII; Roe 1979, 41).

Three of the 18 barrows examined by Charles Smith near Shrewton in 1958 included Beaker pottery: Shrewton 5a, 5e, and 5k (Green and Rollo-Smith 1984). Of these, Shrewton 5k is especially important because the grave contained a Group B Beaker associated with a small copper dagger with the remains of an organic hilt adhering to the tang and a bone pommel (52). Typologically, the dagger is of the Roundway class and may be assigned to Burgess' metallurgical Stage II within his Mount Pleasant Phase (1980, 71–8). A radiocarbon determination on bone from the primary burial provides a date of 2480–2200 BC (3900±40 BP: BM-3017) and makes this the earliest securely dated copper dagger in Britain. Rock art was also represented on the east wall of the central shaft-grave. This small panel comprises groups of intercutting straight lines incised into the chalk (Green and Rollo-Smith 1984, figure 12).

Southwest of Stonehenge, three of the four barrows excavated in 1958 by Ernest Greenfield at Wilsford – barrows 51, 52, and 54 – contained burials accompanied by Beaker pottery (Smith 1991). Barrow 51 had a causewayed ditch and is discussed below. Barrow 54

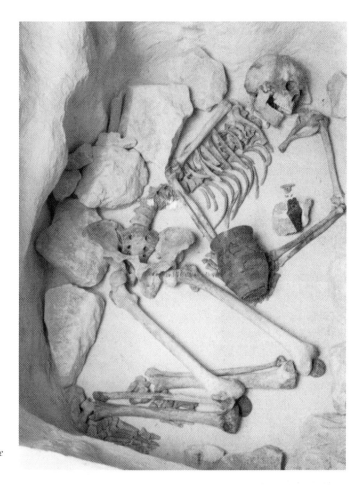

52 Reconstruction of the Beaker burial found in Shrewton 5k. *Photograph: Salisbury and South Wiltshire Museum, copyright reserved*

was a ditchless bowl barrow and is important because the primary grave, which was found to be heavily disturbed and may contain more than one phase of burial, contained at least three Beaker pots, six barbed and tanged arrowheads, a bronze dagger of Gerloff's Type Butterwick (1975, 42), and a stone battleaxe of Roe's Calais Wold Group made from spotted dolerite from the Preseli Hills of Pembrokeshire (Group XIII; Smith 1991, 27–9; 53).

Some round barrows containing graves with Beaker pottery seem to have had a long life as a series of burials accumulated. At Wilsford 1, for example, excavations by E V Field in 1960 revealed a large bowl barrow over 15m in diameter with at least 11 burials in all. The central grave contained two inhumations and a cremation associated with a Style 1 Beaker and some deer antlers rather reminiscent of Durrington 7 already referred to. The remaining eight burials were all on the north side of the barrow, six of them infants with associated Beaker pottery, one an infant with some kind of urn, and finally the crouched burial of a young adult with Beaker pottery and a slate replica of an Irish bronze flat axe (Anon 1961, 30).

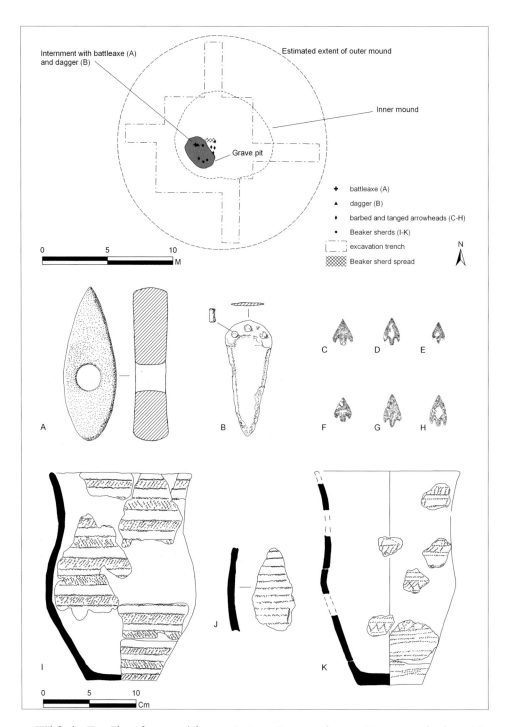

53 Wilsford 4. Top: Plan of excavated features. Bottom: Grave goods comprising a stone battleaxe (A), bronze dagger (B), barbed and tanged flint arrowheads (C–H), and Beaker pottery (I–K). *Drawing by Vanessa Constant: after Smith 1991, figures 10 and 11*

Excavations in advance of construction work for a school on the southeast edge of Amesbury in spring 2002 revealed two previously unknown burials of the late third millennium BC (WA 2002; Fitzpatrick 2002; 2003a; and see also Shanks 2004 for critical comment). The first probably lay beneath a small ditchless round barrow. Within a large rectangular grave-pit were the remains of an adult male aged perhaps 35–45 together with nearly 100 grave goods including two stone wrist-guards, three copper knives, a pair of gold earrings or tress-rings, five Beaker pots, and many other stone, bone, and flint objects. Dubbed the 'King of Stonehenge' or the 'Stonehenge Archer' by the popular press, this is the richest Beaker grave yet found in northwest Europe in terms of the number and quality of items represented. Provisionally dated to 2400–2200 BC, this burial is more-or-less the same age as that below Shrewton 5k which also contains an early copper dagger. Oxygen isotope studies of the Stonehenge Archer's teeth suggest that he spent at least some of his life in or around the Alps, reopening the possibility of long-distance contacts between communities living in the Stonehenge landscape and groups elsewhere in central and southern Europe. Jackie McKinley's study of the skeletal remains suggests that for much of his life the Stonehenge Archer had been disabled as a result of a traumatic injury to his left knee which would have caused him to limp. Many of the artefacts were probably locally made, but the metal used in one of the copper knive/daggers is Spanish, the gold could well be continental, and many of the stone objects come from sources at least 50km distant.

About 5m away from this burial was another, a companion perhaps, also contained in a rock-cut pit and perhaps sealed below a ditchless barrow (Fitzpatrick 2003a, 150). This was also a male, younger at about 20–25, and perhaps related to the first because they share minor abnormalities in their foot-bones. Radiocarbon determinations suggest that this burial is very slightly later than the first so they could be siblings or father and son. The younger man was accompanied by rather fewer grave goods: a single boar's tusk and a pair of gold earrings or tress-rings. Together, these burials raise many questions about the extended trade networks and long-distance social ties of the period, as well as emphasizing the need for vigilance in monitoring development activity throughout the Stonehenge landscape. There is also the question of why they travelled to the Stonehenge area: to find a cure for their ailments at a renowned healing centre and oracle perhaps?

Other burials accompanied by Beaker pottery under round barrows include: Amesbury 51 and 54 (Annable and Simpson 1964, 39); Durrington 36 and 67 (Annable and Simpson 1964, 39–40); Wilsford 1, 2b, and 62 (Annable and Simpson 1964, 40 and 43); Winterbourne Stoke 10, 43, and 54 (Annable and Simpson 1964, 38 and 40; Ozanne 1972).

Causewayed barrows

A new and distinctive type of round barrow typical of the early third millennium BC is that with causewayed ditches, visible simply as segmented ring-ditches when plough-levelled (54). At Wilsford 51, excavated in 1958, several phases of construction were recognized in an area extensively used in earlier times to judge by the amount of residual material. The first phase comprises a segmented ring-ditch dug to provide material for a small mound to cover an oblong grave containing the skeleton of a young adult associated with Beaker pottery (Smith 1991, 13–18). Amesbury 51, immediately south of the Stonehenge Cursus, was also surrounded by a segmented ring-ditch (Ashbee 1978a). The central primary burial and a series of secondary burials in the ditch and mound were all accompanied by Beaker pottery. The head of one of the burials in the central grave had been trephined, suggesting major surgery to relieve pressure on the brain; again perhaps someone seeking relief from the gods. Wood from a mortuary house containing the primary burial yielded a radiocarbon date of 2310–1950 BC (BM-287: 3738±55 BP). Beaker pottery was also associated with the primary grave in the two-phase bowl barrow Shrewton 24 (Green and Rollo-Smith 1984, 285–6). The first phase of the mound was surrounded by a segmented ditch, the whole eventually being covered by a much larger mound with a continuous surrounding ditch.

Plough-levelled causewayed barrows are perhaps represented by the segmented ring-ditch near the Longbarrow Crossroads, coincident with barrow Winterbourne Stoke 72 (RCHM 1979, 3; David and Payne 1997, figure 13B). Another has been identified at Amesbury (RCHM 1979, 2 (no. 146); Harding and Lee 1987, 284), and yet another is suggested by cropmarks immediately north of The Egg near Woodhenge (McOmish 2001, figure 4). The four rectangular pits arranged around the circumference of a circle about 11m in diameter uncovered at Butterfield Down in advance of house-building are probably the remains of another causewayed barrow, adjacent to which was a more conventional ring-ditch some 20m across, although neither monument contained preserved burial deposits (Rawlings and Fitzpatrick 1996, 10).

Flat graves

Flat graves containing inhumation burials of the third millennium BC, often associated with Beaker pottery, are well represented in the Stonehenge landscape. These include examples within monuments such as Stonehenge (Evans 1984), Woodhenge (Cunnington 1929, 52), and Durrington Walls (Wainwright and Longworth 1971, 4). Seemingly isolated inhumation burials in flat graves or pit graves of the same period include those near Durrington Walls (RCHM 1979, 7), at Larkhill Camp (Short 1946), and Totterdown Clump (Wainwright and Longworth 1971, 5). It may be noted, however, that many of these last-mentioned sites were chance discoveries and were mainly recorded with little attention to establishing context or associations.

Investigations in May 2003 about 700m away from the Amesbury Archer's burial, during the course of monitoring the laying of a pipeline at Boscombe Down, revealed a rather different kind of burial of the late third millennium BC (Fitzpatrick 2003b; 2004a; Fitzpatrick et al. 2004). Here a large rectangular pit contained the partly disarticulated remains of three adult males, a teenage male, and three children, together with eight Beakers, flint tools, five barbed and tanged flint arrowheads, a boar's tusk, and a bone toggle used as a clothes fastener. The burials had been inserted on several occasions over

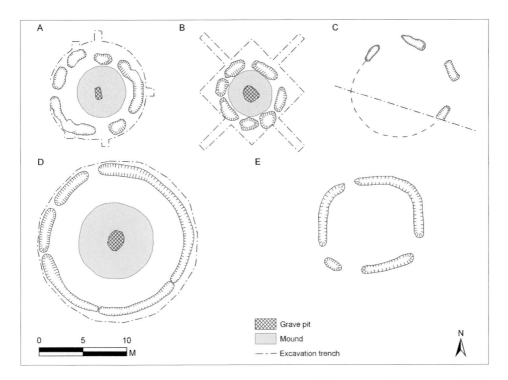

54 Causewayed barrows. A: Wilsford 51. B: Amesbury 51. C: Butterfield Down. D: Shrewton 24. E. North of The Egg, Durrington. *Drawing by Vanessa Constant: A after Smith 1991, figure 2; B after Ashbee 1978a, figure 2; C after Rawlings and Fitzpatrick 1996, figure 6; D after Green and Rollo-Smith 1984, figure 16; E after McOmish 2001, figure 4.3*

a period of time. Initially a man aged between 30 and 45 had been buried on his left side with his legs tucked up and with his head to the north. Close to his head were the remains of three children (one cremated). The teenager, aged about 15–18, and the other two men, both aged 25–30 at death, were placed around the body of the older man. Scientific studies of these burials, dubbed 'The Boscombe Bowmen', suggest that the teenager and adults at least were all from the same family and isotope analysis of samples of tooth enamel suggests that they may have spent some time in southwest Wales, the area known to have been the source of stones used in the construction of Stonehenge Phases 3i–v (Fitzpatrick 2004a; Fitzpatrick et al. 2004).

A STRUCTURED LANDSCAPE

Throughout the third millennium BC the Stonehenge landscape was a busy place. Occupation seems to have been concentrated along the Avon Valley and the higher ground along its western flank – what is known as the Durrington Zone – answering rather emphatically the often-posed question of where the builders and users of Stonehenge lived. Wilsford Down and the northeastern part of Durrington Down may have been flint working areas with flint mines present east of Durrington Down. In the centre of the interfluve between the Avon and the Till there is Stonehenge itself, the cursuses and long enclosures, barrows, burial places, and ceremonial sites that suggest a sacred sector.

Physical subdivisions of various kinds existed across the landscape in some areas and these are occasionally found below later monuments that have served to protect them. For example, a fence represented as a line of postholes was sealed below Shrewton 23 (Green and Rollo-Smith 1984, 281–5) while five postholes on a NNW–SSE alignment below Woodhenge Circle 1 (Durrington 67) may also be interpreted as a fence (Cunnington 1929, plate 39; RCHM 1979, 23). A similar line of six postholes was found on the northern edge of the northern bank at Durrington Walls although their exact date is unknown (Wainwright and Longworth 1971, 15–16). All of these glimpses of what appear to be fragments of rather larger features suggest that by about 2000 BC parts at least of the Stonehenge landscape were being formally parcelled up.

Some of these land divisions may be connected with an expansion of arable cultivation represented in the fill sequences of a number of ditches. At the Amesbury 42 long barrow changes in the mollusca populations and soil matrix suggest the onset of cultivation in levels associated with Beaker pottery (Richards 1990, 108). Below the neighbouring Amesbury 70 and 71 barrows there is evidence for pre-barrow cultivation in the form of rip-ard marks cutting into the chalk bedrock (Christie 1967, 347).

Stray finds datable to the third millennium BC found widely across the Stonehenge landscape show the intensity of activity beyond the confines of the main monuments, and serve as a reminder that we must see the landscape as a totality rather than as a series of defined archaeological sites. At least 15 flint and stone axes have been picked up as casual finds, two of the stone examples being of Cornish origin. Three of the flint examples seem to be roughouts lost in the course of production. Rather surprising in view of the presence of early metalwork in graves is the apparent absence of early copper or bronze axe as stray finds from the surrounding landscape.

At an altogether different level the landscape may also have been structured in a way influenced by the same sorts of cosmologies and belief systems that can be seen determining the layout and use of particular monuments. At a regional scale Nick Thorpe and Colin Richards have noted the widespread associations between Beaker and Peterborough Ware across Wessex as against the very rare and localized associations of Beaker and Grooved Ware (1984, figure 6.2). Within the Stonehenge landscape Beaker and Peterborough Ware commonly occur together westwards and southwards of Stonehenge while Beaker and Grooved Ware associations are restricted to the northern and eastern sectors (1984, figure 6.3). This they attribute to the way that users of Beaker pottery consciously sought to acknowledge and reuse earlier centres of power in the landscape. Elsewhere I have suggested a quartering of the landscape during the third millennium BC, based on a simple cosmological scheme grounded in

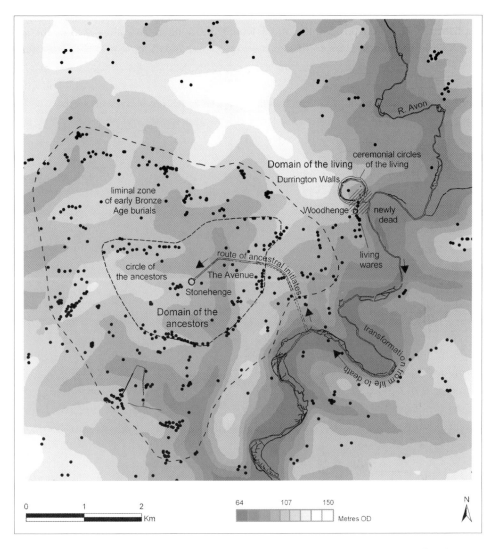

55 A model of the social use of space around Stonehenge. Monuments are shown in outline, barrows as dots. *Drawing by Vanessa Constant: after Parker Pearson and Ramilisonina 1998, figure 7 with topography from EDX Engineering Inc. data at 50m intervals*

a fourfold subdivision of space structured around the movements of the sun (Darvill 1997a, 182–9, and cf. Pollard and Ruggles 2001 for a similar pattern within Stonehenge itself). Parker Pearson and Retsihisate Ramilisonina (1998) by contrast prefer a slightly different scheme in which space was structured and conceived in terms of a domain of the ancestors centred on Stonehenge and a domain of the living centred on Durrington Walls. In this model the River Avon acted as a conduit for the transformation from life to death, the Stonehenge Avenue providing a route for ancestral initiates to move from the River Avon to the circle of the ancestors. Oppositions between life and death were expressed in the deposition of ceramics and the metaphorical use of timber structures in the domain of the living as opposed to stone in the domain of the ancestors (55). It is a simple and seductive model, but it is far from certain that the Avenue extended as far as the River Avon at this time, and with purposeful uses embedded in the structure of Stonehenge itself it might be better seen as a centre for the living seeking to know the future and find a cure for their ailments.

At a still larger scale, long-distance contacts are represented in the movements of people themselves, items of material culture brought to the area from many directions, the integration of ideas from western Britain and the continental mainland in the design of Stonehenge, and the cross-regional cosmologies embedded in the design and use of the monument. All suggest that by about 2000 BC this corner of central southern England had built a reputation that had already spread far and wide. The regional affiliations of the Beaker pottery from the Stonehenge landscape serve to emphasize a continuity with earlier times where the area lay towards the eastern side of a cultural territory that extended westwards across southwestern England and South Wales. Such connections are also well marked by the sources of stone used in making Stonehenge and the imported objects found to date. It is clear, however, that links southwards with communities living on the far side of the English Channel were also gaining in significance. Movements of people, whether as pilgrims, traders, or kinsfolk, should not be underestimated. A study of Beaker burials in central Europe showed that as many as 63 per cent of the sampled population had moved significant distances during their lifetime (Price et al. 2004). This accords well with the presence of the Amesbury Archer who travelled from Alpine Europe to southern Britain, and the Boscombe Bowmen whose travels seem to have paralleled the movements of the bluestones and who may well have participated in their transportation. People moved about a lot in the third millennium BC. To travel may well have been a sign of status or a source of power, but it may equally be related to the healing powers believed to reside in Stonehenge. A surprising number of the burials of third-millennium BC date, including the Amesbury Archer, were suffering from long-term health problems which they may have hoped would be cured by presenting themselves to the gods at Stonehenge just as pilgrims travelling to Santiago de Compostela hoped for relief during the Middle Ages (Mullins 1974). As such, for a while at least, Stonehenge was perhaps a beacon of hope whose influence was widely felt and whose presence structured the way the landscape around about developed.

6

LANDS OF THE ANCESTORS
(2000–1200 BC)

The power of place can be awesome and last long beyond the natural life of a monument or structure. During the third millennium BC Stonehenge changed and developed rapidly, as did its landscape. Approached along the Avenue in about 2000 BC it would have looked spectacular (56), and standing at its focus on a solstice with rock art to left and right would have been moving for anyone allowed that privilege. But over the following centuries its status altered and it changed from being active in people's lives to being a relic from a by-gone age, memories of which lingered. For life was changing. The world was moving on. Early in the second millennium BC the styles of pottery, worked flint, and metalwork changed fairly markedly in southern England, as too the form and use of funerary monuments and settlements. The circulation of Beaker pottery ended by about 1800 BC (Kinnes et al. 1991; Case 1995), its place in funerary contexts initially being taken by Collared Urns, Food Vessels, and Cordoned Urns; Wessex Biconical Urns and early forms of Deverel-Rimbury Ware following a few centuries later. Gold and bronze metal ornaments, tools and weapons became the new symbols of status and power (Burgess 1980, 80–131; Needham 1996, 130–3). Imported objects and copies of things found in continental Europe provided inspiration. Links between central southern Britain and northern France, Brittany, and Normandy especially, demonstrated alliances and structured the political geography of the region.

The early second millennium BC is synonymous with what Stuart Piggott dubbed the Wessex Culture (Piggott 1938; 1973d). This was defined by the distinctive material culture represented by a series of richly furnished graves found widely across the chalklands of southern England and extending northwards into the upper Thames basin and the Cotswolds. Of the hundred or so Wessex Culture graves originally listed by Piggott (1938, 102–6), 35 lie within the Stonehenge landscape, emphasizing the significance of this area.

Originally, the Wessex Culture was seen as resulting from the incursion of a dominant aristocracy from Brittany. Richard Atkinson linked the presence of these people to the quest for metal ore and the opportunities offered by trading raw material obtained from the west of Britain for unusual tools, weapons, and ornaments made by continental craftsmen in metal and exotic stone (Atkinson 1979, 163). In this view the Wessex chieftains grew

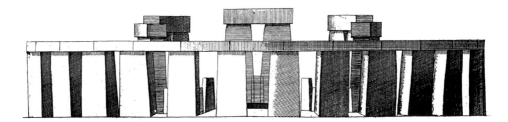

56 Stonehenge from the northeast. William Stukeley's reconstructed orthography of the monument viewed from ground level. *From Stukeley 1740, TAB. XII*

rich as middlemen. Since the 1970s, increasing emphasis has been placed on the essentially indigenous character of the main body of archaeological material for the period with the proposal that these rather exceptional well-furnished burials 'were the graves of the rich and powerful in each chiefdom' (Burgess 1980, 99). Humphrey Case has argued for a high degree of continuity between Beaker-using communities and those responsible for the Wessex graves on the basis of finds from Wilsford 7 (Case 2003). Here, part of a Group B Beaker was found alongside a primary series Collared Urn, the two vessels sharing some decorative motifs, especially criss-cross patterns, zonal lozenges, and zonal herringbone motifs. Also accompanying the extended inhumation in the primary grave was an unspecified number of exotic objects including an accessory vessel (grape cup) and a group of beads and pendants made of gold sheet, amber, jet or shale, and fossil encrinite. However, care must be taken in working out the balance between local developments and the wider influences, as the discovery of the extravagantly rich burial of the Amesbury Archer clearly illustrates. This burial is the most richly furnished grave of its period so far known in northwest Europe, and superficially at least suggests the emergence of wealthy elites well ahead of the Wessex Culture. But scientific analysis shows that the Amesbury Archer himself came from a homeland far away in central Europe (Fitzpatrick 2002; 2003a). He was certainly a traveller, possibly an immigrant or a pilgrim, and may have acquired the range of material that to local eyes in Wessex looked like wealth beyond measure along the way. More scientific analysis is needed to be sure, but one possibility developed in Chapter 5 is the idea that some of the wealthy burials in the area were the final resting places of travellers drawn to the area to visit Stonehenge and enjoy the powers it held as the sanctuary of a powerful deity, an oracle, or a source for miracle cures. One snag was whether the reputation that Stonehenge developed in the later third millennium BC could be maintained.

REACHING THE RIVER

One of the fundamental changes to Stonehenge around 2600 BC was the construction of a ceremonial way or Avenue running northeastwards on the newly established principal axis of the stone circles to link the earthwork enclosure with Stonehenge Bottom. In Chapter 5 it was suggested that what is now a dry valley held a small stream during the third millennium BC, and certainly the form of the valley and the alluvium fill supports such a proposal. Chalkland streams are renowned for being sensitive to slight changes in the local water table, quickly turning to seasonal 'winterbournes' and sometimes running underground as the water table falls. J A Taylor (1980, 123) has noted that with the onset of the Sub-Boreal climatic phase around 2000 BC drier and increasingly cooler continental conditions prevailed, with seasonal combinations of quite fine and vigorous summers and generally harder and longer winters. Such conditions may well have caused the interruption if not the cessation of the Stonehenge Bottom watercourse, and provided a context for extending the Avenue eastwards and then southwards to join the much more reliable River Avon at West Amesbury, a distance of about 2km (57).

The Avenue between Stonehenge Bottom and the River Avon has been excavated in six places and is demonstrably far less regular in its construction that the first section between Stonehenge and Stonehenge Bottom. It is also wider, about 34m between its flanking ditches, and less robustly built with smaller ditches and, presumably, lower banks although none now survive. As noted in Chapter 5, it was Richard Atkinson (1979, 214–15) who first argued for a two-stage Avenue, combining archaeological intuition with early radiocarbon determinations. His views have been developed by others (RCHM 1979, 11; Pitts 1982, 129; Richards 1990, 276–7), but also fiercely contested (Cleal et al. 1995, 319–27). The results of two early radiocarbon determinations have, quite reasonably, been rejected, but no new evidence has come to light to support either a single-phase or a two-phase construction. The critical section of the Avenue has never been excavated, and the geophysical surveys provide an ambiguous picture. The strongest evidence remains the careful earthwork surveys of the Royal Commission on the Historic Monuments of England (RCHM 1979, figure 5) which clearly show a disjunction in the line of both flanking boundary works at 'The Elbow' just above Stonehenge Bottom. Only one acceptable radiocarbon date is available from the eastern extension, 2470–2200 BC (OxA-4905: 3865±40 BP) from a piece of cattle pelvis in the bottom of the southern ditch where the Avenue is crossed by the modern A303. This compares with a secure date of 2580–2280 BC (OxA-4884: 3935±50 BP) from an antler on the floor of the northern ditch, and two dates of 2340–1910 BC (HAR-2013: 3720±70 BP) and 2290–1880 (BM-1164: 3678±68 BP) from antlers recovered from rather less secure contexts in the fill of the southern and northern ditches respectively. Some localized recutting of the ditch was certainly represented in the ditches near Stonehenge itself and perhaps further east as well (Cleal et al. 1995, 307), but refurbishment of the primary section might well be expected when the Avenue as a whole was lengthened.

Whether extended or simply refurbished in places, the Avenue certainly linked the Avon with Stonehenge during the early centuries of the second millennium BC, and presumably provided the main ceremonial approach to the monument. How heavily the route was used and how many people visited Stonehenge is not known, but it may be

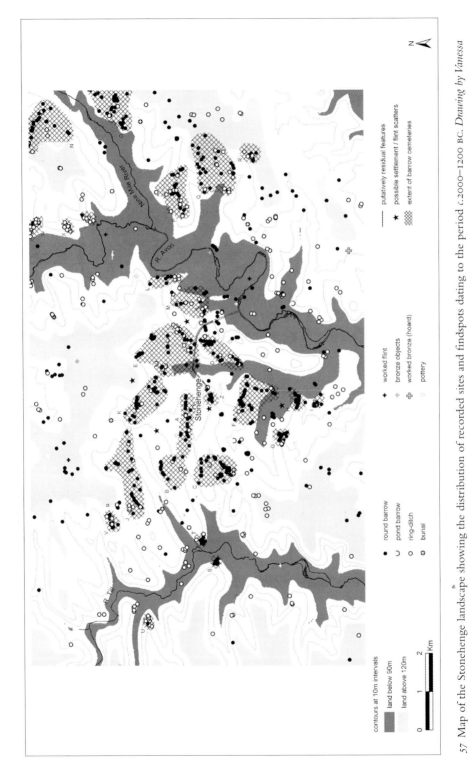

57 Map of the Stonehenge landscape showing the distribution of recorded sites and findspots dating to the period *c.*2000–1200 BC. *Drawing by Vanessa Constant. Wiltshire SMR and various archaeological sources over mapping from EDX Engineering Inc. data at 50m intervals and Ordnance Survey © Crown Copyright 2006. All rights reserved. Licence 100045276*

significant that the Avenue did not accommodate so much movement that it became a hollow-way. Also relevant is the rather small amount of pottery in Food Vessel or Collared Urn traditions from Stonehenge itself. Much the same story can be seen at Durrington Walls where relatively little seems to be happening after 2000 BC. Two hearths part way up the fill of the northern ditch section excavated in 1966–8 date to 2350–1650 BC (BM-286: 3630±110 BC) and 2300–1500 BC (BM-285: 3560±120 BP) suggesting that the original use of the site was over by this time (Wainwright and Longworth 1971, 20–1). Both Durrington Walls and Stonehenge may have been living on past glories, but there is evidence of one enduring tradition at both: pit-digging.

PITS IN RINGS

Digging pits is a recurrent theme of life in the Stonehenge landscape. Down until the third millennium BC such digging was mainly rather sporadic, characterised by irregular clusters of holes and scoops. The excavation of pits into the top of some of the Aubrey Holes at Stonehenge around 2700 BC perhaps marks the start of a new, more regular, approach involving arrangements of pits in rings (*58*). These may be a link to the increased cosmological referencing of the sun and to the solar, lunar, and life cycles noted in Chapter 5. Certainly, the construction of pit circles is something that continued. At Boscombe Down to the west of Amesbury, excavations in 2004 revealed over 30 pits marking the circumference of a circle about 50m across (Fitzpatrick 2004b). A few of the pits showed that at one time they had held posts, but most had not. In many ways this ephemeral monument is rather similar to the ring of Aubrey Holes at Stonehenge, but is probably of slightly later date and may well have developed over more than a century in the late third or early second millennium BC. Grooved Ware, Beaker, and Collared Urn Pottery were all found in association.

At Durrington Walls pit-digging is clearly related to the presence of an earlier structure: the Southern Circle. Here deposits of ash-rich soil intermixed with broken pottery, worked flint, and animal bone were found in the top of some of the postholes. At the time this was interpreted as a result of natural decay processes whereby the rotting timber posts would leave weathering cones into which debris that was formerly piled up against the post would collapse (Wainwright and Longworth 1971, 25). Experimental work elsewhere shows that in practice this does not happen as the post-pipe becomes a void and fills with material while the post is still in place on the surface (Reynolds 1994). In fact, the published section drawings of the Durrington Walls circles are so good that it is easy to reinterpret the evidence and suggest that once the posts were well rotted, and perhaps only visible as stumps, people dug rings of pits following four out of the six post circuits of the timber structure (*58* and *59*). Some of the pits were considerably larger than the post-pipes they cut through, others are imprecisely located over the original post, hinting that perhaps some timbers had disappeared from view. The material used

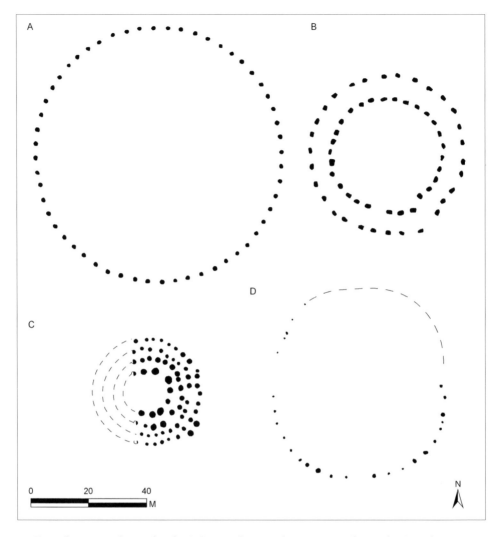

58 Pit circles. A: Y- and Z-Holes, the Aubrey Holes, Stonehenge. B: Y- and Z-Holes, Stonehenge. c: Southern Circle, Durrington Walls. D: Boscombe Down, Amesbury. *Drawing by Vanessa Constant: A and B after Cleal* et al. *1995, figures 36 and 151; C after Wainwright and Longworth 1971, figure 12; D based on information supplied by Andrew Fitzpatrick of Wessex Archaeology*

to refill these pits was mainly a mix of domestic refuse in an ashy soil matrix that could perhaps have been obtained from the midden on the northeast side of the structure or simply scraped up from the surrounding surface. In a few cases more structured deposits were inserted, including fragments from a single heavily decorated Grooved Ware pot (P470) found in the pair of pits dug over former postholes 22 and 23 either side of the main entrance. Beaker pottery was present in nine pits, but this seems to be the latest pottery represented (Wainwright and Longworth 1971, 141 and 71–3).

At Stonehenge two more-or-less concentric rings of pits were dug outside the Sarsen Circle. Known as the Y- and Z-Holes (58B) they each comprise circuits of 30 oblong pits up to 2m long and 1m deep (Cleal et al. 1995, 256–65). In plan they are fairly regularly spaced, but there is a larger gap to the southeast suggesting an entrance at this point; interestingly, their arrangement shows no regard for the earlier principal axis or northeastern entrance into the stone circles. The fill of the Y- and Z-Holes uniformly comprises a primary layer of chalk rubble from the weathering of the holes above which is a reddish earthy fill that looks to have accumulated fairly naturally. Examination of this material suggests that some at least was wind-blown and is thus taken to support the idea of a relatively dry climate at the time (Cornwall 1953, 138–40). Finds were few, although fragments of bluestone and worked flint were present in most. Hole Y30 had a group of three complete red deer antlers and two antler picks resting on the base of the pit. This is the only possible case of structured deposition, all the more significant perhaps as it lies more-or-less on the

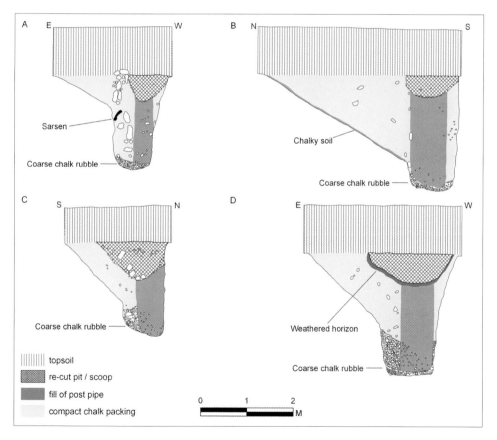

59 Interpretative sections showing pits cut into postholes at the Southern Circle, Durrington Walls. A: Posthole 42; B: Posthole 43; C: Posthole 70; D: Posthole 81. *Drawing by Vanessa Constant: after Wainwright and Longworth 1971, figures 120, 121, 125, and 127*

principal axis of earlier phases. There is no indication that the Y- and Z-Holes ever held stones or were intended to. Radiocarbon dates on antler taken from both rings of pits suggest that the inner Z-Holes are the earliest at 2030–1750 BC, with the Y-Holes a little later at 1640–1520 BC (Cleal et al. 1995, 534). This broadly accords with what is known of the other pit circles in the area and suggests a gradual accumulation that results in a coherent-looking plan even though few may have been open at any one time.

A review of the published sections of the postholes excavated at Woodhenge suggests that here too there may have been a phase of pit-digging following the partial decay of the posts as some post-pipes are shown truncated by other fills (Cunnington 1929, plate 12). Pit circles are increasingly being recognized at other sites across the British Isles (e.g. Ford 1991; Whittle et al. 1992, 162–6) and seem to have been relatively common constructions. In most cases it appears that the circle was created by episodically digging pits to seal off the central area, neutralizing it, and through the act of digging the pit reminding participants and observers alike of the status or meaning of what lies within. Digging the pits perhaps evoked specific memories, but more likely conjured up secondary perceptions of the traditions that made these places special. Remembering the past in this way may also provide a context for what was happening across the hilltops overlooking Stonehenge: the development of barrow cemeteries and burial grounds on a vast scale as if somehow reinforcing links back to some half-remembered or imagined ancestral past.

BARROWS AND CEMETERIES

There are more than 670 round barrows in the Stonehenge landscape, a density of about five barrows per square kilometre, which makes this one of the most heavily populated areas of the British Isles in terms of the number of burial monuments of this period. Some, of course, were built in the fourth and third millennia BC, but the majority date to the first half of the second millennium BC. In places preservation is extremely good, as for example along King Barrow Ridge where light woodland protected the mounds from hostile land-use and the attentions of antiquarian excavators through the nineteenth and much of the twentieth centuries (Cleal and Allen 1994). Sadly though, across most of the area many of the barrows have been levelled and 309 (46 per cent) are currently known only as ring-ditches revealed by cropmarks identified on aerial photographs.

Available records suggest that about 40 per cent of known round barrows in the Stonehenge landscape have been excavated to some degree, although the vast majority of these relate to nineteenth-century diggings with the result that rather little is now known about what was found. Re-excavation has proved successful and deserves to be more widely applied, especially where formerly upstanding mounds have been heavily damaged. Relatively little work has been done with the ring-ditches in the area, although a group of six were excavated at Earl's Down Farm, Amesbury, in 2002

(Anon 2004, 300) and previously unrecorded examples were found in the Avon Valley near Netheravon during the construction of pipe-trenches in 1991 and 1995 (Graham and Newman 1993; McKinley 1999). This group of four or five ring-ditches also serves to illustrate the potential for finding more such sites on the lower ground along the river valleys. At Butterfield Down, Amesbury, the planning and sample excavation of a ring-ditch showed no evidence of a central burial, but a pit-grave immediately outside the ring-ditch on the northeast side contained the burial of a child accompanied by one sherd of pottery believed to be from an accessory vessel (Rawlings and Fitzpatrick 1996, 10–11).

The distribution of known round barrows extends into all areas of the Stonehenge landscape (see *57*). The greatest concentrations are found on the Avon–Till interfluve, especially around Stonehenge itself. Fair numbers are known east of the Avon, slightly fewer to the west of the Till. What is perhaps most remarkable is the relatively low density of round barrows immediately adjacent to Stonehenge itself. The nearest barrow is Amesbury 11, 100m to the east (*colour plate 15*), a fine bell barrow excavated by Richard Colt Hoare (1812, 127–8) who found a cremation accompanied by a pair of bone tweezers beneath a large inverted urn. Almost as near, but to the southwest is a cluster of six bowl barrows and a disc barrow (Amesbury 4–10) that are now completely levelled although well recorded through geophysical survey (David and Payne 1997, figures 6 and 7). All were investigated by Colt Hoare with varying results (Grinsell 1957, 149–50), barrow 4 being the richest with a primary cremation accompanied by a bronze dagger and awl.

Independently, Ann and Peter Woodward (1996) and the present author (Darvill 1997a, 194) recognized a concentric patterning to the distribution of round barrows in two rings around Stonehenge and suggested that this might somehow reflect belief systems and the physical representation of a bipartite cosmological order. Since then Clarke and Kirby (2003) have suggested the possibility of a third, outer, ring of barrows that would extend the pattern still further into the surrounding landscape.

Julian Richards (1990, 273) has noted that many of the barrows around Stonehenge are set on the crests of low ridges, positions in which the mounds of the more substantial barrows are silhouetted against the skyline (*colour plate 17*). It is an area that needs more investigation as the visibility of selected barrows within the landscape is clearly important (Field 1998, 315–16). In one study, Frances Peters defined two main kinds of barrow mound – conspicuous and inconspicuous – the former being mainly built in the early second millennium BC on ridges and high ground (2000, 355). Within the Stonehenge landscape, the largest and most conspicuous round barrow is Milston 12 on Silk Hill, 45m in diameter and 6m high, which is surrounded by a bank and external ditch (Grinsell 1957, 226). Other large mounds include Amesbury 55, the 'Monarch of the Plain' as Colt Hoare called it, a bell barrow nearly 30m in diameter and 2.2m high at the western end of the Cursus cemetery (*60*).

Cemeteries

Numerically, most of the round barrows in the Stonehenge landscape form relatively discrete clusters which are usually considered to be barrow cemeteries. As Leslie Grinsell long ago pointed out, such cemeteries tend to focus around an earlier barrow which can perhaps be seen as a founder's barrow or an ancestral monument of some kind, usually a long barrow, oval barrow, or Beaker phase round barrow. Each cemetery then developed organically, one barrow at a time, gradually expanding to the full extent that can be recognized today (*61*).

Three main kinds of round barrow cemetery can be recognized on the basis of how the barrows are arranged: linear, nucleated, and dispersed (*62*). Curiously, the dispersed cemeteries tend to be in the northern part of the landscape, the linear cemeteries cluster around Stonehenge, while the nucleated examples lie mainly to the south. In all, some 26 round barrow cemeteries can tentatively be identified within the Stonehenge landscape (see *57*):

A	Cursus (Linear)
B	Lesser Cursus (Dispersed)
C	Winterbourne Stoke/Longbarrow Crossroads (Linear)
D	New King Barrows (Linear)
E	Old King Barrows (Dispersed)
F	Normanton Down (Linear)
G	Lake (Nucleated)
H	Wilsford (Nucleated)
I	Lake Down (Dispersed)
J	Rollestone Barrows (Dispersed)
K	Durrington Down (Nucleated)
L	Countess Road/Woodhenge (Linear)
M	Countess Farm (Linear)
N	Silk Hill (Dispersed)
O	Milston Down West (Dispersed)
P	New Barn Down (Linear)
Q	Earl's Farm Down (Dispersed)
R	Boscombe Down West (Nucleated)
S	Parsonage Down (Nucleated)
T	Addestone (Nucleated)
U	Maddington (Nucleated)
V	Elston Hill (Linear)
W	Ablington (Nucleated)
X	Brigmerston (Nucleated)
Y	Bulford Field (Nucleated)
Z	Stonehenge Down (Nucleated)

60 Large bell barrow at the west end of the Cursus Group (Amesbury 55) known as the 'Monarch of the Plain'. *Photograph: Timothy Darvill, copyright reserved*

61 Winterbourne Stoke barrow cemetery to the northeast of Longbarrow Crossroads. Aerial view looking southwest towards the long barrow (Winterbourne Stoke 1) and the modern roundabout on the A303. *Photograph: Mick Aston, copyright reserved*

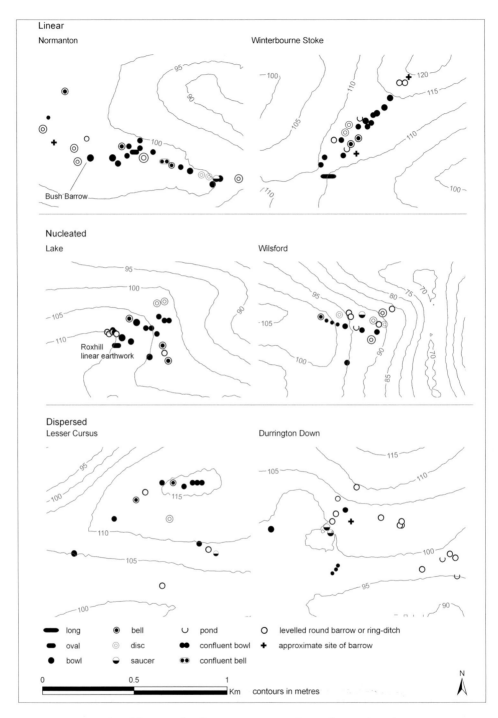

62 Barrow cemeteries of the second millennium BC arranged according to their dominant arrangement: linear, nucleated, and dispersed. *Drawing by Vanessa Constant: after Grinsell 1978a and RCHM 1979, Map 2 with topography from EDX Engineering Inc. data at 50m intervals*

On present evidence the dispersed cemeteries are the largest and may contain several foci; the nucleated cemeteries are usually relatively small. Linear cemeteries often incorporate a penumbral-like scatter of loosely associated barrows. Unfortunately, none of the barrow cemeteries have been completely excavated, nor have any of the large ones been subject to detailed geophysical survey. A nucleated group of barrows within the Stonehenge triangle (57z, the Stonehenge Down cemetery) has, however, been surveyed using magnetometry with good results that emphasize the great diversity of barrow forms even within the seven barrows represented (David and Payne 1997, 83–7).

Small groups of barrows outside these major cemeteries may also be similar. At Earl's Farm Down, Amesbury, the excavation of six ring-ditches in 2002 revealed burials in Collared Urns. One urn, perhaps imported to the region from southwestern England, contained beads of faience, jet, amber, and shale (Anon 2004, 300).

Round barrow construction and form

Since the work of William Stukeley in the eighteenth century round barrows have been classified on morphological grounds as bowl barrows (the most long-lived form which extends back into the fourth millennium BC) together with a series of so-called fancy barrows comprising: bell barrows, disc barrows, saucer barrows, and pond barrows (cf. Thurnam 1868, plate xi (based on Stukeley); Grinsell 1936, 14–25; Ashbee 1960, 24–6). In general, barrows that survive well, or which were recorded by fieldworkers who were able to observe them prior to any recent damage, can be classified according to this system; however, many others remain unclassifiable with the result that it is now impossible to provide more than an impressionistic analysis of the main types represented (*Table C*).

Table C Summary of the main types of round barrow represented in the Stonehenge landscape.

Round barrow type	Number	%
Bowl barrows[†]	425	43
Bell barrows	47	5
Disk barrows	51	5
Saucer barrows	15	2
Pond barrows	18	2
Unclassified	115	11
Ring-ditches	309	32
Totals	980	100

† Including examples dated to the third and fourth millennia BC

Structurally, the early second-millennium BC round barrows typically comprise a turf or loam core covered by an envelope of chalk rubble derived from the perimeter ditch. The examination of sections revealed by storm damage to barrows on King Barrow Ridge (*colour plate 18*) suggests that here there were two main kinds of construction: the conventional turf mound and chalk envelope, and a less common form involving only a turf and soil mound without a chalk capping (Cleal and Allen 1994). Some structural elaboration is, however, represented. Amesbury 61 had a stake circle around the central burial and perhaps a rectangular stake-built structure in the centre (Ashbee 1984a, 55); a stake circle was also found at Amesbury 71 (Christie 1967); and at Amesbury 70 a single posthole marked the centre of the mound (Christie 1964, 32). Stakeholes noted below Winterbourne Stoke 32, 33, and 38 formed no coherent pattern. In contrast, barrows 39, 47, and 50 each had a central setting enclosed by a ring of stakeholes and further groups of stakeholes both inside and outside the perimeter ditch (Gingell 1988). All these features fall comfortably within the range of stake-circle structures characteristic of British and continental round barrows at this time (Ashbee 1960, 60–5). In some cases they probably demarcated a burial place that would be later covered by a mound; in other cases they may have strengthen the core of the mound and given it greater longevity.

Most barrows of this period have a central burial pit for the primary burial. At Winterbourne Stoke 9, Colt Hoare recorded the presence of a boat-shaped wooden coffin; grave goods here included a necklace of shale and amber beads, a bronze dagger, a bronze awl, and a small ceramic vessel with impressed dot-motif decoration (Grinsell 1957, 201). At bell barrow Winterbourne Stoke 4 the cremation and a rich collection of grave goods had been contained within a wooden box (Grinsell 1957, 212). At Amesbury 85, excavations in 1930 showed that the central burial, an adult male aged about 50, had been laid on a carpet of moss and yew branches, the remains of which were preserved by the corrosion products on a bronze dagger placed in the grave with the burial (Newall 1931, 440).

Annable and Simpson (1964, 30) recognized a series of small, low mounds generally less than 10m across with poorly defined encircling ditches that formed part of some barrow cemeteries. These appear to be late in the overall series of barrow types, some being associated with Deverel-Rimbury pottery but most covering simple unaccompanied cremations (Richards 1990, 277).

Associations and grave goods
There is great variety in the quantity and diversity of material accompanying the dead under round barrows. In some cases there was nothing at all with the inhumed or cremated corpse, on other occasions up to a dozen objects. Overall, there are about 40 richly furnished graves known from the Stonehenge landscape, just 6 per cent of the 670 or so known extant round barrows or just 4 per cent if the ring-ditches included. Stuart Piggott (1938) considered all these graves to be part of his Wessex Culture. Following Arthur ApSimon's (1954) study of the daggers this was conventionally divided into an early phase (Wessex I) in which richly furnished inhumations predominate, and a late

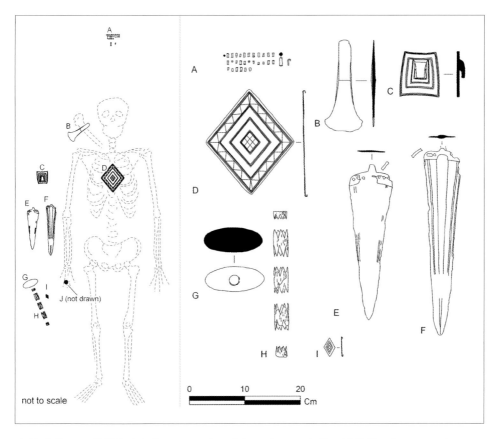

63 Bush Barrow (Wilsford 5). Reconstruction of the main recorded burial (left) and grave goods (right). *Drawing by Vanessa Constant: after Ashbee 1960, figure 24 and Annable and Simpson 1964, items 168–78*

phase (Wessex II) in which cremation is more usual and the range of grave goods more restricted (Annable and Simpson 1964, 21–8). However, dating has always been poor and it is far from certain that the two traditions are chronologically successive. The only dated Wessex Culture grave in the Stonehenge landscape is the cremation burial accompanied by a jet button and jet and amber beads from Amesbury 39 on the western slope of King Barrow Ridge. On typological grounds this would be assigned to Wessex II, but the rather early date of 2300–1650 BC (HAR-1237: 3620±90 BP) is hard to explain unless it is argued that the oak charcoal used for the determination derived from wood several centuries old when it was burnt prior to the construction of the barrow (Ashbee 1986, 84–5). It is this and other dates from elsewhere in southern Britain that have provided support for a minimalist view of the Wessex Culture, first suggested by John Coles and Joan Taylor, in which 'the "Wessex Culture" grave goods in the Wessex area need not stretch over several centuries, but represent a relatively short period without distinctive divisions' (1971, 13). More recently, Taylor has shown that some of the gold used in what would traditionally be seen as successive phases of the Wessex Culture actually came from the same melt and therefore must be contemporary. She suggested that differences between co-existing burial traditions should be regarded as reflections of social status and identity (2005), but what that really means in social terms has yet to be worked out.

The single most richly furnished and best-known burial of the early second millennium BC is that from Bush Barrow on Normanton Down to the southwest of Stonehenge (*colour plate 16*). This barrow was investigated by William Cunnington and Richard Colt Hoare in September 1808 to reveal the burial of an elderly adult male set north–south on the floor of the barrow (Colt Hoare 1812, 202–4). Grave goods with this burial include (*63*): a bronze axe, three bronze daggers (one with gold nails in the hilt; one since lost), two quadrangular gold plates, one gold scabbard-mounting or belt-hook, the stone head and bone inlay of a sceptre, and other fragments of bronze and wood. Linen impressions in the corrosion products of the slightly flanged axe suggest that fine cloth may have been worn by this individual (Piggott 1938, 105; Ashbee 1960, 76–8; Annable and Simpson 1964, 45–6; Burgess 1980, 101). Some of these pieces were imported to the region. The daggers are by far the largest examples from southern Britain and may have been brought from the continent while the oval macehead is a fossil Stomatoporid (*Amphipora ramosa*) quite probably from near Teignmouth in Devon. It is far from certain that this burial was the primary interment in the barrow, and given that the human remains were reburied this is a site that deserved reinvestigation before too long. Some of the grave goods attracted much attention, and not a little controversy, when they were cleaned and restored at the British Museum during the 1980s (Corfield 1988; Kinnes et al. 1988; Shell and Robinson 1988). Alexander Thom and colleagues have speculated that the markings on the gold lozenge from Bush Barrow might allow it to have been used as an alidade-type instrument to fix the dates of key epochs in a 16-month calendar (Thom et al. 1988), a proposition that could find support from the discovery in 2002 of a 'sky-disc' on the Mittelberg, near Nebra, Germany, which appears to show a basic cosmological scheme for the second millennium BC and might also have been used to calibrate a calendar (Meller 2004).

The range of finds recovered from other excavations at round barrows is impressive and very considerable. It includes not only the usual selection of pottery, ornaments, and weaponry (well described by Piggott 1973d), but also some extremely unusual pieces such as the bone whistle made from the hollow long bone of a swan from Wilsford 23 (Annable and Simpson 1964, 44–5; Megaw 1960) and a bronze two-pronged object from Wilsford 58 which has sometimes been seen as a 'standard' of some kind or part of a double handle and chain from a cauldron or similar vessel (Grinsell 1957, 212; Annable and Simpson 1964, 47–8). The two unusual shale cups believed to be from the Amesbury area also probably came from barrows, although the circumstances under which they were found are not known (Piggott 1973d, 369; Newall 1929b). Evidence of cloth, wood, and leather has been found in corrosion on the surface of several metal objects, as for example the dagger from Amesbury 58 (Ashbee 1984a, 69–70 and 81). J J Taylor (1980, 87–8) records the presence of gold objects in six barrows within the Stonehenge landscape: two lozenge plates, a belt-

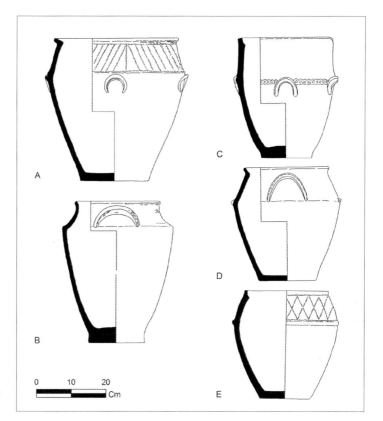

64 Wessex Biconical Urns from burials in the Stonehenge landscape. A: Bulford 47. B: Amesbury 71. C: Bulford 40. D: Bulford 47. E: Winterbourne Monkton 2. *Drawing by Vanessa Constant: after Piggott 1973e, figure 23a, e–g and j*

hook and pins ornamenting a dagger hilt in Bush Barrow (Wilsford 5); a bead and a bead cover from Wilsford 7; an amber-hilted halberd pendant with gold bands; two pendants, a button cover, and two gold-bound amber disks from Wilsford 8; two pairs of gold disks from Wilsford 50a; gold pins from a dagger hilt from Winterbourne Stoke; and a gold-bound amber disk probably from a barrow near Stonehenge.

Several different styles of urn are represented in the graves, including the ubiquitous Collared Urns found widely across the British Isles. Ian Longworth (1984, 281–92) lists 36 examples from the Stonehenge landscape, of which the greatest concentration comprises eight vessels from the Lake cemetery. More regionally distinctive are the Wessex Biconical Urns (also known as Wessex Handled Urns or Horseshoe Handled Urns) which date to the period 1400–1200 BC (*64*). A fine Wessex Biconical Urn was found as a secondary burial at Bulford 27 (Hawley 1910, 617), emphasizing the evolving traditions of urn construction. Well before 1200 BC, Deverel-Rimbury style urns were also being used in the area but, in the Stonehenge landscape at least, most appear to have been deposited with secondary burials cut into round barrows and are dealt with in Chapter 7. The exceptions are related to what seem to be the very small late-style bowl barrows associated with some major cemeteries.

Secondary burials dug into earlier barrows are also known, as for example the male and female burials associated with a Food Vessel Urn cut into the Winterbourne Stoke 1 long barrow (Grinsell 1957, 146).

INTERNATIONAL LINKS

As long ago as the late nineteenth century, the possibility of contact between communities in central southern Britain and the eastern Mediterranean was discussed in all seriousness. In a paper to the British Archaeological Association in August 1880, Dr John Phené reviewed analogies between Stonehenge and sites in the Mediterranean, noting especially the Cyclopean walling and other architectural details found in the fortified citadels of Mycenean Greece. It was a link later picked up by Oscar Montelius (1902) and others, and reinforced by the recognition that at least some of the rich grave goods in barrows of the Wessex Culture could be paralleled amongst objects from the shaft graves of Mycenae (and see Piggott 1938, 94–6; Atkinson 1979, 165–6). Yet more support was provided by the recognition of what was interpreted as a Mycenean dagger of Karo B type amongst the rock art discovered at Stonehenge in the early 1950s (Crawford 1954, 27: see Chapter 5). By 1956, Richard Atkinson felt able to ask: 'is it then any more incredible that the architect of Stonehenge should himself have been a Mycenean, than that the monument should have been designed and erected, with all its unique and sophisticated detail, by mere barbarians?' (Atkinson 1956, 164). A decade later this Aegean view, and the diffusionist perspective that it represented, were called into question by Colin Renfrew (1968; 1973b; 1973c) when it became apparent from radiocarbon dating that the main features of Stonehenge were more than 1000 years older than the supposed prototypes in Greece.

Breaking the links between Stonehenge itself and the Mediterranean was relatively straightforward; sorting out some of the other possibilities has caused a great deal of discussion and debate (e.g. Branigan 1970; Coles and Taylor 1971; Selkirk 1972; Watkins 1976; Barfield 1991). Critical here is the recognition that the rich burials around Stonehenge post-date the construction of Stonehenge itself. The burials belong firmly to the middle centuries of the second millennium BC and thus do overlap chronologically with the Mycenean shaft graves and associated Late Mycenean/Late Helladic cultures now dated to the period 1600–1200 BC (Harding 1984, 12–15).

Technical and stylistic studies suggest that most of the items once considered as possible imports were locally made. The goldwork, for example, probably derives from a single 'Wessex' workshop (Coles and Taylor 1971, 12; Taylor 2005) and the shale objects are all probably British in origin too (Brussell et al. 1981). The blue star- and quoit-shaped faience beads probably derive from north European sources, as too most, if not all, of the analysed segmented beads (Newton and Renfrew 1970; McKerrell 1972; Shepherd and Shepherd 2001, 110–20). Amongst items that may have been imported from the Mediterranean are: the crescentic earring from Wilsford Barrow 8 (Branigan 1970, 95–7); some of the gold-bound disks; and the bone mounts on the Bush Barrow sceptre. A large red glass bead from the Wilsford 42 bell barrow in the Lake cemetery is another likely import from the east Mediterranean, although other sources cannot be ruled out (Guido et al. 1984; Henderson 1988, 448). Amber spacer plates may have been moving in the opposite direction, from northern Europe to the Mediterranean (Harding 1984, 263).

In 1970 Keith Branigan considered the links between Wessex and Mycena in terms not just of the items from the barrows but also of distributions of Minoan and Mycenean objects including bronze double-axes, daggers, and rapiers across Europe generally. He concluded 'that the British finds are not an isolated phenomenon but part of a wide and relatively uniform European pattern' (1970, 105). Such optimism for long-distance contacts was not, however, shared by Anthony Harding who concluded his exhaustive review of the Myceneans overseas by pessimistically noting that 'one has no alternative but to reject the possibility of any regular contact between Britain and Mycenean Greece … sporadic contact … can be accounted for by very few individual acts of exchange' (1984, 265). This assumes, however, more-or-less direct exchange when in fact a more indirect model based on a network of interactions between communities spread across wide areas is more credible. Branigan suggested a mechanism for this when he proposed a chain of linkages from Greece through to the Aeolian Islands, from there on to southern France, onwards again to Brittany, and thence to southern Britain (1970, 105). The first stage of such a journey is marked by the movement of pottery as well as exotic items; the last part reflects a well-established network so strong that some writers have talked about a single cultural province extending from southern Britain across the English Channel into northern France (Megaw and Simpson 1979, 223). Stuart Needham (2000) plays down the movement of people across the Channel, suggesting instead that apparent similarities were driven by the procurement of exotic materials and goods through what he calls 'cosmological acquisition'. One item that was perhaps moved in this way is an Armorican *vase à anses* from Winterbourne Stoke 5 (Tomalin 1988, 209–10), but in all this it is hard to see the material remains in isolation without also thinking of the people behind them.

The very nature of the objects most likely to have moved the greatest distances – small personal items such as ornaments – suggests that perhaps the idea of trade and exchange exaggerates what was happening and that it is more realistic to think in terms of a few people engaging in journeys that allowed them to collect souvenirs of distant lands. As suggested for earlier times, status might have been determined by an ability to travel widely, visit sacred places, and see the known wonders of the world at that time. Indeed, is it just possible that the scanty exotica in these Wessex graves somehow reflects journeys between Britain and Greece in ancient times hinted at by Diodorus and his sources (Oldfather 1935, 39).

Connections were not only southwards towards the Mediterranean. Looking eastwards along the English Channel, mention may also be made of connections represented by the use of stake circles within barrow mounds. This has long been recognized as a regular feature of monuments on both sides of the English Channel, but especially in southern England and the Netherlands (van Giffen 1938; Glasbergen 1954; Gibson 1998a, 70–5). There are also close similarities in the design of some metal artefacts between these areas, and in the form and decoration of the associated ceramic vessels, especially the Wessex Biconical Urns and their counterparts the Hilversum and Drakenstein Urns of the Netherlands and surrounding areas as far west as Brittany (Butler and Smith 1956; ApSimon 1972; Briard 1993, 187). Sabine Gerloff's (1975) study of early British daggers shows that their origins can be traced through a network of links to communities falling within the Reinecke A1–B1 horizons of central Europe.

Nor should long-distance links between communities in the Stonehenge landscape and other parts of Europe be ruled out. In 1962 Stuart Piggott published a remarkable paper entitled 'Salisbury Plain to south Siberia' in which he explored the relationships of the perforated bone points and associated objects from Upton Lovell barrow 4, Wiltshire, finding parallels in a 'well defined but scattered series of similar interments stretching across Eurasia from the Baltic Sea to Lake Baikal' (Piggott 1962b, 93). The Upton Lovell barrow lies 17km west of Stonehenge but well within the central distribution of Wessex Culture barrows. That the occupant of the grave might be a shaman was tentatively considered by Piggott (1962b, 96) and has been taken up by others since (e.g. Burl 1987, 167–8). Colin Shell (2000) has also raised the possibility, originally noted by John Thurnam, that this is the grave of a metalworker.

OCCUPATION AND INDUSTRY

Settlements of the early second millennium BC are poorly represented in the Stonehenge landscape, although the Stonehenge Environs Survey did reveal four concentrations of pottery which might represent occupation areas and would perhaps repay further investigation: around Longbarrow Crossroads; east of Fargo Plantation between the Cursus and the Packway; on Durrington Down; and west of Stonehenge (Richards 1990, 272). Worked flint was found more widely, with slight concentrations not connected with pottery spreads on Wilsford Down and King Barrow Ridge.

Early second-millennium BC flint assemblages have also been recovered from a number of excavations, notably those by Patricia Christie between 1959 and 1964 later analysed by Alan Saville (1978). Although tentatively considered as essentially domestic assemblages that happen to be preserved at, or recovered from, barrow excavations (Saville 1978, 22), another possibility is that the barrow sites provided a context for flint knapping either because of their ancestral connections or because they were by this time 'out of the way' places (cf. Fasham 1978). Excavation of a ring-ditch at Butterfield Down, Amesbury, also revealed a substantial quantity of primary knapping debris in the ditch fills (Rawlings and Fitzpatrick 1996, 10), suggesting that perhaps such structures had similar roles to round barrows in respect of flint working.

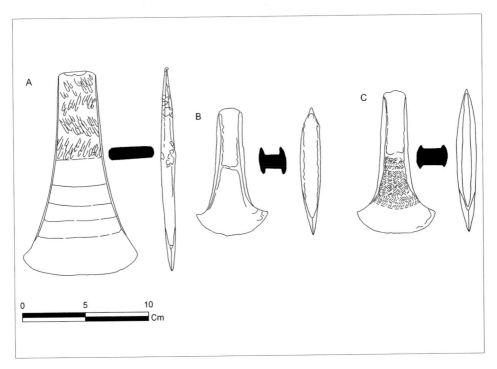

65 Early bronze tools from the Stonehenge landscape. A: Figheldean. B: Durnford. C: Stonehenge Down. *Drawing by Vanessa Constant: A after Moore and Rowlands 1972, plate VI.4; B after Saunders 1972, figure 1; C after Stone 1953, 31*

Another indication of the possible extent of settlement at this time is the scatter of stray finds, especially pieces of metalwork (see *57*). These include eight early bronze axes of Burgess' (1980, 80–131) Overton and Bedd Branwen Phases (*65*). Three come from around Stonehenge: a flanged example simply recorded as from 'near Stonehenge' (Grinsell 1957, 29); a flanged axe from between Stonehenge and Fargo (Grinsell 1957, 29); and a decorated flanged axe of Irish type found on Stonehenge Down (Stone 1953). Five come from further afield: a flanged axe with slight stop-ridge from Durnford (Saunders 1972); a short flanged axe from Beacon Hill, Bulford (Grinsell 1957, 52); an axe of Irish origin with hammered chevron decoration on its butt found north of the recreation ground at Figheldean (SM 1958, 10); a flat axe with a slight stop-ridge from between Figheldean and Netheravon (Saunders 1976); and a simple flanged axe from Wilsford (Grinsell 1957, 123). Of slightly later date is a rapier from Wilsford Down (Grinsell 1957, 122).

The most significant find of metalwork is a hoard of bronze ornaments found in 1834 near Durnford (*66*), perhaps in or near a barrow (Moore and Rowlands 1972, 61–3). The hoard comprises 14 items, including twisted bar torcs, bracelets, and rings, and is typical of the Ornament Horizon of the Taunton industrial phase of the twelfth and eleventh centuries BC (Burgess 1980, 131–58; Needham et al. 1997, 84–6).

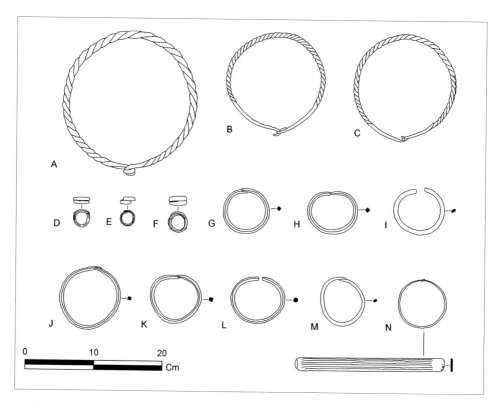

66 The Durnford Hoard. *Drawings by Vanessa Constant of items in Devizes Museum (B,C,G–N) and Salisbury and South Wiltshire Museum (A, D–F)*

BIG BANGS, DARK SKIES, AND WATER

Whether the apparent poverty of occupation in the Stonehenge landscape during the early and middle second millennium BC is real or not remains to be seen, but present evidence fits well with Andrew Fleming's model of settlement systems in Wessex at the time. On the basis of an analysis of barrow groupings right across the chalklands he suggests the presence of relatively mobile pastoralist communities living within seasonally defined territories who were anchored to the land by their ancestral barrow cemeteries that they periodically visited when near by (Fleming 1971). It is an attractive idea and sits comfortably with the notion that many of the cemeteries around Stonehenge overlook the central monument, allowing those interred in the mounds to forever gaze over such a sacred and revered place, perhaps gaining status and power through association with it. The gradual accumulation of generation after generation within these cemeteries served to strengthen such bonds, perpetuate myths, and give both context and meaning to oral traditions that even by this time were perhaps only half understood by those reciting them. But why did Stonehenge lose its power and interest in its maintenance wane?

One possibility has been raised by Mike Baillie in another context, but perhaps of relevance here. Through studies of tree-rings and ice-cores he has identified a number of cataclysmic events during the second millennium BC, two of which were very significant indeed. In 1628 BC the eruption of Santorini in the south Aegean sent shock waves around the globe as skies darkened and a period of environmental instability ensued. It may also be linked with a bombardment of the earth by one or more comets. And according to Baillie something similar also happened around 1159 BC (1999, 210-11), but by that time the occupants of the Stonehenge landscape had perhaps shifted their attention from the sky to focus on the other significant sphere of their cosmology: water.

Soon after 1500 BC the Wilsford Shaft to the southwest of Stonehenge was either dug as a new feature or, more likely in view of the radiocarbon dates from its lowest fill, given a new lease of life (Ashbee et al. 1989; and see Chapter 4). This 30m-deep shaft cut through solid chalk may have been a well and/or a direct link to the watery underworld. Amongst the objects from waterlogged layers dated to the mid-second millennium BC are a shale ring, amber beads, perforated-head bone pins, and pieces of buckets and other wooden containers, gifts perhaps to the deities believed to reside deep in the earth. Away to the east, dated to 1520–1040 BC (OxA-139: 3070±90 BC), is a crouched inhumation burial within a grave right beside the River Avon at Durrington, post-dating a buried land surface associated with deposits of burnt flints (Hedges et al. 1989, 220).

7

FIELDS OF GOLD
(1200 BC – AD 50)

By 1200 BC the Stonehenge landscape was relatively open compared with earlier times, its extensive grasslands giving it a wholly new complexion. What appears to have been a period of relative quietude in the middle of the second millennium BC broke down as the centuries rolled by and a succession of deep-seated and far-reaching social and economic changes came into play. Dating these changes is difficult as the separately developed sequences of pottery and metalwork do not mesh well or sit comfortably with the absolute chronology offered by radiocarbon dating. In conventional terms the later second and early first millennia BC equate with the later part of Burgess' Knighton Heath Phase (1980, 131–59) followed by the Penard, Wilburton, Ewart Park, and Llyn Fawr industrial traditions (1968). This coincides with the later currency of Deverel-Rimbury Ware which John Barrett (1980, 309) argues continued to be used in the Wessex chalklands at least as late as associations with Penard metalwork in the eleventh century BC. The appearance of plain post-Deverel-Rimbury Ware (PPDR) at about 1000 BC, contemporary with late Wilburton and Ewart Park metalworking traditions, provides a fairly secure horizon against which to match the archaeological evidence, and seems to be connected with a period of increased contact with continental Europe, further discussed below.

The first few centuries of the period covered here can be regarded therefore as a phase of transition that marks the end of many traditions whose ancestry stretches back millennia. These include finally abandoning the monumental structures and burial places that were so visible on the face of the landscape and which in many cases have survived down to the present day through benign neglect and fear of the unfamiliar. At Stonehenge itself there is very little evidence for activity at all: a small amount of Deverel-Rimbury Ware and occasional finds such as a bone point from the upper fill of Stonehole 8 (Cleal et al. 1995, 334 and 491). The use of the Wilsford Shaft either as a well or as a connection with the underworld ended as the shaft filled up with soil and occasional pieces of pottery and bone such that by about 700 BC it was just a hollow in the ground. Deverel-Rimbury Ware is fairly well represented through these fills, closely associated environmental evidence indicating a fairly open agricultural landscape around about (Ashbee et al. 1989).

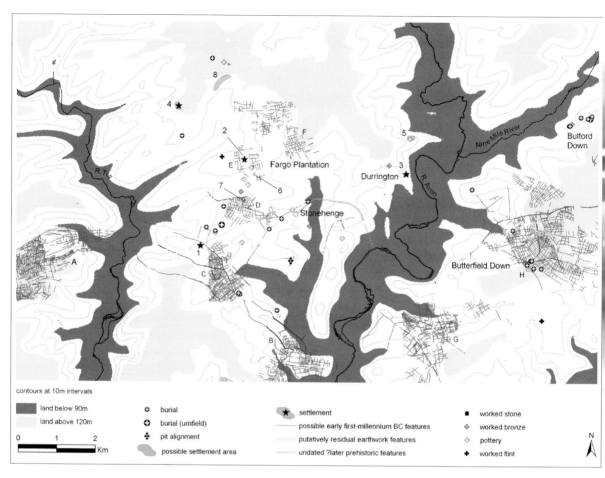

67 Map of the Stonehenge landscape showing the distribution of recorded sites and findspots dating to the period *c.*1200–600 BC. Fieldsystems A–H; 1: Longbarrow Crossroads. 2: Fargo Plantation. 3: The Egg. 4: Rollestone Grain Store. 5: Packway. 6: Durrington Down. 7: West of Stonehenge. 8: East of Robin Hood's Ball. *Drawing by Vanessa Constant: Wiltshire SMR and various archaeological sources over mapping from EDX Engineering Inc. data at 50m intervals and Ordnance Survey © Crown Copyright 2006. All rights reserved. Licence 100045276*

AN AFTERLIFE FOR ROUND BARROWS

The last round barrows to be built in the Stonehenge landscape seem to be the small bowl barrows with poorly defined ditches. These occur in clusters within or around the far larger mounds of the main cemeteries such as at Lake (Wilsford 36f, 36g, 38a, and 39), northwest of Longbarrow Crossroads cemetery (Winterbourne Stoke 17–21b), and as a discrete group on Wilsford Down (Wilsford 35–36e). Excavations by W F Grimes at Lake in 1959 revealed that Wilsford 39 had been grafted into the southeast side of the much larger Wilsford 38, its centrally placed burial being a simple cremation. The smallest of the late barrows was Wilsford 36g with a mound less than 5m across. It covered the cremation of an adult male that was probably contained within a Deverel-Rimbury style pot (Grimes 1964).

From the mid-second millennium BC onwards burials were increasingly deposited as secondary burials added to existing barrows (67). It was a tradition well represented in the Stonehenge landscape, starting with Collared Urns and Wessex Biconical Urns (see Chapter 6) and continuing after 1500 BC with various styles of Deverel-Rimbury Ware, including what are called Bucket Urns, Globular Urns, and Barrel Urns in older literature. No examples have yet been reported from long barrows or oval barrows, but Bulford 45 bowl barrow is one earlier monument that seems to have contained a secondary Deverel-Rimbury style pot (Grinsell 1957, 163). A Barrel Urn with applied cordons decorated with fingertip impressions used to contain a secondary cremation added to Amesbury 3 is one of the largest ceramic vessels from the area at nearly 0.6m high (Annable and Simpson 1964, 68). It is colloquially known as the Stonehenge Urn and was found by Richard Colt Hoare under a stone slab (Colt Hoare 1812, 126).

By the last few centuries of the second millennium BC extensive cremation cemeteries were fairly common, often developing around the edge of extant barrows, spilling across the ditches and beyond. The burials themselves comprise cremated remains in small pits or in ceramic vessels which were normally deposited inverted so as to both cover and contain the associated burial deposits. One of the largest excavated examples of such a cemetery is at Shrewton 5a (68). Here, the primary barrow covered the grave of an adult male associated with a Style 3 Beaker dated to 2030–1740 BC (BM-2517: 3560±50 BP). Extending across the southeastern part of the barrow and its surrounding ditch were 19 secondary burials in a tightly clustered cemetery. Six of these were contained within Deverel-Rimbury style pots, all but one buried inverted. Burial 20 differed from the others in being covered by a small cairn of burnt sarsen and was associated with a small hearth that was presumably the scene of some kind of ritual. Radiocarbon dates of 1700–1100 BC (HAR-4827: 3170±90 BC) for burial 5 and 1700–1050 BC (HAR-4827: 3120±100 BP) for burial 6 suggest a fairly short period of use for this cemetery (Green and Rollo-Smith 1984, 262–3). Among other recorded cremation cemeteries are Woodford 12 (15 burials: Gingell 1988, 26–7); Amesbury 71 (7 burials: Christie 1967); Winterbourne Stoke 10 (7 burials; Grinsell 1957, 201); and Bulford 49 (4 burials; Hawley 1910, 618–20). Broken pottery from superficial contexts at and around other barrow sites might suggest the former existence of a cremation cemetery broken up and scattered by later ploughing, as at Durrington 7 (Richards 1990, 171–84).

Typically, these cremation cemeteries were placed on the southwest side of the host barrow, and experience elsewhere in central southern England suggests that many lay between 100m and 500m from an associated contemporary settlement which was usually intervisible (Bradley 1981).

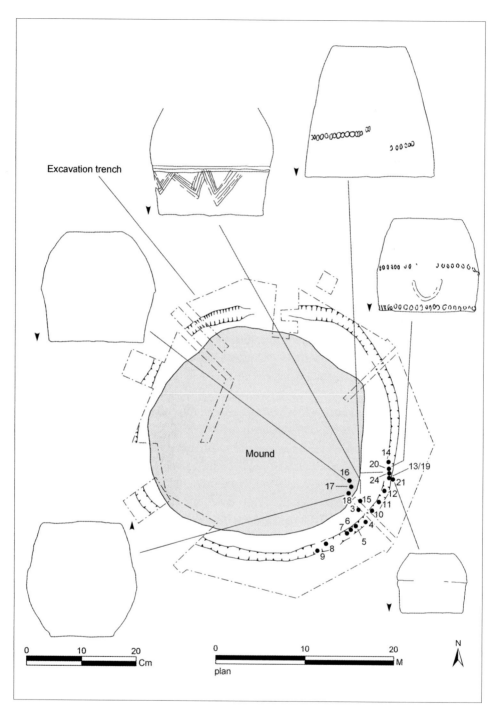

68 Shrewton 5a and later Deverel-Rimbury cremation cemetery. The cremation cemetery comprised 19 burials, of which 6 were within ceramic vessels. *Drawing by Vanessa Constant: after Green and Rollo-Smith 1984, figure 4*

SETTLEMENTS TO 1000 BC

Four settlements datable to the later second millennium BC have been recorded in the Stonehenge landscape, although none have been very fully investigated to modern standards (see *67*). Others no doubt await discovery or closer definition.

At Longbarrow Crossroads watching briefs and recording work during the construction of a new roundabout at the A303/A360 junction in 1967 revealed the presence of at least three circular structures, probably houses, with substantial south-facing porches (Richards 1990, 208–10). Not all could have been contemporary, and it can be suggested that structures 1 and 2 were later replaced by structure 3 (*69B*). A working hollow containing burnt flint in front of structure 2 appears to have been covered by or incorporated within structure 3. A few sherds of Deverel-Rimbury Ware from the area provide the only dating evidence. A palisaded ditch to the west of the structures may be part of a surrounding enclosure, but has not been dated. Notably, the area around Longbarrow Crossroads has a fair scatter of small, putatively late bowl barrows and cremations cemeteries containing Deverel-Rimbury vessels.

A second settlement is represented by a scatter of pottery and burnt flint towards the northern end of Fargo Plantation. Test-pitting and the excavation of five 5m by 5m sample squares yielded substantial amounts of finds but little structural evidence (Richards 1990, 194–208). Subsequent work in the area in connection with the evaluation of a possible access route to the proposed visitor centre at Larkhill sampled a substantial ditch and yielded a bronze side-looped spearhead (WA 1991, 13). This site may originally have been enclosed.

A third settlement is represented at an enclosure known as The Egg, situated a little to the south of Woodhenge on the western slopes of the Avon Valley at Durrington (*69A*). Discovered through aerial photography at the same time as Woodhenge, this enclosure was sampled through excavation by Benjamin and Maud Cunnington (Cunnington 1929, 49–51; Wainwright and Longworth 1971, 6; RCHM 1979, 23). The enclosure boundary comprised a palisade trench that had formerly held close-spaced upright timbers each about 0.3m in diameter. One terminal of the enclosure was extended in a straight line southwards where it meets a linear ditch. In the interior were 25 pits, one containing carbonized barley. Sheep bones were found in the fill of the enclosure boundary and red deer bones in one of the pits in the interior. Subsequent analysis of aerial photographs and finds recovered from monitoring a pipe trench suggest that The Egg is part of a more extensive spread of occupation that would repay detailed investigation (RCHM 1979, 24). A ditch found beside the Packway Enclosure north of Durrington Walls may also be part of the same system of boundaries (Wainwright and Longworth 1971, 324).

The fourth site is at Rollestone Grain Store, Shrewton. Here, field evaluations and excavations in advance of an expansion to the Wiltshire Grain Facility in 1996 revealed an enclosure some 60m by 50m in extent, bounded by a ditch 2m wide and over 1m deep. A single entrance lay in the middle of the western side. Inside the enclosure was a dew-pond (Anon 1998, 163–4).

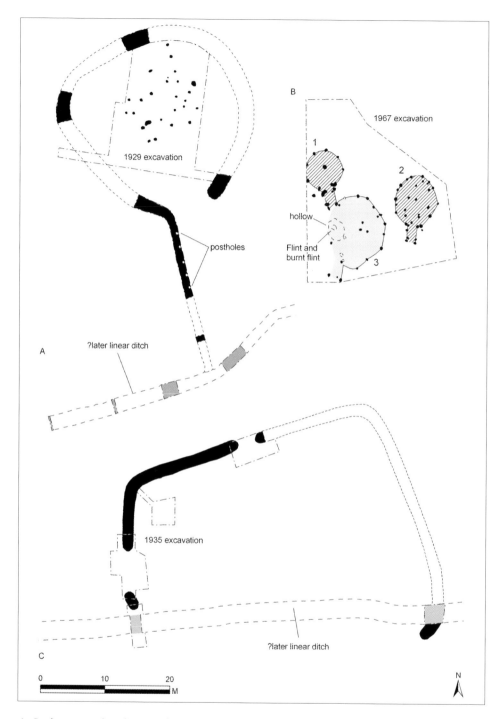

69 Settlements and enclosures of the early first millennium BC. A: The Egg, Durrington. B:
Longbarrow Crossroads, Winterbourne Stoke. C: Boscombe Down East. *Drawing by Vanessa Constant:*
A after Cunnington 1929, plate 45; B after Richards 1990, figure 148; C after Stone 1936, plate 1

Other settlement sites may be indicated by spreads of ceramics, burnt flint, and quern fragments recovered during the Stonehenge Environs Survey and subsequent field evaluations, for example: around the Packway north of Fargo Plantation; on Durrington Down; to the west of Stonehenge (Richards 1990, 276); and within an enclosure east of Robin Hood's Ball (Anon 2003, 236).

Taken as a whole these certain and possible settlements appear to be fairly well spaced at intervals across the Avon–Till interfluve, but to date there is little sign of occupation west of the Till or east of the Avon. It is no doubt only a matter of time before this changes as there are burials and evidence for farming in the form of fieldsystems in both these areas.

FIELDSYSTEMS

One of the most extensive archaeological features that can, in part at least, tentatively be assigned to the later second millennium BC is the arrangement of fieldsystems – the so-called Celtic fields. These have been discussed and described several times (RCHM 1979, xiii and 29–31; Richards 1990, 277–9; McOmish et al. 2002, 51–6), as a result of which eight main blocks can be recognized (67A–G):

West of the Till
      A   Parsonage Down/Shrewton system

Between the Till and the Avon
      B   Rox Hill and Wilsford Down
      C   Longbarrow Crossroads/Winterbourne Stoke Crossroads
      D   Stonehenge Down
      E   Fargo Plantation
      F   Durrington Down

East of the Avon
      G   Amesbury Down
      H   Earl's Farm Down

Not all these systems are necessarily contemporary, nor are all the components visible within them as earthworks or recorded as cropmarks on aerial photographs of the same period. Some important stratigraphy is, however, visible, including the spread of field boundaries connected with the Fargo Plantation system across the western end of the Cursus. This emphasizes how finally the power of the ancient monuments in this landscape had been eclipsed by the late second millennium BC.

The present 'blocking' of recognizable chunks of fieldsystem is almost certainly as much to do with survival patterns as with the original extent of coherent units. Some now remain only as very low-relief earthworks and shallow subsurface features (*colour plate 21*). All of those systems recognized around the edge of the Stonehenge landscape as defined here continue into adjacent areas (see McOmish et al. 2002, figure 3.1 for example) and cannot easily be considered in isolation. Moreover, although it is widely believed that these systems have their origins in the mid or late second millennium BC, they are generally poorly dated, in many cases probably multi-phase. Even a superficial examination of their plans and structural arrangement suggests that several quite different patterns are represented. A great deal of unpicking is needed to establish the nature of particular systems at given points in their development as well as the overall sequence. What comes through rather clearly, however, is that within each there is a strong co-axial element to their layout. Such a pattern, dominated by close-set parallel boundaries following a dominant axis, is typical of early fieldsystems across northwestern Europe. In the British Isles they are especially well preserved on Dartmoor (Fleming 1988), but they have been recognized in many other areas too. Apparently associated enclosures can be recognized on Rox Hill (RCHM 1979, 24), north of Normanton (RCHM 1979, 24), and southwest of Fargo Plantation (RCHM 1979, 24–5), but the date of these is not known.

Close correspondence can be seen between the fieldsystems and the known settlements and clusters of late second-millennium BC burials. Only The Egg at Durrington seems to be unassociated with a fieldsystem. Unfortunately, there are no useful environmental sequences from amid these blocks of fieldsystems so it has to be taken at face value that they were used wholly or partly as cultivation plots. They were the first real fields in the modern sense, and would have glistened gold every late summer as the crops ripened. Prolonged usage is what gave rise to the formation of lynchets such as still survive in a few areas. Away from the fieldsystems there are relevant environmental sequences, but these all suggest grassland as might be expected: Wilsford Shaft (Ashbee et al. 1989, 103); north ditch of the Stonehenge Cursus (Allen 1997, 130); and the eastern ditch of the Amesbury 42 long barrow (Richards 1990, 106). In these areas it is possible to recognize a second kind of agricultural feature: linear earthworks or 'ranch boundaries' as they are sometimes called.

RANCH BOUNDARIES

Many open grassland areas in Wessex appear to have been subdivided by a network of linear earthworks in the later second millennium BC. These comprise substantial banks with associated ditches and variously pre-date, join, delimit, or post-date blocks of fieldsystem in a way that emphasizes the complexity of these early landscapes (see 67). Such boundaries are especially notable on the southern part of the Avon–Till interfluve (RCHM 1979, xii and 25–9), but one major boundary known as the Earl's Farm Linear and several smaller boundaries are known east of the Avon. To date, none have been identified west of the Till.

As with the fieldsystems, dating is difficult. The best preserved are those on Lake Down and Wilsford Down southwest of Stonehenge (*colour plate 22*). Two sections were cut through those on Wilsford Down as part of the Stonehenge Environs Project (Richards 1990, 192–3), confirming the presence of substantial, although different, bedrock-cut ditches. However, neither yielded dating evidence for the initial construction of the ditches. Closely related may be a pit-alignment, perhaps also of the early first millennium BC, noted south of Normanton Down.

East of the Avon there have been numerous sections cut through the Earl's Farm Linear (Bradley et al. 1994, figure 22). One section at Butterfield Down, Amesbury, showed the scale of the ditch but failed to yield firm dating evidence for its construction (Rawlings and Fitzpatrick 1996, 38). The same applies at two further sections on Earl's Farm Down excavated in 1991. Here the ditch was about 3m wide and 1.5m deep, but again neither cutting contained diagnostic dating evidence from primary contexts (Cleal et al. 2004, 234–41). Molluscan sequences from both ditches confirmed that they lay within an essentially open downland environment.

Overall, the linear boundaries within the Stonehenge landscape form part of a much more extensive series of boundaries on Salisbury Plain (Bradley et al. 1994) and seem to have been for both territorial demarcation and the subdivision of agricultural land.

STRAY FINDS AND METALWORK

Stray finds of the later second and early first millennia BC are surprisingly rare within the Stonehenge landscape. The scatters of Deverel-Rimbury Ware generally match the areas of known settlement evidence and early fieldsystems (Richards 1990, figure 160). Best represented are the finds of metalwork to complement that found with burials. An unlooped palstave was found west of Fargo Plantation (Anon 1978, 204) perhaps associated with the settlement in the area referred to above; a socketed bronze knife was residual in a later context at Fargo Road southwest of Durrington Walls (Wainwright 1971, 82); two socketed axes were found on Durrington Down in the late nineteenth century (Grinsell 1957, 66); a bronze spearhead and a small socketed axe came from Wilsford Down (Grinsell 1957, 122); a bronze spearhead was found during building work at Bulford Camp in 1914 (Goddard 1919, 360); a socketed spearhead came from the Amesbury area (Grinsell 1957, 29); and a side-looped spearhead came from the top of a barrow southwest of Stonehenge (Grinsell 1957, 29). At Oldfield near Stonehenge a socketed axe, a class II razor, and a tanged tracer are said to have been found together, perhaps in or near a barrow (Piggott 1946, 138, no. 54). A miniature bronze axe was found by a metal detectorist at Upavon (Robinson 1995, 62, no. 9), and an unlooped palstave of Werrar type and a socketed axe of Hädemarschen type were found in Steeple Langford parish just west of the Stonehenge landscape (Moore and Rowlands 1972, 55).

Evidence of metalworking has been recorded in the Stonehenge landscape, including a possible fragment of a mould from Stonehenge itself (Cleal et al. 1995, 395). More substantial is the piece of a stone mould for casting socketed axes found by the Nine Mile Water in Bulford (Grinsell 1957, 52 with earlier references). The stone is recorded as syenite, a type of igneous rock that is very rare in the British Isles but whose identification is often confused with that of granite. One side of the mould has a matrix for casting South Welsh axes of the type found widely across southern Wales, southwest England, Wessex, the Channel Islands, and northern France (especially Brittany, Normandy, and the Loire basin). An axe that is very similar, if not identical, to those produced in the Bulford mould was found at Sandleheath on the Wiltshire/Hampshire border (Moore and Rowlands 1972, 28; and see Needham 1981). The other side of the Bulford mould has a matrix for casting a very rare kind of socketed axe which has two loops on different levels. Overall, the mould belongs within Burgess' Ewart Park industrial phase (Burgess 1968, 17–26), a period of diversification and change. Moore and Rowlands (1972, 33) suggest that peripatetic axe-smiths working in this tradition often set up their workshops close to river crossings – a very suitable context for the Bulford mould. Rather important, however, are the regional connections this find illustrates, linking the Stonehenge area with its traditional hinterland away to the west and southwest at a time when communities living not far to the east became intimately involved in new developments originating across the channel.

TRADE AND TRANSITIONS

Ewart Park metalworkers in the Thames Valley and southeastern Britain became part of an extensive trade and exchange network that extended across the North Sea and English Channel into the Low Countries and northern France, and from there eastwards into central Europe and beyond. Marking the extent of this network is the distribution of Carp's Tongue Complex metalwork (Burgess 1968, 17–19), named after the distinctive bronze swords. The workmanship and traditions represented by this complex indicate an industrial revolution in terms of the range of items produced and the technologies used. Sheet metalwork was developed at this time, as too the use of lead-bronze and possibly the first appearance of iron alongside bronze. Horse-gear cast in bronze shows the growing importance of riding. The Carp's Tongue swords are especially suitable for use by cavalry, and the presence of bronze chapes suggests the need to draw swords while riding. Knives and many other tools indicate that the bronzesmiths were underpinning the work of many other crafts. And closely associated with changes in metalworking tradition are new styles of pottery, the so-called post Deverel-Rimbury Wares (PDR) that seem to originate in southeastern Britain (Barrett 1980). At first these are mainly plain (PPDR) and draw on styles found in continental Urnfield assemblages from the Low Countries (Champion 1975, 136–8), but after about 800 BC many assemblages have a high proportion of decorated wares (DPDR).

Communities around Stonehenge lay just outside the area in which these developments first appeared (Champion 2001), but they soon caught up as illustrated by the site of Boscombe Down East which lies on the east side of the River Bourne just outside the Stonehenge landscape as defined here. Excavations by J F S Stone in June 1935 revealed a pair of ditches defining a three-sided enclosure (Stone 1936; 69C). Similar enclosures are known fairly widely across central southern England, the best dated being at Down Farm on Cranborne Chase, Dorset, which was built in the last quarter of the second millennium BC (Barrett et al. 1991, 206–11). The Boscombe Down East example pre-dates a linear ditch/ranch boundary, and is directly associated with Globular Urns, Bucket Urns, and bowls of Deverel-Rimbury Ware, intermixed with small quantities of PPDR. Pieces of slag from ironworking were found low in the fill of the ditch and may be among the earliest evidence for this novel form of metalworking in the region (Stone 1936, 470).

Increasing integration with communities in southeast Britain and perhaps beyond is also indicated by the hoard of about 25 bronze socketed axes found in 1971 on Figheldean Down some 2km north of the Stonehenge landscape (Coombs 1979; Needham 1981). All the axes were of the Sompting type, large, heavy, and with a rectangular section and decoration in the form of ribs, pellets, and roundels in various combinations on the outer faces. Most of the axes are in an 'as cast' condition, unshaped and unfinished; several had been made in the same mould. At the time of its discovery the Figheldean Hoard was the largest of its kind from the British Isles and these were quite possibly products from a local workshop. Colin Burgess (1968, 28) notes similarities between Sompting axes and Armorican axes, suggesting the possibility of trade links across the English Channel in the early first millennium BC, a set of connections with a long ancestry for those living in the Stonehenge area.

SETTLEMENT 1000–600 BC

Evidence of occupation in the Stonehenge landscape during the first three or four centuries of the first millennium BC is very poor. The surface collections of the Stonehenge Environs Project found no pottery or other material of this period (Richards 1990, 15–39). DPDR ware is extremely scarce, as too the distinctive angular All Cannings Cross wares and haematite coated bowls of the eighth and seventh centuries (Cunliffe 1973a; 1991, 61–8). Ros Cleal has identified a few sherds of this period at three barrows on Winterbourne Stoke Down (Richards 1990, 242), and this is one area where future work might usefully be concentrated. Also of interest is a working hollow and associated pits excavated at Boscombe Down West in 1949 (Richardson 1951, 127–9). The working hollow comprised a cluster of more than 30 intercutting pits, some of which were probably open at the same time. The fill comprised soil with pockets of ash, lumps of sand and chalk, and few finds except a clay spindle whorl, a bone gouge, and sherds of haematite coated bowls with omphalos bases and furrowed bowls, all probably

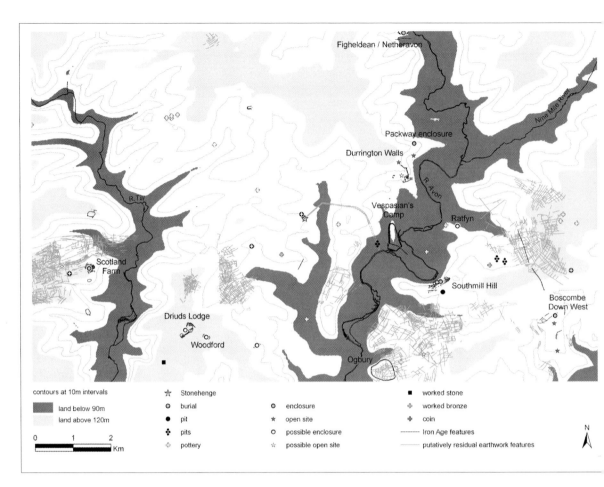

70 Map of the Stonehenge landscape showing the distribution of recorded sites and findspots dating to the period *c.*600 BC – AD 50. *Drawing by Vanessa Constant: Wiltshire SMR and various archaeological sources over mapping from EDX Engineering Inc. data at 50m intervals and Ordnance Survey © Crown Copyright 2006. All rights reserved. Licence 100045276*

of ninth- or eighth-century BC date. The overall impression is that this is the base of a midden that may once have included an upstanding element similar perhaps to the much larger and better-preserved examples at Potterne (Lawson 2000) and East Chisenbury (McOmish et al. 2002, 73–4) deeper into Salisbury Plain to the north.

A few sherds of pottery, all unstratified or from the upper fills of long-forgotten features, are the only signs that anyone visited Stonehenge during this period. The only possible exception is a small collection of sherds from a single proto-saucepan pot or jar perhaps of fourth- to second-century BC date from the top of Z-Hole 12 in the southern sector of the site. This may just be a deliberate deposition and suggest that not everyone had forgotten the ancient significance of the place.

Overall, one is forced to conclude that after a period of transformation in the later second millennium BC the pace of change slowed down again in the early first millennium. It is tempting to link such a hiatus to the onset of the Sub-Atlantic climatic phase around 1000 BC, marked by a period of climatic deterioration (Turner 1981, 256–61) and perhaps changes in settlement patterns in upland and western parts of the British Isles (Burgess 1985). But that is probably too simplistic and ignores the social and political changes going on at the time. It is unlikely that the Stonehenge landscape was abandoned; rather the activities that went on there are archaeologically difficult to see – for example grazing livestock – or we are looking in the wrong places. Whichever was the case, by about 600 BC archaeological evidence is again visible and a wide range of occupation sites are represented, including hillforts and farmsteads (*70*).

HILLFORTS

The best-known and most visible monuments of the middle and late first millennium BC are hillforts, of which numerous variants have been recognized (Cunliffe 1973b; 1991, 312–70). Within the Stonehenge landscape there are two examples: Ogbury and Vespasian's Camp.

Ogbury, the larger of the two, overlooks the River Avon from the east side at Great Durnford (*71c*). This poorly known site is a univallate enclosure of 26ha but it has never been adequately surveyed and is an obvious candidate for future study. Crawford and Keiller (1928, 150–2) provide the best description and illustrate their account with a fine near-vertical aerial photograph; accounts of the site extend back to Stukeley's visit in the early eighteenth century. Internal boundaries have been noted and Grinsell (1957, 65) records finding pottery datable to the fifth or sixth century BC at the site in 1951. Worked flints have also been reported and it has tentatively been suggested that what can be seen today represents a multi-phase site with elements extending back into earlier prehistory (Darvill 1997a, 182: note 6).

The second hillfort, Vespasian's Camp, lies on the west bank of the Avon west of Amesbury (*71e* and *72*). Although there have been recent investigations and a comprehensive survey (RCHM 1979, 20–2; Hunter-Mann 1999), there is still much to learn about this site. It is a univallate enclosure of 16ha with two phases of glacis-type rampart constructed about 500 BC.

All around the Stonehenge landscape there are other hillforts whose existence was no doubt relevant to those living in the area. About 1.5km to the southwest is the multivallate hillfort of Yarnbury Castle and a series of associated settlements and enclosures at Steeple Langford and Hanging Langford (Cunnington 1933b, 198–217). Slightly further away, 5km to the south, is Old Sarum (RCHM 1981, 1–24), and 4km to the southeast is Figsbury Rings (Cunnington 1925; Guido and Smith 1981). About 4km to the northeast is Sidbury (Applebaum 1954; McOmish et al. 2002, figures 3.6 and 3.25), and 6.5km to the north Casterley Camp (Cunnington and Cunnington 1913; McOmish et al. 2002,

71 Comparative plans of mid and late first-millennium BC hillforts and enclosures. A: Packway Enclosure, Durrington. B: Boscombe Down West. C: Ogbury. D: Netheravon/Figheldean. E: Vespasian's Camp, Amesbury. *Drawing by Vanessa Constant: A after Wainwright and Longworth 1971, figure 99; B after Richardson 1951, figure 1; C after Crawford and Keiller 1928, figure 35; D after McOmish et al. 2002, figure 3.31; E after RCHM 1979, figure 13b. Topography based on EDX Engineering Inc. data*

figures 3.7 and 3.28). All these sites, and others in the vicinity too, illustrate the point that much of the high-order settlement pattern of the area has to be seen in a regional rather than a local context. In the mid-first millennium BC the Wessex chalklands supported a scatter of hillforts of various kinds each serving relatively small local territories in some way (Cunliffe 1991, 348–52). In this pattern, Ogbury and Vespasian's Camp (72) have important positions relative to the 'East Avon' routeway between Britain's south coast and the Irish Sea proposed by Andrew Sherratt (1996b, figure 2), but the Stonehenge landscape itself is only one small part of the wider picture. By the fourth century BC there were rather fewer, but larger, hillforts (developed hillforts) with much more extensive territories around them. By this time the Stonehenge landscape lay on the junction of the putative territories of four developed hillforts outwith the landscape itself: Yarnbury, Old Sarum, Casterley Camp, and Sidbury (Cunliffe 1971, figure 14).

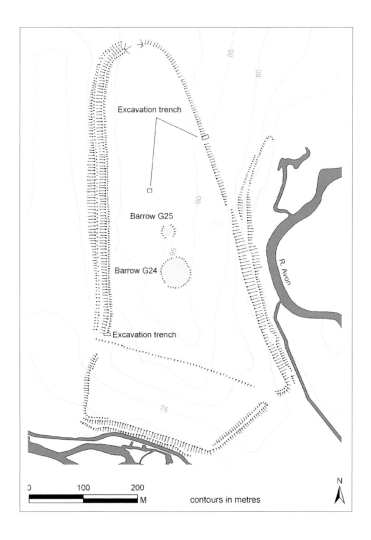

72 Vespasian's Camp, Amesbury. *Drawing by Vanessa Constant: after RCHM 1979, figure 13b. Topography based on EDX Engineering Inc. data*

ENCLOSURES AND FARMSTEADS

Between and around the hillforts are various other settlements, some enclosed and some not. It is tempting to see them as much smaller than the hillforts, but this is not always so (*71*). Importantly though, these non-hillfort sites represent the basic settlement pattern of compounds, hamlets, and farmsteads. The distribution of sites shows contrasts with earlier times, with a focus along the Avon Valley, east of the Avon, and west of the Till (*70*).

To the southwest of Durrington Walls a series of excavations carried out in 1970, in advance of tree-planting, revealed a few pits associated with pottery datable to the fifth to first centuries BC (Wainwright 1971, 82–3). Within Durrington Walls a small cluster of pits containing Little Woodbury style pottery was recorded in 1951 (Stone et al. 1954, 164), and the 1966–8 excavations also recorded features of this date inside the henge-enclosure. This included a palisade trench forming the boundary of a small compound, and groups of pits and postholes (Wainwright and Longworth 1971, 312–28).

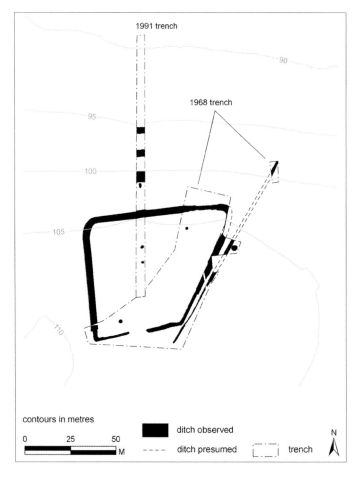

73 The Packway Enclosure, Durrington. *Drawing by Vanessa Constant: after Wainwright and Longworth 1971, figure 99. Topography based on EDX Engineering Inc. data*

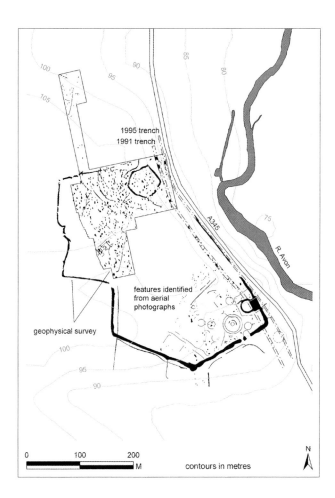

74 Polygonal enclosure west
of the Avon at Netheravon/
Figheldean. *Drawing by Vanessa
Constant: after McOmish* et al.
*2002, figure 3.31 with additions.
Topography based on EDX
Engineering Inc. data*

Immediately north of Durrington Walls is the Packway Enclosure, partially excavated
in 1968 during the construction of a roundabout on the A345 west of the Stonehenge
Inn (*71A* and *73*). This kite-shaped enclosure had an entrance on the south side. Little was
recovered from the inside because of the circumstances of discovery which had truncated
the natural chalk surface and it remains poorly dated within the late first millennium BC
(Wainwright and Longworth 1971, 307–11; and see Graham and Newman 1993, 52–5).

Northwards of Durrington Walls at Netheravon/Figheldean in the Avon Valley
excavations in connection with pipeline construction in 1991 and 1995 revealed a large
multi-sided ditched enclosure on the west side of the river (*71D* and *74*). Within the main
boundary are numerous small compounds and suggestions from geophysical surveys of
round houses and pits (McKinley 1999 with earlier references; McOmish et al. 2002,
figure 3.31). Finds included an iron strip brooch of the early first century AD, and a
bronze Nauheim-derivative brooch of the same date, but no pottery of this period. This
site continued in use through into the Roman period (see Chapter 8).

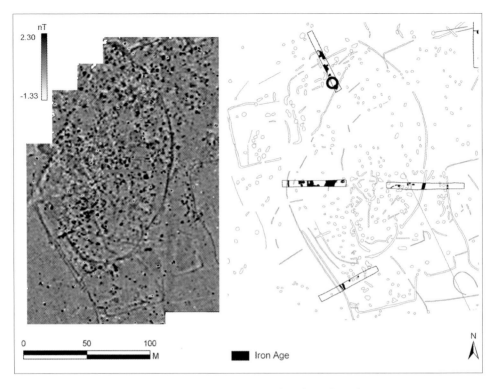

75 Enclosure at Scotland Farm, Winterbourne Stoke. A: Plot of geophysical survey. B: interpretative plan combining geophysical survey, plotting of aerial photographs, and results from field evaluations. *Drawing by Vanessa Constant: survey data kindly supplied by English Heritage and Gifford and Partners*

Another major group of middle and late first-millennium BC sites was investigated at Boscombe Down West by Kitty Richardson and others in 1948–9 in advance of the construction of the Boscombe Down RAF station (Richardson 1951). In the sixth or fifth century BC this settlement comprised an extensive spread of pits and working hollows on the northern part of the site (Area Q) while about 650m to the south (Area R) was a second area that included pits perhaps set within a small ditched enclosure. The pits were generally large and contained a rich material culture. After the third century BC the site was remodelled with the addition of a double-ditched enclosure, roughly circular in plan with an internal space some 200m across (71B). Many pits were found in the interior, but few were investigated (Richardson 1951). Further evidence of pits and a posthole were recorded at Boscombe Down in 1998 by Wessex Archaeology and may be part of the same settlement.

Several separate finds at Southmill Hill, Amesbury, suggest the presence of a settlement dating to the third and second centuries BC. Numerous pits and a V-sectioned ditch have been reported over a period of more than 50 years (Grinsell 1957, 29; Anon 1976, 134).

West of the River Till, geophysical surveys and evaluation excavations connected with the rerouting of the A303 have provided valuable information about a large site at Scotland

Farm, Winterbourne Stoke, previously known from aerial photography (75). Pits and postholes suggest intensive occupation, but full assessment must await the publication of these investigations.

These sites are probably only a part of what existed in the later first millennium BC. More can be glimpsed from accidental finds and poorly documented remains: storage pits and pottery recorded east of Ogbury Camp by Colt Hoare (1812, 220; Crawford and Keiller 1928, 151); two pits revealed during excavations of the Stonehenge Avenue near West Amesbury (Smith 1973, 50–2); a large circular earthwork at Ratfyn discovered during the construction of a railway line in about 1908 (Hawley 1928, 166–7); a pair of conjoining curvilinear enclosures north of Druid's Lodge, Berwick St James (RCHM 1979, 22); a square-shaped enclosure north of Normanton (RCHM 1979, 24); and a circular example southeast of Druid's Lodge in Woodford parish (RCHM 1979, 25). Stray finds of this date from the area include pottery from superficial contexts at half a dozen or so barrows and a large saddle quern from Druid's Head Wood, Stapleford (Grinsell 1957, 107).

FIELDS AND FARMING

Several of these settlements are closely associated with blocks of fieldsystem whose origins lay back in the late second millennium but which continued in use and were presumably modified and extended during the later first millennium BC. The physical connection between the Parsonage Down system and the hillfort at Yarnbury to the west of the River Till is especially strong. The Scotland Farm settlement seems to bracket the fields to the east with Yarnbury to the west.

Direct evidence for land-use during the later first millennium BC is rather poor. In the Avon Valley a mixture of tillage and pasture is indicated by analysis of colluvium deposits at Fighledean (Graham and Newman 1993, 45–50) while at Vespasian's Camp molluscan evidence suggests the presence nearby of pasture (Hunter-Mann 1999, 49–50).

Connecting the fields and settlements was a series of trackways. Most are now lost although glimpses can be seen in the arrangements of boundaries visible on aerial photographs. Hunter-Mann (1999, 39) suggests that an ancient track known as the Harrow Way may connect the Stonehenge area with southeastern England; it runs past the northern side of Vespasian's Camp.

BURIALS

Burials datable to the later first millennium BC are rare in southern Britain, but several have been found in the Stonehenge landscape. In 1967, a crouched adult inhumation dated to 770–410 BC (UB-3820: 2468±27 BP) was found in a grave cut into the top of the Stonehenge Palisade Ditch (Cleal et al. 1995, 161). Others include: a flexed inhumation in a pit on Parsonage Down, Winterbourne Stoke (Newall 1926); an oval pit in Area R at Boscombe Down West which contained an inhumation burial (Richardson 1951, 131); disarticulated human remains mixed with animal bones and pottery dated to the period 760–400 BC in the upper fill of the Wilsford Shaft (Ashbee et al. 1989, 69); and two pits containing burials at Southmill Hill, Amesbury (Anon 1976, 134). It is also possible that a La Tène I bronze bow brooch from Bush Barrow (Grinsell 1957, 123) once accompanied a burial added to the mound in the third century BC.

TERRITORIES AND TRADE

By the first century AD the Stonehenge area lay on the periphery of several major territorial units, perhaps tribal lands or small kingdoms: the Durotriges to the southwest, the Dobunni to the northwest, the Atrebates to the northeast, and the Belgae to the southeast (76). Coins of the Durotriges in particular have been found in the area: silver staters from Middle Farm, Shrewton, and from Stonehenge or near-by (Robinson 1991), a bronze stater found near Amesbury before 1891 (Grinsell 1957, 29); and another coin said to have been found at Amesbury (Robinson 1991, 119).

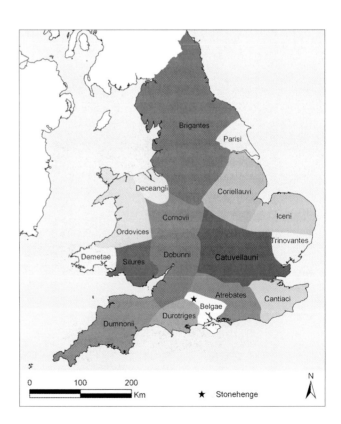

76 Late prehistoric tribal territories in southern Britain. *Drawing by Vanessa Constant: based on Cunliffe 1993, figure 8.1*

The Stonehenge area also lay on the boundary between the southeastern tribes which are sometimes seen as occupying a core area closely tied to the Roman world, and the peripheral tribes who had much less international contact and were perhaps more traditional in their social organization and lifestyles (Cunliffe 1973c; 1991, figure 14.38). One of the very few placenames in the Stonehenge landscape that have survived from later prehistory is that of the River Avon, the Old British *abonā* simply meaning 'river' (Gover et al. 1939, 1; Coles 1994). The direct link provided by this river southwards to the coast may be significant, especially with the development of Hengistbury Head and Poole Harbour as key trading ports on Britain's southern shore. Indeed, a selection of rather unusual coins from the Stonehenge landscape hint that perhaps a few curious travellers from the Mediterranean made their way to Salisbury Plain in much the same way that Pythesus is known to have sailed through the western seaways around 325 BC (Cunliffe 2001). A bronze drachma of the Hellenistic King Menander (*c.*140–80 BC) from 'near Stonehenge' was found before 1880 (Grinsell 1957, 29); a Carthaginian bronze coin was found in March 1956 north of the Boscombe to Amesbury Road; and an Armorican gold stater of the Aulerci Cenomani tribe is known from Lake, Wilsford (Robinson 1991, 119). These could be written off as modern imports, but there is no reason to doubt their ancient credentials (De Jersey 1999). With Gaul under Roman rule from 58 BC it should not be surprising to find connections with the classical world. Against such a background the changing political circumstances consequent on the Roman invasion of AD 43 may not have been such a surprise to the people of the Stonehenge landscape.

8

THE EMPIRE STRIKES BACK
(AD 50–400)

For over a century, southern Britain lay just a short sea-voyage beyond the territorial limits of one of the ancient world's greatest empires. Forays across the Channel by Julius Caesar's armies in 55 and 54 BC seem to have had little impact even on the far southeast of Britain where the forces landed; to those living in the Stonehenge landscape these raids would have registered as scary news reports no doubt hyped by those fearful of change. What exactly the relationship was between southern Britain and Gaul during this period is far from clear: perhaps refugees left Gaul for the relative safety of Britain; maybe Britain resourced local resistance in Gaul; Roman prospectors possibly viewed the natural resources of Britain with envy; maybe old alliances had to supported; certainly there was trade.

Whether Claudius' invasion of AD 43 led by Aulus Plautius and Sentius Saturninus focused on Kent and the far southeast of Britain as traditionally claimed (Frere 1987; Frere and Fulford 2001), or whether it was communities further west in Sussex and Hampshire that found themselves on the front line (Hind 1989), Salisbury Plain was well away from the initial land-falls. Nonetheless, the Stonehenge landscape was within the area taken during the first few years of the conquest as Vespasian and the *Legio II Augusta* advanced westwards (Branigan 1973; Cunliffe 1973d). The area was well to the southeast of the Fosse Way frontier believed to have been established by AD 47 as the new, albeit temporary, edge to the Empire. Manning (1976, 19) notes, however, that north of Old Sarum, across what is now Salisbury Plain, there are no known Roman forts and very little evidence for the presence of the Roman army. The reason is probably the peripheral position of the region relative to the centres of the surrounding tribal territories that were the focus of Roman attention.

Like so many historically imposed life-defining moments, the episode itself is often remembered more fully than events before or after. AD 43 was one such moment for the people of the Stonehenge landscape and over much of southern Britain too. Looked at in the broad terms of everyday lives nothing much changed, even if there was short-term unrest, talk of who to support, and localized tragedy. Within the Stonehenge landscape it is clear that most, if not all, existing settlements continued and perhaps expanded. This is certainly the case at Boscombe Down West, where settlement drift is evident. The double-ditched enclosure discussed in Chapter 7 was the focus of occupation from the later first millennium BC down into the second century AD, but moved northwestwards in the third and fourth centuries AD to create a living area with a cemetery to the south (Richardson 1951, 136). Rather significant in all this are the imported butt beakers and St Remy Ware found in Area P which perhaps arrived from Gaul via Hengistbury Head or Poole Harbour, and the imitation *Terra Nigra* platters brought from eastern England (Richardson 1951, 149–53). These were fine tablewares associated with new ways of celebrating old traditions: eating and drinking. As explained below, much the same happened at Netheravon/Figheldean where occupation of the large, multi-sided enclosure established beside the River Avon in the first or second century BC continued in use, albeit as an unenclosed site, through into the second century AD, to be followed later by the construction of a Roman villa.

A similar picture can be seen in other parts of Salisbury Plain (Bowen and Fowler 1966), with the strongest evidence coming from the Great Ridge – the Nadder/Wylye interfluve – southwest of the Stonehenge landscape. Here are well-preserved single and multi-ditched enclosures and villages such as Ebsbury, Hamshill Ditches, Hanging Langford, and Stockton (Cunnington 1930, 194–5; Corney 1989).

The traditional view of Salisbury Plain in the second to fourth centuries AD is that it was an imperial estate, a *saltus*, and for this reason contained rather few large Roman settlements and villas of the kind found elsewhere across southern Britain (Collingwood and Myres 1937, 224; Branigan 1976, 123). But this view is being gradually eroded by the accumulating evidence (Cunliffe 1973e; 1973f; Graham and Newman 1993, 51–2). Within the Stonehenge landscape the Avon Valley in particular became the focus for occupation with what appear to be villa-based settlements at fairly regular intervals.

FARMS, VILLAS, AND HAMLETS

Settlements dating to the early first millennium AD mainly occur along and around the two main river valleys (77), with a strong focus on the downlands overlooking the river catchments. Many of these settlements were identified by antiquarian finds and early rescue excavations but it is really only since the mid-1980s that firm indications of their nature have come to light as a result of field evaluation and recording work at development sites. In all cases it seems that the areas available for investigation were peripheral to the main occupation zones so there is considerable potential for further research. It is also worth noting that northwards, within the Salisbury Plain Training Area (SPTA), what appear to be rather different kinds of settlement involving compact villages, linear villages, and extensive evidence of cultivation have been revealed by detailed ground survey and the study of aerial photographs (McOmish et al. 2002, 88–106). Whether similar arrangements were also present on the downlands around Stonehenge remains to be seen.

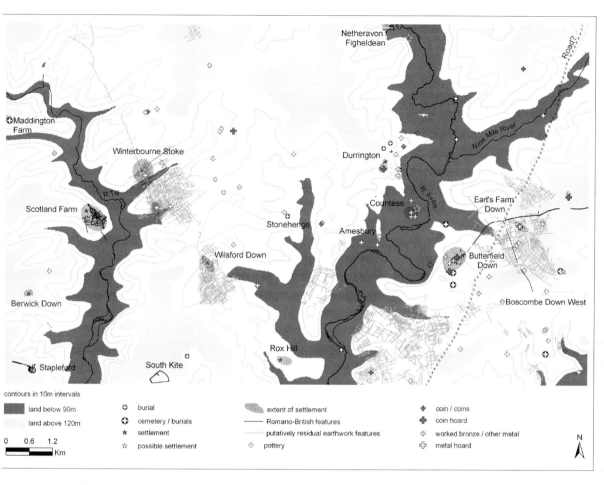

77 Map of the Stonehenge landscape showing the distribution of recorded sites and findspots dating to the period *c.*AD 50–450. *Drawing by Vanessa Constant: Wiltshire SMR and various archaeological sources over mapping from EDX Engineering Inc. data at 50m intervals and Ordnance Survey © Crown Copyright 2006. All rights reserved. Licence 100045276*

East of the Avon

At Butterfield Down, Amesbury, a substantial unenclosed hamlet of about 6ha has been pieced together from a series of field evaluations and excavations over several years (Rawlings and Fitzpatrick 1996, 38–40). Unlike some of the settlements already mentioned this site begins in the second century AD. Rectangular timber-framed buildings with cobwalls seem to have been built. Most were roofed with thatch but some had ceramic or stone tiles. A T-shaped corn-drying oven lay between buildings, while lines of small postholes suggest that the settlement was divided by fences into a series of compounds. Hollow-ways led through the site and out into the surrounding countryside. Cattle and sheep were the most common farm animals represented, the cattle in particular being butchered in such a way as to provide complete hides. Pigs were also eaten, as too were hares and chickens. Horses were rarely eaten but were used for riding and as beasts of burden. Wheat and barley grains as well as crop-processing waste suggest arable cultivation in the area; millstones show grain was converted to flour on-site. Infant burials were found within the settlement; a common Roman practice. A shallow ring-gully possibly represents the remains of a shrine. A bronze and iron sceptre-head showing a bird, perhaps an eagle, perched on a branch came from above the ring-gully, while the deliberate burial of a crow in a pit some distance away to the east may somehow form part of connected rituals. Most of the pottery from the site came from either the New Forest industries to the south or the Oxfordshire industries to the northeast, but finewares included Samian and Rhenish Ware from Gaul. An ivory pin from the fill of the corn-drier has a neat spherical head, dates to the period after AD 200, and was probably imported from the Mediterranean as a hair-pin or garment fastener. Excavations nearby in advance of constructing a new school on the eastern outskirts of Amesbury revealed an inhumation cemetery of the third and fourth centuries AD that may be the burial ground of the Butterfield Down community. Some of the 36 inhumation burials lay within what has been interpreted as a garden of remembrance, and there is some suggestion that these may be early Christian burials (Fitzpatrick 2003a, 147).

Occupation at Boscombe Down West was long-lived and, as already mentioned, started here in the later first millennium BC (Richardson 1951). The inner ditch of the prehistoric enclosure seems to have filled up by the time of the Roman conquest, but the outer ditch remained open and delimited a settlement that continued well into the second century AD. In the late third century the focus of settlement shifted but again the primary evidence is from pits that contained mainly New Forest Ware. About 500m to the south was an enclosed inhumation cemetery of 17 or more graves. Four of the burials were in wooden coffins. Some of the corpses, males and females, had been buried with their boots on; three had simple grave goods including a bronze dolphin brooch, a bone comb, and a small pottery vessel. Plant remains included emmer wheat, bread wheat, club wheat, spelt, and barley; birch, holly, beech, birch, and oak charcoal illustrated the range of wood species exploited by the users of the site. Animal bones represent cattle, horse, sheep/goat, pig, red deer, fox, raven, and frog. Compared with Boscombe Down this seems to be a much smaller, simpler, and poorer settlement in the later Roman period.

A third settlement in this area is on Earl's Farm Down (Cunnington 1930, 173; Grinsell 1957, 30). The foundations of buildings together with a scatter of pottery suggest a substantial site but it has not been explored in any detail. Other possible settlements also need further investigation to define their character.

Avon Valley
Just north of the Stonehenge landscape is what appears to be a Roman villa to the southwest of Netheravon House. Discovered in 1907 during the construction of a military base, the site was the scene of a *Time Team* investigation for Channel 4 television in 1996 (Grinsell 1957, 90–1; Rawlings 2001). A hoard of coins is said to have been found

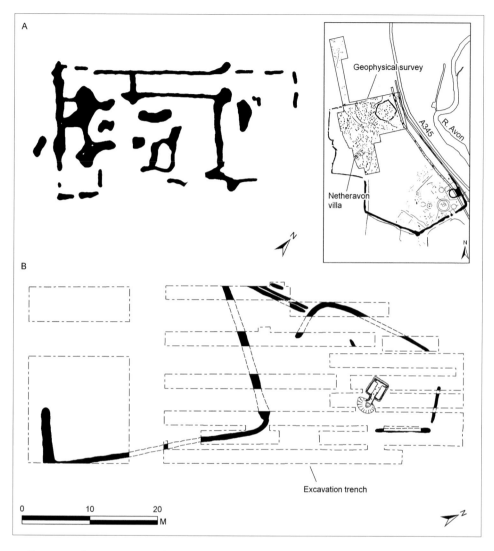

78 Roman settlements. A: Corridor-type villa at Netheravon. B: Enclosures and agricultural facilities at Durrington Walls. *Drawing by Vanessa Constant: A after McOmish et al. 2002, figure 3.31; B after Wainwright 1971, figures 5 and 6*

nearby and may be associated (Cunnington 1930, 198). The discoveries to date show that the main building that it was built and used in the third and early fourth centuries AD, that it had stone walls, and was roofed with stone tiles of several different colours. A mosaic floor was found in 1907, and possibly also a bath. Painted wall plaster was recovered, but insufficient detail of the walls and floors is known to allow a ground-plan of the building to be reconstructed. The 1996 evaluations suggest earlier phases to the use of the site, including a ditch of the first or second century AD.

Moving southwards, excavations in 1991 and 1995 for pipelines west of the River Avon at Netheravon and Figheldean on the extreme edge of the Stonehenge landscape revealed a long-lived settlement already referred to above (Graham and Newman 1993, 34–6; McKinley 1999). The boundary of the polygonal enclosure seems to have become filled by the first century AD, but occupation continued within and around it. A small, rectangular ditched compound was built in the southeastern quarter, and numerous linear boundaries suggest drainage works related to cultivation nearby. A T-shaped corn-drying kiln was also found, together with ceramic building materials and stone slates suggesting the presence of fairly substantial structures. Good samples of animal bones and carbonized plant remains show the importance of wheat and barley to an economy that focused on grazing sheep/goats with lesser amounts of cattle. The range of wild plants and weeds from the site gives an impression of the diversity represented in the Roman landscape: corn gromwell, campions, orache, goosefoot, lesser knapweed, medicks, poppies, plantain, knotgrass, sheep's sorrel, buttercups, cleavers, eyebright, bartsia, corn salad, fat hen, chickweed, bindweed, dock, tare, red clover, mugwort, mayweed, foxtail, various grasses and other legumes. Very little imported fineware was present amongst the pottery, most being Samian and Oxfordshire Ware. Coarsewares included Savernake Ware and New Forest Ware, with a little Black Burnished Ware imported from kilns around Poole Harbour. Subsequent geophysical surveys in the area have revealed the presence of a corridor-type villa building in the northwestern sector of the enclosure (McOmish et al. 2002, figure 3.31; 78A). This building lies about 100m west of an area in which nine burials were found in 1991 and 1995; although scattered they suggest the presence of a small associated cemetery. Most of the corpses had been buried with their boots on. Grave 61 was rather unusual in that it contained the remains of a dog whose tail had been cut off and placed in front of the face of the human burial, presumably the dog's owner (Graham and Newman 1993, 23).

About 4km south again is another area of Romano-British settlement of later third- and fourth-century date sampled by excavation prior to tree-planting west of Durrington Walls (Wainwright 1971; and see RCHM 1979, 24). Postholes, pits, gullies, and hollows were recorded south of Fargo Road, while on the north side were two small ditched enclosures, one containing a corn-drying kiln and two infant burials (78B). These features were regarded as peripheral agricultural facilities, with the main focus of the settlement, perhaps a villa of some kind, lying on the higher ground to the west. Pieces of stone and ceramic roofing tile from the excavations hint at a substantial structure in the vicinity, and the quality of finds, which includes a handful of coins and a fair amount of fine pottery, suggests a well-appointed site in this commanding position. Sheep were again best represented among the animal remains, cattle second, with lesser amounts of dog, horse, and pig. The scale of the site is considerable to judge from quantities of Samian and other pottery recovered over many years from both sides of Fargo Road on Durrington Down (Cunnington 1930, 186; and see Richards 1990, figure 17). An inhumation burial set within a ditched enclosure was found at the Durrington Reservoir in 1991 (Cleal et al. 2004) and may be associated with this settlement. However, an analysis of cropmarks revealed on aerial photographs of the area west of Woodhenge suggests at least two other enclosures and the boundary works of a fieldsystem spread over an area of 20ha that can plausibly be connected to the Durrington Walls settlement. There is also what appears to be a small compact cemetery on the southwest side of this extensive complex (McOmish 2001, figure 4.3).

South again, around Countess Farm and to the northwest of the Countess Roundabout, is a scatter of Roman material found by metal detectorists (Darvill 1993b, 63–8). This has since been confirmed as an area of late Roman occupation as a result of field evaluations for the proposed Stonehenge visitor centre on the east side of Countess Road (WA 2003; 2004).

South of Amesbury evidence of Roman settlement appears less abundant but this is probably a result of fewer opportunities to uncover it. Finds made over a long period at Boscombe Road/New Covert in Amesbury suggest another extensive site here, but further investigations are needed to show its nature. A pot containing a hoard of bronze and silver coins and three silver finger-rings was found in *c*.1842; more recently a midden and pits were seen by Mr St John Booth (Cunnington 1930, 172; Grinsell 1957, 30).

A small bronze figure of Mercury from near Durnford on the southern limits of the Stonehenge landscape (Henig 2003) may suggest the presence of another settlement or shrine hereabouts.

Avon–Till interfluve

On the high ground between the Avon and the Till there is evidence for occupation in four areas, although none has been investigated. Wilsford Down has yielded a number of brooches, ornaments, and ironwork (Cunnington 1930, 208; Grinsell 1957, 122) and was revealed by a pottery scatter in the fieldwalking undertaken for the Stonehenge Environs Project (Richards 1990, figure 17). At Normanton Ditch, Wilsford, a hoard of pewter is recorded as having been ploughed up *c*.1635 (Cunnington 1930, 208; Grinsell 1957, 123).

A second area of Roman settlement is represented by earthworks and two groups of finds, connected by a linear ditch or hollow-way (*79*), one either side of the Amesbury to Shrewton road on Winterbourne Stoke Down (Colt Hoare 1812, plan opp. 170; Cunnington 1930, 209).

A third area of settlement may lie on Rox Hill to judge from a scatter of Roman pottery recorded during the Stonehenge Environs Project (Richards 1990, figure 17), possibly the Romano-British village referred to by Colt Hoare (1812, 227; Cunnington 1930, 208).

Finally, a trapezoidal enclosure known as the South Kite, Stapleford, may be of early Roman date. No investigations have been carried out, but nearby is a single burial that may also be of this period.

Till Valley and west of the Till

West of the Till, there are again substantial traces of Roman occupation at four sites. The most extensively studied is Maddington Farm, Shrewton, on the very far western side of

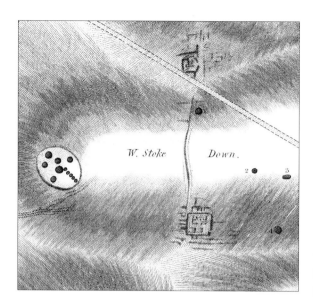

79 Romano-British settlement on Winterbourne Stoke Down depicted by Colt Hoare. *From Colt Hoare 1812, plan opp. 170*

the Stonehenge landscape. Here, two burials found during the construction of a pipeline led to the excavation of a wider area and the identification of a small farmstead of third- and fourth-century date together with an associated inhumation cemetery (McKinley and Heaton 1996). Nine burials were found altogether, including two laid in a crouched position and one that was accompanied by a small dog. As at sites in the Avon Valley, wheat and barley were represented in the palaeobotanical assemblages while sheep/goat were most numerous among the animal bones. Cattle, horse, pig, and dog were also present, as well as fowl and eel. Finewares from the Oxfordshire and New Forest industries, and small amounts of Samian made up 7 per cent of the ceramic assemblage, a higher proportion than at Durrington, Butterfield Down, or Figheldean. Coarsewares include Black Burnished Ware, New Forest Ware, and vessels from the North Wiltshire industries.

Cunnington (1930, 209) recorded another settlement on High Down, Winterbourne Stoke, northwest of the Coniger, confirmed as Roman by Colt Hoare (1812, 95). On Berwick Down in the southwest corner of the Stonehenge landscape there is further extensive evidence of Roman occupation, tested 'by the spade' by Colt Hoare in the nineteenth century (Cunnington 1930, 174). This site is adjacent to the D-shaped enclosure at Scotland Farm on the north side of the A303 (see 75). And further south still the small enclosure at Stapleford may also be of this date.

FIELDS AND ECONOMY

Some of the fieldsystems within the Stonehenge landscape undoubtedly originated in the early first millennium AD, while many earlier ones continued in use. The Fargo Road settlement noted above is located on the periphery of a major fieldsystem and lynchets were recognized within the excavation areas (Wainwright 1971). The same applies at Netheravon/Figheldean. Overall, the investigated sites show a remarkably consistent pattern of mixed agriculture, involving cereal cultivation and animal husbandry with a heavy reliance on sheep/goats which were presumably grazed on the adjacent downland. Cattle and pigs were perhaps kept in and around the settlement itself, the cattle grazing the lower ground. Every farm seems to have had a dog, and horses would have been a common sight.

Investment in agricultural infrastructure was important, with several reported grain-driers. These may well have been used as malting floors for the processing of barley for use in brewing beer (Reynolds 1979). Few if any of the sites were wealthy in the way that villas in the Cotswolds or the Chilterns seem to have been, but they had wide links into local markets that in turn connected to the main pottery producers in central southern Britain and also stocked finewares from Gaul and beyond.

VISITING THE PAST

Many of the prehistoric monuments in the landscape seem to have attracted attention and perhaps occasional visits during Roman times as pottery and coins have been recovered at several barrows (see for example Cunnington 1929; Newall 1931, 432; Ashbee 1980; Hunter-Mann 1999). Stonehenge itself was clearly frequented during the Roman period as a fairly substantial collection of finds suggests: 20 coins ranging in date from AD 41–50 through to AD 330–95; pottery (1857 sherds found in twentieth-century excavations); and personal ornaments, brooches, pins, toilet equipment, and possibly some graffiti (Cleal et al. 1995, 431–5 and 491). At Woodhenge the excavations of 1926–8 revealed the remains of infant burials in the upper ditch fills associated with Romano-British pottery and there is a possibility that the infant buried in the centrally placed grave at the site is also of this date (Cunnington 1929, 60). Whether these visits were made out of curiosity or convenience, or because of some residual significance attached to the place, is not known.

Apart from the possible shrine at Butterfield Down, Romano-Celtic temples are rather rare in central southern Britain. Notable, however, is the example 45km northwest of Stonehenge at Nettleton Scrubb, Wiltshire, which, rather interestingly, was dedicated to Apollo (Wedlake 1982).

BURIALS AND CEMETERIES

Where extensive excavations have taken place it seems that most settlements had associated burial grounds nearby, typically within 500m or so, and these have been described in

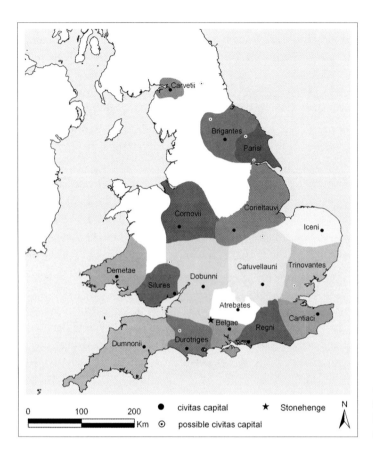

80 Roman *civitates* in southern Britain. *Drawing by Vanessa Constant:* based on *Frere 1967, 1*

previous sections. Elsewhere in the landscape, graves of this period have been recorded at three other sites: inhumations at Idmiston, excavated in 1995 but not yet published, and Ratfyn (Grinsell 1957, 29); and a cremation southeast of Milston Farmhouse, Figheldean. Most probably, these burials signal further settlements in the vicinity.

Anne Foster (2001) has emphasized the continuity of inhumation burial in Wiltshire from later prehistoric times into the first millennium AD, well shown by the presence of two crouched burials seemingly of the third or fourth century AD at Maddington Farm, Shrewton. Throughout the area grave goods are relatively rare and some at least of the undated burials known in the Stonehenge landscape may well be of Romano-British date.

LANDSCAPES AND TERRITORIES

Running through the Stonehenge landscape there would have been a network of roads and tracks, connecting the villas and farmsteads together and linking the area with major long-distance routes. The only substantial Roman road identified within the Stonehenge landscape is the Old Sarum (*Sorviodunum*) to Mildenhall (*Cvetio*) road that is likely to be a Romanized trackway established in the first millennium BC. The trackway passes just east of Amesbury, running in a north-northeasterly direction, through Boscombe Down Camp and Bulford Camp, although its precise route on the ground has never been tested (Margary 1973, 99–100). Other nearby routeways include the Harrow Way, and the Old Sarum to Mendip Hills road that passed just south of the Stonehenge landscape (Margary 1973, 101–3).

The nearest major settlement for communities living in the Stonehenge landscape was 5km to the south at *Sorviodunum* beside the River Avon around Old Sarum and modern-day Stratford-sub-Castle (James 2002). Here a fairly substantial settlement developed around a junction of four or five roads, comparable in size to many of the 'small towns' across southern Britain (Burnham and Watcher 1990). The nearest major town, the local *civitas* capital, was Winchester (*Venta Belgarum*) about 35km to the southeast, easily accessible by main road from *Sorviodunum*. As in earlier times, the Stonehenge landscape lies right on the edge of several territories (*80*) and there may have been some ambivalence about which tribal unit or *civitas* people hereabouts were affiliated to. Even in the late Roman period when these small political units had been replaced by larger regions the people of Stonehenge lived very near a major boundary, that between *Britannia Prima* to the west and *Maxima Caesariensis* to the east (Jones and Mattingly 2002, 148).

Overall, the density of occupation during the early first millennium AD, the fairly regular spacing of settlement sites, and the homogeneity of the local economy suggests that this was a stable and productive area, prosperous but not rich. By the late fourth century the main river valleys had become the focus of settlement, and on the basis of much earlier land divisions and fieldsystems had access to valley-land and adjacent upland that well suited a mixed agricultural economy.

9

FROM AMBROSIUS TO DOMESDAY
(AD 400–1100)

The disintegration of the Roman Empire in the early fifth century AD had ramifications throughout northern Europe, including the Stonehenge landscape, but the cracks started much earlier. Many towns became de-urbanized after about AD 300 and while a degree of prosperity can be seen in rural settlements during the fourth century these too decline from AD 350 onwards. By the later fourth century things had changed, and changed drastically. Richard Reece has gone so far as to suggest that people at this time were 'turning their back on wholesome Roman society with its careful safeguards and limiting ordnances for the wildness of the hairy Dark Age potentate, or perhaps leaving the effete Roman administration with its silks and perfumes, even for the so-called men, for the homespun roughness and basic sense of the British cattle-raider. Moving out of light and organization, for a penumbra of cured hams, sheeps wool and only local knowledge' (1988, 124). Economic uncertainty, religious division, administrative weakness, and a revulsion from fashion, it is perhaps small wonder that an essentially tribal organization re-emerged, strangely reminiscent of how things had been perhaps 500 years before. Local warlords protected their people, but unlike earlier times the names of some of these colourful characters have come down to us through oral traditions and legend: Ambrosius, Arthur, Eldol, Vortigern, and others. The great deeds of these heroes were narrated, however inaccurately, in the writings of the first British chroniclers and historians, many of whom were churchmen. These include Gildas (*c.*AD 516–70), Bede (*c.*AD 673–735), Nennius (*c.*AD 760–810), Henry of Huntingdon (*c.*AD 1084–155), and Geoffrey of Monmouth (*c.*AD 1100–1155), the last two of which also discuss Stonehenge (see Chapter 2). And from this point forward it becomes necessary to integrate the purely archaeological evidence with tradition, myth, folklore, and early written historical sources, a task that is never easy.

Immigrants from lands across the North Sea and beyond may well have been a familiar sight in southern Britain during late Roman times, and their numbers probably increased through the fifth century. Personal ornaments and small-scale traditions projecting their identity and in some small way preserving their cultural heritage betray their existence,

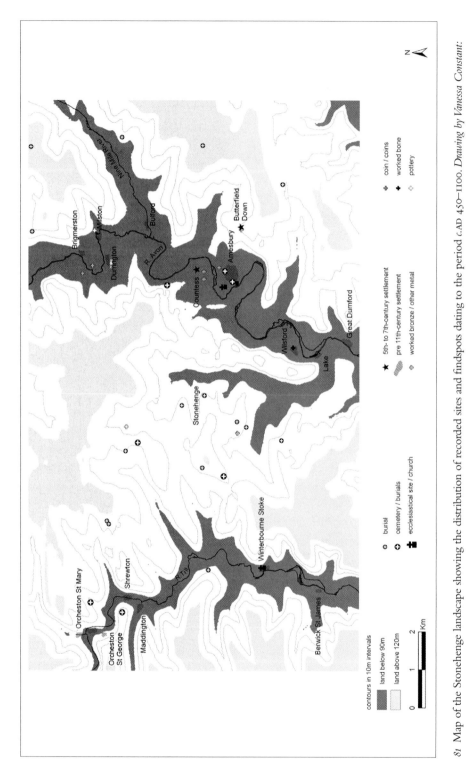

81 Map of the Stonehenge landscape showing the distribution of recorded sites and findspots dating to the period *c.*AD 450–1100. *Drawing by Vanessa Constant: Wiltshire SMR and various archaeological sources over mapping from EDX Engineering Inc. data at 50m intervals and Ordnance Survey © Crown Copyright 2006. All rights reserved. Licence 100045276*

but like so many who came here in later centuries their names are rarely recorded and from the fifth century we know of few besides the brothers Hengist and Horsa.

Bruce Eagles (2001) has argued that Germanic migrations into Wiltshire took place within the framework of the former Romano-British *civitates*, with the Avon Valley seeing an Anglo-Saxon presence relatively early, accompanied by the development of new cultural identities and social order among local communities. The River Avon itself was undoubtedly a significant route into Wessex from the south coast, and recent finds around Breamore south of Salisbury have led to suggestions that the river below Charford was within Jutish territory (Yorke 1989) while its northern part was firmly within Anglo-Saxon lands, perhaps the territory of the *Wilsaete* (Eagles 1994; 2004, 93).

Within a landscape populated by groups of diverse ethnic origin and affinity unrest was endemic and conflict common. Numerous battles between Britons and Saxons and later between Saxons and Danes have been recorded, and attempts made to pinpoint the battlegrounds and map the changing political geography of the later first millennium AD (Alcock 1971). During the later fifth century AD the Stonehenge area was perhaps in the hands of Aurelius Ambrosius, a native Briton mentioned by several early historians. His reputation was so great that in Geoffrey of Monmouth's account he was ultimately responsible for the construction of Stonehenge as a memorial to the 480 British chiefs treacherously massacred by the Jutish mercenary Hengist (Thorpe 1973, 190). Who came after Ambrosius we do not know, but the *Anglo-Saxon Chronicle* records that in about AD 552 the Britons hereabout lost a battle with the Saxons led by Cynric at a place called *Searoburgh* (Garmonsway 1972, 16) which is generally recognized as Old Sarum (Gover et al. 1939, xiii). As a result the pagan Saxons controlled the chalklands of Salisbury Plain from the mid-sixth century onwards. Any pockets of Roman Christianity that had developed during the fourth century no doubt went underground or largely disappeared.

LATE ROMAN AND ANGLO-SAXON SETTLEMENT

At least two of the main Roman settlements in the eastern part of the Stonehenge landscape show evidence of more-or-less continuous occupation into the fifth century and perhaps beyond (*81*). At Butterfield Down on the high ground east of the Avon excavations in 1990–3 revealed a sunken-floor building containing much third- and fourth-century AD pottery (Rawlings and Fitzpatrick 1996, 13–14; *82*), perhaps an example of the increasingly widely recognized class of late Roman native British sunken-floor or terraced structures seen also at Figheldean Site A (Graham and Newman 1983, 19–22) and further afield at Poundbury, Dorset, and Godshill, Hampshire (Eagles 2001, 210). At Butterfield Down further evidence of early fifth-century occupation is a hoard of coins, eight gold and one silver, found by a metal detectorist outside the area of the excavations. The hoard was probably deposited in a small New Forest Ware globular beaker and dates to sometime after AD 405. The eight gold coins were *solidi*, one of Gratian (AD 367–83), two of Valentinian II (AD 375–92), one of Arcadius (AD 383–408), and four of Honorius (AD 393–423). The silver coin was a *siliqua* of Arcadius. This is one of the latest Roman coin hoards found in Britain to date, and in contemporary terms represented a small fortune (Rawlings and Fitzpatrick 1996, 19).

The second site, perhaps slightly later in date, lies in the Avon Valley around the present-day Countess Roundabout on the A303. Anglo-Saxon pottery was found during field evaluations on the site of the proposed Stonehenge visitor centre northeast of Countess Roundabout in 1995 (WA 1995, 19) and at least two brooches of the same period have been found in the area (Darvill 1993b, 63–8). Other finds of mid-first-millennium AD date have been reported from the Avon Valley north of Amesbury (McOmish et al. 2002, 109 and figure 5.1) but the focus of this activity was not identified until 2003–4 when further field evaluations were undertaken on the site of the proposed visitor centre (WA 2003; 2004). During this work five sunken-floor buildings were recorded, seemingly all of the classic Germanic *Grubenhaus* form with a large posthole at either end of the sunken area. Pottery attributable to the period from the fifth to eighth centuries AD, including organic tempered ware, was recovered, together with charred cereal grain and animal bone representing sheep, cattle, and chicken. These are the first such buildings to have been found in the Stonehenge landscape and they suggest a substantial settlement in this fairly low-lying area. The discovery in 1834 of a group of inhumation burials, long considered sub-Roman or early Saxon in date, about 300m south of the Countess settlement suggests the strong possibility of a contemporary cemetery (Bonney 1982; Chandler and Goodhugh 1989, 6); further burials were noted in London Road in 2003 but not dated (Anon 2003, 349).

It is likely that other nearby sites were occupied at this time, as for example Vespasian's Camp (Hunter-Mann 1999, 51), but in all cases firm archaeological evidence is lacking. However, a clear indication of the widespread, and fairly intensive, Pagan Saxon settlement of the area comes from the distribution of burials.

BURIALS AND CEMETERIES

Leslie Grinsell (1959, 61–4) has noted that in southern Britain it was common for a prehistoric burial monument reused in the later first millennium AD to be referred to as a *beorh* or *hlaew*, whereas only the word *hlaew* was normally used for newly constructed barrows. Although no new Anglo-Saxon barrows appear to have been built in the Stonehenge landscape, numerous earlier mounds were reused even though their names have not survived. Grinsell (1957) gives examples from all but three of the 16 modern parishes that include territory within the Stonehenge landscape (*81*), and to these can be added other burials and finds that probably derive from disturbed burials or which have been found since Grinsell compiled his listing:

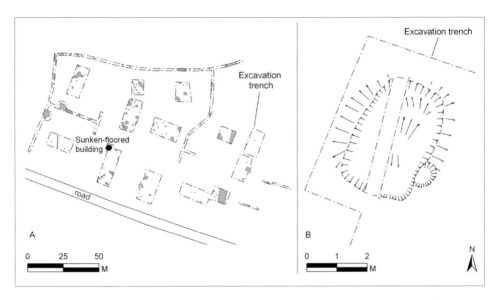

82 Sunken-floor hut and related features at Butterfield Down, Amesbury. A: General plan of excavation trenches and features. B: Detail of the sunken-floored building. *Drawing by Vanessa Constant: after Rawlings and Fitzpatrick 1996, figures 8 and 10*

Amesbury: Barrow 44, intrusive interment. Barrow 85, socketed iron spearhead and other objects perhaps associated with an intrusive interment. Stonehenge, up to three burials (see below).

Bulford: socketed iron spearhead found on Bulford Down in 1861 and a similar piece found at Bulford Camp in 1906.

Durnford: Barrow 1 or 2, intrusive interment.

Durrington: Barrow ?, a skull possibly from an intrusive interment. Possible cemetery site of 30+ graves (see below).

Figheldean: Barrow 25, intrusive interment inferred from the socketed iron spearhead found. Netheravon Aerodrome, find of an interment believed to have been deposited in a wooden coffin. A bronze late Saxon mount from Knighton Farm (Robinson 1992, 66, no. 5) suggests a nearby settlement.

Idmiston: Barrow 23, intrusive interment with iron shield-boss that is unlikely to be later than the mid-sixth century AD, socketed iron spearhead, and wooden bucket with bronze mounts.

Milston: Barrow 3, intrusive interment. Barrow 7, intrusive interment; small pot and fragment from a comb above a chalkpit.

Netheravon: two burials found during the construction of the Aviation School in 1913, one accompanied by weapons, a bronze pin, and perhaps a bucket.

Orcheston: Elston, inhumations (one adult and one youth) with an iron knife found before 1856 (Robinson 1987).

Shrewton: Shrewton Windmill, inhumation accompanied by a bronze armlet, ?girdle-hanger, iron knife, and pot. A second burial was found in the same area in 1968. A split iron spearhead suggests a third unlocated burial in the parish. Northwest of the allotment gardens at Maddington, a substantial inhumation cemetery (Wilson and Hurst 1968, 241).

Wilsford: Barrow 3, intrusive interment. Barrow 50b, intrusive interment. Long barrow 30, intrusive interment.

Winterbourne Stoke: Barrow 4, five intrusive interments. Barrow 61, intrusive interment. Barrow 23a, glass bead of Saxon type suggestive of an intrusive burial.

Woodford: socketed iron spearhead found in 1863.

The possible cemetery on Durrington Down found in 1864 is intriguing. Grinsell (1957, 66) suggested that it is near Fargo and that the graves were oriented north to south. Ruddle (1901, 331) indicated that they were in an arable field near the Durrington/Winterbourne Stoke boundary and that while 30 were found only two were laid north to south. He also mentioned that these two burials had flints set like a low wall around and over the skeletons (and see RCHM 1979, 7). Unfortunately, the exact position of this find is not known. It may be significant, however, that the examination of Durrington 7 on Durrington Down as part of the Stonehenge Environs Project revealed a scatter of grass-tempered Saxon pottery (Richards 1990, 182). In addition, Maud Cunnington found a group of 11 inhumations in shallow graves intrusive to barrow Durrington 67 (Cunnington 1929, 43–4; RCHM 1979, 7). Taken together these finds suggest the strong possibility of one or more Saxon occupation sites and cemeteries along the high ground between Fargo Road and Fargo Plantation, perhaps related to the continued use of the Roman site west of Durrington Walls (see Chapter 8).

Much the same applies to the discoveries around Shrewton, most of which are from northwest of the modern village not far from Roman site at Maddington Farm, although it is notable that nothing later than about AD 400 was found there during excavations in 1993 (McKinley and Heaton 1996).

Not all burials in the area followed conventional Pagan Saxon traditions; two in particular illuminate quite different aspects of how the dead were treated. The first is an extraordinary 'bog burial' at Lake in the Woodford Valley (McKinley 2003). Radiocarbon dated to AD 400–620 (GU-4921: 1560±50 BP), this was the burial of a young adult female aged about 20–25 years at death. She had been buried fully prone and extended, with the left arm flexed with the hand resting on the abdomen and the right arm fully extended. The body had been covered with at least 18 oak planks (*83*). The position of the grave adjacent to the River Avon in a wetland context raises the question of whether this was a ritual burial or a sacrifice of some kind, and also shows a persistent interest in the traditional power of watery places in the landscape (see Chapter 6).

The second unusual burial comes from Stonehenge itself, an inhumation found by Hawley in November 1923 adjacent to Y-Hole 9, just outside the Sarsen Circle in the

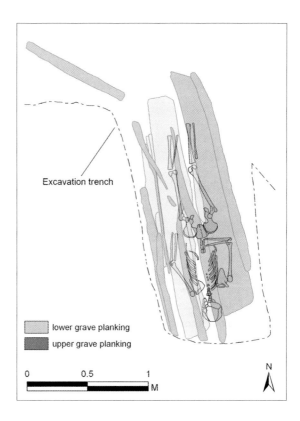

Excavation trench

lower grave planking
upper grave planking

83 Bog-burial at Lake. *Drawing by Vanessa Constant: after McKinley 2003, figure 2*

0   0.5   1
M

N

southeast sector. At the time of excavation it was discounted as Roman or later and of no great interest (Hawley 1925, 30–1). The roughly cut, rather shallow grave contained the slightly contracted remains of an adult male aged about 28–32 years at death. The grave was flanked by two postholes (*84*). Radiocarbon determinations have now shown it to be of the seventh century AD (AS 610–780 (OxA-9361: 1359±38 BP) and AD 430–660 (OxA-9921: 1490±60 BP)) and forensic analysis suggests a traumatic death through decapitation by a single blow with a sharp blade from the rear-right side of the back of the neck. Scientific studies of the individual's tooth enamel suggest that during his childhood he lived fairly locally, to the northeast of Stonehenge (Pitts 2001a, 319–20; Pitts et al. 2002). In the light of this evidence the two postholes near the burial can be interpreted as the remains of a gallows and the possibility raised that Stonehenge was an execution site in middle Saxon times. At least two other undated inhumations were found by Hawley at Stonehenge, one in the outer ditch and another within the Bluestone Horseshoe, while a human tarsal was found near the Heelstone in a context containing medieval pottery (Pitts 1982, 90). In addition, a small amount of organic tempered Saxon pottery and a penny of Aethelred II (Cleal et al. 1995, 432–5) serve to strengthen the evidence for considerable activity at the site in the later first millennium AD. Cunnington (1933a, 171) also refers to an Anglo-Saxon silver belt ornament from the site in Salisbury Museum.

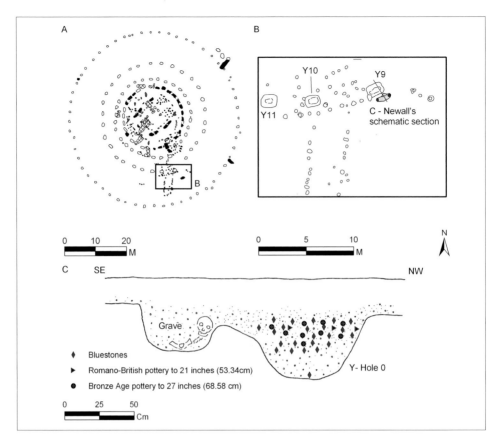

84 Burial and possible gallows at Stonehenge. A: Stonehenge with the area of the detailed plan (B) indicated. C: Section through the grave and Stonehole Y-Hole 9. *Drawing by Vanessa Constant: after Pitts* et al. *2002, figure 2*

The liminal position of Stonehenge and its powerful associations with an ancient order made the site ideal for executions, a point that links with David Hinton's comments on the derivation of the very name of the site – the stone hanging place (Hinton 1998; and see Pitts et al. 2002, 139–43).

Further evidence of execution may be provided by the cleft skull of one of the intrusive burials in the Wilsford 3 long barrow near the Wilsford–Charlton parish boundary (Cunnington 1914, 403).

LANDSCAPE AND POLITICAL ORGANIZATION

It was during the later first millennium AD, after the conquests by the West Saxons, that many of the administrative units so familiar in later times first came into being. Some of the units that were later known as hundreds (see below) may have been established as early as the seventh century (Yorke 1995, 89–90), perhaps reflecting a post-Roman tribal landscape of so-called 'micro-kingdoms' (Pitts et al. 2002, 143). And at a still wider geographical scale a pattern of relatively stable kingdoms had become established by the ninth century, the Stonehenge landscape being comfortably within the Kingdom of Wessex (*85*), which rather interestingly shows many similarities with the much earlier territories within which Stonehenge lay.

Increasing centralization of administration during the tenth and eleventh centuries favoured the royal centre at Wilton in the Wylye Valley as a focal point, such that by the reign of Alfred (AD 871–99) the people of the whole region between the Thames and Cranborne Chase regarded the royal village as their capital.

Throughout this process some traditional placenames remained but many were supplanted by names better understood by the new elite, while creations such as the barrows already referred to were given names meaningful to the Germanic tongue. Most of the settlements along the Avon Valley and the Till Valley have names ending in *–tun*, an Old English suffix generally meaning a piece of enclosed land with dwellings on it,

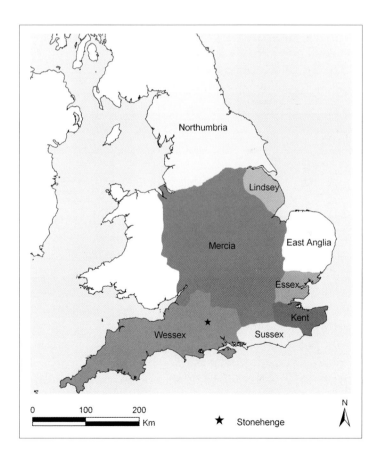

85 Anglo-Saxon and contemporary kingdoms in southern Britain. *Drawing by Vanessa Constant: based on Hill 1981, figure 42*

as in Milston, Shrewton, and Orcheston for example (Mawer and Stenton 1969, 61–2). Slightly more complicated are the *–ington* names in the Avon Valley, Durrington and Allington, where the first part of the name refers to a former owner of the land, in this case perhaps *Dēora* and *Ealda* respectively (Gover et al. 1939, 358 and 365). Also common are names with the suffix *–ford*, as for example in Durnford, Bulford, and Wilsford which simply denote river crossings. There are two names with *–burh* suffixes that come down to us as Ogbury and Amesbury, both meaning a fortified place (Mawer and Stenton 1969, 10). In the case of Ogbury it is probably an ancient fortification that is being referred to, but with *Ambresbyrig*, modern-day Amesbury, it probably relates to the development of a small *burh* within a much broader network of defended sites providing a measure of security for the inhabitants of the Kingdom of Wessex (Hinton 1977, 75).

AMESBURY

The town of Amesbury has been subject to several historical investigations which together provide a tentative picture of its early development and the relocation of occupation from the strongly defended Vespasian's Camp eastwards into the valley of the Avon (Hinton 1975; Haslam 1984, 130; Chandler and Goodhugh 1989). The first references to Amesbury are in Saxon land charters: the will of King Alfred (d.899) bequeathing (*aet*) *Ambresbyrig* to his younger son Aethelweard, and lands left in King Eadred's (d.955) will to his mother Eadgifu (Finberg 1964). It has been suggested that the placename *aet Ambresbyrig* probably indicates its early existence as a *burh* or fortification belonging to *Ambre* (Gover et al. 1939, 358). Indeed, the placename *Ambre* may have pre-Saxon origins and perhaps represents the name of the semi-mythical hero Ambrosius, legends of whom were well established by the eighth century (Gover et al. 1939, 358; Morris 1973, 100). If so, it may support the notion that Ambrosius Aurelianus established a garrison as resistance against the Saxon invaders during the third quarter of the fifth century (Bond 1991, 385). Alternatively, the personal element could represent *Ambri*, who is mentioned in Geoffrey of Monmouth's legend of Stonehenge, and 'of the hill of *Ambrius*', although Geoffrey does not specify where this was (Chandler and Goodhugh 1989, 5).

If the origins of Amesbury are obscure, so too is the detail of its early development. Even the location of its ancient heart is largely conjectural, the best estimate being that it lies somewhere near the river crossing at Queensbury Bridge, east of Vespasian's Camp, perhaps extending along the present High Street (Chandler and Goodhugh 1987, 7). If it was the centre of a royal estate, as has been suggested (Haslam 1976, 5), then it may have been the main settlement for estate staff and in time have become a small town (Hinton 1975, 27–8). It is also possible that there was a minster church here, a headquarters for priests working throughout the estate and a mother church for all local Christian worshippers. The king certainly held assemblies (the Witan) at Amesbury in AD 932 and AD 995 (Bond 1991, 386), and in AD 979 a Benedictine abbey was founded by Queen

Aelfthryth, third wife of King Edgar (Hinton 1979). It was one of only two churches in the country with a dedication to St Melor, a boy saint of Brittany murdered by his uncle. Legend records that relics of St Melor were brought to Amesbury, but what happened to them is not known (Diverres 1979).

As an institution the abbey survived down to AD 1177, but where exactly it stood and what it comprised is not known. Most likely, it occupied the site of the present parish church, initially perhaps as a few simple wooden buildings comprising a church and associated accommodation. Support for this view is provided by the discovery of fragments from two Saxon crosses which came to light during restoration works in 1907 (Ball 1979). Both are displayed in the present parish church. One takes the form of a simple plain equal-armed cross with chamfered edges and a central recessed disc containing a concentric ring of small bosses (86B). It probably dates to the late eleventh

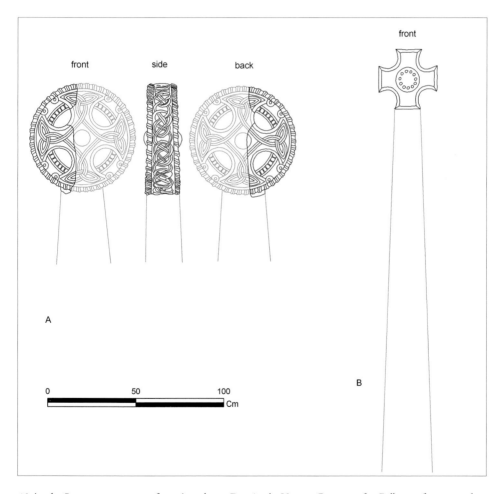

86 Anglo-Saxon stone crosses from Amesbury. *Drawing by Vanessa Constant: after Ball 1979, figures 1 and 10*

or early twelfth century. The other is more ornate, represented now by two joining fragments from a wheelhead cross of the tenth or eleventh century (*86A*). It is made of sandstone and the design includes two concentric wheels with a continuous interlacing design on the faces and edges. Also relevant is the fact that the generously proportioned Romanesque nave of the present church dates to 1125–50 and would therefore have been built during the life of the abbey (RCHM 1987, 106), perhaps reflecting the increasing wealth of the house in the early part of the twelfth century.

It is likely that both the early settlement and the associated ecclesiastical complex were enclosed by an earthwork of some sort, perhaps the large ditch recorded at 15 Church Street in 1999 (Anon 2001, 243). Given the apparent importance of Amesbury in the late Saxon period a royal palace might also be expected, but none has yet been found.

THE LATE SAXON LANDSCAPE

Domesday records that Amesbury was held by the king in 1066. It had never paid geld nor had it been assessed in hides which was the usual form of taxation. Instead, tax had been paid in kind, probably the earliest form of formalized taxation known in England and generally dating at least as far back as the seventh century (Chandler and Goodhugh 1989, 6). By the eleventh century, Amesbury was the focal point for a hundred, an administrative area almost certainly based on the original royal estate and extending from Biddesden in Chute Forest to below Durnford in the Avon Valley, and eastwards to the Hampshire border (Thorn and Thorn 1979).

Amesbury Hundred is accredited with substantial areas of woodland, but downland must have been the dominant land type. Over the following centuries Amesbury continued to expand and consolidate its position as the principal settlement in the area, and in the countryside around about many of the smaller settlements must also have been developing, especially along the Avon and Till valleys, in situations that suited the mixed farming economies (see McOmish et al. 2002, figure 5.2 for the Avon Valley). The majority of the present settlements already existed at the time of the Domesday Survey in 1086. For the most part they would have comprised clusters of timber-framed farmsteads; Winterbourne Stoke in the Till Valley is recorded as having a church; Amesbury perhaps served communities in the Avon Valley.

None of the late Saxon settlements seem to be directly over the site of later Roman and Pagan Saxon settlements, although Maddington in the Till Valley and Durrington in the Avon Valley are certainly close to earlier settlements and could easily have shifted nearer to the river at this time. Once established, these settlements seem to have thrived and in the immediate post-Domesday period developed as focal points within a territorial system of township/parish units which frequently utilized prehistoric barrow cemeteries or individual barrows as boundary markers (Bonney 1966; 1976) and may well be based on traditions established much earlier in the life of this landscape.

10

LIFE IN THE SHIRE
(AD 1100–1800)

In the centuries following the Norman Conquest of the mid-eleventh century the Crown and the Church become increasingly formative agents in the development of the landscape. Castles, palaces, churches, monasteries, towns, villages, hamlets, and farmsteads were key elements in a complicated, densely packed (*87*), and structured system, although it is not until about AD 1500 that the communities living in the Stonehenge landscape come into sharper focus as additional written and cartographic sources become available.

The Conquest period is represented by a simple horseshoe-shaped ringwork castle at Stapleford in the Till Valley in the southwest corner of the Stonehenge landscape. The ringwork was later expanded to operate in a manorial capacity with the addition of a fishpond and suite of paddocks, but the core remains (Creighton 2000, 111). A much larger castle was established in what became a major royal and ecclesiastical centre at Old Sarum, about 6km south of the Stonehenge landscape on the east bank of the Avon (RCHM 1981).

Political and administrative centralization during the eleventh century favoured the 'shire' as the main jurisdiction, emerging no doubt from earlier subdivisions of the Kingdom of Wessex. The change is clearly seen through the development of the name that comes down to us as Wiltshire. As late as AD 900 the term *Wilsaetan* was widely applied, meaning the 'people of the Wylye (River)'. But by the compilation of the Domesday Book in AD 1086 this had become the more recognizable form *Wiltescire* (Gover et al. 1939, xvi). In this way an expression of identity through deeply embedded associations between people and the land they occupied, an essentially tribal system, had been replaced by an emphasis on place and governance which in large measure underpins the emergence of a simple state.

Hundreds were the principal subdivision of the shire, the Stonehenge landscape mainly comprising elements of Dole to the west and Amesbury to the east, with small portions of Branch, Underditch, and Alderbury to the south and Elstub to the north (*88*). As so often in its history, Stonehenge itself stands near the boundary of the territory in which it lies – Amesbury Hundred – wholly irrelevant to the everyday lives of those living and working in its surrounding landscape, but occasionally perhaps haunting those versed in folklore and tradition.

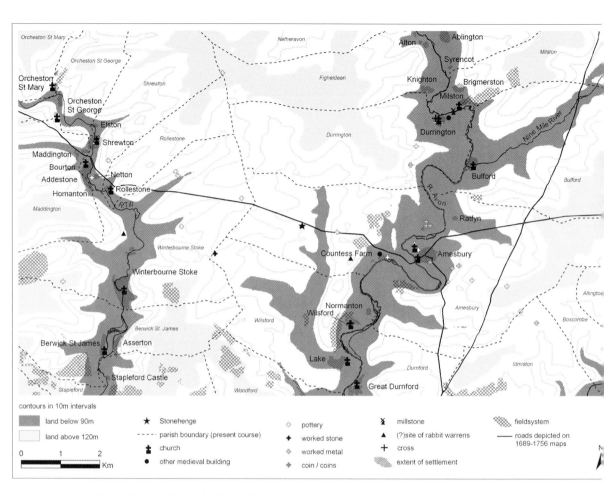

87 Map of the Stonehenge landscape showing the distribution of recorded sites and findspots dating to the period *c.*AD 1100–1600. Modern parish boundaries shown. *Drawing by Vanessa Constant: Wiltshire SMR and various archaeological sources over mapping from EDX Engineering Inc. data at 50m intervals, EDINA UKBorders, and Ordnance Survey © Crown Copyright 2006. All rights reserved. Licence 100045276*

Local people, by now a seamless fusion of folk with roots extending back millennia together with Germanic immigrants, dominated the area. There are few certain Norman-French placenames within the Stonehenge landscape to suggest further immigration at that period, although there can be no doubt that, as the nobility changed, their influence was felt lower down the social order. All the estates and manors within the Stonehenge landscape were placed in the hands of Normans after the Conquest. Rollestone in the Till Valley is a post-conquest name, first recorded in 1242, which may refer to a twelfth- or thirteenth-century owner of the estate named *Rolf*, a Norman personal name of Scandinavian origin (Gover et al. 1939, 235). Likewise, Normanton to the southwest of Stonehenge, first recorded in the fourteenth century, may be a late use of the *tun*-formation referring back to a twelfth- or thirteenth-century French owner (Gover et al. 1939, 372). More visible, however, is the effect of Anglo-Norman culture on the area, especially the high level of investment in new churches between the late eleventh and mid-twelfth centuries, and also the impact of Norman and Plantagenet royalty on the town of Amesbury.

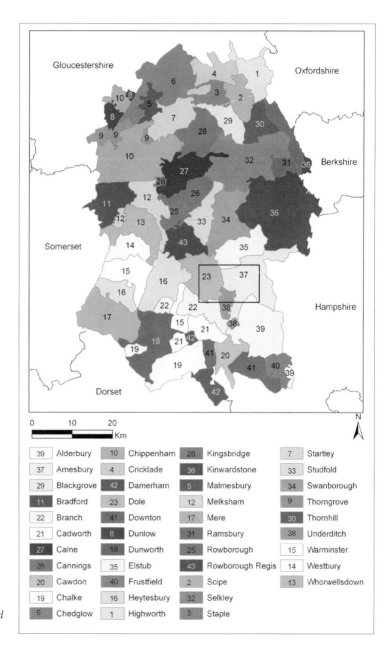

88 The medieval Hundreds of Wiltshire. *Drawing by Vanessa Constant: based on Gover* et al. *1939*

39	Alderbury	10	Chippenham	28	Kingsbridge	7	Startley
37	Amesbury	4	Cricklade	36	Kinwardstone	33	Studfold
29	Blackgrove	42	Damerham	5	Malmesbury	34	Swanborough
11	Bradford	23	Dole	12	Melksham	9	Thorngrove
22	Branch	41	Downton	17	Mere	30	Thornhill
21	Cadworth	8	Dunlow	31	Ramsbury	38	Underditch
27	Calne	18	Dunworth	25	Rowborough	15	Warminster
26	Cannings	35	Elstub	43	Rowborough Regis	14	Westbury
20	Cawdon	40	Frustfield	2	Scipe	13	Whorwellsdown
19	Chalke	16	Heytesbury	32	Selkley		
6	Chedglow	1	Highworth	3	Staple		

AMESBURY

Amesbury remained the largest settlement throughout the medieval period. In 1066 it was held by the king, Edward the Confessor; after the Conquest it was held by William I who took from it the yearly cost of keeping his household for one day. This royal ownership continued down until at least the 1140s and strongly influenced the development of the town. But if the overall ownership of the estate is relatively straightforward, the feudal arrangement of its holdings is complicated. From Pugh's (1948) study of the manors of Amesbury it seems that during the later eleventh century the single royal estate of Amesbury was divided into two smaller manors. In 1086 both were held by Edward of Salisbury, Sheriff of Wiltshire, passing to his son Walter and then in 1147 to his grandson, Patrick, who by that time had been created Earl of Salisbury (Bond 1991, 392). For some four centuries the Amesbury manors and associated lands passed through many hands and were divided, detached under multiple ownership, and finally reunited with almost all of their lands intact in 1541. Edward, Duke of Somerset and Earl of Hertford, acquired the manor of Amesbury Earls in 1536 and Amesbury Priors in 1541.

In 1177 the old Benedictine Amesbury Abbey was closed and in its place Henry II created a new foundation, a double-house for nuns and brothers as a priory attached to the Order of Fontevrault based in Anjou, France (Farmer 1979). Amesbury Priory's new conventual buildings, including a church, were constructed between 1177 and 1186 on land now occupied by Amesbury Abbey (confusingly, renamed as such after the Dissolution) at the considerable cost to the king of £881 (Colvin 1963, 88–90). Nothing now survives of these buildings above ground, although in 1859–60 extensive foundations were revealed north of the present house, including a rectangular room with a stone bench around the walls and a richly tiled floor (Kite 1901, 439–45). The precinct in which the priory stood was defined on the north and west sides by the Avon and on the northeast and southeast by a wall. Over the following centuries this new priory enjoyed much royal favour and flourished, gradually increasing in size and wealth. The mother of Edward I, Queen Eleanor, chose to live out her last days in the priory and was buried there in June 1291, while the king's daughter Mary was a nun there all her life (RCHM 1987, 233). In 1256, there were 76 nuns; by 1318 it housed 117 nuns with 14 chaplains (Bettey 1986, 74). By the fifteenth century, Amesbury Priory had become the second wealthiest and fifth largest in England (Haslam 1984).

A much-debated question is the fate of the church associated with Amesbury Abbey when it was closed in favour of the newly created priory (RCHM 1987, 233–5). By 1177 the church was a simple stone Romanesque building of rectangular or cruciform plan. It may simply have been turned into a parish church served by chaplains from the priory (Crowley 1995, 50–1), its generous size being a reflection of the importance of Amesbury as a royal estate. But its progressive development and enlargement over the following centuries seems rather elaborate for that. The crossing, transept, and chancel were added in the mid-thirteenth century, three transeptal chapels sometime later; new windows were inserted in the nave in the early fourteenth century, and a south aisle added in the late fifteenth century (RCHM 1987, 103). It is possible, therefore, that its fortune was bound up with that of the priory and, following the suggestion made by C H Talbot in 1899, the nave belonged to the parish while the crossing and chancel were rebuilt by the priory to accommodate the male canons while their female counterparts worshipped in the new church within the main conventual buildings (Talbot 1901; RCHM 1987, 234). At the Dissolution, if not before, the entire church would have been at the disposal of the parish (*colour plate 23*).

The settlement of Amesbury grew up alongside the priory during its prosperous years, but little is known of the town from an archaeological perspective (*89*). The main entrance into the priory precinct was half way along High Street, on the northwest side, approached via what is now known as Abbey Lane. Opposite was a long, narrow triangular market place that dates from the thirteenth century, and by the 1540s contained a market house. Markets were held on Wednesdays, Thursdays, and Saturdays.

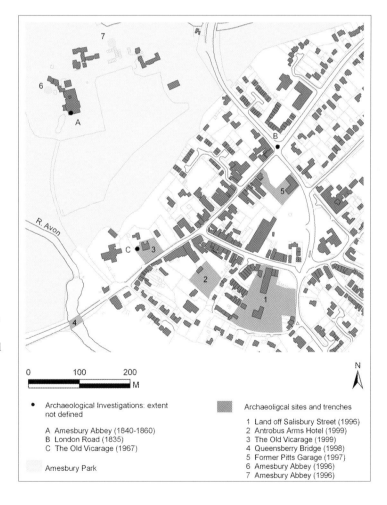

89 Amesbury. Plan of the modern town showing the position and extent of early features and principal excavations. *Drawing by Vanessa Constant: Wiltshire SMR and various archaeological sources over Ordnance Survey © Crown Copyright 2006. All rights reserved. Licence 100045276*

0   100   200
M

N

• Archaeological Investigations: extent not defined

A Amesbury Abbey (1840-1860)
B London Road (1835)
C The Old Vicarage (1967)

Amesbury Park

Archaeoligcal sites and trenches

1 Land off Salisbury Street (1996)
2 Antrobus Arms Hotel (1999)
3 The Old Vicarage (1999)
4 Queensberry Bridge (1998)
5 Former Pitts Garage (1997)
6 Amesbury Abbey (1996)
7 Amesbury Abbey (1996)

90 Queensberry Bridge, Amesbury, carrying the road into the town from the west over the River Avon. Built in 1775. *Photograph: Timothy Darvill, copyright reserved*

Four or five inns stood in the town by the early sixteenth century, the George being the only surviving example that can trace its name back to 1522, possibly still occupying its original site.

Many of the houses in the town at this time would have been timber-framed, and have long since vanished. The only known surviving domestic medieval building of the period seems to be West Amesbury House. With a fifteenth-century core, medieval screens passage with an *in situ* wooden screen, arched doorways, and a medieval arch-braced and wind-braced roof in the west wing, the medieval building possibly lay within a grange of Amesbury Priory (Chandler and Goodhugh 1989).

Something of the scale of the town can be gauged by the existence of 22 burgage plots held by Amesbury manor in 1364. Each plot would have held a substantial house and associated outbuildings and yards. In 1377 the parish of Amesbury had 375 taxpayers (Crowley 1995, 18). It was a local administrative centre and the hundred court was held there.

At its dissolution in 1540 the main conventual buildings of Amesbury Priory passed to Edward Seymour, the future Protector and Duke of Somerset, who dismantled most of the buildings in fairly short order, keeping only the prioress' lodging and some associated buildings to form a private house (Jackson 1867). Between 1595 and 1601 a new mansion house was built over the site of the former priory and given the name Amesbury Abbey. Over the following decades Abbey Lane, formerly the main access, was closed off, the precinct was consolidated, and Diana House and Kent House were built as lodges in the northeast and east corners of the precinct respectively (Crowley 1995, 21).

Robbed of its priory, Amesbury remained a small and rather poor town through the post-medieval period. High Street remained built up, with many cottages and smaller houses behind. Very little work was done to maintain the church and there are no major reconstructions or additions of this period. Two seventeenth-century cottages survive: one in Frog Lane and one at the southwest end of Coldharbour. West Amesbury House was extensively altered during the late seventeenth century, an entirely new stone and flint exterior being added, together with a new gabled and symmetrically fenestrated frontage with mullioned windows.

A short period of prosperity occurred during the occupancy by Charles Douglas, Duke of Queensbury, of Amesbury Abbey between 1725 and 1778. The fine Queensberry Bridge with five arches and a solid parapet was built in 1775 and provided a magnificent entry into town from the west (*90*). From the 1780s, however, the town declined in significance locally and regionally. In 1809 the market hall was taken down, and by 1812 there were vacant sites on both sides of the High Street (Crowley 1995, 22).

FORESTS AND PARKS

Throughout the medieval period, Amesbury Hundred constituted part of the very extensive Royal Forest of Chute, the earliest known documentary evidence for which dates from the twelfth century (Bond 1994, 123). However, the name is ancient, probably pre-Roman, and derives from the Old British word *cēto* meaning wood (Gover et al. 1939, 12).

The creation of parks for hunting was a feature of the Wiltshire countryside from the twelfth century onwards, but the Stonehenge landscape is remarkably devoid of known examples (Watts 1996, figure 2). Only with increasing interest in recreational/ornamental uses for parkland in the sixteenth century do we find emparkment taking place, and that in the rather special context of Amesbury Abbey.

Edward Seymour procured the manor of Amesbury Priors in 1541 after the dissolution of Amesbury Priory (Chandler and Goodhugh 1989, 25–6). Five years earlier he had been bequeathed Amesbury Earls manor. Combined, these estates comprised the whole of Amesbury, but for a variety of reasons they changed hands a number of times during the later sixteenth and early seventeenth centuries. In 1661, one notable owner, the Duke of Somerset, commissioned architect John Webb to design a magnificent house in the Inigo Jones style. An illustration in *Vitruvius Britannicus* in 1725 shows the full glory of the place which Pevsner described as 'a noble edifice of a kind yet very rare in England, purely classical, of nine bays, with a pedimented giant portico of two columns and two angle pillars rising above a rusticated ground floor' (1975, 91). In 1676 the Bruce family acquired the manor, but in 1720 sold it to Lord Carleton who, before his death in 1725, devised it to his nephew, Charles Douglas, the third Duke of Queensberry. Upon the Duke's death in 1778, the estate passed to his cousin, William Douglas, the fourth Duke of Queensberry, who died in 1810 (Pugh 1948, 70–110).

These changes in land ownership affected the character of the former landscape and the extent of innovation and development within it, especially the development of Amesbury Park which grew out of the former monastic precinct in a series of marked stages (English Heritage 1987; Chandler 2002; Mowl 2004, 68–70). The first period of improvement and expansion was under Charles Douglas, who lived at Amesbury from 1725 onwards. Initially attention was focused on the land around the house, with the construction of a formal garden and extensive tree-planting (91B). The house itself was extended at this time to designs attributed to Henry Flitcroft. New entrance gates were erected near Kent House and a formal ride, later called Lord's Walk, was planted to provide a new approach to the Abbey.

Things changed again in the early 1730s when the formal garden was removed and open parkland brought close to the house, separated by a ha-ha ditch. In 1735 the Duke purchased West Amesbury manor which included land to the west of Vespasian's Camp and across Stonehenge Down. This allowed him to expand the parkland progressively westwards (91C) and introduce many new contemporary ideas. Originally designed by Charles Bridgeman, features west of the river included tree-planting within Vespasian's Camp (previously arable land); the creation of a grotto known as Gay's Cave; establishing a number of serpentine and straight walks, glades, and radiating vistas such as the prospect towards Stonehenge; and building a Chinese temple designed by Chambers on a bridge over the Avon (Bond 1991, 419). Not all of the features in Bridgeman's original scheme were ever completed, but expansion continued.

By 1773, the Duke had extended the park further to the north and west, incorporating the Seven Barrows and engulfing existing open fields at West Amesbury and Amesbury Countess. The line of a trackway running northwards from West Amesbury towards Durrington and Shrewton was probably diverted westwards at this time (91D). In 1777 he constructed the Baluster Bridge over the Avon, and by the time of his death in 1778 the park covered about 120ha. There followed a period of neglect and decline between 1778 and 1810 when the fourth Duke was mainly absent. Until about 1800 most of the park was under pasture, but over the ensuing two decades most of it was ploughed up and it remained in arable usage at least until the tithe commutation of 1846 (Chandler 2002, 15).

During the third Duke's occupation, the wider estate also experienced a period of investment. The Countess Court Farmhouse, originally constructed in the early to mid-seventeenth century, received a new three-bay façade in the Georgian style. To the south of the house, a five-bayed timber-framed stave barn and granary were constructed (Slocombe 1989, 26–7). Estate cottages were also built on Countess Road, but have since been demolished for the construction of Amesbury bypass (Chandler and Goodhugh 1989, 71).

Fishing, fowling, hunting, hawking, and hare coursing were regular sports at Amesbury from the sixteenth century onwards, much of it undertaken within and around the park associated with Amesbury Abbey (Crowley 1995, 18–19).

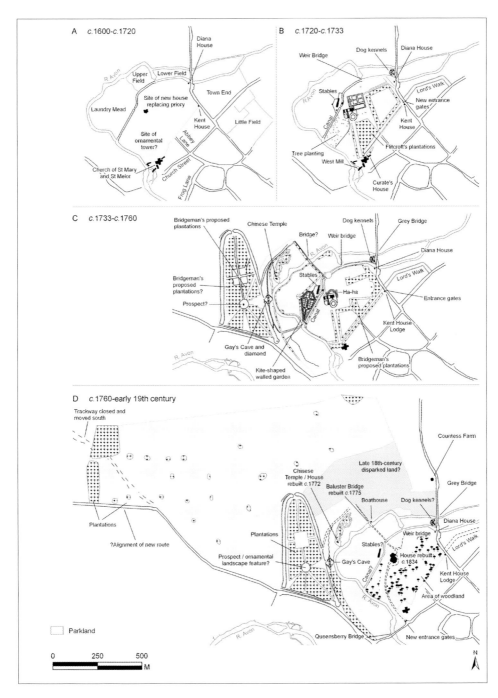

91 Amesbury Park. A: Early ornamental park to c.1773 planned by Charles Bridgeman. B: Later expansion north and west c.1773–8. *Drawing by Vanessa Constant: Wiltshire SMR, English Heritage Parks and Gardens Register and various archaeological sources over Ordnance Survey © Crown Copyright 2006. All rights reserved. Licence 100045276*

VILLAGES, HAMLETS, AND TOWNSHIPS

Beyond the town of Amesbury was a series of smaller settlements – villages and hamlets – strung out along the Avon Valley to the north and south at intervals of between 2–4km. The same pattern can also be seen in the Till Valley (see *87*). One or more of these settlements within a single jurisdiction can be considered a 'township', many of which are coterminous with what later became recognized as ecclesiastical parishes. Each township included a mix of three main types of land: meadow on the valley bottom forming a valuable source for grazing and hay production; arable open fields on the lower slopes; and downland in common pasture on the higher, more remote areas. In some cases there may also have been patches of woodland, but these were rare. There is some evidence to support enclosure (see below), but most of the arable land remained in open fields until at least the eighteenth century. Indeed, the basic pattern of three land types can still be seen in many of the modern parishes (cf. Aston 1985, figure 15). The pattern is clearly evident from the arrangement of parish boundaries which fossilized earlier patterns and have shifted little over recent centuries; every parish includes an amount of each kind of land in a way that created strip-parishes whose short sides meet along the rivers and along the watersheds between.

In a very real sense the villages and hamlets that we recognize today developed during this period. Anglo-Saxon placenames prevail, and the main villages were already extant by the Domesday Survey of 1086 (*Table D*); some may extend back still further, if not on exactly the same spot then at least within the compass of localized settlement drift as one focus was eclipsed by the next.

The zenith of occupation in the villages was between the early twelfth and the fifteenth centuries. During their early history most of the buildings would have been timber-framed structures. Later, stone, flint rubble, and brick began to be used, first for the churches and then for domestic architecture. The earliest recognized structural elements in the extant churches are typically Romanesque, suggesting a period of investment, prosperity, and religious fervour during the eleventh and twelfth centuries. Many churches show later alterations and additions through the thirteenth, fourteenth, and fifteenth centuries, all changing from a simple rectangular plan into a cruciform shape (*92*). Not until the sixteenth century were domestic buildings built in stone, and then still only occasionally. Throughout this period villages tended to be either compact nucleated agglomerations or regular rows with contiguous tofts running parallel with the valley (Lewis 1994, 173–4).

AVON VALLEY SETTLEMENTS

Starting in the Avon Valley, the most northerly settlements within the Stonehenge landscape are Alton, Ablington, Syrencot, and Knighton, all part of Figheldean township whose focus at Figheldean itself lies a kilometre or so to the north. The first main village is therefore Milston with its twin Brigmerston, both Saxon in origin. Small and compact, they lie on the east side of the Avon with a townland extending onto the uplands of Brigmerston Field and Milston Down. In 1377 there were 55 taxpayers; 139 in 1801 (Crowley 1995, 137). The parish church stands in Milston. It dates from the late thirteenth century but little early work survived the restorations of 1860 and 1906. Since at least 1763 it has been dedicated to St Mary. Old House overlooking the churchyard has a date of 1613.

Close by to the south is Durrington, a larger settlement on the west side of the Avon that again has pre-Norman origins. Its extensive townland runs eastwards onto Larkhill and Durrington Down as far as the watershed with the River Till. In 1377 there were 139 taxpayers; 339 in 1801 (Crowley 1995, 95). Durrington church, dedicated to All Saints after 1851, was standing in the early twelfth century. As seen today, much of the exterior fabric results from the extensive restorations to designs by J W Hugall of Pontefract carried out in 1851, but many existing features were reused, including the north door dating to *c.*1125 now reset in the south aisle. Inside, much of the old church is preserved and illustrates progressive development through the twelfth and thirteenth centuries. The original south aisle dates to the late twelfth century, the chancel is of the mid-thirteenth century, and the west tower was added *c.*1500 (RCHM 1987, 136). Northwest of the church is the base of the former village cross, later used as a plinth for the village War Memorial (*93*); much of the main street plan of the medieval village can still be traced.

South again is Bulford, east of the Avon and named after a ford across the river that was replaced by a bridge in the early 1760s. Saxon in origin, Bulford was part of the lands of Amesbury Abbey at the time of the Domesday Survey. The township runs eastwards onto Bulford Down and includes Beacon Hill as the highest point in the area at 204m OD. The settlement of Hindurrington, also a holding of Amesbury Abbey, lay within the parish but has since largely disappeared. In 1377 there were 125 taxpayers; 228 in 1801 (Crowley 1995, 63). St Leonard's church, until about 1900 dedicated to St John the Evangelist, shows traces of Romanesque architecture and was clearly a substantial building during the twelfth and thirteenth centuries, the tower was added about 1600 (RCHM 1987, 117). Many later alterations also survived the restorations of 1902–11 to designs by C E Ponting. The large manor house southwest of the church is seventeenth century in origin and was one of several substantial buildings along the old road, now Church Lane, on the east side of the Avon.

South of Amesbury is the small village of Wilsford in Underditch Hundred, west of the Avon, which is now the focus of a large parish that includes its own townland as well as the formerly detached part of Durnford Parish known as Normanton and the lands associated with the village of Lake to the south. All seem to have been settlements established in Saxon times. The church of St Michael in Wilsford has a fine mid-twelfth-century west tower, and various other contemporary architectural elements that survived restorations by T H Wyatt in 1851 (Pevsner 1975, 575–6). Lake House was originally built by clothier George Duke in the late sixteenth century, but it was gutted by fire in 1912 and has since been reinstated.

Table D Medieval settlements and their churches within the Stonehenge landscape.

Settlement	Domesday Name[1]	Dedication of the Church	Earliest structural remains	Main architectural styles represented in extant fabric	Modern restorations
Avon Valley					
Amesbury	Ambresberie	St Mary and St Melor	Norman	C13 (crossing, transepts, and chancel); C14; C15; C18	1852-3 by W Butterfield; 1905 by C E Ponting and D Blow
Bulford	–	St Leonard (1900, formerly St John the Evangelist)	Norman	C13; C14; C16; C17	1902-11 by C E Ponting
Durrington	Derintone	All Saints (1851)	Norman	C13 (chancel); C16 (tower); C17	1851 by J W Hugall
Durnford	Darneford	St Andrew	Norman	C13 (chancel and tower); C14; C15; C17; C18	1903-4 by C E Ponting
Milston	Mildestone	St Mary	C13	?	1860 and 1906
Wilsford	Wiflesforde	St Nicholas	Norman	EE/Perp	
Till Valley					
Berwick St James	Wintreburne	St James	Norman	C13 (north chapel, chancel, and tower) C14; C15; C17	
Maddington★	Wintreburne	St Mary	Norman	C13 (chancel and tower); C14; C17	1843-53 by T H Wyatt and D Brandon
Orcheston St Mary	Orcestone	St Mary	Norman	C13 (aisle and tower); C14; C16	1832-3
Orcheston St George	Orcestone	St George	Norman	C12; C14	
Rollestone★	Wintreburne	St Andrew	C13	C14	
Shrewton★	Wintreburne	St Mary	Norman	C15 (tower); C16	1855 by T H Wyatt
Stapleford	Stapleford	St Mary	Norman	C14; C16	
Winterbourne Stoke	Wintreburnestoch	St Peter	Norman	C13 (crossing); C14 (tower); C15; C16	1880-1 and 1835

1 – Based on Gover et al. 1939.

★ – Elements of the Shrewton polyfocal village

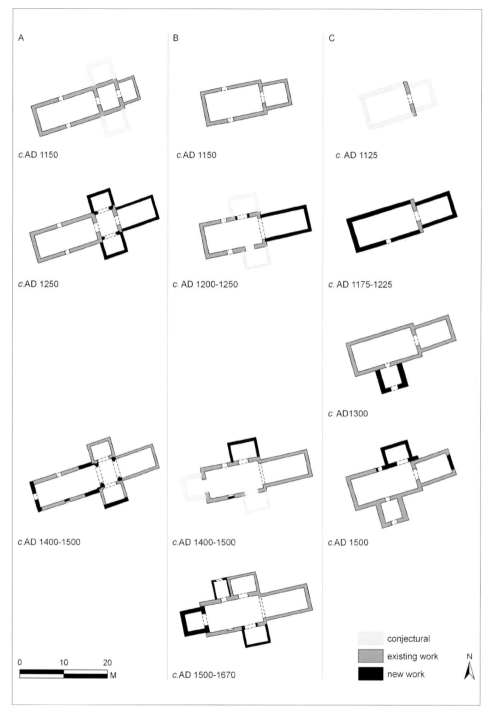

A

*c.*AD 1150

*c.*AD 1250

*c.*AD 1400-1500

0   10   20
M

B

*c.*AD 1150

c. AD 1200-1250

*c.*AD 1400-1500

*c.*AD 1500-1670

C

c. AD 1125

c. AD 1175-1225

c. AD1300

*c.*AD 1500

conjectural

existing work

new work

N

92 Developing church plans in the Stonehenge landscape. A: Winterbourne Stoke. B: Berwick St James. C: Bulford. *Drawing by Vanessa Constant: after* RCHM *1987, figures 238, 257 and 537*

93 Base of the medieval village cross at Durrington, later used as a plinth for a War Memorial.
Photograph: Timothy Darvill, copyright reserved

Finally, Great Durnford is the main settlement of the parish of Durnford that also includes Little Durnford, Newtown, and Netton to the east of the Avon, and the detached area of Normanton west of the river transferred to Wilsford parish in 1885. Unusually for this area, Durnford has a long river frontage to the west; Little Down, Netton Down, and Salterton Down served as upland to the east. The main village and most of the hamlets seem to be Saxon in origin, the name Durnford referring to a hidden or secret ford across the Avon (Gover et al. 1939, 363). In 1377 there were 162 taxpayers; 399 in 1801 (Crowley 1995, 80). St Andrew's church is still substantially Romanesque in appearance, remarkably spacious inside, with two surviving Norman doorways showing the width of the nave has not changed since the twelfth century (Pevsner 1975, 226). The chancel is mid-thirteenth century, the tower late thirteenth century (RCHM 1987, 133). Durnford Manor, north of the church, is a late eighteenth-century brick house. Little Durnford is a six-bay mid-eighteenth-century house in flint and stone.

TILL VALLEY SETTLEMENTS

Turning to the Till Valley there are five main settlements. By the late eleventh century the large Saxon estate of Orcheston in the northern part of the valley had been divided into four smaller estates, two forming Orcheston St Mary and two Orcheston St George. The name Orcheston probably refers to *Ordric's Farm* (Gover et al. 1939, 234); perhaps the owner of the original Saxon estate. The two main settlements lie physically close together, one each side of the river, and both have lands extending northeastwards out of the valley onto Orcheston Down.

Orcheston St Mary is a small, compact settlement on the east bank of the Till. In 1377 there were just 26 taxpayers; 133 in 1801 (Crowley 1995, 229). The church of St Mary is possibly Norman in origin, but most of what can be seen is thirteenth century and later. The principal farmhouse of the village was The Rookery, situated north of the church, heavily repaired in 1753 (Crowley 1995, 229). Other seventeenth- and eighteenth-century buildings south of the church show that development at this time occurred between the two villages, the pair finally coalescing during the twentieth century, united as a single parish in 1934.

Orcheston St George lies on the west bank of the Till and its fortunes were closely bound up with those of Orcheston St Mary. The church, dedicated of course to St George, retains Norman architectural features, but much of what is visible is of thirteenth- and fourteenth-century date in the Perpendicular style (Pevsner 1975, 367). Elston lay within Orcheston St George parish, although it may have been more closely connected to the group of settlements immediately to the south.

Next, southwards, is a rather different kind of settlement: a polyfocal village based on Shrewton. In the eleventh century this comprised a series of estates all called *Wintreburne* which at the time was the name applied to the River Till (Gover et al. 1939, 236). This unit developed into eight separate hamlets: Shrewton, Maddington, Netton, Rollestone, Homanton, Addestone, Bourton, and perhaps Elston to the north. Later these became three parishes – Shrewton, Rollestone, and Maddington – but the associated settlements remained as a single conglomeration along the river valley (94). Shrewton was on the east side with lands extending eastwards as far as the watershed of the Till. In 1377 there were just 49 taxpayers in the parish but this increased considerably to 269 by 1801 (Crowley 1995, 244). The church, dedicated to St Mary, has some remaining Romanesque and Early English architectural details but was heavily restored by T H Wyatt in 1855 (Pevsner 1975, 471). Around the village are a few remaining seventeenth- and eighteenth-century cottages and small houses. Also noteworthy is the domed lock-up dating to c.1700; it was moved a few metres south to its present position in 1974 (95).

Maddington lies west of the Till and includes the smaller settlements of Addestone, Bourton, Homanton, and Newport. Its lands extend westwards onto Homanton Down, Cow Down, and Tenantry Down. In 1377 there were 115 taxpayers in the parish and this rose to 327 by 1801 (Crowley 1995, 203). The church, dedicated to St Mary from 1763, contains fragments of twelfth-century stonework but most of the older work visible today dates from the thirteenth century and later and has survived restorations in 1843–53 and later (Crowley 1995, 212). The church was declared redundant in 1975.

Rollestone on the east side of the Till south of Maddington formed the third parish of this polyfocal settlement, its townland extending eastwards onto Rollestone Down as far as the watershed with the Avon. As already noted, name suggests that in the early post-conquest period this area was held by someone named *Rolf*, a Norman personal name of Scandinavian origin (Gover et al. 1939, 235). Its church, dedicated to St Andrew, dates mainly from the thirteenth century and later (Pevsner 1975, 382).

Two kilometres south of Shrewton is the village of Winterbourne Stoke, again named after the river. Situated on the east bank of the Till this very large parish contained extensive uplands across Fore Down, High Down, Winterbourne Stoke Down, and Oatlands Hill east as far as the watershed with the Avon. There was also some land to the west across Parsonage Down. The village is mainly arranged along a single street south of the modern A303. In 1377 there were 93 taxpayers in the parish and this rose to 256 by 1801 (Crowley 1995, 276). A church at Winterbourne Stoke is recorded in the Domesday Survey of 1086, but the earliest features of the present church, dedicated to St Peter, are parts of the nave which date to c.1150 (RCHM 1987, 227). Two Norman doorways show the width of the nave has remained unchanged since the twelfth century, but all around are signs of vigorous development through the thirteenth and fourteenth centuries, the tower being added in the fifteenth century. The Manor House and several cottages in the village date to the seventeenth century (Pevsner 1975, 592).

Berwick St James lies south again, focused on the east side the river but with lands extending westwards to Berwick Down and Yarnbury, and eastwards to Druid's Lodge. Again the village is focused along a single main street with the church towards the south end. In 1377 there were 80 taxpayers in the parish and this had risen to 226 by

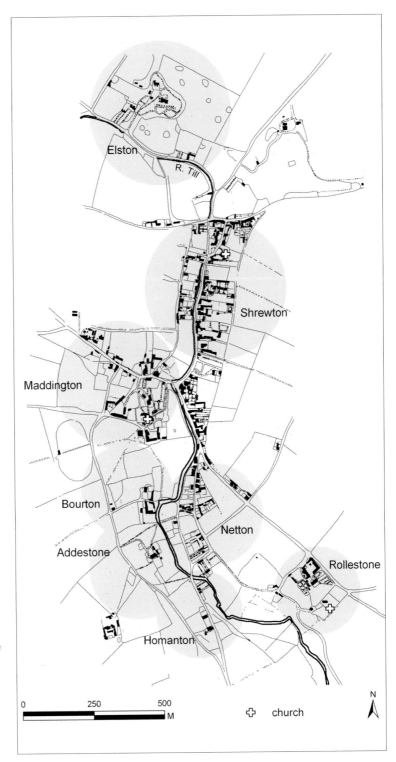

94 Shrewton: a
polyfocal village.
*Drawing by Vanessa
Constant: based on
Aston 1985, figure
41 over Ordnance
Survey © Crown
Copyright 2006.
All rights reserved.
Licence 100045276*

Elston

R. Till

Shrewton

Maddington

Bourton

Netton

Addestone

Rollestone

Homanton

0   250   500
M

✚ church

N

95 Shrewton lock-up built *c.*1700 and moved to its present position in 1974. *Photograph: Timothy Darvill, copyright reserved*

1801 (Crowley 1995, 169). The church of St James (*colour plate 24*) was standing by the mid-twelfth century; two Norman doors and the font survived numerous alterations and additions made between the thirteenth and fifteenth centuries (Pevsner 1975, 108). Manor Farm has a wing dating back to *c.*1600, and Godwins and the Boot Inn both date back to the seventeenth century.

The smaller settlement of Asserton lies within the parish of Berwick St James while Uppington and Staple Castle lie within Stapleford parish, the focus of which lies south of the Stonehenge landscape considered here.

Desertion and shrinkage

Growth in these villages and hamlets just described was not continuous or even. From the early sixteenth century at least there is landscape and documentary evidence for settlement desertion and shrinkage along the valleys of the Till and the Avon (Aston 1982, 11; 1983, 11). Durrington has been the subject of detailed study and shows a decline from 30 customary tenant families in the mid-fourteenth century down to 19 at the end of the fifteenth century. By 1506 12 virgates of land (about 144ha) were held by five tenants in contrast to the situation in the thirteenth century when there was individual virgate ownership (Hare 1981, 167). In common with many chalkland settlements in Wessex,

Durrington shows a varied pattern of shrinkage and desertion while still maintaining its traditional agricultural and settlement character (Hare 1980). Shrewton with its eight separate hamlets declined too, Homanton, Addestone, and Bourton became deserted, while Elston, Netton, Maddington, and Rollestone drastically shrank.

Shrinkage can also be seen elsewhere within the Stonehenge landscape. Empty crofts and paddocks, for example, have been found at the small compact hamlet of West Amesbury, and at Ratfyn, which now only exists as a single farm. The documentary record also provides evidence in support of deserted settlement. Hindurrington, a 'lost' hamlet in Bulford parish, is recorded in Lay Subsidy and Poll Tax returns of the fourteenth century, but not in the field (Aston 1985, 41). Detailed surveys of Orcheston (McOmish et al. 2002, 126–7) show that large parts of both villages were deserted and now survive only as earthworks. Overall, Beresford and Hurst (1971, 206–7) record eight deserted/shrunken villages and farmsteads within the Stonehenge landscape, but none has been examined in sufficient detail to shed light on the exact date or cause of desertion.

Townships and parishes

Several of the modern parishes have been created by the amalgamation of medieval tithings or townships, but some original medieval land units still remain. As observed on modern Ordnance Survey maps, Wilsford-cum-Lake, for example, was created out of the medieval townships of Normanton, Lake, and Wilsford. Also, Shrewton incorporated the medieval townships of Netton, Shrewton, Bourton, Addestone, and part of Elston (Aston 1985, 40–1 and 79–80). As noted in Chapter 9, some township units seem to have incorporated prehistoric features at certain points on their boundaries, perhaps reflecting earlier land divisions. West Amesbury, Winterbourne Stoke, and Normanton townships, for instance, converge at barrow 10 in the Longbarrow Crossroads cemetery. Amongst others, potential prehistoric boundaries can be found at bell barrow Amesbury 55, where Amesbury Countess, West Amesbury, and Winterbourne Stoke converge, while the north bank of the Cursus forms part of the Durrington/Amesbury boundary (Bond 1991, 394).

FARMING

The lands between settlements were far from empty; farming at this time was a labour-intensive business. The economy of the area between the eleventh and nineteenth centuries was predominantly agricultural, based on arable cultivation and animal husbandry. The balance between arable and pasture land changed over time, dictated by social, economic, and political circumstances. In general, the higher ground, remote from the settlements along the main river valleys, was open grassland. Land nearer the settlements had a higher incidence of cultivated ground. Other forms of farming were relevant to the sustainability of communities as well and these too have left their mark on the landscape.

Cultivation

Archaeological evidence of strip cultivation in the form of ridge and furrow earthworks can be seen cutting earlier fieldsystems in several areas, for example south of Longbarrow Crossroads, and on Rox Hill (RCHM 1979, xiv). Ridge and furrow cultivation is also visible on aerial photographs of the land east of King Barrow Ridge (RCHM 1979, plate 9). However, these areas are only part of the picture as every townland had cultivated land that was typically worked on the two-field or three-field system. In order to produce and maintain good yields of wheat and barley the characteristically thin soils of the area required sheep to be folded on the fields to fertilize the land between cropping. Accordingly, sheep were sent out to pasture on the chalk downland during the day and close-folded on the arable land of the lower slopes at night (Bond 1991, 407). It has been proposed that the 'extensive pasture resources and more balanced economy' of the Wiltshire chalklands enabled communities here to resist the late medieval agricultural depression experienced elsewhere in the country even though some evidence in support of settlement shrinkage exists during this period (Bond 1991, 397).

The expansion of arable farming from the seventeenth century, with the subsequent diminution of the downland, also contributed to the changing character of the physical and cultural landscape. Widespread evidence from placenames shows the extent of these changes (Kerridge 1959, 49–52). The fieldname 'Burnbake' on later maps is indicative of a method of turf removal, known as 'burnbeating', 'burnbaking', or 'devonshiring'. Examples can be found on the south side of Durrington Down where new fields were created, and in the fields of Amesbury Countess where existing arable fields were extended beyond the Seven Barrows on King Barrow Ridge (Bond 1991, 409).

Placenames also contribute to an understanding of the development of agriculture and farming, and subsequently the changing character of the landscape. For instance, a Tithe Award for Durnford gives the fieldname 'Sainfoin Piece' to land on the northern boundary of Normanton tithing; it suggests that the leguminous crop sainfoin was cultivated here, presumably to reduce the length of the fallow period.

Concerns over the impact on archaeological remains of expanding arable agriculture on the downland were expressed by antiquarians as far back as the eighteenth century. William Stukeley, for example, records that (1740, 1):

> The Wiltshire downs, or Salisbury plain, (as commonly call'd) for extent and beauty, is, without controversy, one of the moft delightful parts of Britain. But of late years great encroachments have been made upon it by the plough, which threatens the ruin of this fine champain, and of all the monuments of antiquity thereabouts.

Penning and grazing

Sheep were the main livestock of the area, kept mainly for their meat and wool. In some villages they would be taken out to the downs during the day and brought back to the village at night, but for longer periods grazing the downs, and especially if they were over-wintered on the downs some form of shelter or penning was needed. These are usually rectangular or square, banked enclosures. Two lie on Wilsford Down close beside one another, each measuring about 200m by 140m, and others are known as earthworks enclosing about 0.5ha on Orcheston Down and Figheldean Down (McOmish et al. 2002, 116–17). An undated rectangular enclosure on Winterbourne Stoke Down identified through aerial photography may be another example (RCHM 1979, 25), as too a square enclosure identified on King Barrow Ridge (Darvill 1995, figure 4.6). A rather smaller sheepfold was cut into the southwestern side of Bush Barrow with a small spinney of thorn bushes planted for shelter on top (Bond 1991, 417; RCHM 1979, title page and xxi).

Warrening

Rabbits provided a sustainable food source that could be farmed intensively in dedicated warrens and formed an important part of the rural economy of the area (RCHM 1979, xxi; Betty 2004). The placename Coneybury Hill in West Amesbury refers to a rabbit warren in the area. The earliest records date to an Inquisition of 1382 in which the Lord of Totness and Harringworth granted the manor of Amesbury an area of land called 'le Conynger' (Bond 1991, 398). Later, in the early seventeenth century, the planned introduction of rabbits to the barrows at Amesbury Abbey is well recorded. An account of AD 1609–10 shows that in 1605 'Two round connye berryes were made to his Lordship's appointment and at the same time 14 couple of conies put into the ground. Which 14 couple of cunnies with theire encrease did breade and feed there' (RCHM 1979, xxi).

A very sizable warren can be seen at the Coniger, an earthwork enclosure at Winterbourne Stoke, first mentioned in 1574 and recorded as encompassing a number of prehistoric barrows (RCHM 1979, xxi). More typically, warrens comprised pillow mounds: low, rectangular mounds of earth covering narrow wooden or stone tunnels in which rabbits or hares could live and breed and which led to fixed entrances on the outer surface. When a warrener wished to harvest some rabbits he simply placed nets over the entrances to the tunnels and sent a ferret into the warren so the rabbits would flee and get caught in one of the nets. Excavations around the North Kite by W F Grimes in the late 1950s included the examination of a pillow mound southwest of Druid's Lodge.

Prehistoric barrows may have been used as ready-made warrens, not least because rabbits often colonize such mounds quite naturally. Indeed Stonehenge itself had become an established rabbit warren by the early 1720s, although by the later eighteenth century rabbits were regarded locally as a nuisance and the tradition of keeping them declined (Bond 1991, 420).

Water meadows

A significant change to the Stonehenge landscape during the seventeenth century was the introduction of floated meadows or water meadows along the valley bottoms (Kerridge 1953; 1954; Atwood 1963). Floated meadows were created at Wylye and

Chalke in around 1635; many other villages followed their lead later in the 1640s (Aubrey 1969). The Amesbury water meadows were also constructed during the seventeenth century, some time before 1680, as written records mention repairs and replacements to machinery (Bettey 1979; Cowan 1982). The water meadows along the west bank of the Avon at Woodford were also constructed in the seventeenth century, an act that drew a lawsuit claiming that construction of the bay and weir dammed the excellent fishing on this section of the river (McKinley 2003, 8–9).

Enclosure

Enclosure began relatively late in the Stonehenge landscape, probably during the second half of the eighteenth century. However, no Parliamentary acts or awards have been found for Amesbury, Bulford, or Wilsford and it must therefore be assumed that enclosure here was by agreement. Written sources suggest that, at least for Amesbury, open fields were still used up until the mid-eighteenth century, after which they were piecemeal and limited in extent. Towards the end of the eighteenth century all the land owned by the third Duke of Queensberry (largely around Amesbury) was enclosed and divided between six farms: West Amesbury; Countess Court; Red House; Earl's Court; Kent House; and South Ham (Bond 1991, 419). Durrington, Shrewton, and Winterbourne Stoke were not enclosed until the nineteenth century. Elsewhere, essentially medieval patterns of land ownership were reorganized with a propensity towards the merging of smaller holdings and the development of existing larger farms (Bond 1991).

ANCIENT SITES IN A NEW LANDSCAPE

Stonehenge itself is first mentioned in available written sources around AD 1130, presumably as a place of interest and intrigue, and the source of patriotic and mythical schemes for early British history (Chippindale 2004, 6). To what extent Stonehenge was robbed of some of its stones during later medieval and post-medieval times has been a matter of some discussion. Newall (1921, 435) records a fragment of bluestone, perhaps originally from Stonehenge, in a cottage garden at Lake, and two sarsens thought to have come from Stonehenge have been recorded at Berwick St James some 6.5km to the southwest, although their status is far from certain. Following earlier writers, Atkinson (1979, 85–6; cf. Long 1876, 75–7) favoured the deliberate destruction of parts of the site, perhaps in the Roman or early medieval period, but Ashbee (1998) suggests that non-completion may have as much to do with its present condition as slighting and dilapidation. The discovery of pottery dating to about AD 1400 inside the main cist of the primary burial at Amesbury 85 suggests that here at least there was robbing or investigation of the mound (Newall 1931, 433). A bronze skillet handle of medieval date found within Durrington Walls (Short 1956, 393) may similarly indicate activity at this much earlier monument.

96 Eighteenth-century trippers at Stonehenge. *From Stukeley 1740, TAB. XXII*

Intellectual interest in Stonehenge and its surroundings increased with visits by notable antiquarians of the day: Inigo Jones between 1633 and 1652, John Aubrey in the 1660s, William Stukeley in the 1720s, and John Wood in 1747 amongst them. The wider interest they promoted no doubt led to others making visits and it is interesting that several views of the site show casual visitors (*96*), some of whom arrived by carriage or on horseback. One picture of 1790 shows a shepherd-guide wearing a smock showing two gentlemen and a lady one of the Sarsen Trilithons. Graffiti carved into the stones from the seventeenth century onwards is further evidence of its attraction to visitors (*97*), in some cases perhaps because of the midsummer games that in 1781, at least, included a sack-race, cricket, wrestling, and bowling (Goulstone 1985, 52). In 1680 a fair at Stonehenge was granted to the Lord of West Amesbury manor on 25–26 September each year (Crowley 1995, 46). This was probably a sheep fair, but how long it continued is not known. Other ancient monuments in the area also found novel community uses, as with the Prophet Barrow (Wilsford 43 in the Lake cemetery) which according to local tradition was used as a preaching place by French prophets in the early 1700s (Grinsell 1978a, 38).

It was intellectual developments away from the sites themselves that were to have the most profound long-term effects, especially the reinvention of the Druids. Stuart Piggott has masterfully documented this development (1975), noting how the availability of classical writings by Caesar, Pliny, Tacitus, and others during the sixteenth century led Renaissance scholars to consider possible links between the Druids as portrayed by these ancient authors and the ancient stone circles of northern Europe. Writing in 1649, John Aubrey was amongst the first to suggest that Stonehenge might have been one of the temples used by the Druids, a view that he embellished by using reports from the New World concerning what were considered 'primitive peoples' or 'noble savages'. In the words of Stuart Piggott, Aubrey had 'drawn inferences from his archaeological fieldwork in Wiltshire which were to have unexpected far-reaching repercussions on the creation of the Druids-as-wished-for which have lasted until today' (Piggott 1975, 130). In the mid-eighteenth century William Stukeley expanded on the idea of the Druids being the architects of Stonehenge (1740), and provided what has become one of the iconic images of a Druid in the tradition of soft primitivism (98). This merely served to reinforce and consolidate what is now a piece of national folklore.

97 Stonehenge: eighteenth-century graffiti (above) and prehistoric rock art (below) on Stone 53. *Photograph: Timothy Darvill, copyright reserved*

98 William Stukeley's vision of a British Druid. *From Stukeley 1740, TAB. I*

99 Tollhouse built in 1762 for the Amesbury Trust beside the Amesbury to Marlborough Road (modern A345) north of the town. *Photograph: Timothy Darvill, copyright reserved*

ROADS AND TRACKS

Direct evidence for roads and trackways within the Stonehenge landscape before the seventeenth century is rather limited. A road from Marlborough through Bulford and thence across to Shrewton and on to Warminster is known as the Packway and is recorded from the 1550s (Crowley 1995, 95). Ogilby's road book of about 1675 shows the line of the London–Barnstaple road just north of the present A344, possibly the line marked by an apparently unfinished road still visible as an earthwork (RCHM 1979, 31–2 and see below). The eighteenth- and early nineteenth-century documentary record is slightly more comprehensive, and includes Andrews and Drury's county map of 1773, the map of the Amesbury Hundred published by Colt Hoare in 1826, the first edition OS map (1817), and various manorial court records. Many of the tracks and roads which appear on the Andrews and Drury map have ceased to exist, or exist in a relocated and realigned form in the present landscape. These include parts of the old Amesbury to Market Lavington road, a track from the Avenue in Stonehenge Bottom northeastwards towards Durrington, and part of the Old Marlborough Road running northwards from Salisbury (Bond 1991, 421).

The main road through the area is that leading southwestwards from London via Andover towards Mere, a route now followed by the A303. In medieval times this road crossed the River Avon in Amesbury. The Amesbury Turnpike Trust was created in 1761 by Act of Parliament and turnpiked the London road from Thruxton (Hampshire) through to Amesbury and also from Amesbury through to Mere. At about the same time this Trust attempted to build a branch from King Barrow Ridge on the London Road across to Warminster via Shrewton. It was never finished but in part now survives as an earthwork (RCHM 1979, xxii) and may have been shown on some early maps. A little later, in 1773, a new straight turnpike was made northwestwards from Stonehenge Bottom, close to the north side of Stonehenge, and on to Shrewton and Devizes; the A344 and A360 now follow this line. The present Salisbury to Devizes road (A360) was turnpiked in 1760. Other roads turnpiked in the late eighteenth century include the A345 running north from Amesbury, and what is the minor road between Folly Bottom (Amesbury) and villages such as Bulford and Milston on the east side of the Avon (Crowley 1995, 15).

As well as the roads themselves, there are a few tollhouses remaining in the Stonehenge area. One on the A345 north of Amesbury was built in 1762 for the Amesbury Trust (*99*) while another, for the same Trust, was built before 1800 on the road leading westwards out of Amesbury towards Stonehenge (Haynes and Slocombe 2004, 4–5). There is also a fair amount of street furniture associated with these roads, including some fine milestones (*100*).

100 Eighteenth-century milestone beside the modern A344 northeast of Stonehenge telling the traveller that they are 75 miles from London and 2 miles from Amesbury. *Photograph: Timothy Darvill, copyright reserved*

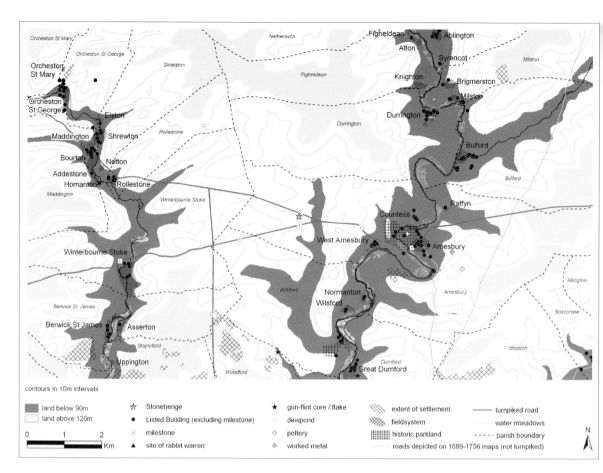

101 Map of the Stonehenge landscape showing the distribution of recorded sites and findspots dating to the period *c*.AD 1600–1800. Modern parish boundaries shown. *Drawing by Vanessa Constant: various archaeological sources over mapping from EDX Engineering Inc. data at 50m intervals, EDINA UKBorders, and Ordnance Survey © Crown Copyright 2006. All rights reserved. Licence 100045276*

INDUSTRY

Although the economy of the Stonehenge landscape was largely based upon sheep–crop husbandry, there is considerable evidence for various industrial activities around Amesbury and in some of the larger villages. The increasing trend for stone buildings in many of the villages from about 1600 onwards, many of the early examples now Listed Buildings (*101*), promoted new skills in the construction industry.

Mills were present along both of the main rivers, some perhaps on earlier sites. In 1086 there were eight mills on the king's estate at Amesbury (Crowley 1995, 45). A millstone and a number of timbers have been recorded at Durrington, suggesting that archaeological remains may await investigation.

Amesbury Priory may have had a tile factory in the town during the thirteenth century (Crowley 1995, 46). In 1662 Thomas Fuller wrote that 'the best [tobacco pipes] for shape and colour … are made at Amesbury' (Brown 1959). This accolade seems to relate to a clay-pipe factory owned by the Gauntlet family from *c.*1600 to 1698. It was situated at Wrestler's Gate outside the Priory Manor between Normanton and West Amesbury. Remnants of clay-pits were found at the site in *c.*1840 (Ruddle 1895). Other industries in the town included malting, tanning, lime-burning, clothmaking, tailoring, shoemaking, and soap-making. Wool-staplers are recorded at Durnford and there were weavers at Durrington and Figheldean in the sixteenth and seventeenth centuries. Gunflint-making sites have been identified on Rox Hill and at Rox Hill Clump, part of a little-researched but seemingly fairly extensive industry around the Salisbury area (Fowler and Needham 1995). Although small-scale, all of these industries promoted connections with other parts of southern Britain and played a part in expanding the horizons of those living and working in the area during the following century.

11

TURNPIKES, TRIPPERS, AND TROOPS
(AD 1800–1900)

The nineteenth century was a time of transition for the Stonehenge landscape, a time when essentially medieval traditions finally disappeared and new roles began to be defined. The pattern of settlement strung along the two main river valleys continued unaltered, but all the villages grew bigger in terms of their population and more extensive in the area they covered. Many were still focused around collections of farms and a church, but over the course of the nineteenth century more cottages were added to the villages.

Settlement beyond the established villages also developed. Prompted by the abandonment of communal farming techniques and the spread of enclosure, isolated farmsteads and field barns out on the downs appear during the nineteenth century: Durrington Down Barn by 1811; Fargo Cottages west of Stonehenge in 1847; Grant's Barn in Winterbourne Stoke by 1841; and Greenland Farm by 1887. For the first time in over a thousand years, settlement again reached beyond the valleys as the downland was effectively recolonized.

Amesbury remained a small town, larger than the surrounding villages, but with no industrial base it stayed impoverished. With a population of about 720 in 1801, the number of inhabitants may have been at its lowest level since the early Middle Ages (Crowley 1995, 18). Despite a small increase during the mid-nineteenth century, the population in 1901 was still only 1143. In the town itself it was mainly the seventeenth- and eighteenth-century houses that remained in use; areas such as the west side of Back Lane being cleared of cottages in 1851. At about the same time several large houses were built on the southeast side of High Street, including Wyndersham House in 1848. The Amesbury Union Workhouse was built on Salisbury Road in 1837 to designs by W B Moffatt and Sir Gilbert Scott. A lock-up was built in the northeast corner of High Street in 1827, and a police station in the 1880s. In 1852–3 St Mary and St Melor's church was restored to designs by William Butterfield, who evidently intended to remove all features later than c.1400, and largely succeeded (Crowley 1995, 51). There were at least four schools in Amesbury in the early nineteenth century, including Rose's School founded by John Rose in 1677. In 1818 there were a total of 21 pupils spread through the various schools.

102 Amesbury Abbey house, designed by Thomas Hopper for Sir Edmund Antrobus and built in the 1830s on the foundations of the previous house. *Photograph: Timothy Darvill, copyright reserved*

After the turbulent times of the eighteenth century, Sir Edmund Antrobus acquired Amesbury Abbey in 1825, whereafter it passed through three generations of the family all of whom had the same christian name. The second Sir Edmund rebuilt the main house in the 1830s, engaging the architect Thomas Hopper to design it (Pevsner 1975, 91). Parts of the original foundations were reused, but the new house was taller and wider than its predecessor. Hopper kept the nine-bay front but made the portico of six instead of four columns (*102*). The main gateway into the grounds was moved to a position west of the church, the entrance being flanked by two very fine seventeenth-century piers reused from an earlier entrance (*103*).

ENCLOSURE AND AGRICULTURE

Enclosure through Act of Parliament played a major role in altering the physical organization of the countryside during the nineteenth century. Amongst the earliest parishes to enclose open fields and downland through Parliamentary procedures were Shrewton and Winterbourne Stoke in 1812, and Durrington in 1823 (Bond 1991, 424). Later piecemeal mergers and subdivisions have also contributed to the present form of the field boundaries. Available Tithe Award maps from the period 1840–50 illustrate very well the complexity of the defined land-parcels, especially along the Avon Valley where much of the land was under cultivation (*104*).

Not all areas were enclosed however. Extensive tracts of the higher ground remained under permanent pasture, retaining their existing characteristics; these included Tenantry Down; Durrington Down; Normanton Down; Countess Court Down; West Amesbury Down; Winterbourne Stoke Middle Down; and Wilsford Down.

In general the Stonehenge landscape was farmed from relatively few large farms. In Amesbury parish, for example, between 1778 and 1900 the 5800 acres (2347ha) of agricultural land was worked by Park Farm, Earl's Farm, Red Farm, and Southam Farm (Crowley 1995, 41). Most of the farms had a mixture of land types, well illustrated by Ratfyn Farm which in 1846 covered 502 acres (203ha), of which about 5.5 per cent was water meadow, 1.5 per cent lowland pasture, 67 per cent arable land, and 26 per cent downland pasture (Crowley 1995, 45).

103 Seventeenth-century gate piers relocated to flank the main entrance to the grounds of Amesbury Abbey in the early nineteenth century. *Photograph: Timothy Darvill, copyright reserved*

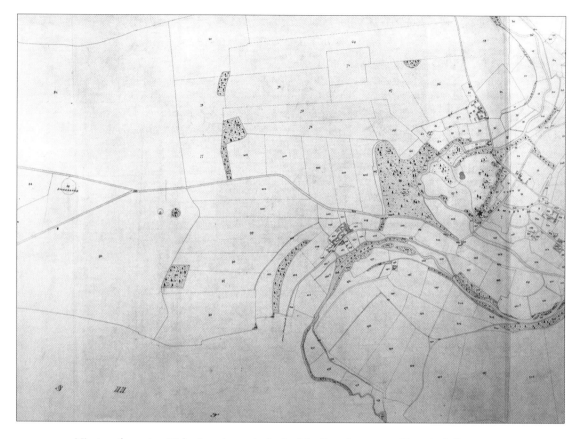

104 Nineteenth-century Tithe Award map (*c.*1840) of the Stonehenge area. Vespasian's Camp can be seen as a wooded area centre right; Stonehenge is centre left. *Reproduced courtesy of the Wiltshire Buildings Record, copyright reserved*

Sheep remained the mainstay of animal husbandry in the area, although most farms also kept cattle and pigs. Wheat and barley were the principal crops grown. Many of the farms comprised accommodation as well as storage and processing facilities for arable crops, as in the case of Countess Farm where the main buildings were arranged around a central yard (*105*).

Water meadows created in the eighteenth century continued in use and benefited from the introduction of better mechanical systems for sluices and drainage. Most were in the Avon Valley below Ham Hatches, at Durrington, and at Winterbourne Stoke in the Till Valley.

Although attempts to rear rabbits in formal warrens had ceased by the early nineteenth century, the rabbit population of the area remained high and Long (1876, 118) notes how in 1863 the under-gamekeeper of Sir Edmund Antrobus was digging deeply for rabbits in the vicinity of the fallen trilithon at Stonehenge.

WOODS AND WOODLAND

The eighteenth century was probably the all-time low-point in the level of woodland cover in the landscape. Deliberate planting began soon after, and in the nineteenth century a number of fairly substantial plantations were added, including Fargo Plantation and Luxenborough Plantation. In some cases these developed into mature stands, incidentally protecting ancient monuments within them. Many of these early nineteenth-century plantings were to provide shelterbelts, game coverts, and ornamental clumps, and this is reflected in their shape and form. They include the Long Barrow Plantation in Wilsford; Normanton Gorse (also known as Furze Cover); Fargo Plantation; and Luxemborough Plantation (Bond 1991, 425).

Extending to the north of Vespasian's Camp and to the west towards King Barrows are dispersed ornamental clumps which first appear on the Ordnance Survey map of 1879. Since the 1960s it has been widely believed that these clumps represent the disposition of ships at the opening of the Battle of the Nile (1798) or Trafalgar (1805). However, there is no evidence to support this idea (RCHM 1979, xxi), and recent studies have concluded that in fact the clumps were planted about 1770 as part of the expansion of the parkland associated with Amesbury Abbey, and cannot therefore have anything to do with either battle (Chandler 2002, 15–16).

ROADS AND TRANSPORT

Improved communication was one of the main changes of the nineteenth century. In addition to the turnpike roads established in the late eighteenth century many others were created, for the most part connecting major centres of population to north and south, east and west. The Swindon, Marlborough and Everleigh Trust turnpiked the modern A345 Amesbury to Old Sarum road in 1836, and in 1840 the Amesbury to Rushall to East Kennett road was turnpiked by the Kennett and Amesbury Trust. Like the earlier turnpikes, some of the street furniture from the period remains although it is often of lesser quality than in earlier centuries (*106*). A number of public and private roads in Durrington and Winterbourne Stoke were constructed to replace unfenced tracks and open-field baulk and headland ways. By 1871, however, turnpikes were out of fashion and all the existing turnpikes in the area were de-turnpiked (Crowley 1995, 15).

In 1883 the Bristol and London and South Western Junction Railway company proposed to construct a railway through the Stonehenge landscape from east of Amesbury through to west of Shrewton. As proposed it would have run in a cutting north of Vespasian's Camp, demolished several round barrows and the Avenue on King Barrow Ridge, run across Stonehenge Bottom on an embankment, passed 500m north of Stonehenge itself, run along part of the Cursus, and finally bisected the Lesser Cursus. Through the efforts of Sir John Lubbock and others this scheme was averted (Freshfield

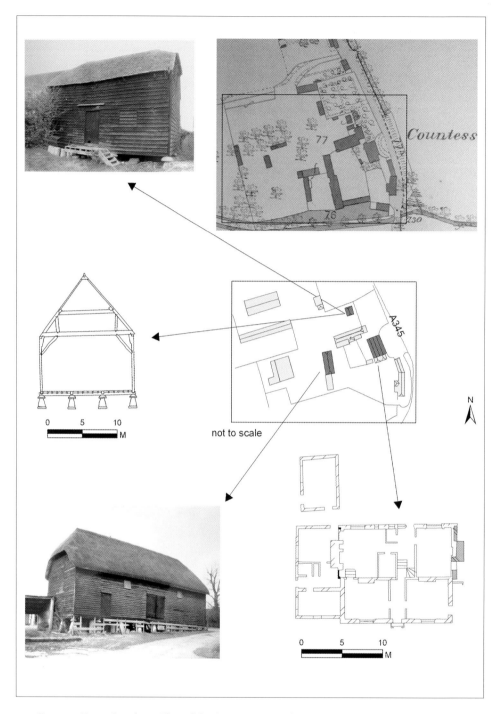

105 Countess Farm, Amesbury. Plan of the farm in 1887 and 2003 with plans and photographs of the main surviving buildings. *Drawing by Vanessa Constant: pictures reproduced courtesy of the National Trust and the Wiltshire Buildings Record*

and Carnarvon 1883, 293–5). Ten years later the Great Western Railway proposed a line from Pewsey southwards to include a station for Stonehenge and Amesbury, but this scheme also failed (Chippindale 2004, 158). It was not until 1902 that Amesbury was eventually linked to the London and South Western Railway via the Amesbury and Military Camp Light Railway that at first ran from a station south of London Road in Amesbury through to a junction with the main line at Grateley (Hampshire).

106 Nineteenth-century milestone with a metal plate fixed to a stone block on the Salisbury to Devizes road (A360) near Airman's Cross. Compare the design of this with the eighteenth-century milestone beside the A344 near Stonehenge in illustration 100. *Photograph: Timothy Darvill, copyright reserved*

STONEHENGE, TRIPPERS, AND THE NEO-DRUIDS

New and better roads and the availability of cheap railway travel were undoubtedly factors that led to an increase in the scale of visitor interest in Stonehenge through the nineteenth century, as it became a destination for outings and social occasions. As early as 1770 the Amesbury Turnpike Trust advertised its roads as being good for viewing Stonehenge (Crowley 1995, 17).

Between about 1882 and 1880 Henry Browne and his son Joseph, both of whom lived in Amesbury, acted as guides to the site and sold models and paintings of it (Chippindale 2004, 143–7). From the 1860s a Mr Judd ran a photographic business at the site photographing visitors and then developing the pictures in a mobile darkroom for visitors to take away as a souvenir (*107*). It was not only photographs that were taken, for pieces of stone from the site were believed to have curative powers. Hammers were available, but the custodians attempted to dissuade visitors from damaging the stones (Chippindale 2004, 159). Goulstone (1986) has drawn attention to a mid-nineteenth-century description of hare-coursing around Stonehenge, and suggests the presence of a turf-cut geoglyph or emblem in the form of a shepherd's crook at or near Stonehenge itself. Concerts were performed at Stonehenge in the late nineteenth century, one on Friday 18 September 1896 featuring the Magpie Musicians from Crystal Palace (Chippindale et al.1990, 102).

As well as members of the public interested to see the site, several renowned artists used it as a subject for their work, amongst them James Bridges in about 1820, J M W Turner in 1828, and John Constable in 1835 (Chippindale 1986a; 1987; 2004).

It was also during the nineteenth century that links between Druids and Stonehenge changed from being a purely academic proposition relating to the interpretation of the site to being a piece of theatre at the site itself. Central to this development was Edward Williams, also known by the bardic nom-de-plume of Iolo Morganwg, a stonemason from Glamorgan. In the late eighteenth century he claimed that Glamorganshire bards had preserved more-or-less in tact the lore and wisdom of the ancient Druids. In 1792 the first ceremony in celebration of these traditions was held at a hastily constructed stone circle – the Maen Gorsedd – on Primrose Hill in London, and later he rather opportunistically grafted these increasingly elaborate Gorsedd ceremonies onto the traditional annual meeting of Welsh Bards known as the Eisteddfod (Piggott 1975, 159–82). As well as the Gorsedd Druids numerous other groups sprang up, including: the Ancient Order of Druids founded in London in 1781 by Henry Hurle; the United Ancient Order of Druids established as a friendly society in 1833; and the Order of Druids in 1858. The Ancient Druid Order may be the oldest such group; their list of Chosen Chiefs apparently extends back to 1717, although some early names may have been included retrospectively (Grinsell 1978b, 13). Participants in all these orders believed they were actually Druids, and dressed up in a range of costumes that mixed replica prehistoric objects with vaguely classical robes.

107 Members of the author's family posed for a group photograph during a visit to Stonehenge in the 1880s. *Photograph: Darvill family archive, copyright reserved*

It is not exactly known when Neo-Druidic ceremonies commenced at Stonehenge. Searches of local newspapers by Leslie Grinsell suggest that the first documented visit may have been on Monday 21 June 1909 (Grinsell 1978b, 14), although Stuart Piggott and others have suggested that Druidical ceremonies were held at Stonehenge during the late nineteenth century (Worthington 2004, 57). Piggott also noted that in 1901 a contretemps between Sir Edmund Antrobus and the Chief Druid led to the Druids being ejected from Stonehenge by the police, an act that apparently led to the public cursing of Sir Edmund (Piggott 1975, 181).

Gatherings at Stonehenge to witness the midsummer sunrise seem to have increased in popularity through the late nineteenth century. Grinsell notes that in 1872 there were about 35 visitors present, in 1878 perhaps as many as 300. Adam Stout suggests that they were arriving in their thousands by the late nineteenth century, quoting for example the *Devizes Chronicle* saying 'they journeyed from far and near – some in brakes, waggonettes, and traps, while the majority travelled by bicycles. The roads leading to the place presented a very animated appearance' (Stout 2003, 38). By 1899 it was already necessary for 15 policemen to be present following disorderly scenes in previous years (Grinsell 1978b, 22).

108 Druid's Lodge Cottages, built *c.*1900 beside the A360. *Photograph: Timothy Darvill, copyright reserved*

Reinforcing the link between Druids, stone circles, and Stonehenge were a whole series of literary and artistic representations. Druids regularly appeared in pictures of Stonehenge, and, quite inexplicably, Stonehenge appears as a background feature in a range of pictures featuring Druids or mystical visions of the landscape. In William Blake's *Jerusalem*, 'All things begin and end in Albion's ancient Druid rocky shore' with great Stonehenge-derived trilithons straddling the landscape on one engraved page (Blake 1820, plate 27). Perhaps drawing on the same basic themes, a small settlement called Druid's Head was established in Woodford parish *c.*1800 and became the centre of a substantial estate. Druid's Lodge, a plain redbrick house, was built in *c.*1895, the associated cottages beside the main road a few years later (*108*).

LANDS FOR MILITARY TRAINING

Perhaps the biggest change of the nineteenth century, and one that has had a far-reaching impact ever since, was the acquisition of land around Stonehenge for military training. In 1897 the Army purchased 40,000 acres (16,187ha) for about £10 per acre, mainly west of the Avon around Durrington and Rollestone, but some east of the Avon around Bulford. This became the core of one of the largest military training grounds in the British Isles – now known as Salisbury Plain Training Area (SPTA). In 1899 the area north of Durrington was used for artillery practice, the gunners being housed in a camp on Durrington Down (James 1983, 8–9). Rifle ranges were set up at Bulford in 1898, and here both hutted and tented camps were established.

Quite unexpectedly, the military presence established in and around the training area transformed the surrounding landscape and provided a new source of wealth and prosperity for the area in the twentieth century.

12

SWEET DREAMS AND FLYING MACHINES (AD 1900–2000)

Horse-drawn ploughs and cavalry training could be seen in the Stonehenge landscape in 1900. Just a century later five-furrow ploughs pulled by tractors rated at 110 horse-power till the downs, helicopters fitted with the very latest computer-controlled weapon systems practise their airborne manoeuvres, and the very ground shakes as guns pound the target areas away to the north in the heart of the Plain. The twentieth century was a period of profound change for the Stonehenge landscape, every bit as great in its impact as the works of the early farmers more than 5000 years before if the different levels of technology are taken into account.

The population of the Stonehenge landscape rose considerably during the twentieth century, much of it directly or indirectly attributable to the increasing scale of military occupation. In Bulford, for example, there were 341 residents in 1891, 4000 by 1941, and 5255 in 1991 (Bettey 1986, 288; Crowley 1995, 64). Much the same can be seen in Durrington parish, which includes Larkhill: 427 in 1901, 3005 in 1921, and 6926 in 1991 (Crowley 1995, 95). Many of the other villages expanded too, although less dramatically than those closely associated with military camps. The town of Amesbury grew not just in terms of its population but also in the range of services available and the amount of industry. By the end of the twentieth century its eastward expansion physically connected it to Boscombe Down as a continuous settlement, and more expansion is planned.

MILITARY MANOEUVRES

Following the acquisition by the army of land in the southern part of Salisbury Plain in 1897 (see Chapter 11) the military presence has been indelibly marked on the landscape with its own variety of distinctive archaeology (Schofield and Lake 1995; Dobinson et al. 1997; Bond 1991; WA 1998), including marker-stones emphasizing the boundary of the military estate (*109*).

109 Concrete marker on the boundary of War Department land at Larkhill. *Photograph: Timothy Darvill, copyright reserved*

In 1902, a permanent camp was established at Bulford Barracks, the most easterly part of the Stonehenge landscape (Bond 1991) and later, in 1914, Larkhill was made a permanent base for the School of Artillery (Watkin 1979, 115). Numerous temporary camps were established for anything between a few days and several years, including the 'extensive hutted encampment' constructed at the eastern end of the Stonehenge Cursus during the First World War and still in place into the 1920s (RCHM 1979, xxiv; Bond 1991, 435).

Balloons were the first aircraft used by the army and came to play an important role in the Boer War (1899–1902). War balloons were launched on Salisbury Plain and the earliest aerial photographs of Stonehenge were taken from such a platform in 1906 (Capper 1907). Larkhill Airfield is one of the earliest surviving military airfields, constructed in 1909, and was one of the very first flying schools in England (Watkin 1979, 115). As flying machines became more sophisticated it was involved in training pilots for duty in the First World War (WA 1998, 16). The aeroplane sheds at Larkhill, built during this time, still stand. The remains of other airfields can also be found dotted around the Stonehenge landscape, including Stonehenge Down (*110*), Lake Down, Rollestone Balloon School, Oatlands, Shrewton, Bulford Fields, and the still operational Boscombe Down.

From 1906 onwards Salisbury Plain has been extensively used as a practice ground for target exercises (James 1983, 20). Former military sites also include railways, hospitals, housing, memorials, defensive structures, paraphernalia such as pillboxes and anti-tank obstacles, and recreational facilities. Army records reveal sites previously unknown, for example the Fargo Camp Military Hospital. Although out of use as a hospital by 1925 it was still occupied, albeit on a reduced scale, until at least 1939, when it was known as Fargo Lodge (Bond 1991, 436). Narrow-gauge railways and standard-gauge military railways built from 1916 onwards were used for moving military supplies and for tank firing practice (Cross 1971).

War graves are known at Durrington, Bulford Village, Maddington, Orcheston St Mary, Hewettson Cross in Fargo Plantation (*111*), and the Lorraine/Wilson Cross at Airman's Cross on the A360/A344/B3046 junction (*colour plate 25*). At Wood Road, Larkhill, a brass plaque marks the site of the first military airfield on Salisbury Plain. The Bulford Kiwi is a modern geoglyph cut into the chalk hillside east of Bulford Camp by New Zealand troops stationed at Sling Camp in 1918 (Newman 1997, 202–3).

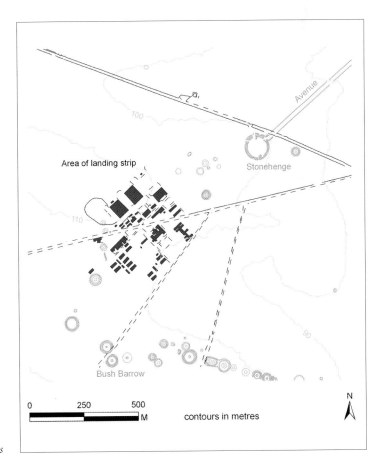

110 Stonehenge Airfield *c*.1917. *Drawing by Vanessa Constant: various sources*

111 Cross in Fargo Plantation
erected as a memorial to Major
Alexander William Hewettson,
killed while flying nearby in July
1913. *Photograph: Timothy Darvill,
copyright reserved*

The peak of military usage in terms of the area of land occupied came at the end of the Second World War, since when the military estate in this area has contracted slightly and consolidated in the northern part of the landscape. When military land was released back into agricultural use it was not always cleared of infrastructure straightaway. Thus Stonehenge Airfield appears on maps of the 1920s as the Pedigree Stock Farm, and the camp west of the Cursus was used as a pig farm for a short while. It is hard to visualize now, but in the late 1940s the Stonehenge landscape looked more like a disaster zone than open downland.

Clearance did eventually come, accompanied by government schemes to increase agricultural productivity which had the disturbing consequence that many extant ancient earthworks were levelled. At the west end of the Cursus, for example, not only was the camp removed but so too the earthworks of the Cursus west of Fargo Plantation and a previously upstanding round barrow that stood within the Cursus. Excavations did not take place until after they have been flattened (Christie 1963); some years later the barrow (Winterbourne Stoke 30) and the earthwork forming the western terminal of the Cursus were restored. But it was not only the agricultural landscape that was undergoing change.

GROUNDWORKS AND ROADWORKS

Railways became a feature of the Stonehenge landscape in the early twentieth century (Crowley 1995, 16). Amesbury railway station opened in 1902, serviced by a branch of the London and South Western Railway. The line was extended under the A303 via Ratfyn to Bulford and Bulford Camp in 1906, and a short spur served Boscombe Down airfield from about 1918. In 1914–15 the Larkhill Light Military Railway was opened, running from Ratfyn junction across to Druid's Lodge, Wilsford. It followed a northerly route that passed through the Larkhill army camp; there was a spur to serve Stonehenge Airfield. Although run by the military from a camp in Countess Road, the Larkhill Railway was available for some public use. All these lines were short-lived. The military routes had been closed down by 1928; the Grateley to Bulford line was closed to passengers in 1952 and to goods trains in 1963. The track was lifted in 1965 and thus ended an era (Harding 1991, 3).

Coincident with the dismantling of the railways in the area was the first major improvement to the road network for some decades. In 1958 the main road linking London with the West Country was reclassified as a Trunk Road, the A303(T). Local to Stonehenge, the single biggest change was the creation of the Amesbury bypass on the A303 in 1967–8, a task accompanied by limited archaeological recording of features such as the Stonehenge Avenue (Cleal et al. 1995, 296). Associated work was carried out on the A345 in 1966–8, including major excavations at Durrington Walls (Wainwright and Longworth 1971), and around Longbarrow Crossroads in 1967 (Richards 1990, 208–10).

STONEHENGE AND ITS VISITORS

The turn of the twentieth century was a turbulent time for Stonehenge and a difficult period for the Antrobus family who owned the site and the estate on which it lay. In April 1898 Sir Edmund Antrobus died and was succeeded by his nephew of the same name. In August 1899 the new baronet announced that he was willing to sell Stonehenge, together with 1300 acres (5265ha) of downland, to the nation for £125,000 (Chippindale 1976, 112–13). The price was considered too high, and despite rumours of interest from across the Atlantic no purchaser was found. The fall of Stone 22 and its lintel Stone 122 on 31 December 1900, together with the increasing public interest in the monument, raised questions about safety and how the site should be preserved. Wooden props were inserted to support the stones, and a joint committee of three leading amenity societies – the Wiltshire Archaeological and Natural History Society, the Society of Antiquaries of London, and the Society for the Protection of Ancient Buildings – was set up under the chairmanship of Viscount Dilhorne to consider the future. Amongst their recommendations was a proposal to enclose the monument by a wire fence, divert the Netheravon to Larkhill track to the west of the stones, and restore specific stones. The fence was duly erected in the early summer of 1901, and in August and September Professor William Gowland excavated at the base of Stone 56 in advance of setting it back upright. Moving the track, an undisputed public road, proved more difficult and after various legal battles it was left in place until it was finally diverted after the First World War. More significantly perhaps, rows and lawsuits also focused on a quite different issue: freedom of access.

At an early stage in deliberations on the future of Stonehenge the renowned Liberal parliamentarian Sir John Lubbock resigned from the joint advisory committee because he considered that it was not sufficiently insistent on the rights of access for the public. And he was right. After the fence was erected Sir Edmund Antrobus charged an entry fee of one shilling (5p), something that was considered an outage by those who energetically campaigned against it, first with letters to the press, and then, in March 1904, by recourse to the High Court. The court found in favour of Sir Edmund, who thereafter continued to make admission changes, although the problem of free access to all has never really gone away.

112 Stonehenge and associated visitor facilities, view westward from Stonehenge Bottom in 1930 with the Custodian's cottages to the left and the Stonehenge Café to the right. *Photograph: English Heritage, copyright reserved*

In 1913 the passing of the *Ancient Monuments Consolidation and Amendment Act* provided additional legal protection of the site, what today would be called 'scheduling', which was applied to Stonehenge in November 1913. In the same year the Antrobus family finally announced its intention to sell the Amesbury Estate which was eventually auctioned in several lots on 21 September 1915. Bidding for Stonehenge started at £5,000 and finished at £6,600 when the hammer came down on a bid by local landowner Cecil Chubb of Bemerton (Chippindale 1976, 120). With an annual income from visitors of £360 Chubb should perhaps have hung onto his purchase, but, in 1918, he generously presented it to the nation in whose care it has remained ever since.

A second programme of restoration was instigated by the Ministry of Works between 1919 and 1926, accompanied by a series of research excavations directed by William Hawley for the Society of Antiquaries of London (Chippindale 2004, 179–83; Cleal et al. 1995). Much of the surrounding land was acquired by the National Trust piecemeal from 1927 onwards when about 587ha was purchased following a public appeal; by 1990 the estate totalled about 760ha (1875 acres).

Visitor numbers rose steadily, with the Ministry of Works and its successor departments looking after the site: 38,000 in 1922, 124,000 in 1951, 666,000 in 1975, and 830,000 in 2004 (Crowley 1995, 17; English Heritage 2005). In 1918 a pair of cottages were built southeast of the stones as accommodation for the custodians, and in 1927 a privately run café was built north of the A344 (*112*); both were demolished in the 1930s (Crowley 1995, 17). Further excavations took place at Stonehenge itself most years between 1950 and 1959, with some later work in 1964 and 1978–81 (Cleal et al. 1995, 11–12). In 1967–8 a major infrastructure development took place north of the A344 to create car-parks, visitor facilities, and an underpass to provide access to the monument.

Midsummer festivals became an increasingly visible part of the Stonehenge tradition through the twentieth century, the rise of which has been well documented by Adam Stout (2003) and Andy Worthington (2002; 2004). Neo-Druid groups were amongst the most vocal opponents of the admission charges and controls on access to Stonehenge, disregarding the High Court's ruling and the Ministry of Works' attempts to regulate the festivities. In 1925 they rushed the turnstiles so that more than 1000 worshipped at the site for free, a break for freedom that earned them a ban for several years (Stout 2003, 40). The following year they met at midsummer some distance from the stones and heard speeches from the Chief Druid who spoke up in support of the miners who were still holding out after the collapse of the General Strike. Here, perhaps not for the first time and certainly not for the last, Stonehenge and its problems were directly connected to wider social issues and provided a high-profile platform that allowed comment to be heard by a wider audience.

The Neo-Druids were back at Stonehenge in the late 1920s, but seem to have become more marginal as the 1930s wore on and were irregular attenders by the end of the decade. Their place in 1939 was taken by Wiltshire Folk Dancers who seemingly performed traditional dances to the tune of an accordion (Stout 2003, 41). After the

Second World War the Neo-Druids were back in force every midsummer, supported by crowds of people from all over the world: 3000 were present in 1960. Music was a regular feature of the partying alongside the festival, skiffle, jazz, and rock-and-roll, each style associated with its distinctive sub-culture and each of course offensive to all but devotees. Druid-baiting was part of the scene, with thunderflashes being lobbed at the white-robed celebrants in 1956. The Summer Solstice had become an event where anti-Establishment feelings could be vented and the mores of a counter-culture celebrated. Many blamed the Neo-Druids, including Glyn Daniel, then editor of the influential journal *Antiquity*, who suggested that the authorities should 'clear Stonehenge of modern Druidic follies' (1978, 177). In 1964, and again in subsequent years over the next decade or so, barbed wire barricades were set up around the stones and only the Neo-Druids, a few local people, and a handful of press photographers were allowed within the stones on midsummer morning; everyone else had to view the scene from a distance (*113*).

Ten years later, in 1974, Wally Hope and others promoted the idea of a 'Free Stoned Henge' festival to coincide with the solstice. Flyers by Phil Russell and airplay on Radio Caroline attracted a crowd of about 500; the name of the festival perhaps recalling the title of the album *Stonedhenge* released by Ten Years After in 1968. Recollections of the event vary, but early pioneers of synthesizer-driven prog-rock Zorch played from a small stage facing the stones. After the solstice around 30 people decided not to leave straightaway and set up a camp to continue the festival beside the by-way to the west of Stonehenge calling themselves the Wallies of Wessex. Their open camp, known as Fort Wally, remained in the area through until the Winter Solstice (Worthington 2004, 38–40). The following year a much bigger festival was planned, posters designed by Roger Hutchinson promoting the event being widely circulated across southern England (*114*). The gathering was focused on King Barrow Ridge east of Stonehenge and the hot sunny weather attracted a crowd of about 3000 to hear two bands – Hawkwind and Here and Now – open the show on midsummer's eve. The festival lasted about ten days and was generally judged to be a success. It was repeated in 1976 back to the west of Stonehenge, and continued there annually through to 1984.

Over the course of a decade or so, the Stonehenge Free Festival became increasingly associated with a counter-culture that, while maintaining an interest in the stones, gradually drifted away from its hippie-dominated roots. The anarchy of punk lifestyles, the rise of the Peace Movement, anti-Thatcherism protests, riots against the Poll Tax, militant animal-rights campaigns, attacks on the Establishment, and the nihilistic culture of Rave were all ingredients for trouble that in 1984 finally mixed together in what has been claimed as the largest free festival in the British Isles. To many observers it was thus no surprise that when English Heritage and the National Trust announced that they would not permit a festival in 1985 the move was seen as provocative and a step too far in terms of restricting personal freedoms and controlling the will of counter-cultures. Stonehenge and the Stonehenge Festival became the focus of confrontation

113 Summer solstice at Stonehenge in the 1970s when only a party of Neo-Druids, local people, and a few photographers were allowed within the stones. *Photograph: Timothy Darvill, copyright reserved*

and conflict which erupted into violence on 2 June 1985 when Wiltshire Police stopped a convoy of would-be festival goers heading for Stonehenge on the A338. Their convoy was chased into a field near Cholderton where ensued what the press dubbed the 'Battle of Beanfield' between police and protestors, well documented by Chris Chippindale (1986b) and Andy Worthington (2005) and taken as the theme for a rebellious song of the same name by indie-rockers The Levellers (1991, track 10).

People shrewdly asked 'Who owns Stonehenge?' (Chippindale et al. 1990), but little changed over the following years as English Heritage and the National Trust resolutely refused to allow not just the festival but any access to Stonehenge at all over the solstice period. Exclusion orders were imposed and a heavy police presence maintained year after year, things that riled those opposing the ban and provoked confrontation both peaceful and otherwise (Dobinson 1992; Bender 1998). Various proposals were made to provide a more worthwhile celebration (e.g. Chippindale 1985b) but it was not until 2000 that general access to the stones at the Summer Solstice was restored, a move that initially prompted a mixed reaction (Dennison 2000). It took more than a decade for the anger and uptightness of the 1980s to seep away, but in 2001 about 14,000 people turned up for what was a very peaceful and enjoyable night of celebrations. In subsequent years more than 20,000 have been present for the sunrise and a sense of occasion once more fills the circle as folk of all ages and myriad cultures soak up the essence of what is going on (*colour plate 26*). But as one problem was solved, another was fermenting.

114 Poster drawn by Roger Hutchinson advertising the 1975 Free Festival at Stonehenge: copies widely adorned noticeboards and lamp-posts across southern Britain. *Poster by Roger Hutchinson, copyright reserved*

CONSERVATION AND MANAGEMENT

Looking after Stonehenge and the landscape around about has been a problem throughout the twentieth century, and as noted already various measures were taken to provide access and facilities. From the mid-1970s, Stonehenge became the only ancient monument in England to be subject to its own piece of parliamentary legislation with the passing of the *Stonehenge Regulations* revised in 1983 and updated again in 1997 (Statutory Instrument 1997 No. 2038). These regulations provide controls over public access to Stonehenge and its surroundings.

Through the 1970s heavy visitor use of the monument meant that on busy days it was almost impossible to see the stones for people, while the stones themselves were getting smoothed and were loosing their natural patina as people stroked them, hugged them, or just rubbed against them in the crush. In 1978 visitors were excluded from walking amongst the stones except through special access arrangements out of normal opening hours. A new enclosure and visitor pathway through the site were made in 1981 (Bond 1982), the route being changed to a circular one more recently with the construction of a bridge/viewing platform over the Avenue. These though were simple solutions to short-term problems that stand alongside much of the other day-to-day maintenance. Looming overhead were two much bigger problems: the overall inadequacy of the visitor facilities and the desire to remove the A344 cutting through the edge of the site; and the need to upgrade the A303 as it passes through this sensitive and archaeologically rich landscape.

Resolving these two issues represents one of the longest-running sagas in conservation archaeology, but both came into sharper focus in 1986 when the Stonehenge landscape was inscribed as a World Heritage Site, half of the 'Stonehenge, Avebury, and Associated Sites' designation that signalled international recognition of the universal value of these prehistoric remains to the common heritage of mankind. As appropriate to a World Heritage Site, a series of plans and strategies have since been developed and widely discussed (Addyman 1989; Wainwright 2000a), now published as the *Stonehenge World Heritage Site Management Plan* (English Heritage 2000); the *Stonehenge Estate Land Use Plan* (National Trust 2001); and the *Stonehenge World Heritage Site Archaeological Research Framework* (Darvill 2005). Proposals to deal with the two overarching issues of the visitor centre and the A303 improvements were set out in the *Stonehenge Master Plan* (English Heritage and National Trust 1999), sweet dreams that will become reality through the Stonehenge Project. Both elements of the scheme have provoked controversy and divided opinions, not least because much bigger social, economic, and political issues (e.g. national transport policy, globalization, climate change, and the meaning of World Heritage Site designation) have found their way into the arguments and Stonehenge has again become a rallying ground for those pursuing a whole raft of divergent agendas.

Stonehenge visitor centre

The idea of improving visitor access to, and facilities for, Stonehenge has been discussed for decades, as too the associated closure of the A344 that cuts through the north side of Stonehenge and the Avenue (Chippindale 1983b; 1985a; 2004, 259–77; DoE 1979; Heritage Projects 1984; LH 1997). On many days of the year Stonehenge is simply swamped by vehicles and people (*115*), and in 1993 the facilities were famously described by Parliament's House of Commons Public Accounts Committee as 'a national disgrace'. More than a dozen possible sites have been considered for the relocation of the visitor centre and many studies and evaluations have been carried out to assess the likely impacts of each (*116*).

By 1990 extensive consultations and researches focused on a site adjacent to Durrington Down Farm at Larkhill that was highly suitable for a new visitor centre. An Environmental Impact Assessment was carried out (Darvill 1991) and a planning application submitted. Following many debates and a failure to agree some basic

115 Summertime at Stonehenge, viewed from the by-way northwest of the monument. The car-parks and visitor facilities dwarf the view of Stonehenge itself (top left). *Photograph: Timothy Darvill, copyright reserved*

principles of conservation the proposal was withdrawn in December 1991 and further possible sites reviewed (Darvill 1993a; 1993b; 1993c; 1994). Eventually, a piece of land outside the World Heritage Site beside the River Avon east of Countess Road was selected and after appropriate assessment (Darvill 1995; WA 1995; 2003; 2004) was purchased by English Heritage in December 2000. Denton Corker Marshall, a well-respected international architectural practice, designed the new centre amid much debate as to whether Countess Road East was indeed the best site, how it should be used, and how exactly visitors will circulate within the landscape around Stonehenge (Baxter and Chippindale 2002; Pitts and Richards 2003; Chippindale and Baxter 2003). In 2004 an Environmental Impact Statement (Chris Blandford Associates 2004) and planning application was submitted to Salisbury District Council. Unexpectedly, opposition to the proposals seems to have prevailed and the Local Planning Authority refused the application in July 2005, leaving English Heritage the option of mounting an appeal or submitting a revised proposal.

Improving the A303

Plans for the upgrading and improving of the A303 from King Barrow Ridge through to Berwick Down have been debated almost as long as the visitor centre proposals. Although English Heritage commissioned various studies to assist in early discussions about alternative routes, the majority of the work has been co-ordinated by the Highways Agency. Overall, more than 50 possible routes and permutations thereof involving cuttings and tunnels were examined in detail between 1991 and 1999.

In June 1999 Transport Minister Lord Whitty announced the Government's preferred route for the improvement of the A303, a mainly on-line solution for the eastern section with a 2km long tunnel south of Stonehenge itself and a northern by-pass for Winterbourne Stoke. Autumn 1999 saw the appointment of Mott MacDonald as the lead consultants on the development of these proposals, including the contentious matters of how long the tunnel should be and how it should be constructed. However, after considerable public pressure, in December 2002 the Government announced that a 2.1km-long bored tunnel would be included in the scheme, and on 5 June 2003 Draft Orders and an Environmental Impact Statement (BBCHG 2003) were published, initiating a period of public consultation.

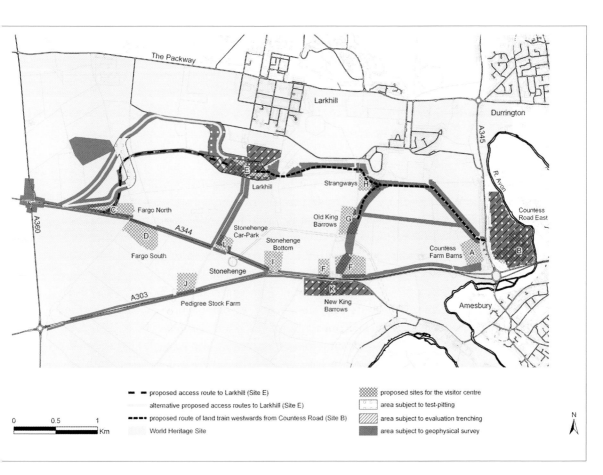

116 Map showing the distribution and extent of the main sites assessed as possible locations for a new visitor centre for Stonehenge. The site at Countess Road East has been selected for development. *Drawing by Vanessa Constant: based on Darvill 1993a; 1997b; English Heritage and National Trust 1999, with additional data kindly supplied by Wessex Archaeology, Gifford and Co., and English Heritage over Ordnance Survey © Crown Copyright 2006. All rights reserved. Licence 100045276*

A Public Inquiry into the proposals opened in Salisbury on 17 February 2004 and sat for 37 days until its close on 11 May 2004. The inspector's report, received by the Department of Transport in January 2005 but not published until July (DFT 2005), recommended adoption of the on-line solution with a 2.1km-long bored tunnel, but in the time taken to work through the planning and consultation on the scheme the estimated costs of building it rose substantially from £284m to £470m. As a result Government ministers initiated a further round of public consultation to identify and review lower cost options.

SPRING 2006

At the time of going to press both elements of the Stonehenge Project have become bogged down in bureaucratic and democratic processes. All sides agree that something needs to be done, but no one can agree exactly what that something should be. As with the question of access to Stonehenge at the Summer Solstice, there is unlikely to be a solution to the visitor centre and road improvement schemes until attention focuses solely on what is best for Stonehenge and its landscape while the bigger issues are drawn off and debated in another arena.

AN ICON: A LIFE

Stonehenge has truly become a legend in its own lifetime, the monument itself being the internationally recognized face of one of the richest archaeological landscapes in the world. Stonehenge was among the 12 icons proposed by the Department of Culture, Media and Sport as part of a portrait of England (DCMS 2006). It appears in pictures, photographs, sculptures, in literature, poetry, and music. Stonehenge features in advertising campaigns for products as diverse as Benson and Hedges cigarettes, Sellotape, and Renault cars. There are at least half-a-dozen replicas of it around the world, some in stone or concrete but more unusual is Autohenge built by sculptor Bill Lishman from crushed cars at Blackstock, Ontario, in Canada which once featured on the cover of a Steely Dan album (1993). Throughout the Stonehenge landscape and beyond there are numerous references to Stonehenge. There is the long-established Stonehenge Inn at Durrington (*117*) and the Amesbury Archer public house in the Solstice Centre service station beside the A303 at Boscombe Down opened in 2005. The Stonehenge Comprehensive School is in Amesbury, which is also the base for Stonehenge Construction and numerous other firms and businesses that use the name. A wall painting in the Rajpoot Tandoori Restaurant in Fisherton Street, Salisbury, shows Stonehenge as it is today, one of many representations on murals. And on a still wider canvas there is a bewildering range of direct and indirect references to Stonehenge and its surroundings in popular literature, art, film, and music (Darvill 2004a).

117 The Stonehenge Inn, Durrington. *Photograph: Timothy Darvill, copyright reserved*

Aspects of the prehistoric past are also re-created from time to time in the Stonehenge landscape – references to a by-gone era. A stone circle was built on the edge of a new housing development at Butterfield Down, Amesbury, in 1998 (*colour plate 27*); in June 2005 'Foamhenge' was created near Stockton for a television programme (*118*); and a couple of months later a full-scale reconstruction of the southern circle at Durrington Walls was made in timber at Upavon for a Channel 4 *Time Team* programme (see *37*).

It seems impossible now to escape the gaze of this landscape, yet looking back over the millennia through which the Stonehenge landscape has been part of the life of so many people it is clear that the landscape itself has not one but several tiers of existence, interlocking cycles of life and death that relate back to the visions of time considered in Chapter 1. Looked at from one direction, the Stonehenge landscape is still youthful, its skin still soft and smooth, its rivers running freely, and the communities it supports all healthy and vibrant. There is a long way to go before the next Ice Age or some devastating tectonic movement calls time by fundamentally reorganizing its structure and form.

Looked at another way, there are numerous medium-term cycles that come and go. History repeats itself every thousand years or so as things are shaken up. After upheavals that might been seen as some rite of passage the landscape emerges invigorated or reclothed in some new style: the development of farming, the influx of sacred

118 Foamhenge. A life-sized polystyrene reconstruction of Stonehenge built near Stockton for a Channel 5 TV documentary programme screened on 21 and 22 June 2005. *Photograph: Timothy Darvill, copyright reserved*

monuments, the expansion of agriculture, the localization of settlement in the river valleys, and the spread of the military. Nothing stays new, and as the twenty-first century unfolds it will be interesting to see what happens next.

Getting still closer to the landscape there is a third element to the cycle, shorter in duration and still more personal. For however well we know the Stonehenge landscape in its totality, the reality is that any one person can only actually experience it, and engage with it, for, at most, the span of a single life. We can each go to the landscape, enjoy it, learn from it, and take some insight from it, but always we have to recognize that it will outlive us; there is always more to come, another chapter in the constantly unfolding biography of a richly textured, deeply ancient, and truly remarkable land.

BIBLIOGRAPHY

Adamson, T, 2002, Stonehenge: the stone mason and his craft. *Antiquity*, 76, 41–2

Addyman, P, 1989, The Stonehenge we deserve. In H Cleere (ed.), *Archaeological heritage management in the modern world*. London: Unwin Hyman. 265–71

Albarella, U, & Payne, S, 2005, Neolithic pigs from Durrington Walls, Wiltshire, England: a biometrical database. *Journal of Archaeological Science*, 32, 589–99

Albarella, U, & Serjeantson, D, 2002, A passion for pork: meat consumption at the British late Neolithic site of Durrington Walls. In P Miracle & N Milner (eds.), *Consuming passions and patterns of consumption*. Cambridge: McDonald Institute for Archaeological Research. 33–49

Alcock, L, 1971, *Arthur's Britain*. London: Allen Lane

Alcock, S E, & Osborne, R (eds.), 1994, *Placing the gods: sanctuaries and sacred space in ancient Greece*. Oxford: Clarendon Press

Allen, M, 1995, Before Stonehenge. In R M J Cleal, K E Walker, & R Montague, *Stonehenge in its twentieth century landscape* (English Heritage Archaeological Report 10). London: English Heritage. 41–62

Allen, M, 1997, Environment and land-use: the economic development of the communities who built Stonehenge (an economy to support the stones). *Proceedings of the British Academy*, 92, 115–44

Anderson, C, Planel, P, & Stone, P, 1996, *Teacher's handbook to Stonehenge*. London: English Heritage

Annable, F K, 1959, Excavation and fieldwork in Wiltshire: 1958. *Wiltshire Archaeological and Natural History Magazine*, 57, 227–39

Annable, F K, & Simpson, D D A, 1964, *Guide catalogue of the Neolithic and Bronze Age collections in Devizes Museum*. Devizes: Wiltshire Archaeological and Natural History Society

Anon, 1930, A villa at Netheravon. *Wiltshire Archaeological and Natural History Magazine*, 45, 490–1

Anon, 1961, Excavation and fieldwork in Wiltshire. *Wiltshire Archaeological and Natural History Magazine*, 58, 30–8

Anon, 1973, Winterbourne Stoke. *CBA Groups XII and XIII Archaeological Review*, 7, 20

Anon, 1976, Wiltshire Archaeological Register for 1974–5. *Wiltshire Archaeological and Natural History Magazine*, 70/71, 132–8

Anon, 1978, Wiltshire Archaeological Register for 1976–7. *Wiltshire Archaeological and Natural History Magazine*, 72/73, 201–8

Anon, 1992, Excavation and fieldwork in Wiltshire 1990. *Wiltshire Archaeological and Natural History Magazine*, 85, 156–62

Anon, 1998, Excavation and fieldwork in Wiltshire 1996. *Wiltshire Archaeological and Natural History Magazine*, 91, 152–66

Anon, 2001, Excavation and fieldwork in Wiltshire 1999. *Wiltshire Archaeological and Natural History Magazine*, 94, 243–55

Anon, 2003, Excavation and fieldwork in Wiltshire 2001. *Wiltshire Archaeological and Natural History Magazine*, 96, 229–37

Anon, 2004, Excavation and fieldwork in Wiltshire 2002. *Wiltshire Archaeological and Natural History Magazine*, 97, 300–8

Anon, 2005, Excavation and fieldwork in Wiltshire 2003. *Wiltshire Archaeological and Natural History Magazine*, 98, 349–56

Applebaum, S, 1954, The agriculture of the British Early Iron Age as exemplified at Figheldean Down, Wiltshire. *Proceedings of the Prehistoric Society*, 20, 103–13

ApSimon, A M, 1954, Dagger graves in the 'Wessex' Bronze Age. *Annual Report of the University of London Institute of Archaeology*, 10, 37–62

ApSimon, A M, 1972, Biconical urns outside Wessex. In F Lynch & C Burgess (eds.), *Prehistoric man in Wales and the west*. Bath: Adams and Dart. 141–60

Ashbee, P, 1960, *The Bronze Age round barrow in Britain*. London: Phoenix

Ashbee, P, 1978a, Amesbury Barrow 51: excavation 1960. *Wiltshire Archaeological and Natural History Magazine*, 70/71, 1–60

Ashbee, P, 1978b, *The ancient British*. Norwich: Geo Books

Ashbee, P, 1980, Amesbury barrow 39: excavations 1960. *Wiltshire Archaeological and Natural History Magazine*, 74/75, 1–34

Ashbee, P, 1984a, The excavation of Amesbury Barrows 58, 61a, 61, 72. *Wiltshire Archaeological and Natural History Magazine*, 79, 39–91

Ashbee, P, 1984b, *The earthen long barrow in Britain* (second edition). Norwich: Geo Books.

Ashbee, P, 1986, The excavation of Milton Lilbourne Barrows 1–5. *Wiltshire Archaeological and Natural History Magazine*, 80, 23–96

Ashbee, P, 1998, Stonehenge: its possible non-completion, slighting and dilapidation. *Wiltshire Archaeological and Natural History Magazine*, 91, 139–42

Ashbee, P, Bell, M, & Proudfoot, E, 1989, *Wilsford Shaft excavations, 1960–62* (HBMCE Archaeological Report 11). London: English Heritage

Aston, M, 1982, Wiltshire. *Medieval Villages Research Group Annual Report*, 30, 11

Aston, M, 1983, Wiltshire. *Medieval Villages Research Group Annual Report*, 31, 11–12

Aston, M, 1985, *Interpreting the landscape*. London: Batsford

Aston, M, & Lewis, C, 1994, Introduction. In M Aston & C Lewis (eds.), *The medieval landscape of Wessex* (Oxbow Monograph 46). Oxford: Oxbow Books. 1–12

Atkinson, R J C, 1951a, The excavations at Dorchester, Oxfordshire, 1946–51. *Archaeological Newsletter*, 4.4, 56–9

Atkinson, R J C, 1951b, The henge monuments of Great Britain. In R J C Atkinson, C M, Piggott & N K Sandars, *Excavations at Dorchester, Oxon. First report*. Oxford: Ashmolean Museum. 81–107

Atkinson, R J C, 1956, *Stonehenge*. London: Hamish Hamilton

Atkinson, R J C, 1961, Neolithic engineering. *Antiquity*, 35, 292–9

Atkinson, R J C, 1966, Moonshine on Stonehenge. *Antiquity*, 40, 212–16

Atkinson, R J C, 1974, The Stonehenge bluestones. *Antiquity*, 48, 62–3

Atkinson, R J C, 1978, Some new measurements on Stonehenge. *Nature*, 275 (no. 5675), 50–2

Atkinson, R J C, 1979, *Stonehenge* (second edition). Harmondsworth: Penguin Books

Atkinson, R J C, 1984, Barrows excavated by William Stukeley near Stonehenge, 1723–4. *Wiltshire Archaeological and Natural History Magazine*, 79, 244–6

Atkinson, R J C, 1987, *Stonehenge and neighbouring monuments* (revised edition). London: English Heritage

Atkinson, R J C, Piggott, S, & Stone, J F S, 1952, The excavation of two additional holes at Stonehenge, and new evidence for the date of the monument. *Antiquaries Journal*, 32, 14–20

Atwood, G, 1963, A study of Wiltshire water-meadows. *Wiltshire Archaeological and Natural History Society Magazine*, 58, 403–12

Aubrey, J, 1693a (ed. J Fowles, 1980), *Monumenta Britannica, or, a miscellany of British antiquities. I (Parts 1 and 2)*. Sherborne: Dorset Publishing Co.

Aubrey, J, 1693b (ed. J Fowles, 1982), *Monumenta Britannica, or, a miscellany of British antiquities II (Part 3 and index)*. Sherborne: Dorset Publishing Co.

Aubrey, J (ed. K G Ponting), 1969, *Aubrey's natural history of Wiltshire: a reprint of the natural history of Wiltshire*. Newton Abbot: David and Charles

Baillie, M, 1999, *Exodus to Arthur: catastrophic encounters with comets*. London: Batsford

Bakker, J A, 1979, Lucas de Heere's Stonehenge. *Antiquity*, 53, 107–11

Ball, P F, 1979, The Saxon crosses at Amesbury. In J H Chandler (ed.), *The Amesbury millennium lectures*. Amesbury: The Amesbury Society. 32–46

Barber, M, 2005, Stonehenge from the air in 1900: the ballooning adventures of the Reverend John McKenzie Bacon. *AARGnews*, 30, 9–17

Barber, M, Field, D, & Topping, P, 1999, *The Neolithic flint mines of England*. Swindon: English Heritage

Barclay, A, & Harding, J (eds.), 1999, *Pathways and ceremonies: the cursus monuments of Britain and Ireland* (Neolithic Studies Group Seminar Papers 4). Oxford: Oxbow Books

Barclay, E, 1895, *Stonehenge and its earthworks*. London: Nutt

Barfield, L, 1991, Wessex with and without Mycenae: new evidence from Switzerland. *Antiquity*, 65, 102–7

Barnatt, J, 1989, *Stone circles of Britain* (BAR British Series 215). Oxford: British Archaeological Reports (2 vols.)

Barrett, J C, 1980, The pottery of the later Bronze Age in lowland England. *Proceedings of the Prehistoric Society*, 46, 297–319

Barrett, J C, 1994, *Fragments from antiquity*. Oxford: Blackwell

Barrett, J C, 1997, Stonehenge, land, sky and the seasons. *British Archaeology*, 29, 8–9

Barrett, J C, Bradley, R, & Green, M, 1991, *Landscape, monuments and society. The prehistory of Cranborne Chase*. Cambridge: Cambridge University Press

Barton, N, 1992, *Hengistbury Head, Dorset. Volume 2: the late upper Palaeolithic and early Mesolithic sites* (OUCA Monograph 34). Oxford: Oxford University Committee for Archaeology

Barton, N, 1999, The lateglacial or late and final upper Palaeolithic colonization of Britain. In J Hunter & I Ralston (eds.), *The archaeology of Britain: an introduction from the upper Palaeolithic to the Industrial Revolution*. London: Routledge. 13–34

Batchelor, D, 1997, Mapping the Stonehenge landscape. *Proceedings of the British Academy*, 92, 61–72

Baxter, I, & Chippindale, C, 2002, Stonehenge: the 'brownfield' approach. *Current Archaeology*, 16.3 (no. 183), 94–6

Bayliss, A, Bronk Ramsey, C, & McCormac, F G, 1997, Dating Stonehenge. *Proceedings of the British Academy*, 92, 39–59

BBCHG [Balfour Beatty-Costain Halcrow-Gifford], 2003, *A303 Stonehenge Improvement: environmental statement*. London: Balfour Beatty-Costain Halcrow-Gifford for the Highways Agency [limited circulation printed report, 2 vols. plus non-technical summary]

Beck, C, & Shennan, S, 1991, *Amber in prehistoric Britain* (Oxbow Monograph 8). Oxford: Oxbow Books

Beckensall, S, 1999, *British prehistoric rock art*. Stroud: Tempus

Bender, B, 1992, Theorizing landscapes, and the prehistoric landscapes of Stonehenge. *Man* (ns), 27, 735–55

Bender, B, 1993, Stonehenge – contested landscapes (medieval to present day). In B Bender (ed.), *Landscape: politics and perspectives*. Oxford: Berg. 245–80

Bender, B, 1998, *Stonehenge: making space*. Oxford: Berg

Beresford, M, & Hurst, J G (eds.), 1971, *Deserted medieval village studies*. London: Lutterworth

Bergström, T, 1974, *Stonehenge*. London and New York: Boyle Books

Bettey, J H, 1979, Farming and community life in Amesbury and district during the sixteenth and seventeenth centuries. In J Chandler (ed.), *The Amesbury millennium lectures*. Amesbury: Amesbury Society. 58–69

Bettey, J H, 1986, *Wessex from AD 1000*. London: Longman

Betty, J H, 2004, The production of rabbits in Wiltshire during the seventeenth century. *Antiquaries Journal*, 84, 380–93

Bevins, R E, Lees, G J, & Roach, R A, 1989, Ordovician intrusions of the Strumble Head – Mynydd Preseli region, Wales: lateral extensions of the Fishguard volcanic complex. *Journal of the Geological Society of London*, 146, 113–23

Bewley, R H, Crutchley, S P, & Shell, C A, 2005, New light on an ancient landscape: LiDAR survey in the Stonehenge World Heritage Site. *Antiquity*, 79, 636–47

Bintliff, J, 1991, The construction of an *Annaliste*/structural history approach to archaeology. In J Bintliff (ed.), *The Annales School and archaeology*. Leicester: Leicester University Press. 1–33

Blake, W, 1820, *Jerusalem: the emanation of the giant Albion*. London: Privately Printed

Bollongino, R, Edwards, C J, Alt, K W, Burger, J, & Bradley, D G, 2005, Early history of European domestic cattle as revealed by ancient DNA. *Biology Letters*, 2.1, 155–9

Bolton, E, 1627, *Nero Caesar or Monarchie depraved* (second edition). London

Bond, D, 1982, An excavation at Stonehenge, 1981. *Wiltshire Archaeological and Natural History Magazine*, 77, 39–44

Bond, J, 1991, Appendix H: landscape regression analysis. In T C Darvill (ed.), *Stonehenge Conservation and Management Project: environmental statement*. London: Debenham Tewson and Chinnocks [limited circulation printed report, 3 vols.]. 383–444

Bond, J, 1994, Forests, chases, warrens and parks in medieval Wessex. In M Aston & C Lewis (eds.), *The medieval landscape of Wessex* (Oxbow Monograph 46). Oxford: Oxbow Books. 115–58

Bonney, D, 1966, Pagan Saxon burials and boundaries in Wiltshire. *Wiltshire Archaeological and Natural History Magazine*, 61, 25–30

Bonney, D, 1976, Early boundaries and estates in southern England. In P H Sawyer (ed.), *Medieval settlement*. London: Edward Arnold. 72–82

Bonney, D, 1981, Megaliths near Stonehenge. *Wiltshire Archaeological and Natural History Magazine*, 76, 166–7

Bonney, D, 1982, Pagan Saxon burials at Amesbury. *Wiltshire Archaeological and Natural History Magazine*, 77, 150

Booth, A St S, and Stone, J F S, 1952, A trial flint mine at Durrington. *Wiltshire Archaeological and Natural History Magazine*, 54, 381

Bowen, C, & Fowler, P J, 1966, Romano-British rural settlements in Dorset and Wiltshire. In C Thomas (ed.), *Rural settlement in Roman Britain* (Council for British Archaeology Research Report 7). London: Council for British Archaeology. 43–67

Bowen C, & Smith, I F, 1977, Sarsen stones in Wessex: the Society's first investigations in the evolution of the landscape project. *Antiquaries Journal*, 57, 186–96

Bradley, R, 1981, Various styles of urn-cemeteries and settlement in southern England *c*.1400–1000 bc. In R Chapman, I Kinnes & K Randsborg (eds.), *The archaeology of death*. Cambridge: Cambridge University Press. 93–104

Bradley, R, 1992, The excavation of an oval barrow beside the Abingdon causewayed enclosure, Oxfordshire. *Proceedings of the Prehistoric Society*, 58, 127–42

Bradley, R, 1993, *Altering the earth: the origin of monuments in Britain and continental Europe* (Society of Antiquaries of Scotland Monograph Series 8). Edinburgh: Society of Antiquaries of Scotland

Bradley, R, 1998, *The significance of monuments*. London: Routledge

Bradley, R, 2000, *The good stones: a new investigation of the Clava Cairns* (Society of Antiquaries of Scotland Monograph 17). Edinburgh: Society of Antiquaries of Scotland

Bradley, R, 2005, *Ritual and domestic life in prehistoric Europe*. London: Routledge

Bradley, R, & Chambers, R, 1988, A new study of the cursus complex at Dorchester-on-Thames. *Oxford Journal of Archaeology*, 7, 271–89

Bradley, R, Entwistle, R, & Raymond, F, 1994, *Prehistoric land divisions on Salisbury Plain* (English Heritage Archaeological Report 2). London: English Heritage

Branigan, K, 1970, Wessex and Mycenae: some evidence reviewed. *Wiltshire Archaeological and Natural History Magazine*, 65, 89–107

Branigan, K, 1973, Vespasian in the south-west. *Proceedings of the Dorset Natural History and Archaeological Society*, 95, 50–7

Branigan, K, 1976, Villa settlement in the West Country. In K Branigan & P Fowler (eds.), *The Roman west country*. Newton Abbot: David and Charles. 120–41

Breest, K, & Veil, S, 1991, The late upper Palaeolithic site of Schweskau, Ldkr, Lüchow-Dannenberg, Germany, and some comments on the relationship between Magdalenian and Hamburgian. In N Barton, A J Roberts & D A Roe (eds.), *The late glacial in north-west Europe* (Council for British Archaeology Research Report 77). London: Council for British Archaeology. 82–99

Briard, J, 1993, Relations between Brittany and Great Britain during the Bronze Age. In C Scarre & F Healy (eds.), *Trade and exchange in prehistoric Europe. Oxbow Monographs 33*. Oxford: Oxbow Books 33. 183–90

Bridgland, D R, 2001, The Pleistocene evolution and Palaeolithic occupation of the Solent River. In F F Wenban-Smith & R Hosfield (eds.), *Palaeolithic archaeology of the Solent River* (Lithic Studies Society Occasional Paper 7). London: Lithic Studies Society. 15–26

Britton, D, 1961, A study of the composition of Wessex Culture bronzes. *Archaeometry*, 4, 39–52

Bronk Ramsey, C, 2000, *OxCal – Radiocarbon calibration programme version 3.5*. Oxford: Oxford University Laboratory for Archaeology and Art History

Brophy, K, 1999, The cursus monuments of Scotland. In A Barclay & J Harding (eds.), *Pathways and ceremonies: the cursus monuments of Britain and Ireland* (Neolithic Studies Group Seminar Papers 4). Oxford: Oxbow Books. 119–29

Brussell, G D, Pollard, A M, & Baird, D C, 1981, The characterization of early Bronze Age jet and jet-like material by x-ray fluorescence. *Wiltshire Archaeological and Natural History Magazine*, 76, 27–32

Brown, W E, 1959, Tobacco and clay pipes. In E Crittall (ed.), *A history of Wiltshire. Volume IV*. London: University of London Institute of Historical Research, Victoria History of the Counties of England. 240–4

Burgess, C, 1968, The later Bronze Age in the British Isles and north-western France. *Archaeological Journal*, 125, 1–45

Burgess, C, 1980, *The age of Stonehenge*. London: Dent

Burgess, C, 1985, Population, climate and upland settlement. In D Spratt & C Burgess (eds.), *Upland settlement in Britain: the second millennium BC and after* (BAR British Series 143). Oxford: British Archaeological Reports. 195–229

Burl, A, 1985, Geoffrey of Monmouth and the Stonehenge bluestones. *Wiltshire Archaeological and Natural History Magazine*, 79, 178–83

Burl, A, 1987, *The Stonehenge people*. London: Dent

Burl, A, 1991, The Heel Stone, Stonehenge: a study in misfortunes. *Wiltshire Archaeological and Natural History Magazine*, 84, 1–10

Burl, A, 1994, Stonehenge: slaughter, sacrifice and sunshine. *Wiltshire Archaeological and Natural History Magazine*, 87, 85–95.

Burl, A, 1997, The sarsen horseshoe inside Stonehenge: a rider. *Wiltshire Archaeological and Natural History Magazine*, 90, 1–12

Burl, A, 2000a, *The stone circles of Britain, Ireland, and Brittany*. New Haven and London: Yale University Press

Burl, A, 2000b, Myth-conceptions. *3rd Stone*, 37, 6–9

Burl, A, 2001, The Third Stone. The Altar Stone at Stonehenge: prone to doubt. *3rd Stone*, 40, 48–55

Burl, A, 2003, New angles on stone circles. Brittany, the British Isles and the land that archaeology forgot. *3rd Stone*, 47, 8–15

Burnham, B C, & Wacher, J, 1990, *The 'small towns' of Roman Britain*. London: Batsford.

Butler, J J, & Smith, I F, 1956, Razors, urns, and the British middle Bronze Age. *University of London Institute of Archaeology Annual Report*, 12, 20–52

Campbell Smith, W, 1963, Jade axes from sites in the British Isles. *Proceedings of the Prehistoric Society*, 29, 133–72

Campbell Smith, W, 1965, The distribution of jade axes from sites in Europe with a supplement to the catalogue of those from the British Isles. *Proceedings of the Prehistoric Society*, 31, 25–33

Canham, R, 1983, *Archaeology in the Salisbury Plain Training Area*. Trowbridge: Wiltshire County Council [limited circulation printed report]

Capper, J C, 1907, Photographs of Stonehenge as seen from a war balloon. *Archaeologia*, 60, 571–2

Case, H, 1973, A ritual site in north-east Ireland. In G Daniel & P Kjaerum (eds.), *Megalithic graves and ritual. Papers presented at the III Atlantic Colloquium, Moesgård 1969*. Copenhagen: Jutland Archaeological Society Publications. 173–96

Case, H, 1993, Beakers: deconstruction and after. *Proceedings of the Prehistoric Society*, 59, 241–68

Case, H, 1995, Some Wiltshire Beakers and their contexts. *Wiltshire Archaeological and Natural History Magazine*, 88, 1–17

Case, H, 1997, Stonehenge revisited. A review article. *Wiltshire Archaeological and Natural History Magazine*, 90, 161–8

Case, H, 2003, Beaker presence at Wilsford 7. *Wiltshire Archaeological and Natural History Magazine*, 96, 161–94

Castleden, R, 1993, *The making of Stonehenge*. London: Routledge

Castleden, R, 2001, The epic of the Stonehenge bluestones: were they moved by ice, or by people? *3rd Stone*, 39, 12–25

Champion, T, 1975, Britain in the European Iron Age. *Archaeologia Atlantica*, 1.2, 127–46

Champion, T, 2001, The beginnings of Iron Age archaeology in Wessex. In J Collis (ed.), *Society and settlement in Iron Age Europe* (Sheffield Archaeology Monograph 11). Sheffield: J R Collis Publishing. 9–22

Chandler, J H, 2002, *A303 Stonehenge Historic Landscape Survey (Draft)*. Cambridge: Mott MacDonald for the Highways Agency [limited circulation printed report]

Chandler, J H, & Goodhugh, P, 1989, *Amesbury: history and description of a south Wiltshire Town* (second edition). Amesbury: The Amesbury Society

Charleton, W, 1663, *Chorea Gigantum*. London

Childe, V G, 1940, *Prehistoric communities of the British Isles*. London: Chambers

Chippindale, C, 1976, The enclosure of Stonehenge. *Wiltshire Archaeological and Natural History Magazine*, 70/71, 109–23

Chippindale, C, 1983a, *Stonehenge complete*. London: Thames and Hudson

Chippindale, C, 1983b, What future for Stonehenge? *Antiquity*, 57, 172–80

Chippindale, C, 1985a, English Heritage and the future of Stonehenge, *Antiquity*, 59, 132–7

Chippindale, C, 1985b, Time for a Stonehenge celebration. *Current Archaeology*, 9.3 (no. 98), 84–5

Chippindale, C, 1986a, James Bridges's Stonehenge. *Wiltshire Archaeological and Natural History Magazine*, 80, 230–2

Chippindale, C, 1986b, Stoned Henge: events and issues at the summer solstice, 1985. *World Archaeology*, 18.1, 38–58

Chippindale, C, 1987, *Visions of Stonehenge 1350–1987*. Southampton: Southampton City Art Gallery [folder with handlist, illustrated essay, and posters]

Chippindale, C, 2004, *Stonehenge complete* (new and expanded edition). London: Thames and Hudson

Chippindale, C, & Baxter, I, 2003, Stonehenge and English Heritage attitudes. *Current Archaeology*, 16.7 (no. 187), 313–17

Chippindale, C, Devereux, P, Fowler, P, Jones, R, & Sabastian, T, 1990, *Who owns Stonehenge?* London: Batsford

Chris Blandford Associates, 2004, *Stonehenge visitor facilities and access scheme: environmental statement*. London: Chris Blandford Associates for English Heritage [limited circulation printed report, 2 vols. and non-technical summary. Also available on-line at <www.thestonehengeproject.org>]

Christie, P M, 1963, The Stonehenge Cursus. *Wiltshire Archaeological and Natural History Magazine*, 58, 370–82

Christie, P M, 1964, A Bronze Age round barrow on Earl's Farm Down, Amesbury. *Wiltshire Archaeological and Natural History Magazine*, 59, 30–45

Christie, P M, 1967, A barrow cemetery of the second millennium BC in Wiltshire, England. *Proceedings of the Prehistoric Society*, 33, 336–66

Christie, P M, 1970, A round barrow on Greenland Farm, Winterbourne Stoke. *Wiltshire Archaeological and Natural History Magazine*, 65, 64–73

Clark, A, 1990, *Seeing beneath the soil*. London: Batsford

Clark, J G D, 1952, *Prehistoric Europe: the economic basis*. London: Methuen

Clark, J G D, Higgs, E S, & Longworth, I H, 1960, Excavations at the Neolithic site at Hurst Fen, Mildenhall, Suffolk, 1954, 1957 and 1958. *Proceedings of the Prehistoric Society*, 26, 202–45

Clarke, B, & Kirby, C, 2003, A newly discovered round barrow and proposed dispersed linear cemetery at Boscombe Down West. *Wiltshire Archaeological and Natural History Magazine*, 96, 215–18

Cleal, R M J, & Allen, M, 1994, Investigation of tree-damaged barrows on King Barrow Ridge and Luxenborough Plantation, Amesbury. *Wiltshire Archaeological and Natural History Magazine*, 87, 54–84

Cleal, R M J, Allen, M J, & Newman, C, 2004, An archaeological and environmental study of the Neolithic and later prehistoric landscape of the Avon Valley and Durrington Walls environs. *Wiltshire Archaeological and Natural History Magazine*, 97, 218–48

Cleal, R M J, Walker, K E, & Montague, R, 1995, *Stonehenge in its landscape: twentieth-century excavations* (English Heritage Archaeological Report 10). London: English Heritage.

Coady, I, 2004, *What is the nature and extent of early Holocene activity within the Stonehenge environs?* Unpublished undergraduate thesis, School of Conservation Sciences, Bournemouth University

Coles, B J, 1994, *Trisantona* rivers: a landscape approach to the interpretation of river names. *Oxford Journal of Archaeology*, 13.3, 295–312

Coles, J, & Taylor, J, 1971, The Wessex Culture: a minimal view. *Antiquity*, 45, 6–14

Collingwood, R G, & Myres, J N L, 1937, *Roman Britain and the English settlements*. Oxford: Oxford University Press

Colt Hoare, Sir R, 1812, *The ancient history of Wiltshire. Volume I.* London: William Miller [reprinted with an introduction by J Simmons and D D A Simpson, 1975, Wakefield: EP Publishing]

Colt Hoare, Sir R, 1821, *The ancient history of Wiltshire. Volume II.* London: William Miller [reprinted with an introduction by J Simmons and D D A Simpson, 1975, Wakefield: EP Publishing]

Colton, R, & Martin, R, 1967, Eclipse prediction at Stonehenge. *Nature*, 211, 1011–12

Colton, R, & Martin, R, 1969, Eclipse cycles and eclipses at Stonehenge. *Nature*, 213, 476–8

Colvin, H M (ed.), 1963, *History of the King's Works: the Middle Ages*. London: HMSO (2 vols.)

Condit, T, & Simpson, D, 1998, Irish hengiform enclosures and related monuments: a review. In A Gibson & D Simpson (eds.), *Prehistoric ritual and religion. Essays in honour of Aubrey Burl.* Stroud: Sutton Publishing. 45–61

Coombs, D, 1979, The Figheldean hoard, Wiltshire. In C Burgess & D Coombs (eds.), *Bronze Age hoards: some finds old and new* (BAR British Series 67). Oxford: British Archaeological Reports. 253–68

Cope, J, 1998, *The modern antiquarian: a pre-millennial odyssey through megalithic Britain*. London: Thorsons

Corcoran, J X W P, 1969, The Cotswold-Severn group. In T G E Powell, J X W P Corcoran, F Lynch & J G Scott, *Megalithic enquiries in the west of Britain*. Liverpool: Liverpool University Press. 13–106 and 273–95

Corfield, M, 1988, The reshaping of metal objects: some ethical considerations. *Antiquity*, 62, 261–5

Corney, M, 1989, Multiple ditch systems and late Iron Age settlement in central Wessex. In M Bowden, D Mackay, & P Topping (eds.), *From Cornwall to Caithness: some aspects of British field archaeology* (BAR British Series 209). Oxford: British Archaeological Reports. 111–28

Cornwell, B, 1999, *Stonehenge: a novel of 2000 BC*. London: Harper Collins

Cornwell, I W, 1953, Soil science and archaeology with illustrations from some British Bronze Age monuments. *Proceedings of the Prehistoric Society*, 19, 129–47

Cornwell, I W, & Hodges, H W M, 1964, Thin section of British Neolithic pottery; Windmill Hill – a test-site. *Bulletin of the Institute of Archaeology*, 4, 29–33

Cowan, M, 1982, *Floated water meadows in the Salisbury area* (South Wiltshire Industrial Archaeology Society, Historical Monograph 9). Salisbury: South Wiltshire Industrial Archaeology Society

Crawford, O G S, 1929, Durrington Walls. *Antiquity*, 3, 49–59

Crawford, O G S, 1954, The symbols carved at Stonehenge. *Antiquity*, 28, 221–4

Crawford, O G S, & Keiller, A, 1928, *Wessex from the air*. Oxford: Clarendon Press

Creighton, O H, 2000, Early castles in the medieval landscape of Wiltshire. *Wiltshire Archaeological and Natural History Magazine*, 93, 105–19

Crittall, E (ed.), 1973, *A history of Wiltshire. Volume I.2.* London: University of London Institute of Historical Research, Victoria History of the Counties of England

Cross, D A E, 1971, Narrow-gauge railways on Salisbury Plain. *Wiltshire Archaeological and Natural History Magazine*, 66, 184–5

Crowley, D A (ed.), 1995, *A history of Wiltshire. Volume XV. Amesbury Hundred, and Branch and Dole Hundred.* London: University of London Institute of Historical Research, Victoria History of the Counties of England

Cunliffe, B, 1971, Some aspects of hill-forts and their cultural environments. In M Jesson & D Hill (eds.), *The Iron Age and its hill-forts.* Southampton: Southampton University Archaeological Society. 53–70

Cunliffe, B, 1973a, The early pre-Roman Iron Age 650–400 BC. In E Crittall (ed.), *A history of Wiltshire. Volume I.2.* London: University of London Institute of Historical Research, Victoria History of the Counties of England. 408–16

Cunliffe, B, 1973b, The middle pre-Roman Iron Age, 400–100 BC. In E Crittall (ed.), *A history of Wiltshire. Volume I.2.* London: University of London Institute of Historical Research, Victoria History of the Counties of England. 417–25

Cunliffe, B, 1973c, The late pre-Roman Iron Age 100 BC to AD 43. In E Crittall (ed.), *A history of Wiltshire. Volume I.2.* London: University of London Institute of Historical Research, Victoria History of the Counties of England. 426–38

Cunliffe, B, 1973d, The period of Romanizaton, 43–250. In E Crittall (ed.), *A history of Wiltshire. Volume I.2.* London: University of London Institute of Historical Research, Victoria History of the Counties of England. 439–52

Cunliffe, B, 1973e, The later Roman period 250–367. In E Crittall (ed.), *A history of Wiltshire. Volume I.2.* London: University of London Institute of Historical Research, Victoria History of the Counties of England. 453–9

Cunliffe, B, 1973f, The end of the Roman era, 367–500. In E Crittall (ed.), *A history of Wiltshire. Volume I.2.* London: University of London Institute of Historical Research, Victoria History of the Counties of England. 460–7

Cunliffe, B, 1991, *Iron Age communities in Britain* (third edition). London: Routledge

Cunliffe, B, 1993, *Wessex to AD 1000.* London: Longman

Cunliffe, B, 2001, *The extraordinary voyage of Pytheas the Greek.* London: Allen Lane at the Penguin Press

Cunliffe, B, & Renfrew, C (eds.), 1997, *Science and Stonehenge* (Proceedings of the British Academy 92). Oxford: British Academy

Cunnington, B H, 1920, 'Blue hard stone, ye same as at Stonehenge' found in Boles [Bowles] Barrow (Heytesbury I). *Wiltshire Archaeological and Natural History Magazine*, 41, 172–4

Cunnington, B H, 1924, The 'Bluestone' from Boles Barrow. *Wiltshire Archaeological and Natural History Magazine*, 42, 431–7

Cunnington, B H, & Cunnington, M E, 1913, Casterley Camp excavations. *Wiltshire Archaeological and Natural History Magazine*, 38, 53–106

Cunnington, M E, 1914, List of the long barrows of Wiltshire. *Wiltshire Archaeological and Natural History Magazine*, 38, 379–414

Cunnington, M E, 1925, Figsbury Rings. An account of excavations in 1924. *Wiltshire Archaeological and Natural History Magazine*, 43, 48–58

Cunnington, M E, 1929. *Woodhenge: a description of the site as revealed by excavations carried out there by Mr and Mrs B H Cunnington, 1926–7–8. Also of four circles and an earthwork enclosure south of Woodhenge.* Devizes: Privately Published

Cunnington, M E, 1930, Romano-British Wiltshire. *Wiltshire Archaeological and Natural History Magazine*, 45, 166–216

Cunnington, M E, 1931, 'The Sanctuary' on Overton Hill, near Avebury. *Wiltshire Archaeological and Natural History Magazine*, 45, 300–35

Cunnington, M E, 1933a, Wiltshire in Pagan Saxon times. *Wiltshire Archaeological and Natural History Magazine*, 46, 147–75

Cunnington, M E, 1933b, Excavations at Yarnbury Castle, 1932. *Wiltshire Archaeological and Natural History Magazine*, 46, 198–213

Cunnington, M E, 1935, Note on a burial at Amesbury. *Wiltshire Archaeological and Natural History Magazine*, 47, 267

Cunnington, M E, & Goddard, E H, 1934, *Catalogue of antiquities in the museum of the Wiltshire Archaeological and Natural History Society. Part II* (second edition). Devizes: Wiltshire Archaeological and Natural History Society

Cunnington, R H, 1935, *Stonehenge and its date*. London: Methuen

Cunnington, R H, 1975, *From antiquary to archaeologist: a biography of William Cunnington 1754–1810*. Princes Risborough: Shire Publications

Cunnington, W, 1884, Stonehenge notes: the fragments. *Wiltshire Archaeological and Natural History Magazine*, 21, 141–9

Cunnington, W, 1889, Notes on the Bowl's Barrow. *Wiltshire Archaeological and Natural History Magazine*, 24, 104–17

Cunnington, W, & Goddard, E H, 1896, *Catalogue of antiquities in the museum of the Wiltshire Archaeological and Natural History Society at Devizes. Part I – The Stourhead Collection*. Devizes: Wiltshire Archaeological and Natural History Society

Curnow, T, 2004, *The oracles of the ancient world*. London: Duckworth

Curwen, C, 1930, Neolithic camps. *Antiquity*, 4, 22–54

Daniel, G, 1978, Editorial. *Antiquity*, 52, 177–82

Darrah, J, 1993, The bluestones of Stonehenge. *Current Archaeology*, 12.2 (no. 134), 78

Darvill, T (ed.), 1991, *Stonehenge Conservation and Management Project: environmental statement*. London: Debenham Tewson and Chinnocks [limited circulation printed report, 3 vols.]

Darvill, T, 1993a, *Stonehenge Conservation and Management Programme: an archaeological background*. London: English Heritage and the National Trust

Darvill, T, 1993b, *Stonehenge visitor centre (alternative sites), Wiltshire*. London and Bournemouth: DTZ Debenham Thorpe and Timothy Darvill Archaeological Consultants [limited circulation printed report]

Darvill, T, 1993c, *Stonehenge visitor centre, Wiltshire, western approach route corridor: archaeological assessment*. London and Bournemouth: DTZ Debenham Thorpe and Timothy Darvill Archaeological Consultants [limited circulation printed report]

Darvill, T, 1994, *Stonehenge visitor centre, Wiltshire, western approach route corridor: field evaluation*. London and Bournemouth: DTZ Debenham Thorpe and Timothy Darvill Archaeological Consultants [limited circulation printed report]

Darvill, T (ed.), 1995, *Stonehenge visitor centre, Wiltshire. Countess Road and King Barrow Ridge site: field evaluation*. London and Bournemouth: DTZ Debenham Thorpe and Timothy Darvill Archaeological Consultants [limited circulation printed report]

Darvill, T, 1996, Neolithic buildings in England, Wales, and the Isle of Man. In T Darvill & J Thomas (eds.), *Neolithic houses in northwest Europe and beyond* (Neolithic Studies Group Seminar Papers 1). Oxford: Oxbow Books. 77–112

Darvill, T, 1997a, Ever increasing circles: the sacred geography of Stonehenge and its landscape. *Proceedings of the British Academy*, 92, 167–202

Darvill, T, 1997b, *Stonehenge Conservation and Management Programme: a summary of archaeological assessments and field evaluations undertaken 1990–1996*. Bournemouth: Timothy Darvill Archaeological Consultants for English Heritage and the National Trust [limited circulation printed report]

Darvill, T, 2003, Billown and the Neolithic of the Isle of Man. In I Armit, E Murphy, E Nelis, & D Simpson (eds.), *Neolithic settlement in Ireland and western Britain*. Oxford: Oxbow Books. 112–19

Darvill, T, 2004a, Archaeology in rock. In N Brodie & C Hills (eds.), *Material engagements: studies in honour of Colin Renfrew*. Cambridge: McDonald Institute for Archaeological Research Monograph. 55–77

Darvill, T, 2004b, *The long barrows of the Cotswolds and adjacent areas*. Stroud: Tempus

Darvill, T, 2004c, Tales of the land, tales of the sea: people and presence in the Neolithic of Man and beyond. In V Cummings & C Fowler (eds.), *The Neolithic of the Irish Sea: materiality and traditions of practice*. Oxford: Oxbow Books. 46–54

Darvill, T, 2005, *Stonehenge World Heritage Site: an archaeological research framework*. London and Bournemouth: English Heritage and Bournemouth University

Darvill, T, Morgan Evans, D, & Wainwright, G, 2003, Strumble-Preseli Ancient Communities and Environment Study (SPACES): second report 2003. *Archaeology in Wales*, 43, 3–12

Darvill, T, & O'Connor, B, 2005, The Cronk yn Howe Stone and the rock art of the Isle of Man. *Proceedings of the Prehistoric Society*, 71, 283–331

Darvill, T, & Wainwright, G, 2002a, Strumble-Preseli Ancient Communities and Environment Study (SPACES): first report 2002. *Archaeology in Wales*, 42, 17–28

Darvill, T, & Wainwright, G, 2002b, SPACES – exploring Neolithic landscapes in the Strumble-Preseli area of southwest Wales, *Antiquity*, 76, 623–4

Darvill, T, & Wainwright, G, 2003, Stone circles, oval settings and henges in south-west Wales and beyond. *Antiquaries Journal*, 83, 9–46

Darwin, C, 1888, *The formation of vegetable mould through the action of worms with observations on their habits*. London: John Murray

David, A, & Payne, A, 1997, Geophysical surveys within the Stonehenge Landscape: a review of past endeavour and future potential. *Proceedings of the British Academy*, 92. 73–113

Davies, J B, & Thurnam, J, 1865, *Crania Britannica: delineations and descriptions of the skull of the aboriginal and early inhabitants of the British Islands: with notices of their other remains*. London: Privately Printed (2 vols.)

Davies, P, & Wolski, C, 2001, Later Neolithic woodland regeneration in the long barrow fills of the Avebury area: the molluscan evidence. *Oxford Journal of Archaeology*, 20.4, 311–18

DCMS [Department for Culture, Media and Sport], 2006, *ICONS: a portrait of England* [on-line]. London: Department of Culture Media and Sport [available at <http://www.icons.org.uk/theicons> accessed 20 January 2006]

De Jersey, P, 1999, Exotic Celtic coinage in Britain. *Oxford Journal of Archaeology*, 18.2, 189–216

Dennison, S, 2000, Archaeologists divided on Stonehenge solstice. *British Archaeology*, 54, 4

DFT [Department for Transport], 2005, *Report of the Local Inquiry into the A303 Stonehenge Improvement Scheme* [on-line]. London: Department for Transport [available at: <www.dft.gov.uk/stellent/groups/dft_roads/documents/page/dft_roads_039211.hcsp> assessed 28 March 2006]

Dimbleby, D, 2005, *A picture of Britain*. London: BBC and Tate Publishing

Diverres, A H, 1979, Saint Melor: what is the truth behind the legend? In J H Chandler (ed.), *The Amesbury millennium lectures*. Amesbury: The Amesbury Society. 9–19

DLA [Defence Land Agent], 1993, *The archaeology of Salisbury Plain training area: management plans for archaeological site groups*. Salisbury: Defence Land Agent [limited circulation printed report]

Dobinson, C, 1992, Saturday night and Sunday morning. *British Archaeological News*, 7.4, 61–2

Dobinson, C S, Lake, J, & Schofield, A J, 1997, Monuments of war: defining England's 20th century defence heritage. *Antiquity*, 71, 288–99

DoE [Department of the Environment], 1979, *Report of the Stonehenge Working Party*. London: Department of the Environment [limited circulation printed report]

DoE [Department of Environment], 1990, *Archaeology and planning* (PPG16). London: HMSO

Drewett, P, 1975, The excavation of an oval burial mound of the third millennium bc at Alfriston, East Sussex, 1974. *Proceedings of the Prehistoric Society*, 41, 119–52

Drewett, P, 1986, The excavation of a Neolithic oval barrow at North Marden, West Sussex, 1982. *Proceedings of the Prehistoric Society*, 52, 31–51

Drewett, P, 1987, Survey of Mynydd Preseli. *Archaeology in Wales*, 27, 14–16

Duke, E, 1846, *The druidical temples of the county of Wiltshire*. London and Salisbury: J R Smith and W B Brodie and Co.

Eagles, B, 1994, The archaeological evidence for settlement in the fifth to seventh centuries. In M Aston & C Lewis (eds.), *The medieval landscape of Wessex* (Oxbow Monograph 46). Oxford: Oxbow Books. 13–22

Eagles, B, 2001, Anglo-Saxon presence and culture in Wiltshire c.AD 450 – c.675. In P Ellis (ed.), *Roman Wiltshire and after: papers in honour of Ken Annable*. Devizes: Wiltshire Archaeological and Natural History Society. 199–233

Eagles, B, 2004, A mid 5th- to mid 6th-century bridle-fitting of Mediterranean origin from Breamore, Hampshire, England, with a discussion of its local context. In Marc Lodewijckx (ed.), *Bruc Ealles Well: archaeological essays concerning the peoples of north-west Europe in the first millennium AD* (Acta Archaeologica Lovaniensia Monographiae 15). Leuven: Leuven University Press. 87–96

Emerson, R W, 1841, *Essays*. Boston: Munroe and Company

English Heritage, 1987, *Register of parks and gardens of special historic interest in England. Part 46: Wiltshire*. London: English Heritage

English Heritage, 2000, *Stonehenge World Heritage Site: management plan*. London: English Heritage

English Heritage, 2005, *Stonehenge World Heritage Site – Key facts and figures*. London: English Heritage [limited circulation printed fact-sheet dated September 2005]

English Heritage & National Trust, 1999, *Stonehenge: the master plan*. London: English Heritage and The National Trust [brochure and limited circulation printed report]

Evans, J, 1897, *The ancient stone implements, weapons and ornaments of Great Britain* (second edition). London: Longmans, Green and Co.

Evans, J G, 1968, Periglacial deposits on the chalk of Wiltshire. *Wiltshire Archaeological and Natural History Magazine*, 63, 12–26

Evans, J G, 1984, Stonehenge – the environment in the late Neolithic and early Bronze Age and a Beaker-age burial. *Wiltshire Archaeological and Natural History Magazine*, 78, 7–30

Evans, J G, & Wainwright, G J, 1979, The Woodhenge excavations. In G J Wainwright, *Mount Pleasant, Dorset: excavations 1970–71* (Reports of the Research Committee of the Society of Antiquaries of London 37). London: Society of Antiquaries. 71–4 and 192–7

Evans, W D, 1945, The geology of the Prescelly Hills, North Pembrokeshire. *Quarterly Journal of the Geological Society of London*, 64, 273–96

Exon, S, Gaffney, V, Woodward, A, & Yorston, R, 2001, *Stonehenge landscapes: journeys through real-and-imagined worlds*. Oxford: Archaeopress

Fagg, B, 1956, The discovery of multiple rock gongs in Nigeria. *Man*, 56, 17–18

Fagg, B, 1957, Rock gongs and slides. *Man*, 57, 30–2

Farmer, D H, 1997, The refoundation of Amesbury Abbey. In J H Chandler (ed.), *The Amesbury millennium lectures*. Amesbury: The Amesbury Society. 47–57

Fasham, P, 1978, A Bronze Age flint industry from a barrow site in Micheldever Wood, Hampshire. *Proceedings of the Prehistoric Society*, 44, 47–68

Field, D, 1998, Round barrows and the harmonious landscape: placing early Bronze Age burial monuments in south-east England. *Oxford Journal of Archaeology*, 17.3, 309–26

Field, E V, 1961, Excavation and fieldwork in Wiltshire, 1960, Wilsford. *Wiltshire Archaeological and Natural History Magazine*, 58, 30–1

Finberg, H P R, 1964, *The early charters of Wessex*. Leicester: Leicester University Press

Findley, D C, Colbourne, G J N, Cope, D W, Harrod, T R, Hogan, D V, & Staines, S J, 1984, *Soils and their use in south-west England* (Soil Survey of England and Wales Bulletin 14). Rothamsted: Soil Survey

Fitzpatrick, A P, 2002, 'The Amesbury Archer': a well-furnished early Bronze Age burial in southern England. *Antiquity*, 76, 629–30

Fitzpatrick, A P, 2003a, The Amesbury Archer. *Current Archaeology*, 16.4 (no. 184), 146–52

Fitzpatrick, A P, 2003b, Six more bodies found near grave of 'King of Stonehenge'. *Current Archaeology*, 16.6 (no. 186), 233

Fitzpatrick, A P, 2004a, The Boscombe Bowmen: builders of Stonehenge? *Current Archaeology*, 17.1 (no. 193), 10–16

Fitzpatrick, A P, 2004b, A sacred circle on Boscombe Down. *Current Archaeology*, 17.3 (no. 195), 106–7

Fitzpatrick, A P, Evans, J, & Chenery, C, 2004, Was Stonehenge really built by Welshmen? *British Archaeology*, 78, 14–5

Fleming, A, 1971, Territorial patterns in Bronze Age Wessex. *Proceedings of the Prehistoric Society*, 37, 138–66

Fleming, A, 1988, *The Dartmoor Reaves: investigating prehistoric land boundaries*. London: Batsford

Folkersheimer, H, 1562 (ed. 1845), *Zurich letters* (second series). Cambridge: Parker Society

Ford, S, 1991, An early Bronze Age pit circle from Charnham Lane, Hungerford, Berkshire. *Proceedings of the Prehistoric Society*, 57.2, 179–81

Foster, A, 2001, Romano-British burials in Wiltshire. In P Ellis (ed.), *Roman Wiltshire and after: papers in honour of Ken Annable*. Devizes: Wiltshire Archaeological and Natural History Society. 165–77

Fowler, M J F, & Needham, H J, 1995, Gun-flint industries in the Salisbury Region. *Wiltshire Archaeological and Natural History Magazine*, 88, 137–41

Frere, S S, 1987, *Britannia: a history of Roman Britain* (third edition). London: Routledge and Kegan Paul

Frere, S S, & Fulford, M, 2001, The Roman invasion of AD 43. *Britannia*, 32, 45–56

Freshfield, E, & Carnarvon, Earl of, 1883, Anniversary Address, St George's Day, Monday, April 23, 1883. *Proceedings of the Society of Antiquaries of London* (second series), 9, 292–305

Garfitt, J E, 1979, Moving the stones to Stonehenge. *Antiquity*, 53, 190–4

Garfitt, J E, 1980, Raising the lintels at Stonehenge. *Antiquity*, 54, 142–4

Garmonsway, G N (trans.), 1972, *The Anglo-Saxon chronicle*. London: J M Dent and Sons

Garrow, D, Beadsmoore, E, & Knight, M, 2005, Pit clusters and the temporality of occupation: an earlier Neolithic site at Kilverstone, Thetford, Norfolk. *Proceedings of the Prehistoric Society*, 71, 139–58

Gerloff, S, 1975, *The early Bronze Age daggers in Great Britain and a reconsideration of the Wessex Culture* (Prähistorische Bronzefunde VI.2). Munich: C H Beck'sche Verlagsbuch-handlung

Gibson, A, 1998a, *Stonehenge and timber circles*. Stroud: Tempus

Gibson, A, 1998b, Hindwell and the Neolithic palisaded sites of Britain and Ireland. In A Gibson & D Simpson (eds.), *Prehistoric ritual and religion*. Stroud: Sutton Publishing. 68–79

Gibson, A (ed.), 2002, *Behind wooden walls: Neolithic palisaded enclosures in Europe* (BAR International Series 1013). Oxford: Archaeopress

Gingell, C, 1988, Twelve Wiltshire round barrows. Excavations 1959 and 1961 by F de M and H L Vatcher. *Wiltshire Archaeological and Natural History Magazine*, 82, 19–76

Glasbergen, W, 1954, Barrow excavations in the Eight Beatitudes. The Bronze Age cemetery between Toterfout and Halve Mijl, North Brabant, II. The implications. *Palaeohistoria*, 3, 1–204

Goddard, E H, 1913, A list of prehistoric, Roman, and Pagan Saxon antiquities in the county of Wiltshire arranged under parishes. *Wiltshire Archaeological and Natural History Magazine*, 38, 153–378

Goddard, E H, 1919, Bronze implements found in Wiltshire not previously recorded. *Wiltshire Archaeological and Natural History Magazine*, 40, 359–60

Goskar, T A, Carty, A, Cripps, P, Brayne, C, & Vickers, D, 2003, The Stonehenge laser show. *British Archaeology*, 73, 9–13

Goulstone, J, 1985, Folk games at Silbury Hill and Stonehenge. *Antiquity*, 49, 51–3

Goulstone, J, 1986, Stonehenge: the Shepherd's Crook turf carving. *Wiltshire Archaeological and Natural History Magazine*, 80, 230

Gover, J E B, Mawer, A, & Stenton, F M, 1939 (reprinted 1992), *The place-names of Wiltshire* (English Place-Name Society Volume XVI). Nottingham: English Place-Name Society

Gowland, W, 1902, Recent excavations at Stonehenge. *Archaeologia*, 58, 37–82

Graham, A, & Newman, C, 1993, Recent excavations of Iron Age and Romano-British enclosures in the Avon valley, Wiltshire. *Wiltshire Archaeological and Natural History Magazine*, 86, 8–57

Green, C, & Rollo-Smith, S, 1984, The excavation of eighteen round barrows near Shrewton, Wiltshire. *Proceedings of the Prehistoric Society*, 50, 255–318

Green, C P, 1997, The provenance of rocks used in the construction of Stonehenge. *Proceedings of the British Academy*, 92, 257–70

Green, M, 1986, *The gods of the Celts*. Gloucester: Alan Sutton

Green, M, & Allen, M J, 1997, An early prehistoric shaft on Cranborne Chase. *Oxford Journal of Archaeology*, 16.2, 121–32

Grimes, W F, 1929, Pembrokeshire survey. *Bulletin of the Board of Celtic Studies*, 5, 277

Grimes, W F, 1938, Excavations at Meini Gwyr, Carmarthen. *Proceedings of the Prehistoric Society*, 4, 324-25

Grimes, W F, 1939, Bedd y Afanc. *Proceedings of the Prehistoric Society*, 5, 258

Grimes, W F, 1948, Pentre-Ifan burial chamber, Pembrokeshire. *Archaeologia Cambrensis*, 100, 3–23

Grimes, W F, 1964, Excavations of the Lake Group of Barrows, Wiltshire. *Bulletin of the Institute of Archaeology, University of London*, 4, 89–121

Grinsell, L V, 1936, *The ancient burial mounds of England*. London: Methuen

Grinsell, L V, 1957, Archaeological gazetteer. In R B Pugh & E Crittall (eds.), *A history of Wiltshire. Volume I.1*. London: University of London Institute of Historical Research, Victoria History of the Counties of England. 21–279

Grinsell, L V, 1959, *Dorset Barrows*. Dorchester: Dorset Natural History and Archaeological Society

Grinsell, L V, 1975, *Legendary history and folklore of Stonehenge*. St Peter Port: Toucan Press

Grinsell, L V, 1978a, *The Stonehenge barrow groups*. Salisbury: Salisbury and South Wiltshire Museum

Grinsell, L V, 1978b, *The Druids and Stonehenge: the story of a Myth*. St Peter Port: Toucan Press

Grinsell, L V, 1986, Wiltshire prehistoric sites in recent fiction. *Wiltshire Archaeological and Natural History Magazine*, 80, 234–7

Grinsell, L V, 1987, The Christianization of prehistoric and other pagan sites. *Landscape History*, 8, 27–37

Guido, M, Henderson, J, Cable, M, Bayley, J, & Biek, L, 1984, A Bronze Age glass bead from Wilsford, Wiltshire: Barrow G 42 in the Lake Group. *Proceedings of the Prehistoric Society*, 50, 245–54

Guido, M, & Smith, I, 1981, Figsbury Rings: a reconsideration of the inner enclosure. *Wiltshire Archaeological and Natural History Magazine*, 76, 21–6

Guirand, F, 1959, Greek mythology. In F Guirand (ed.), *Larousse encyclopedia of mythology*. London: Paul Hamlyn. 87–212

Harding, A, 1984, *The Mycenaeans and Europe*. London: Academic Press

Harding, A F, & Lee, G E, 1987, *Henge monuments and related sites of Great Britain* (BAR British Series 175). Oxford: British Archaeological Reports

Harding, J, 2000, Later Neolithic ceremonial centres, ritual and pilgrimage: the monument complex at Thornborough, North Yorkshire. In A Ritchie (ed.), *Neolithic Orkney in its European context*. Cambridge: McDonald Institute Monographs. 31–46

Harding, J, 2003, *Henge monuments of the British Isles*. Stroud: Tempus

Harding, P, 1988, The chalk plaque pit, Amesbury. *Proceedings of the Prehistoric Society*, 54, 320–6

Harding, P, 1995, Three handaxes from Stapleford, Wiltshire. *Wiltshire Archaeological and Natural History Magazine*, 88, 120–2

Harding, P, & Bridgland, D R, 1998, Pleistocene deposits and Palaeolithic implements at Godolphin School, Milford Hill, Salisbury. *Wiltshire Archaeological and Natural History Magazine*, 91, 1–10

Harding, P, & Gingell, C, 1986, The excavation of two long barrows by F de M and H F W L Vatcher. *Wiltshire Archaeological and Natural History Magazine*, 80, 7–22

Harding, P A, 1991, *Bulford Branch Line*. Knaphill: Privately Published

Hare, J N, 1980, Durrington: a chalkland village in the later Middle Ages. *Wiltshire Archaeological and Natural History Magazine*, 74/75, 137–47

Hare, J N, 1981, Change and continuity in Wiltshire agriculture in the later Middle Ages. In W Minchinton (ed.), *Agricultural improvement: medieval and modern*. Exeter: Exeter Papers in Economic History

Harrad, L, 2004, Gabbroic clay sources in Cornwall: a petrological study of prehistoric pottery and clay samples. *Oxford Journal of Archaeology*, 23.3, 271–86

Harrison, W J, 1902, A bibliography of the great stone monuments of Wiltshire – Stonehenge and Avebury. *Wiltshire Archaeological and Natural History Magazine*, 32, 1–170

Haslam, J, 1976, *Wiltshire towns: the archaeological potential*. Devizes: Wiltshire Archaeological and Natural History Society

Haslam, J, 1984, The towns of Wiltshire. In J Haslam (ed.), *Anglo-Saxon towns in southern England*. Chichester: Phillimore. 87–148

Hatchwell, R, 1969, *Stonehenge and Avebury: a catalogue of printed books, manuscripts, prints, and drawings ... offered for sale*. Little Somerford: R Hatchwell

Hawkes, J, 1967, God in the machine. *Antiquity*, 41, 174–80

Hawkins, G S, 1964, Stonehenge: a Neolithic computer. *Nature*, 202, 1258–61

Hawkins, G S, 1966a, *Stonehenge decoded*. London: Souvenir Press

Hawkins, G S, 1966b, *Astro-archaeology* (Smithsonian Institution Special Report 226). Cambridge, Mass.: Smithsonian Institution

Hawkins, G S, 1973, *Beyond Stonehenge*. London: Hutchinson

Hawkins, G S, Atkinson, R J C, Thom, A, Newham, C A, Sadler, D H, & Newall, R A, 1967, Hoyle on Stonehenge: some comments. *Antiquity*, 41, 91–8

Hawley, W, 1910, Notes on barrows in south Wiltshire. *Wiltshire Archaeological and Natural History Magazine*, 36, 615–28

Hawley, W, 1921, Stonehenge: interim report in the exploration. *Antiquaries Journal*, 1, 19–41

Hawley, W, 1922, Second report on the excavations at Stonehenge. *Antiquaries Journal*, 2, 36–52

Hawley, W, 1923, Third report on the excavations at Stonehenge. *Antiquaries Journal*, 3, 13–20

Hawley, W, 1924, Fourth report on the excavations at Stonehenge (June to November 1922). *Antiquaries Journal*, 4, 30–9

Hawley, W, 1925, Report on the excavations at Stonehenge during the season of 1923. *Antiquaries Journal*, 5, 21–50

Hawley, W, 1926, Report on the excavations at Stonehenge during the season of 1924. *Antiquaries Journal*, 6, 1–16

Hawley, W, 1928, Report on the excavations at Stonehenge during 1925 and 1926. *Antiquaries Journal*, 8, 149–76

Haynes, R, & Slocombe, I, 2004, *Wiltshire toll houses*. Salisbury: The Hobnob Press

Heath, R, 2002, *Stonehenge* (revised edition). Presteigne: Wooden Books

Heaton, M, & Cleal, R M J, 2000, Beaker pits at Crescent Copse, near Shrewton, Wiltshire, and the effects of arboreal fungi on archaeological remains. *Wiltshire Archaeological and Natural History Magazine*, 93, 71–81

Hedges, R E M, Housley, R A, Law, I A, & Bronk C R, 1989, Radiocarbon dates from the Oxford AMS System: *Archaeometry* datelist 9. *Archaeometry*, 31, 207–34

Henderson, J, 1988, Glass production in Bronze Age Europe. *Antiquity*, 62, 435–51

Henig, M, 2003, A Romano-British figurine of Mercury from near Durnford. *Wiltshire Archaeological and Natural History Magazine*, 96, 225–7

Herbert, A, 1849, *Cyclops Christianus*. London

Heritage Projects, 1984, *The Stonehenge we deserve: proposals for the Stonehenge Prehistory Centre*. York: Heritage Projects Ltd [limited circulation printed report]

Higgs, E S, 1959, The excavation of a late Mesolithic site at Downton, near Salisbury, Wiltshire. *Proceedings of the Prehistoric Society*, 25, 209–32

Hill, D, 1981, *An atlas of Anglo-Saxon England 700–1066*. Oxford: Basil Blackwell

Hind, J G F, 1989, The invasion of Britain in AD 43 – an alternative strategy for Aulus Plautius. *Britannia*, 21, 1–21

Hinton, D A, 1975, Amesbury and the early history of its Abbey. In J Chandler (ed.), *The Amesbury millennium lectures*. Amesbury: The Amesbury Society. 20–31

Hinton, D A, 1977, *Alfred's Kingdom: Wessex and the south 800–1500*. London: Dent

Hinton, D A, 1998, Stonehenge, Merlin, and gallows humour. *British Archaeology*, 34, 18

Hodder, I, 1984, Archaeology in 1984. *Antiquity*, 58, 25–32

Hodson, F R (ed.), 1974, *The place of astronomy in the ancient world*. London: Oxford University Press for The British Academy

Hogg, A H A, 1981. Another way to lift the Stonehenge lintels. *Antiquity*, 55, 131–2

Hosfield, R T, 2001, The Lower Palaeolithic of the Solent: 'site' formation and interpretative frameworks. In F F Wenban-Smith & R Hosfield (eds.), *Palaeolithic archaeology of the Solent River* (Lithic Studies Society Occasional Paper 7). London: Lithic Studies Society. 85–98

Housley, R A, Gamble, C S, Street, M, & Pettitt, P, 1997, Radiocarbon evidence for the lateglacial human recolonization of Northern Europe. *Proceedings of the Prehistoric Society*, 63, 25–54

Hoyle, F, 1966, Speculations on Stonehenge, *Antiquity*, 40, 262–76

Hoyle, F, 1973, *From Stonehenge to modern cosmology*. San Francisco: W H Freeman and Co.

Hoyle, F, 1977, *On Stonehenge*. London: Heinemann

Hunter-Mann, K, 1999, Excavations at Vespasian's Camp Iron Age hillfort. *Wiltshire Archaeological and Natural History Magazine*, 92, 39–52

Hutton, R, 2005, The religion of William Stukeley. *Antiquaries Journal*, 85, 381–94

Ixer, R A, 1997a, Detailed provenancing of the Stonehenge dolerites using reflected light petrology – a return to the light. In A Sinclair, E Slater, & J Gowlett (eds.), *Archaeological sciences 1995* (Oxbow Monograph 64). Oxford: Oxbow. 11–17

Ixer, R, 1997b, Steep Holm 'Bluestones'. *Current Archaeology*, 13.7 (no. 151), 279

Ixer, R A, & Turner, P, 2006, A detailed re-examination of the petrology of the Altar Stone and other non-sarsen sandstones from Stonehenge as a guide to their provenance. *Wiltshire Archaeological and Natural History Magazine*, 99, 1–9

Jackson, J E, 1867, On Amesbury monastery. *Wiltshire Archaeological and Natural History Magazine*, 10, 61–84

Jacobi, R, 1979, Early Flandrian hunters in the south-west. *Proceedings of the Devon Archaeological Society*, 37, 48–93

Jacobi, R, 1991, The Creswellian, Creswell and Cheddar. In N Barton, A J Roberts & D A Roe (eds.), *The late glacial in north-west Europe* (Council for British Archaeology Research Report 77). London: Council for British Archaeology. 128–40

James, D J, 2002, *Sorviodunum* – a review of the archaeological evidence. *Wiltshire Archaeological and Natural History Magazine*, 95, 1–26

James, E O, 1962, *The ancient gods*. London: Weidenfeld and Nicholson

James, N D G, 1983, *Gunners at Larkhill: a history of the Royal School of Artillery*. Salisbury: Hobnob Press

Johnston, R, 1999, An empty path? Processions, memories and the Dorset Cursus. In A Barclay & J Harding (eds.), *Pathways and ceremonies: the cursus monuments of Britain and Ireland* (Neolithic Studies Group Seminar Papers 4). Oxford: Oxbow Books. 39–48

Jones, A, 1999, Local colour: megalithic architecture and colour symbolism in Neolithic Arran. *Oxford Journal of Archaeology*, 18.4, 339–50

Jones, B, & Mattingly, D, 2002, *An atlas of Roman Britain*. Oxford: Oxbow Books

Jones, I, & Webb, J, 1655, *The most notable antiquity of Great Britain, vulgarly called Stone-Heng, on Salisbury Plain, restored*. London

Judd, J W, 1902, Note on the nature and origin of the rock-fragments found in the excavations made at Stonehenge by Mr Gowland in 1901. *Archaeologia*, 58.1, 106–18

Kaiser, D, 2003, Sacred Preseli. *3rd Stone*, 46, 34–7

Kellaway, G A, 1971, Glaciation and the stones of Stonehenge. *Nature*, 232, 30–5

Kellaway, G A, 1991, The older Plio-Pleistocene glaciations of the region around Bath. In G A Kellaway (ed.), *Hot springs of Bath*. Bath: Bath City Council. 243–73

Kellaway, G A, 2002, Glacial and tectonic factors in the emplacement of the bluestones of Salisbury Plain. *The Survey of Bath and District*, 17, 57–71

Kendrick, T D, & Hawkes, C F C, 1932, *Archaeology in England and Wales 1914–1931*. London: Methuen

Kerridge, E, 1953, The floating of the Wiltshire water-meadows. *Wiltshire Archaeological and*

Natural History Magazine, 55, 105–18

Kerridge, E, 1954, The sheepfold in Wiltshire and the floating of the water-meadows. *Economic History Review* (second series), 6, 282–329

Kerridge, E, 1959, Agriculture, 1500–1793. In E Crittall (ed.), *A history of Wiltshire. Volume IV*. London: University of London Institute of Historical Research, Victoria History of the Counties of England. 49–52

Kinnes, I, 1979, *Round barrows and ring-ditches in the British Neolithic* (British Museum Occasional Paper 7). London: British Museum

Kinnes, I, Gibson, A M, Ambers, J, Bowman, S, Leese, M, & Boast, R, 1991, Radiocarbon dating and British Beakers: the British Museum programme. *Scottish Archaeological Review*, 8, 35–68

Kinnes, I A, Longworth, I H, McIntyre, I M, & Oddy, W A, 1988, Bush Barrow gold. *Antiquity*, 62, 24–39

Kite, E, 1901, Notes on Amesbury Monastery, with an account of some discoveries on the site in 1860. *Wiltshire Notes and Queries*, 3 (1899–1901), 115–19, 145–54, 221–7, 258–67, 289–305, 354–66, 433–48

Kristiansen, K, & Larsson, T, 2005, *The rise of Bronze Age society*. Cambridge: Cambridge University Press

Kuhn, T S, 1970, *The structure of scientific revolutions* (second edition). Chicago: University of Chicago Press

Laidler, B, & Young, W E V, 1938, A surface flint industry from a site near Stonehenge. *Wiltshire Archaeological and Natural History Magazine*, 48, 151–60

Lambarde, W, 1580, *Angliae topographicum and historiarum* [first published 1730]

Larson, G, Dobney, K, Albarella, U, Fang, M, Matisoo-Smith, E, Robins, J, Lowden, S, Finlayson, H, Brand, T, Willerslev, E, Rowley-Conwy, P, Andersson, L, & Cooper, A, 2005, Worldwide phylogeography of wild boar reveals multiple centres of pig domestication. *Science*, 307, 1618–21

Lawson, A J, 1993, A late Neolithic chalk plaque from Butterfield Down, Wiltshire. *Antiquaries Journal*, 73, 183–5

Lawson, A J, 2000, *Potterne 1982–5: animal husbandry in later prehistoric Wiltshire* (Wessex Archaeology Report 17). Salisbury: Wessex Archaeology

Leland, J (ed. A Hall), 1709, *Commentarii de Scriptoribus Britannicis*. Oxonii: E Theatro Sheldoniano

Legg, R, 1986, *Stonehenge antiquaries*. Sherborne: Dorset Publishing

Levellers, The, 1991, *Levelling the land*. London: China Records WOLCD1022 [music CD]

Lewis, C, 1994, Medieval settlement of Wiltshire. In M Aston & C Lewis (eds.), *The medieval landscape of Wessex* (Oxbow Monograph 46). Oxford: Oxbow. 171–93

LH [Lords Hansard], 1997, Stonehenge. *Lords Hansard*, 30:6:97 columns 58–72

Lockyer, N, 1909, *Stonehenge and other British stone monuments astronomically considered* (second edition). London: Macmillan

Long, W, 1876, Stonehenge and its barrows. *Wiltshire Archaeological and Natural History Magazine*, 16, 1–244

Longworth, I H, 1984, *Collared Urns of the Bronze Age in Great Britain and Ireland*. Cambridge: Cambridge University Press

Loveday, R, 1999, The origins and implications of the Breton buckler motif. *Oxford Journal of Archaeology*, 18.2, 127–42

Lubbock, J, 1865, *Prehistoric times*. London: Williams and Norgate

Lukis, W C, 1864, Danish cromlechs and burial customs. *Wiltshire Archaeological and Natural History Magazine*, 8, 145–69

Lynch, F, 1972, Ring-cairns and related monuments in Wales. *Scottish Archaeological Forum*, 4,

61–80

Lynch, F, & Musson, C, 2001, A prehistoric and early medieval complex at Llandegai, near Bangor, North Wales. *Archaeologia Cambrensis*, 130, 17–142

McAvoy, F, 2000, The development of a Neolithic monument complex at Godmanchester, Cambridgeshire. In M Dawson (ed.), *Prehistoric, Roman, and post-Roman landscapes of the Great Ouse Valley* (Council for British Archaeology Research Report 119). York: Council for British Archaeology. 51–6

McKerrell, H, 1972, On the origins of British faience beads and some aspects of the Wessex–Mycenae relationship. *Proceedings of the Prehistoric Society*, 38, 286–301

McKinley, J I, 1999, Further excavations of an Iron Age and Romano-British enclosed settlement at Figheldean, near Netheravon. *Wiltshire Archaeological and Natural History Magazine*, 92, 7–32

McKinley, J I, 2003, A Wiltshire 'bog body'? Discussion of a fifth/sixth century AD burial in the Woodford Valley. *Wiltshire Archaeological and Natural History Magazine*, 96, 7–18

McKinley, J I, & Heaton, M, 1996, A Romano-British farmstead and associated burials at Maddington Farm, Shrewton. *Wiltshire Archaeological and Natural History Magazine*, 89, 44–72

McOmish, D S, 2001, Aspects of prehistoric settlement in western Wessex. In J Collis (ed.), *Society and settlement in Iron Age Europe* (Sheffield Archaeology Monograph 11). Sheffield: J R Collis Publishing. 73–81

McOmish, D, Field, D, & Brown, G, 2002, *The field archaeology of the Salisbury Plain Training Area*. London: English Heritage

Malim, T, 1999, Cursuses and related monuments of the Cambridgeshire Ouse. In A Barclay & J Harding (eds.), *Pathways and ceremonies: the cursus monuments of Britain and Ireland* (Neolithic Studies Group Seminar Papers 4). Oxford: Oxbow Books. 77–85

Manning, W H, 1976, The conquest of the west country. In K Branigan & P Fowler (eds.), *The Roman west country*. Newton Abbot: David and Charles. 15–41

Margary, I D, 1973, *Roman roads in Britain*. London: John Baker

Marsden, B M, 1974, *The early barrow diggers*. Princes Risborough: Shire Publications

Maskelyne, N S, 1878, Stonehenge: the petrology of its stones. *Wiltshire Archaeological and Natural History Magazine*, 17, 147–60

Mawer, A, & Stenton, F M, 1969, *Introduction to the survey of English place-names* (English Place-Name Society Volume 1.1). Cambridge: Cambridge University Press

Megaw, J V S, 1960, Penny whistles and prehistory. *Antiquity*, 34, 6–13

Megaw, J V S, & Simpson, D D A (eds.), 1979, *Introduction to British prehistory*. Leicester: Leicester University Press

Meller, H (ed.), 2004, *Der geschmiedete Himmel: die weite Welt im herzen Europas vor 3600 Jahren*. Stuttgart: Landesmuseum für Vorgeschichte

Meyrick, O, 1948, Sir Richard Colt Hoare and William Cunnington. *Wiltshire Archaeological and Natural History Magazine*, 52, 213–18

Miles, D, 2005, *The tribes of Britain*. London: Weidenfeld and Nicholson

Moir, G, 1979, Hoyle on Stonehenge. *Antiquity*, 53, 124–9

Montelius, O, 1908, The chronology of the British Bronze Age. *Archaeologia*, 61, 97–162

Moore, C N, & Rowlands, M, 1972, *Bronze Age metalwork in Salisbury Museum*. Salisbury: Salisbury and South Wiltshire Museum

Morris, J, 1973, *The age of Arthur*. London: Weidenfeld and Nicolson

Mowl, T, 2004, *Historic gardens of Wiltshire*. Stroud: Tempus

Mullins, E, 1974, *The pilgrimage to Santiago*. London: Secker and Warburg

National Trust, 2001, *Stonehenge Estate land-use plan: July 2001*. London: The National Trust [CD-ROM publication also available on-line at: <www.stonehengemasterplan.org>]

Needham, S, 1981, *The Bulford-Helsbury manufacturing tradition: the production of Stogursey socketed axes during the later Bronze Age in southern Britain* (British Museum Occasional Paper 13). London: British Museum

Needham, S, 1996, Chronology and periodization in the British Bronze Age. *Acta Archaeologica*, 67, 121–40

Needham, S, 2000, Power pulses across a cultural divide: cosmologically driven acquisition between Armorica and Wessex. *Proceedings of the Prehistoric Society*, 66, 151–208

Needham, S, 2005, Transforming Beaker Culture in north-west Europe; processes of fusion and fission. *Proceedings of the Prehistoric Society*, 71, 171–217

Needham, S, Bronk Ramsay, C, Coombs, D, Cartwright, & Pettitt, P, 1997, An independent chronology for British Bronze Age metalwork: the results of the Oxford Radiocarbon Accelerator programme. *Archaeological Journal*, 154, 55–107

Newall, R S, 1921, Stonehenge. *Wiltshire Archaeological and Natural History Magazine*, 41, 434–5

Newall, R S, 1926, Pits at Winterbourne Stoke. *Wiltshire Archaeological and Natural History Magazine*, 43, 344–5

Newall, R S, 1929a, Stonehenge. *Antiquity*, 3, 75–88

Newall, R S, 1929b, Two shale cups of the early Bronze Age and other similar cups. *Wiltshire Archaeological and Natural History Magazine*, 44, 111–17

Newall, R S, 1931, Barrow 85 Amesbury. *Wiltshire Archaeological and Natural History Magazine*, 45, 432–43

Newall, R S, 1952, Stonehenge Stone no. 66. *Antiquaries Journal*, 32, 65–7

Newall, R S, 1956, Stonehenge: a review. *Antiquity*, 30, 137–41

Newall, R S, 1959, *Stonehenge, Wiltshire* (third edition). London: HMSO [Ministry of Works Official Guide-book]

Newall, R S, 1966, Megaliths once near Stonehenge. *Wiltshire Archaeological and Natural History Magazine*, 61, 93

Newham, C A, 1966, Stonehenge: a Neolithic observatory. *Nature*, 211, 456–8

Newham, C A, 1972, *The astronomical significance of Stonehenge*. Shirenewton: Moon Publications

Newman, P, 1997, *Lost gods of Albion: chalk hill-figures of Britain*. Stroud: Sutton

Newton, R G, & Renfrew, C, 1970, British faience beads reconsidered. *Antiquity*, 44, 199–206

Nichols, J (ed.), 1790, *Bibliotheca topographica Britannica 3*. London: Privately printed

North, J D, 1996, *Stonehenge: Neolithic man and the cosmos*. London: Harper Collins

Oldfather, C H (trans.), 1935, *Diodorus Siculus: Library of History, II, Books 2.35–4.58*. Harvard: Loeb Classical Library

Olmsted, G S, 1994, *The gods of the Celts and the Indo-Europeans* (Archaeolingua 6). Budapest: Archaeolingua

Oswald, A, Dyer, C, & Barber, M, 2001, *The creation of monuments: Neolithic causewayed enclosures in the British Isles*. Swindon: English Heritage

Ottaway, B, 1974, Cluster analysis of impurity patterns in Armorico-British daggers. *Archaeometry*, 16, 221–31

Ozanne, P, 1972, The excavation of a round barrow on Rollestone Down, Winterbourne Stoke, Wiltshire. *Wiltshire Archaeological and Natural History Magazine*, 67, 43–60

Palmer, S, 1970, The stone industries of the Isle of Portland, Dorset, and the utilisation of Portland Chert as artifact material in southern England. *Proceedings of the Prehistoric Society*, 36, 82–115

Parker Pearson, M, 1993, *Bronze Age Britain*. London: English Heritage and Batsford

Parker Pearson, M, Pollard, J, Richards, C, Thomas, J, Tilley, C, & Welham, K, 2006, A new avenue at Durrington Walls. *Past*, 52, 1–2

Parker Pearson, M, & Ramilisonina, R, 1998, Stonehenge for the ancestors: the stones pass on the message. *Antiquity*, 72, 308–26

Parker Pearson, M, Richards, C, Allen, M, Payne, A, & Welham, K, 2003, The Stonehenge Riverside Project: new approaches to Durrington Walls. *Past*, 45, 6–8

Parker Pearson, M, Richards, C, Allen, M, Payne, A, & Welham, K, 2004, The Stonehenge Riverside Project. Research design and initial results. *Journal of Nordic Archaeological Science*, 14, 45–60

Passmore, A D, 1940, A disc barrow containing curious flints near Stonehenge. *Wiltshire Archaeological and Natural History Magazine*, 49, 238

Peacock, D P S, 1969, Neolithic pottery production in Cornwall. *Antiquity*, 43, 145–8

Perks, A M, & Bailey, D M, 2003, Stonehenge: a view from medicine. *Journal of the Royal Society of Medicine*, 96, 94–7

Peters, F, 2000, Two traditions of Bronze Age burial in the Stonehenge landscape. *Oxford Journal of Archaeology*, 19.4, 343–58

Petrie, F, 1880, *Stonehenge: plans, description, and theories*. London: Edward Stanford

Pevsner, N (revised B Cherry), 1975, *The buildings of England: Wiltshire* (second edition). Harmondsworth: Penguin

Phené, J S, 1881, Existing analogies of Stonehenge and Avebury. Researches in the Mediterranean. *Wiltshire Archaeological and Natural History Magazine*, 19, 235–47

Piggott, C M, 1946, The late Bronze Age razors of the British Isles. *Proceedings of the Prehistoric Society*, 12, 121–41

Piggott, C M, & Piggott, S, 1939, Stone and earth circles in Dorset. *Antiquity*, 13, 138–58

Piggott, S, 1937, Prehistory and the Romantic movement. *Antiquity*, 11, 31–8

Piggott, S, 1938, The early Bronze Age in Wessex. *Proceedings of the Prehistoric Society*, 4, 52–106

Piggott, S, 1940, Timber-circles: a re-examination. *Archaeological Journal*, 96, 193–222

Piggott, S, 1941, The sources of Geoffrey of Monmouth. II. The Stonehenge story. *Antiquity*, 15, 305–19

Piggott, S, 1951, Stonehenge reviewed. In W F Grimes (ed.), *Aspects of archaeology in Britain and beyond*. London: H W Edwards. 274–92

Piggott, S, 1954a, Recent work at Stonehenge. *Antiquity*, 28, 221–4

Piggott, S, 1954b, *The Neolithic cultures of the British Isles*. Cambridge: Cambridge University Press

Piggott, S, 1959a, Stonehenge restored. *Antiquity*, 33, 50–1

Piggott, S, 1959b, The radio-carbon date from Durrington Walls. *Antiquity*, 33, 289–90

Piggott, S, 1962a, *The West Kennet Long Barrow: excavations 1955–56* (Ministry of Works Archaeological Report 4). London: HMSO

Piggott, S, 1962b, From Salisbury Plain to south Siberia. *Wiltshire Archaeological and Natural History Magazine*, 58, 93–7

Piggott, S, 1973a, The beginnings of human settlement: Palaeolithic and Mesolithic periods, to 4000 BC. In E Crittall (ed.), *A history of Wiltshire. Volume I.2*. London: University of London Institute of Historical Research, Victoria History of the Counties of England. 281–3

Piggott, S, 1973b, The first agricultural communities: the Neolithic period. In E Crittall (ed.), *A history of Wiltshire. Volume I.2*. London: University of London Institute of Historical Research, Victoria History of the Counties of England. 284–332

Piggott, S, 1973c, The later Neolithic: single graves and the first metallurgy. In E Crittall (ed.), *A history of Wiltshire. Volume I.2*. London: University of London Institute of Historical Research, Victoria History of the Counties of England. 333–51

Piggott, S, 1973d, The Wessex Culture of the early Bronze Age. In E Crittall (ed.), *A history of Wiltshire. Volume I.2*. London: University of London Institute of Historical Research, Victoria History of the Counties of England. 352–75

Piggott, S, 1973e, The final phase of Bronze technology. In E Crittall (ed.), *A history of Wiltshire. Volume I.2*. London: University of London Institute of Historical Research, Victoria History of the Counties of England. 376–407

Piggott, S, 1975, *The Druids* (revised edition). London: Thames and Hudson

Piggott, S, 1985, *William Stukeley: an eighteenth-century antiquary* (revised edition). London: Thames and Hudson

Piggott, S, 1993, John Thurnam (1810–73) and British prehistory. *Wiltshire Archaeological and Natural History Magazine*, 86, 1–7

Pitts, M, 1980, On two barrows near Stonehenge. *Wiltshire Archaeological and Natural History Magazine*, 74/75, 181–4

Pitts, M, 1982, On the road to Stonehenge: report on the investigations beside the A344 in 1968, 1979, and 1980. *Proceedings of the Prehistoric Society*, 48, 75–132

Pitts, M, 2001a, *Hengeworld* (revised edition). London: Arrow

Pitts, M, 2001b, Excavating the Sanctuary: new investigations on Overton Hill, Avebury. *Wiltshire Archaeological and Natural History Magazine*, 94, 1–23

Pitts, M, Bayliss, A, McKinley, J, Boylston, A, Budd, P, Evans, J, Chenery, C, Reynolds, A, & Semple, S, 2002, An Anglo-Saxon decapitation and burial at Stonehenge. *Wiltshire Archaeological and Natural History Magazine*, 95, 131–46

Pitts, M, & Richards, J, 2003, A future for Stonehenge. *Current Archaeology*, 16.5 (no. 185), 186–201

Pollard, A M, Bussell, G D, & Baird, D C, 1981, The analytical investigation of early Bronze Age jet and jet-like material from the Devizes Museum. *Archaeometry*, 23, 139–67

Pollard, J, 1995a, Inscribing space: formal deposition at the later Neolithic monument of Woodhenge, Wiltshire. *Proceedings of the Prehistoric Society*, 61, 137–56

Pollard, J, 1995b, The Durrington 68 timber circle: a forgotten late Neolithic monument. *Wiltshire Archaeological and Natural History Magazine*, 88, 122–5

Pollard, J, & Ruggles, C L N, 2001, Shifting perceptions: spatial order, cosmology, and patterns of deposition at Stonehenge. *Cambridge Archaeological Journal*, 11.1, 69–90

Polydore Vergil, 1534 (ed. H Ellis, 1846), *Historie of England*. London: Camden Society (2 vols.)

Price, T D, Knipper, C, Grupe, G, & Smrcka, V, 2004, Strontium isotopes and prehistoric human migration: the Bell Beaker period in central Europe. *European Journal of Archaeology*, 7.1, 9–40

Pryor, F, French, C, Crowther, D, Gurney, D, Simpson, G, & Taylor, M, 1985, *The Fenland Project, No. 1: Archaeology and environment in the Lower Welland Valley Volume 1* (East Anglian Archaeology 27.1). Cambridge: Cambridgeshire Archaeological Committee

Pugh, R B, 1948, The early history of the manors in Amesbury. *Wiltshire Archaeological and Natural History Society Magazine*, 52, 70–110

Radley, J, 1969, An archaeological survey and policy for Wiltshire: Part II, Mesolithic. *Wiltshire Archaeological and Natural History Magazine*, 64, 18–20

Rahtz, P A, & ApSimon, A M A, 1962, Neolithic and Beaker sites at Downton, Wiltshire. *Wiltshire Archaeological and Natural History Magazine*, 58, 116–42

Ramsey, A C, Aveline, W T, & Hill, E, 1868, *Geology of parts of Wiltshire and Gloucestershire* (Memoirs of the Geological Survey of Great Britain Sheet 34). London: Geological Survey

Rankine, W F, 1956, Mesolithic finds in Wiltshire. *Wiltshire Archaeological and Natural History Magazine*, 56, 149–61

Rastall, J, 1530, *The patyme of people, or the chronicle of the realm of England.* London

Rawlings, M, 2001, Archaeological investigations at the Roman villa, Netheravon, 1996. *Wiltshire Archaeological and Natural History Magazine*, 94, 148–5

Rawlings, M, & Fitzpatrick, A P, 1996, Prehistoric sites and a Romano-British settlement at Butterfield Down, Amesbury. *Wiltshire Archaeological and Natural History Magazine*, 89, 1–43

RCHM [Royal Commission on Historical Monuments (England)], 1979, *Stonehenge and its environs.* Edinburgh: Edinburgh University Press

RCHM [Royal Commission on Historical Monuments (England)], 1981, *Ancient and historical monuments in the city of Salisbury. Volume I.* London: HMSO

RCHM [Royal Commission on Historical Monuments (England)], 1987, *Churches of southeast Wiltshire.* London: HMSO

Reece, R, 1988, *My Roman Britain.* Cirencester and Oxford: Cotswold Studies/Oxbow Books

Renfrew, C, 1968, Wessex without Mycenae. *Annual of the British School in Athens*, 63, 277–85

Renfrew, C, 1973a, Monuments, mobilization and social organization in Neolithic Wessex. In C Renfrew (ed.), *The explanation of culture change: models in prehistory.* London: Duckworth. 539–58

Renfrew, C, 1973b, *Social archaeology. an inaugural lecture.* Southampton: University of Southampton

Renfrew, C, 1973c, *Before civilization.* London: Jonathan Cape

Renfrew, C, 1974, British prehistory: changing configurations. In C Renfrew (ed.), *British prehistory: a new outline.* London: Duckworth. 1–40

Renfrew, C, 1979, *Investigations in Orkney* (Reports of the Research Committee of the Society of Antiquaries of London 38). London: Thames and Hudson

Renfrew, C, 1987, *Archaeology and language: the puzzle of the Indo-European origins.* London: Jonathan Cape

Renfrew, C, 1996, Language families and the spread of farming. In D Harris (ed.), *The origins and spread of agriculture and pastoralism in Eurasia.* London: UCL Press. 70–92

Reynolds, P J, 1979, Romano-British corn-drying oven: an experiment. *Archaeological Journal*, 136, 27–42

Reynolds, P J, 1994, The life and death of a post-hole. *Interpreting Stratigraphy*, 5, 21–5

Richards, C, & Thomas, J, 1984, Ritual activity and structured deposition in later Neolithic Wessex. In R Bradley & J Gardiner (eds.), *Neolithic studies* (BAR British Series 133). Oxford: British Archaeological Reports. 189–218

Richards, J, 1990, *The Stonehenge Environs Project* (HBMCE Archaeological Report 16). London: English Heritage

Richards, J, 1991, *Stonehenge.* London: English Heritage

Richards, J, 2004, *Stonehenge: a history in photographs.* London: English Heritage

Richards, J, 2005, *Stonehenge.* London: English Heritage [site guidebook]

Richards, J, & Whitby, M, 1997, The engineering of Stonehenge. *Proceedings of the British Academy*, 92, 231–56

Richardson, K M, 1951, The excavation of Iron Age villages on Boscombe Down West. *Wiltshire Archaeological and Natural History Magazine*, 54, 124–68

Ricq-de Bouard, M, 1993, Trade in Neolithic jadeite axes from the Alps: new data. In C Scarre & F Healy (eds.), *Trade and exchange in prehistoric Europe* (Oxbow Monograph 33). Oxford: Oxbow. 61–7

Robinson, P, 1987, Saxon burials at Orcheston. *Wiltshire Archaeological and Natural History Magazine*, 81, 132

Robinson, P, 1991, Durotrigian coin from Stonehenge. *Wiltshire Archaeological and Natural History Magazine*, 84, 119–20

Robinson, P, 1992, Some late Saxon mounts from Wiltshire. *Wiltshire Archaeological and Natural History Magazine*, 85, 63–9

Robinson, P, 1995, Miniature socketed Bronze Age axes from Wiltshire. *Wiltshire Archaeological and Natural History Magazine*, 88, 60–8

Roe, D, 1969, An archaeological survey and policy for Wiltshire: Part I, Palaeolithic. *Wiltshire Archaeological and Natural History Magazine*, 64, 1–17

Roe, D, 1981, *The lower and middle Palaeolithic periods in Britain*. London: Routledge

Roe, F E S, 1979, Typology of stone implements with shaftholes. In T H McK Clough & W A Cummins (eds.), *Stone axe studies* (Council for British Archaeology Research Report 23). London. Council for British Archaeology. 23–48

Ruddle, C S, 1895, Early tobacco pipes. *Wiltshire Notes and Queries*, 1 (1893–5), 282

Ruddle, C S, 1901, Notes on Durrington. *Wiltshire Archaeological and Natural History Magazine*, 31, 331–42

Ruggles, C, 1997, Astronomy and Stonehenge. *Proceedings of the British Academy*, 92, 203–29

Rutherford, E, 1987, *Sarum*. London: Century

Salt, A, & Boutsikas, E, 2005, Knowing when to consult the Oracle at Delphi. *Antiquity*, 79, 573–85

Sandell, R E, 1961, Sir Richard Colt Hoare. *Wiltshire Archaeological and Natural History Magazine*, 58, 1–6

Saunders, P R, 1972, A flanged axe from Durnford. *Wiltshire Archaeological and Natural History Magazine*, 67, 158–9

Saunders, P R, 1976, A flat axe from Figheldean or Netheravon. *Wiltshire Archaeological and Natural History Magazine*, 70/71, 125–6

Saville, A, 1978, Five flint assemblages from excavated sites in Wiltshire. *Wiltshire Archaeological and Natural History Magazine*, 72/73, 1–28

Scarre, C, 1997, Misleading images: Stonehenge and Brittany. *Antiquity*, 71, 1016–20

Schofield, J (ed.), 1998, *Monuments of war: the evaluation, recording and management of twentieth-century military sites*. London: English Heritage

Schofield, J, & Lake, J, 1995, Defining our defence heritage. *Conservation Bulletin*, 13, 12–13

Schulting, R J, & Wysocki, M, 2005, 'In this chambered tumulus were found cleft skulls …': an assessment of the evidence for cranial trauma in the British Neolithic. *Proceedings of the Prehistoric Society*, 71, 107–38

Scourse, J D, 1997, Transport of the Stonehenge bluestones: testing the glacial hypothesis. *Proceedings of the British Academy*, 92, 271–314

Selkirk, A, 1972, The Wessex Culture. *Current Archaeology*, 3.9 (no. 32), 241–4

Shanks, M, 2004, *Archaeological rats* [on-line]. Stamford: Stamford University [available at <http://metamedia.stanford.edu/~mshanks/weblog/index> accessed 19:03:04]

Shell, C, 2000, Metalworker or shaman? Early Bronze Age Upton Lovell G2a burial. *Antiquity*, 74,

271–2

Shell, C A, & Robinson, P, 1988, The recent reconstruction of the Bush Barrow lozenge plate. *Antiquity*, 62, 248–60

Shennan, S, 1982, Exchange and ranking: the role of amber in the earlier Bronze Age of Europe. In C Renfrew & S Shennan (eds.), *Ranking, resource and exchange: aspects of the archaeology of early European society*. Cambridge: Cambridge University Press. 33–45

Shepherd, I A G, & Shepherd, A N 2001, A Cordoned Urn burial with faience from 102 Findhorn, Moray. *Proceedings of the Society of Antiquaries of Scotland*, 131, 101–28

Sherratt, A, 1996a, Settlement patterns or landscape studies? Reconciling reason and romance. *Archaeological Dialogues*, 3.2, 140–59

Sherratt, A, 1996b, Why Wessex? The Avon route and river transport in later British prehistory. *Oxford Journal of Archaeology*, 15.2, 211–34

Short, H de S, 1936, Scrap bronze from south Wiltshire. *Wiltshire Archaeological and Natural History Magazine*, 56, 392–4

Short, H de S, 1946, Bronze Age Beakers from Larkhill and Bulford. *Wiltshire Archaeological and Natural History Magazine*, 51, 381–3

Sidney, Sir P, 1962, The Seven Wonders of England. In W A Ringler (ed.), *Poems*. Oxford: Oxford University Press. 149

Slocombe, P M, 1989, *Wiltshire farm buildings, 1500–1900*. Devizes: Wiltshire Buildings Record

SM [Salisbury Museum], 1958, *Salisbury and South Wiltshire Museum Annual Report*. Salisbury: Salisbury Museum

Smith, A C, 1866, Methods of moving colossal stones, as practised by some of the more advanced nations in antiquity. *Wiltshire Archaeological and Natural History Magazine*, 10, 52–60

Smith, A G, 1981, The Neolithic. In I G Simmons & M J Tooley (eds.), *The environment in British prehistory*. London: Duckworth. 125–209

Smith, G, 1973, Excavations of the Stonehenge Avenue at West Amesbury, Wiltshire. *Wiltshire Archaeological and Natural History Magazine*, 68, 42–56

Smith, I F, 1991, Round barrows, Wilsford cum Lake G51–54: excavations by Ernest Greenfield in 1985. *Wiltshire Archaeological and Natural History Magazine*, 84, 11–39

Smith, J, 1771, *Choir gaur; the grand orrery of the ancient Druids commonly called Stonehenge, on Salisbury Plain, astronomically explained in the earliest ages, for observing the motions of the heavenly bodies*. Salisbury: Privately published

Smith, R W, 1981, *Archaeology in the Salisbury Plain training areas*. Trowbridge: Wiltshire County Council Library and Museum Service [limited circulation printed report]

Smith, R W, 1984, The ecology of Neolithic farming systems as exemplified by the Avebury region of Wiltshire. *Proceedings of the Prehistoric Society*, 50, 99–120

Spender, S, 1974, *Henry Moore: Stonehenge*. London: Ganymed Original Editions Ltd

Steely Dan, 1993, *Remastered: the best of Steely Dan*. London: MCA CD10967 [music CD]

Sterud, G, 1973, A paradigmatic view of prehistory. In C Renfrew (ed.), *The explanation of culture change: models in prehistory*. London: Duckworth. 3–18

Stevens, F, 1921, Durrington. Mammoth tooth. *Wiltshire Archaeological and Natural History Magazine*, 41, 434

Stevens, F, 1924, *Stonehenge today and yesterday*. London: HMSO

Stone, E H, 1923, The age of Stonehenge. *Antiquaries Journal*, 3, 130–4

Stone, E H, 1924a, *The stones of Stonehenge*. London: Robert Scott

Stone, E H, 1924b, The method of erecting the stones of Stonehenge. *Wiltshire Archaeological and Natural History Magazine*, 42, 446–56

Stone, J F S, 1935, Some discoveries at Ratfyn, Amesbury, and their bearing on the date of Woodhenge. *Wiltshire Archaeological and Natural History Magazine*, 47, 55–67

Stone, J F S, 1936, An enclosure on Boscombe Down East. *Wiltshire Archaeological and Natural History Magazine*, 47, 466–89

Stone, J F S, 1939, An early Bronze Age grave in Fargo Plantation near Stonehenge. *Wiltshire Archaeological and Natural History Magazine*, 48, 357–70

Stone, J F S, 1948, The Stonehenge Cursus and its affinities. *Archaeological Journal*, 104, 7–19

Stone, J F S, 1949, Some Grooved Ware pottery from the Woodhenge area. *Proceedings of the Prehistoric Society*, 15, 122–7

Stone, J F S, 1953, A decorated Bronze Age axe from Stonehenge Down. *Wiltshire Archaeological and Natural History Magazine*, 55, 30–3

Stone, J F S, Piggott, S, & Booth, A, 1954, Durrington Walls, Wiltshire: recent excavations at a ceremonial site of the early second millennium BC. *Antiquaries Journal*, 34, 155–77

Stone, J F S, & Young, W E V, 1948, Two pits of Grooved Ware date near Woodhenge. *Wiltshire Archaeological and Natural History Magazine*, 52, 287–306

Stout, A, 2003, The world turned upside down. Stonehenge Summer Solstice before the hippies. *3rd Stone*, 46, 38–46

Stuiver, M, Reimer, P J, Bard, E, Beck, J W, Burr, G S, Hughen, K A, Kromer, B, McCormac, F G, van der Plicht, J, & Spurk, M, 1998, INTCAL98 radiocarbon age calibration 24,000–0 CalBP. *Radiocarbon*, 40, 1041–84

Stukeley, W, 1740, *Stonehenge, a temple restor'd to the British druids*. London: W Innys and R Manby

Talbot, C H, 1901, Amesbury Church. Reasons for thinking it was not the church of the Priory. *Wiltshire Archaeological and Natural History Magazine*, 31, 8–29

Taylor, J A, 1980, Environmental changes in Wales during the Holocene period. In J A Taylor (ed.), *Culture and environment in Prehistoric Wales* (BAR British Series 76). Oxford: British Archaeological Reports. 101–30

Taylor, J J, 1980, *Bronze Age goldwork of the British Isles*. Cambridge: Cambridge University Press

Taylor, J J, 2005, The work of the Wessex Master Goldsmith: its implications. *Wiltshire Archaeological and Natural History Magazine*, 98, 316–26

Teall, J J H, 1894, Notes on sections of Stonehenge rocks belonging to Mr W Cunnington. *Wiltshire Archaeological and Natural History Magazine*, 27, 66–8

Ten Years After, 1968 (reissued 1997), *Stonedhenge*. London: Decca/BGOCD356 [music CD]

Thatcher, A R, 1976, The Station Stones at Stonehenge. *Antiquity*, 50, 144–6

Thom, A, 1974, Stonehenge. *Journal of Historical Astronomy*, 5, 71–90

Thom, A, 1975, Stonehenge as a possible lunar observatory. *Journal of Historical Astronomy*, 6, 19–30

Thom, A S, Ker, J M D, & Burrows, T R, 1988, The Bush Barrow gold lozenge: is it a solar and lunar calendar for Stonehenge? *Antiquity*, 62, 492–502

Thomas, H H, 1923, The source of the stones of Stonehenge. *Antiquaries Journal*, 3, 239–60.

Thomas, J, 1999, *Understanding the Neolithic*. London: Routledge

Thomas, N, 1952, A Neolithic chalk cup from Wilsford in the Devizes Museum: and notes on others. *Wiltshire Archaeological and Natural History Magazine*, 54, 452–63

Thomas, N, 1964, The Neolithic causewayed camp at Robin Hood's Ball, Shrewton. *Wiltshire Archaeological and Natural History Magazine*, 59, 1–27

Thorn, C, & Thorn, F (eds.), 1979, *Domesday Book: Wiltshire*. Chichester: Phillimore

Thorpe, L (trans.), 1973, *Geoffrey of Monmouth: the history of the Kings of Britain*. London: Penguin Books

Thorpe, N, & Richards, C, 1984, The decline of ritual authority and the introduction of Beakers into Britain. In R Bradley & J Gardiner (eds.), *Neolithic studies* (BAR British Series 133). Oxford: British Archaeological Reports. 67–84

Thorpe, R S, Williams-Thorpe, O, Jenkins, D G, & Watson, J, 1991, The geological sources and transport of the bluestones of Stonehenge, Wiltshire, UK. *Proceedings of the Prehistoric Society*, 57, 103–57

Thurnam, J, 1865, On the two principal forms of ancient British and Gaulish skulls. Part II. *Memoirs of the Anthropological Society of London*, 1 (1863–4), 459–519

Thurnam, J, 1866, On an incised marking on the impost of the Great Trilithon at Stonehenge. *Wiltshire Archaeological and Natural History Magazine*, 9, 268–77

Thurnam, J, 1868, On ancient British barrows. Part I – long barrows. *Archaeologia*, 42, 161–244

Thurnam, J, 1869, On leaf and lozenge-shaped flint javelin heads, from an oval barrow near Stonehenge. *Wiltshire Archaeological and Natural History Magazine*, 11, 40–9

Thurnam, J, 1871, On ancient British barrows. Part II – round barrows. *Archaeologia*, 43, 258–552

Tilley, C, 1994, *A phenomenology of landscape*. Oxford: Berg

Tinsley, H M, 1981, The Bronze Age. In I G Simmons & M J Tooley (eds.), *The environment in British prehistory*. London: Duckworth. 210–49

Tomalin, D J, 1988, Armorican vases à anses and their occurrence in southern Britain. *Proceedings of the Prehistoric Society*, 54, 203–21

Topping, P, 1992, The Penrith henges: a survey by the Royal Commission on the Historic Monuments of England. *Proceedings of the Prehistoric Society*, 58, 249–64

Tratman, E K, 1967, The Priddy Circles, Mendip, Somerset, henge monuments. *Proceedings of the University of Bristol Spelaeological Society*, 11.1, 143–67

Turner, J, 1981, The Iron Age. In I G Simmons & M J Tooley (eds.), *The environment in British prehistory*. London: Duckworth. 250–91

van Griffen, A E, 1938, Continental bell- and disc-barrows in Holland. *Proceedings of the Prehistoric Society*, 4, 258–71

Vatcher, F de M, 1961, The excavation of the long mortuary enclosure on Normanton Down, Wiltshire. *Proceedings of the Prehistoric Society*, 27, 160–73

Vatcher, F de M, 1969, Two incised chalk plaques near Stonehenge Bottom. *Antiquity*, 43, 310–11

Vatcher, L, & Vatcher, F de M, 1973, Excavation of three post-holes in the Stonehenge car-park. *Wiltshire Archaeological and Natural History Magazine*, 68, 57–63

WA [Wessex Archaeology], 1991, *Stonehenge Visitor Centre, Wiltshire, western approach route corridor archaeological evaluation stage 1: test pits*. Salisbury: Wessex Archaeology [limited circulation printed report reference W623a]

WA [Wessex Archaeology], 1993a, *Stonehenge Visitor Centre, Wiltshire. Site 12: A303 footbed archaeological evaluation*. Salisbury: Wessex Archaeology for English Heritage [limited circulation printed report reference W639a]

WA [Wessex Archaeology], 1993b, *The Southern Rivers Project Report 1 1991–1992. The upper Thames Valley, the Kennet Valley, and the Solent drainage system*. Salisbury: Wessex Archaeology for English Heritage [limited circulation printed report]

WA [Wessex Archaeology], 1995, *Stonehenge Visitor Centre, Wiltshire SVC – Countess Roundabout archaeological evaluation*. Salisbury: Wessex Archaeology [limited circulation printed report reference 38477]

WA [Wessex Archaeology], 1998, *Stonehenge military installations: a desk-based assessment*. Salisbury: Wessex Archaeology [limited circulation printed report reference 44411]

WA [Wessex Archaeology], 2002, *The Amesbury Archer* [on-line]. Salisbury: Wessex Archaeology [available at: <www.wessexarch.co.uk/projects/amesbury/archer.html> accessed 27 June 2002]

WA [Wessex Archaeology], 2003, *Stonehenge Visitor Centre, Countess East, Amesbury, Wiltshire. Archaeological evaluation: results*. Salisbury: Wessex Archaeology [limited circulation printed report reference 53324.01]

WA [Wessex Archaeology], 2004, *Stonehenge Visitor Centre, Countess East, Amesbury, Wiltshire. Further archaeological evaluation*. Salisbury: Wessex Archaeology [limited circulation printed report reference 54700.01a]

Wainwright, G J, 1962, The excavation of an earthwork at Castell Bryn-Gwyn, Llanidan parish, Anglesey. *Archaeologia Cambrensis*, 111, 25–58

Wainwright, G J, 1969, A review of henge monuments in the light of recent research. *Proceedings of the Prehistoric Society*, 35, 112–33

Wainwright, G J, 1971, The excavation of prehistoric and Romano-British settlements near Durrington Walls, Wiltshire, 1970. *Wiltshire Archaeological and Natural History Magazine*, 66, 76–128

Wainwright, G J, 1973, Prehistoric and Romano-British settlements at Eaton Heath, Norwich. *Archaeological Journal*, 130, 1–43

Wainwright, G J, 1975, Religion and settlement in Wessex, 3000–1700 BC. In P Fowler (ed.), *Recent work in rural archaeology*. Bradford-on-Avon: Moonraker Press. 57–72

Wainwright, G J, 1977, New light on Neolithic habitation sites and early Iron Age settlements in southern Britain: 1963–73. In M R Apted, R Gilyard-Beer, & A D Saunders (eds.), *Ancient monuments and their interpretation*. London: Phillimore. 1–12

Wainwright, G J, 1989, *The henge monuments: ceremony and society in prehistoric Britain*. London: Thames and Hudson

Wainwright, G, 2000a, The Stonehenge we deserve. *Antiquity*, 74, 334–42

Wainwright, G, 2000b, Time please. *Antiquity*, 74, 909–43

Wainwright, G J, & Longworth, I H, 1971, *Durrington Walls excavations, 1966–1968* (Reports of the Research Committee of the Society of Antiquaries of London 29). London: Society of Antiquaries

Watkin, B, 1979, *A history of Wiltshire*. Chichester: Phillimore

Watkins, T, 1976, Wessex without Cyprus: Cypriot daggers in Europe. In J V S Megaw (ed.), *To illustrate the monuments*. London: Thames and Hudson. 135–43

Watts, K, 1996, Wiltshire deer parks: an introductory survey. *Wiltshire Archaeological and Natural History Magazine*, 89, 88–98

Wedlake, W J, 1982, *The excavation of the shrine of Apollo at Nettleton, Wiltshire, 1956–1971* (Reports of the Research Committee of the Society of Antiquaries of London 40). London: Thames and Hudson

Wells, H G, 1934, *Experiment in autobiography*. London: Gollancz

Whittle, A, 1978, Resources and population in the British Neolithic. *Antiquity*, 52, 34–42

Whittle, A W R, 1997a, Remembered and imagined belongings: Stonehenge in its traditions and structures of meaning. *Proceedings of the British Academy*, 92, 145–66

Whittle A, 1997b, *Sacred mound. Holy rings. Silbury Hill and the West Kennet palisade enclosures: a later Neolithic complex in north Wiltshire* (Oxbow Monographs 74). Oxford. Oxbow Books

Whittle, A, Atkinson, R J C, Chambers, R, and Thomas, N, 1992, Excavations in the Neolithic and Bronze Age complex at Dorchester-on-Thames, Oxfordshire, 1947–1952 and 1981. *Proceedings of the Prehistoric Society*, 58, 143–202

Whittle, A, Davies, J J, Dennis, I, Fairbairn, A S, & Hamilton, M A, 2000, Neolithic activity and occupation outside Windmill Hill causewayed enclosure, Wiltshire: a survey and excavation 1992–93. *Wiltshire Archaeological and Natural History Magazine*, 93, 131–80

Williams-Thorpe, O, Green, C P, & Scourse, J D, 1997, The Stonehenge bluestones: discussion. *Proceedings of the British Academy*, 92, 315–34

Williams-Thorpe, O, Jenkins, D G, Jenkins, J, & Watson, J S, 1995, Chlorine-36 dating and the bluestone of Stonehenge. *Antiquity*, 69, 1019–20

Williams-Thorpe, O, Jones, M C, Potts, P J, & Webb, P C, 2006, Preseli dolerite bluestones: axe-heads, Stonehenge monoliths, and outcrop sources. *Oxford Journal of Archaeology*, 25.1, 29–46

Williams-Thorpe, O, Potts, P J, & Jones, M C, 2004, Non-destructive provenancing of bluestone axe-heads in Britain. *Antiquity*, 78, 359–79

Wilson, D M, & Hurst D G, 1968, Medieval Britain in 1968. *Medieval Archaeology*, 12, 230–87

Woodward, A B, & Woodward, P, 1996, The topography of some barrow cemeteries in Bronze Age Wessex. *Proceedings of the Prehistoric Society*, 62, 275–92

Woodward, P, 1988, Pictures of the Neolithic: discoveries from the Flagstones House excavations, Dorchester, Dorset. *Antiquity*, 62, 266–74

Worthington, A, 2002, A brief history of the summer solstice at Stonehenge. *3rd Stone*, 42, 41–7

Worthington, A, 2004, *Stonehenge: celebration and subversion*. Loughborough: Alternative Albion

Worthington, A (ed.), 2005, *The Battle of the Beanfield*. Teignmouth: Enabler Publications

Wymer, J (ed.), 1977, *Gazetteer of Mesolithic sites in England and Wales* (Council for British Archaeology Research Report 20). London: Council for British Archaeology

Wymer, J, 1999, *The Lower Palaeolithic occupation of Britain*. Salisbury and London: Wessex Archaeology and English Heritage

Yorke, B, 1989, The Jutes of Hampshire and Wight and the origins of Wessex. In S Bassett (ed.), *The origins of Anglo-Saxon kingdoms*. Leicester: Leicester University Press. 84–96

Yorke, B, 1995, *Wessex in the early Middle Ages*. Leicester: Leicester University Press

INDEX

Page number of illustrations are shown in italic

Barrow numbers for a parish are shown in bold

CP refers to colour plate numbers